1992

Gadamer's Hermeneutics

Gadamer's Hermeneutics:

A Reading of *Truth and Method*

Joel C. Weinsheimer

Yale University Press
New Haven and London

Designed by James J. Johnson
and set in Times Roman type.
Printed in the United States of America by
Vail-Ballou Press, Binghamton, New York.

Library of Congress Cataloging in Publication Data

Weinsheimer, Joel.
  Gadamer's hermeneutics.

  Bibliography: p. 261
  Includes index.
    1. Gadamer, Hans-Georg, 1900–   Wahrheit und
Methode.   2. Humanities—Methodology.   3. Hermeneutics.
4. Aesthetics.   I. Gadamer, Hans Georg, 1900–
Wahrheit und Methode.   1985.   II. Title.
B3248.G343W4538   1985   111'.83   84–27028
ISBNs 0–300–03320–6 (cloth)
         0–300–04135–7 (pbk.)

10   9   8   7   6   5   4   3

For
Mabel E. Weinsheimer
and
Herbert G. Weinsheimer

Sein Denken jedenfalls war als Ganzes der Versuch, auf eine Frage zu antworten, die Meister Ekkhart gefragt hat: ''Warum gehet ihr aus?'' Noch einmal lautet die Antwort, wie bei Plotin, in der Mystik, bei Fichte, bei Hegel gelautet hat: um heimzufinden.

Philosophische Lehrjahre

Contents

Preface ix

Abbreviations of Gadamer's Main Works xiii

Introduction: Hermeneutics and the Natural Sciences 1

    The Limits of Method 4

    Method and Truth in the Natural Sciences 15

    Method against Itself 36

A Reading of *Truth and Method*

  1. The Critique of Aesthetics 63

    The Prodigal as Paradigm 66

    What Is More than Art? 80

    The Truth about Art 91

    The Player in Truth Is Being Played 100

    Art as History 118

  2. The Critique of Historicism 133

    How History Became Art 134

    Prejudice as a Condition of Truth 164

    Understanding by Applying 184

    Questioning Experience 199

  3. Being at Home in Language 213

    The Spirit of the Letter 220

    The Rise of "Language" 229

    Language and Being: Difference without Distinction 242

Selected Bibliography 261

Index 273

Preface

Already close to retirement in 1960, Hans-Georg Gadamer brought a highly productive philosophical career not to a close but to a climax with the publication of *Truth and Method*. Now, a quarter-century after its appearance, not only is *Truth and Method* internationally recognized as the most important contribution to philosophical hermeneutics since Heidegger's *Being and Time* (1927); Gadamer's thought has left its mark everywhere among the human sciences—in sociology, literary theory, history, theology, law—and indeed in philosophy of natural science.

In English-speaking countries, Gadamer's name is not at all unknown. Both his magnum opus and many of the *Kleine Schriften* are available in English. Thanks to a number of fine introductions, the general conclusions of *Truth and Method* have become familiar; the main texts of the *Hermeneutikstreit* between Gadamer, Habermas, and others have been translated and its issues rehearsed and clarified in numerous commentaries. Gadamer's hermeneutics has thus become a growing force and influence, not just a topic of discussion.

Yet it is still the case that the circle of Gadamer's influence remains much smaller than it could be—and, in my opinion, rightly should be. *Truth and Method* is a book of philosophy directed primarily to philosophers, yet its significance reaches far beyond the confines of that discipline. There are many students of other disciplines who, like me, are not philosophers by profession

ix

but find Gadamer's hermeneutics directly pertinent to their special fields, and yet who have difficulty in penetrating beyond the bare but enticing generalities that are circulated about *Truth and Method*. To such readers in particular this book is addressed.

Its aim is at once modest and ambitious: to offer a detailed, comprehensive, and noncontroversial exposition of *Truth and Method* in a form accessible to the nonspecialist reader. More than an introduction, this exposition does not limit itself to Gadamer's broad conclusions, but also retraces the path of historical analysis and argument that leads to them. It provides a section-by-section consideration of each phase of Gadamer's presentation, so that a reader with a specific interest in a particular part of *Truth and Method* can consult the corresponding section of this explication. Prefacing the detailed exposition, the introductory chapter focuses the central issue of *Truth and Method* announced in its title. From diverse passages it gathers and organizes Gadamer's objections to the notion that scientific method defines the exclusive avenue to truth. But this chapter also questions whether Gadamer's conception of scientific method and its objectives is not in fact askew, and it goes on to suggest some unsuspected affinities of his hermeneutics with mathematical logic that should be of interest to the specialist reader as well. In the opening chapter as elsewhere, however, my intention is not to criticize *Truth and Method* but to make it more accessible and to open its dialogue to greater participation.

No one, it is safe to say, finds Gadamer's work easy going. I certainly have not found it so and have tried to ascertain the sources of difficulty. Not least is the translation—a laborious undertaking that, for the most part, is successful. Yet crucial phrases—notoriously "effective-historical consciousness" (*wirkungsgeschichtliches Bewusstsein*)—leave the reader blankly ignorant.[1] Even in German, as Gadamer himself admits, the phrase was overly ambiguous ("Die Kontinuität der Geschichte," p. 45). Not all the difficulties are due to the reader's deficiencies or the translation's. Early in his career, while still a *Privatdozent*, Gadamer tells us, his lectures tended toward overcomplication. "My friends had even invented a new scientific unit: it was called a 'Gad' and designated a certain measure of unnecessary complexity" (*Philosophische Lehrjahre*, p. 46). Even *Truth and Method*, it is not disrespectful to say, is perhaps too complex by a Gad or two.

Far more interesting, however, is its necessary and irreducible complexity.

---

1. Partly for this reason, I have decided to retranslate all citations from *Wahrheit und Methode*. I am also responsible for translations from other works for which a German title appears in the notes. Otherwise I have availed myself of the published translations.

This stems primarily from two sources. First is the fact that Gadamer's hermeneutic philosophy is itself hermeneutically grounded. As Richard Palmer rightly observes in *Hermeneutics*, "Gadamer's argument rests strongly on his detailed critical analyses of previous thinking about language, historical consciousness, and the aesthetic experience" (p. 166). To scant these analyses, as general overviews are forced to do and the *Hermeneutikstreit* did as well, is either to miss the grounds of Gadamer's hermeneutics entirely or to imply that they are more abstract, unhistorical, and original than they in fact are. The entire structure as well as specific theses of *Truth and Method* militates against overlooking history as its ground of truth. Yet when we do look in detail at Gadamer's critical review of the histories of aesthetics, historicism, and language philosophy, we are confronted with a particular kind of problem. Since Gadamer attempts not only to overcome his predecessors' positions but to assimilate them to his own, it is difficult and ultimately impossible to discriminate absolutely between the two.

"In Heidegger's lectures," Gadamer wrote in *Philosophische Lehrjahre*, "topics came alive to us in a way that we no longer knew: is he speaking of his own concerns or those of Aristotle? It is a great hermeneutic truth which we all began to experience at that time and which I later tried to justify theoretically and represent myself" (p. 216). This truth is precisely the fusion of horizons, and since Gadamer not only justifies but himself performs this fusion in *Truth and Method*, the consequence is that we cannot finally segregate his exposition of Kant or Dilthey or Aquinas from the presentation of his own theses and his critique of theirs. Even the German conditional mood that indicates semidetached, indirect discourse is absent from his exegeses. This fusion of discourses, so that history becomes self-critical, introduces considerable complexity into *Truth and Method* no doubt, but it is a necessary complexity, one intrinsic to the subject.

The second source of immanent difficulty is a corollary of the first. It derives from Gadamer's twin hermeneutic impulses toward the one and the many. Both concentric and eccentric in direction, *Truth and Method* exhibits unity without closure and inclusiveness without dispersion. It breaks down distinctions without obliterating differences. Even the book's title displays this openness. It is not ironic—if that assertion implies the title should really be "Truth or Method." Rather truth and method remain in unresolved tension, not identical certainly, but not dichotomized either. It is hermeneutic rigor itself that resists neat antitheses and neat reconciliations and that fact precludes pat formulations of Gadamer's thought. Gadamer does not think in assertions, statements, and propositions that aim at unequivocal meanings in logical sequence. Rather, he thinks in questions. Even his answers open onto an unsaid, unasserted aura of meaning that cannot be pinned down in univocal statements. For the same reason, Gadamer offers no explicit program for the reformation of hermeneutics that could be formulated here. All these factors make for a necessary complexity that I have not tried to reduce but instead have tried to elucidate.

Having decided to center on *Truth and Method* and to make the elucidation of it as comprehensive as possible, I could not also engage in a running battle with Gadamer's critics on the right and left. Although it is the fate of *Truth and Method* to have been disseminated not by Gadamer's disciples but by his critics, nevertheless the issues raised by this debate have been local and particular, if also serious. These objections and replies have already been frequently and intensively canvassed in the secondary literature, and that is some excuse for relegating them here to the footnotes. But, more important, I have done so because this book is designed to offer its readers a basic and detailed understanding of *Truth and Method* as a whole, one not confined to its more controversial aspects.

Even the modest task of elucidation attempted here has its limits, however. In endeavoring to shed light on the text, this interpretation has necessarily focused its beam: it spotlights certain aspects of *Truth and Method* to the exclusion of others. Thus it cannot be exhaustive. And even those important aspects which it does succeed in highlighting can be obscured by the glare of overclarification. As Gadamer writes with respect to translation, "Like all interpretation, translation is a spotlighting. The translator has no choice but to take on himself the task of spotlighting. He is permitted to leave nothing in the dark, even if it is unclear to him. He must show his colors. Of course there are borderline cases where in the original (and for the 'original reader') there is really something unclear. But in just such hermeneutic borderline cases becomes evident the necessity under which the translator always labors. Here he must resign himself. He must say clearly how he understands. Insofar as he is always in the situation of being unable to give expression to all the dimensions of his text, that means a continual renunciation is necessary for him. Every translation that takes its task seriously is clearer and flatter than the original" (*WM* 363–64; *TM* 348). The same pertains to this interpretation of *Truth and Method*. It too settles for a trade-off and sacrifices resonance and contour for the sake of clarity. But if, for just this reason, it also enables the reader to return better prepared to the original—there to hear the overtones and discern the multi-dimensionality missing here—this book will have served its purpose.

My work on this study was assisted by a faculty development grant from Texas Tech University and by a fellowship from the Alexander von Humboldt Stiftung, supported by Wolfgang Iser. For the generosity of this assistance, I remain indebted and sincerely grateful.

Abbreviations of Gadamer's Main Works

DD   *Dialogue and Dialectic: Eight Hermeneutical Studies on Plato.* Trans. P. Christopher Smith. New Haven: Yale University Press, 1980.

HD   *Hegel's Dialectic: Five Hermeneutical Studies.* Trans. P. Christopher Smith. New Haven: Yale University Press, 1976.

KS   *Kleine Schriften.* 4 vols. Tübingen: J. C. B. Mohr (Paul Siebeck), 1972–79.

PH   *Philosophical Hermeneutics.* Trans. David E. Linge. Berkeley: University of California Press, 1976.

RAS   *Reason in the Age of Science.* Trans. Frederick G. Lawrence. Cambridge: MIT Press, 1981.

TM   *Truth and Method.* Ed. Garrett Barden and John Cumming. New York: Seabury Press, 1975.

WM   *Wahrheit und Methode: Grundzüge einer Philosophischen Hermeneutik.* 4th ed. Tübingen: J. C. B. Mohr (Paul Siebeck), 1975.

Introduction: Hermeneutics and the Natural Sciences

Like truth, method is the subject of the whole of *Truth and Method*, not a topic specifically located in any particular part of it. Although the first subsection of the book bears the title "Das Methodenproblem," Gadamer does not begin by defining method, enumerating its presuppositions, or elaborating its implications.[1] Rather, he proceeds immediately to a history of the nonmethodical avenues to truth which have become available through the "humanistic tradition." That Gadamer leaves method undefined is typical of *Truth and Method* and itself embodies the suspicions about method that inform the book. "To define is to distrust," Laurence Sterne once wrote; and what definition distrusts is the capacity not only of the reader but of conversation itself. Through definition, a word becomes a term: rigid, predictable, and invulnerable to the twists and turns that a word receives both in dialogue and in the history of the language in general. The terminal character of terminology is appropriate to meaning that has been finally determined and about which discussion has stopped. In this sense, definition is the foundation and fruition of methodic knowledge.

If Gadamer does not begin (or end) with a definition of method but rather

---

1. No more does Gadamer define truth: "Hermeneutic reflection is limited to opening up new possibilities for knowledge which would not be perceived without it. Of itself it offers no criterion of truth" (*KS* 4:130).

proceeds to the history of its humanistic alternatives, that is in part because history is itself the alternative to method. *Truth and Method*, however admirable the order of its presentation, cannot be called a systematic demonstration of specifiable theses. It aims to make sense of and legitimate certain ideas, but not to prove them. They cannot be proved, not because of their intrinsic irrationality, still less because they are false, but rather, precisely because they call into question the belief that proof is our sole means of access to truth. As methodical proof calls a halt to history and obviates any further need to consult tradition as a source of knowledge, so also art, philosophy, history—tradition generally—challenge the universality and exhaustiveness of method as the exclusive means whereby knowledge worthy of being called true is disclosed.

Nevertheless, though Gadamer's choice of history over definition is thoughtfully motivated, it is notable and perhaps of fundamental significance that he challenges the dominion of method through a history of the humanistic tradition, and not through a history of method. This implies, first, that method lies outside the humanistic tradition.[2] Second it implies, albeit indirectly, that method, and specifically the method of the natural sciences, has no history: that it sprang full-blown from the heads of Bacon and Descartes and has not altered significantly since then. Especially in contrast to his careful delineation of the history of aesthetics and historiography from the late eighteenth to the early twentieth century, Gadamer's allusions to the historical changes in scientific method are sparse, irregular, and frustratingly sketchy.

This is not to say that his conception of method is superficial—far from it. Yet, since *Truth and Method* lacks even a basic discrimination between the theories of method proposed by Descartes and Bacon—let alone between these and the numerous theories of philosophers of science who have since made contributions to the field—it appears that Gadamer views method and natural science itself as monolithic, homogeneous, and fixed.[3] "What one calls method in modern science," he writes, "is everywhere one and the same, and only

2. On the growth of method within the humanistic tradition, see Ong, *Ramus, Method, and the Decay of Dialogue*, pp. 225ff. This may be the place to mention Gadamer's own method, which he says is phenomenological (*TM* xxiv; *WM* xxiv). Gadamer does not consider the implications of this fact, but it is important to remember that, as Heidegger writes, "the expression 'phenomenological' signifies primarily a *methodological conception*" (*Being and Time*, p. 50). So too Reiner Wiehl remarks, "Phenomenology is less a theory than a method" (in Bubner et al., ed., *Hermeneutik und Dialectik*, p. 170). It would be legitimate to ask whether *Truth and Method* falls under its own critique with respect to its method.

3. Dieter Misgeld observes that Gadamer "never analyses scientific method in terms of a plurality of methods or the relation between theories and methods" ("Gadamer's Hermeneutics," p. 236).

displays itself in an especially exemplary manner in the natural sciences'' (*WM* 5; *TM* 9). This very thesis dates *Truth and Method* as belonging, in respect to its view of science, to the late stages of logical positivism, a movement which we, with the advantage of two decades of hindsight, can see was rapidly drawing to a close (and probably already over) when *Truth and Method* was published in 1960.[4] The influential Unified Science movement, organized before World War II and including Neurath, Carnap, Russell, and Morris among its founding members, had as its aim the construction of just such an integral, universal science as Gadamer seems to assume. To some extent, positivism has always been characterized by its global pretensions; and there is no need to assert any direct influence of the Unified Science movement[5] on Gadamer (though when he writes about Leibniz's *characteristica universalis*, he seems to have Carnap and others in mind). The point is rather that the typically positivist ambition toward totality and exclusiveness makes itself felt in Gadamer's tacit and unquestioned assumption that natural science has—and since its inception has always had—only one method and that we know what that method is.

If Gadamer does tend merely to assume the imperialist ambitions of science (even if only to combat them), it may be that he shares other essential interests with those to whom his thought appears most antipathetic. I will later indicate that, despite Gadamer's telling objections to propositional logic, for example, there is a significant affinity between his denial of Hegelian totalization and Russell's theory of types, Gödel's incompleteness theorem, and Tarski's semantic conception of truth. But here it is important to insist on Gadamer's monolithic notion of natural science and its method for another reason. Although he does not define scientific method, Gadamer does nevertheless conceive it as uniform, determinate, and hence fundamentally definable. The absence of definition seems for this reason to be motivated as much by the idea that method belongs to common and accepted knowledge as by a special hermeneutic rigor. Gadamer's conception of method is abstract and essentially unhistorical, and that fact justifies the endeavor that follows to winnow it out from the dispersed passages of *Truth and Method* where it appears.

On the abstract uniformity of method depends Gadamer's contention that

---

4. One consequence of this belatedness, which we will discuss below, is that Gadamer may ''challenge beliefs hardly anyone since the early days of logical positivism would still entertain'' (Misgeld, ''Gadamer's Hermeneutics,'' p. 223).

5. Despite the lack of direct influence, Habermas may be right that Gadamer ''involuntarily supports the positivist degradation of hermeneutics'' (quoted in Bleicher, *Contemporary Hermeneutics*, p. 155). See also Habermas's review of *TM* in Dallmayr and McCarthy, ed., *Understanding and Social Inquiry*, p. 355.

the human and natural sciences are distinct because what is scientific about the human sciences derives from elsewhere than methodology (*WM* 5; *TM* 9). Thus this abstraction is highly significant. For if it can be shown that the history of method has not remained static, that method varies significantly among the various natural sciences, or that some or all natural sciences depend far less on method than Gadamer assumes, then it may follow either that the human sciences participate in some stage in the history of method, that they approximate the methods of one or more particular natural sciences, or that they in fact share with the natural sciences a fundamental independence from method.[6] If so, the distinction between the human and natural sciences would become less categorical than it often appears in *Truth and Method*.

THE LIMITS OF METHOD

What, then, is Gadamer's conception of method in general? First of all, it must be said that method is the paradigmatic expression of the condition that gave rise to epistemology.[7] The search for the foundations of knowledge—its possibility and legitimacy—remained the dominant theme of philosophy from Descartes to Husserl. Method, and epistemology in general, Gadamer contends, is primarily a response to *Fremdheit*, the condition of being no longer at home in the world. To be at home means to belong, to live in surroundings that are familiar, self-evident, and unobtrusive; its contrary, *Fremdheit*, consists in the schism between past and present, I and others, self and world. Method derives from this sense of living among objects to which one no longer belongs. "As the foreignness which the age of mechanics felt toward nature as the natural world has its epistemological expression in the concept of self-consciousness and in the methodologically developed rule of certainty, of 'clear and distinct perception,' so also the human sciences of the nineteenth century felt a comparable foreignness with respect to the historical world. The spiritual creations of the past, art and history, no longer belong to the self-evident domain of the present but rather are objects relinquished to research, data from which a past allows itself to be represented" (*WM* 61; *TM* 58).

6. On this last possibility, see Kuhn, *Essential Tension*, p. 116. Others have argued for a less categorical division between the humanities and natural science; see Toulmin, "The Construal of Reality"; Rorty, "Reply to Dreyfus and Taylor"; Mary Hesse, "In Defense of Objectivity"; and Richard Bernstein, *Beyond Objectivism and Relativism*.

7. For a detailed contrasting of epistomology and hermeneutics, see Rorty, *Philosophy and the Mirror of Nature*, pp. 315–56. Rorty is professedly indebted to Gadamer for a number of his insights.

Gadamer here mentions a number of essential elements and correlatives of method that unfold like motifs throughout *Truth and Method*: self-consciousness, objectivity, reconstruction, foreignness, regulation, certainty. We will be examining these in detail below. But what he most strongly intimates in this passage is the sense of loss that accompanies the movement from being at home to *Fremdheit*, the movement in which one's world devolves into the materiale of knowledge. "Little we see in nature that is ours," Wordsworth laments; "for this, for everything, we are out of tune." Like nature, art and history no longer belong to us, nor we to them. They no longer belong to the *selbstverständlich*: the things that are to us self-understandable, self-evident matters of course. Method, then, aims to redeem this loss by substituting itself for the kind of understanding that is not reflective knowledge because it understands everything in advance by belonging to it, before knowing and its methodical regulation come into play.[8] But the paradox of the substitute is operative here as elsewhere: method famishes the very craving for homecoming that it is designed to satisfy.

It should be apparent that the genesis of epistemology in *Truth and Method* parallels the genesis of presence-at-hand in Heidegger's *Being and Time*. Both thinkers insist on the phenomenological priority of significance to fact, relation to substance, and understanding to knowledge.[9] The latter are generated by a breakdown whereby some element of the self-evident becomes obtrusive, importunate, and demanding of our attention. It doesn't work right, or fit into its usual relationships, or possess its usual significance. It is not what it is supposed to be, or (as now appears) what *I* supposed it to be. From one's surprise or frustration at this sudden unintelligibility derive both the first and third persons: both *I* and that which stands over against me (*Gegenstand*). Subject and object separate and precipitate out simultaneously. Yet even while separate they remain interdependent, because the breakdown in the world corresponds to a breakdown in understanding. Since subject and object are correlative in this view, "subjectivism" and "objectivism" come to be largely synonymous terms. Both subject and object are derivative and secondary, in that both precipitate out of the more primordial unity of being at home in the world. Further, both are determined negatively: the knowing subject no longer understands, and the object to be known no longer fits. The cognitive remedies for these twin defects are

8. Kruger doubts that this pre-reflective understanding can be opposed to scientific knowledge, because "it is clear that the lifeworld has long since been permeated by science" (in Bubner et al., ed., *Hermeneutik und Dialectik*, p. 8).

9. "The primacy that language and understanding have in Heidegger's thought indicate the priority of the 'relation' over against its relational members" (*PH* 30).

likewise correlative. The object is disassembled, the rules of its functioning are ascertained, and then it is reconstructed according to those rules; so, also, knowledge is analyzed, its rules are determined, and finally it is redeployed as method. The purpose of both remedies is to prevent unanticipated future breakdowns by means of breaking down even further the flawed entity and then synthesizing it artificially. Thus Gadamer speaks of "the ideal of knowledge familiar from natural science, whereby we understand a process only when we can bring it about artificially" (*WM* 355; *TM* 336). Artificial reproduction is the basis of technology in the realm of objects and of method in the realm of subjects.

The question is, how much of what we need to know can be reproduced by rule in this way? Gadamer "does not in the slightest exclude the fact that the methods of the modern natural sciences find application to the social world as well. . . . It never even entered my mind to deny the unavoidability of methodical work within the so-called human sciences" (*WM* xvii; *TM* xvii).[10] But this work, Gadamer suggests, however rigorous and extensive its methodical deployment, cannot of itself exhaust what is to be known. In particular, it cannot exhaust what is to be known of tradition; and that is so because tradition is not like consciousness. It is not rule-governed and hence cannot be reconstructed artificially, by rule. In this respect Gadamer is as close to Kant as to Heidegger; he takes on Dilthey's task of writing a Kantian critique of historical judgment[11] by accepting certain premises from the *Critique of Judgment* and extending them to the realm of history: "However dissatisfactory appears the development paved by Kant toward subjectivism in the newer aesthetics, Kant has convincingly demonstrated the untenability of aesthetic rationalism" (*WM* 455; *TM* 437). "Aesthetic rationalism" refers here to the ideal of French neoclassicism that art can and should be produced by rule, along with its corollary that questions of taste can be determined by proof and argument. Undermining this ideal, Kant defends the autonomy of art against all conceptual knowledge, insisting rather on the free play of genius and its escape from regulation and legislation. Just as for Kant beauty is neither produced nor enjoyed by appeal to any specifiable rule or standard, so for Gadamer history and tradition generally cannot be understood in that way either. "Everywhere where one has to 'come across something'

10. Hilberath rightly emphasizes that "there is no question but that on the one hand [Gadamer] treasures the methodically achieved knowledge of the [natural] sciences and wants to see them applied in hermeneutic practice" (*Theologie*, p. 58).

11. At the center of *Truth and Method* lies an essentially Kantian question: "How is understanding possible?" (*WM* xvii; *TM* xviii). Yet, in answering this question, Gadamer follows not Kant's but Heidegger's path. See Ricoeur, "The Task of Hermeneutics," in Murray, ed., *Heidegger*, pp. 152ff.

which cannot be found by learning and methodical work alone—that is, everywhere where *inventio* emerges, where something is owing to inspiration and not methodical calculation—there it depends on *ingenium*, on genius" (*WM* 50; *TM* 50). For such discoveries, the rules and methods of knowledge are of no help. Thus it is clear why Gadamer disavows any attempt in *Truth and Method* to "develop a system of regulations that could describe or even direct the methodical procedures of the human sciences" (*WM* xvi; *TM* xvi). Such an endeavor would be futile, for there is no art or technique of happening onto things. There is no method of stumbling.

Method is designed rather to avoid stumbling and prevent accidents, whether serendipitous or otherwise. The assumption of methodology, of course, is that haphazard guesses and intuitions whose origins are unknown are rarely felicitous; and this rarity is not merely an empirical infrequency. Rather, it originates in the basic prescription of method, that whatever has not been regularly derived or confirmed should, even if true, be held in suspicion and, for purely methodological reasons, in fact be considered erroneous (*WM* 255; *TM* 240). It is not enough that a conclusion be true; it must be exempt from the suspicion of falsehood, and the presupposition of the Enlightenment is that "a methodically disciplined use of reason can protect against every error. That was Descartes' idea of method" (*WM* 261; *TM* 246). Mistakes are precluded by method because the methodologically controlled mind is aware of its position at all times, knows its origin and the rules that govern its progress; and therefore the end of method is clear and distinct, because the steps of derivation can be retraced, reconstructed, and rechecked at will.[12] Truths accidentally known, as irregular and unrepeatable, are therefore essentially unfounded; and what is not founded by method, what is not repeatable, is suspect. Thus, as method becomes the criterion of truth, history (itself essentially unrepeatable) becomes increasingly unnecessary (*WM* 329; *TM* 311).

We should be under no misapprehension that Gadamer favors making mistakes: whenever they can by method be avoided, of course they should be. "The practice of the legal historian, like that of the judge, has its 'methods' of avoiding errors, and therein I concur entirely with the legal historian. The hermeneutical interest of the philosopher, however, arises only where the avoidance of error has already been achieved" (*WM* xxi; *TM* xxi). What makes this statement so astonishing is that we are inclined to ask: What remains for philosophical hermeneutics if its aim is already achieved and error successfully avoided? What

---

12. "As determined by method, the ideal knowledge consists in tracing the path of knowledge so consciously that it is always possible to retrace it" (*KS* 1:50)

is left? This remainder, first, cannot be called error, for method (per hypothesi) has removed everything that can rightly be called error; and thus the aim of philosophical hermeneutics cannot be to excise anything further of that kind at all. Error is the mistake that can be avoided. What remains, however, is ineluctable and hence not erroneous. That this remainder exists and functions in understanding is Gadamer's thesis. For the moment, we can call it *hap*. It makes its presence felt when one happens onto something, in the haphazard guess, the happenstance situation, in happiness and haplessness. If, for better or worse, hap cannot be avoided, it eludes the hegemony of method.

Assuming the efficacy of hap, the fundamental hubris of method consists in its presumption that it exhausts the sphere of truth.[13] Excepting this presumption, Gadamer has no quarrel with method; but that exception is nevertheless decisive. "The concept of knowledge based on scientific procedures," Gadamer writes, "tolerates no restriction of its claim to universality" (*PH* 54). Basic to method, whether Cartesian or Baconian, is the claim to comprehend (in both senses) all that in truth is. Hap, by contrast, is what occurs to us "beyond our willing and doing" (*WM* xvi; *TM* xvi). And if the advent of truth, like other events, can happen to us without our desiring or intending it, that means that in methodological universalism, there is a distinct exaggeration of sovereignty— of its claim to control what occurs to us and in our world, to control history, and especially to control truth. The ambition of method, in Bacon's words, is to "extend the empire of man over things," to "exercise over the nature of things the authority which properly belongs" to the mind (*Complete Essays*, pp. 263, 155). The peculiar sycophancy of method as Bacon conceives it is that precisely by submitting the mind to the shows of things, which Bacon calls the "humiliation of the human spirit," the mind achieves dominion (p. 161). (One is reminded of the slave's mode of power in Hegel.) When the conditions and laws governing a process have been submissively determined so that it can be brought about artificially, the process can be dominated—that is, produced and prevented at will. To the extent that Bacon is representative, Gadamer is justified in saying that, although basic research in natural science is not directed to any particular practical end,[14] nevertheless, it is rightly conceived as the "willful domination of existents" (*WM* 430; *TM* 412).

13. Grondin suggests that Gadamer consigns the truth of beings to natural science while preserving the truth of being for hermeneutics. Thus "the differentiation between truth and method, rightly understood, is another name for the *ontological* difference, newly discovered by Heidegger, between being and beings" (*Hermeneutische Wahrheit*, p. vii).

14. "For the sciences what is allowed to count as methodically certified experience is distinguished by the fact that it is fundamentally independent of every situation of action and every integration into a context of action" (*KS* 4:173).

Whether this will to power is on the whole a good or a bad thing Gadamer is not concerned to determine. It is futile to prescribe to science in any case. What does concern Gadamer is the equation of the domitability of the objects of objective science with their whole truth. "The truth that science speaks to us," he writes, "is itself relative to a determinate behavior toward the world and cannot at all claim to be the whole" (*WM* 425; *TM* 407). In the specific *Weltverhalten* of objective science, "the concept of 'being in itself' acquires the character" of a *Willenbestimmung*—a dialectical term that means both a delimitation and a destination of the will. First, as a delimitation, "what is in itself is independent of one's willing and choosing. However, [as a destination] in that it is known in its being in itself, it is precisely in this way put at one's disposal, so that one can reckon with it, that is, can direct it to one's own purposes" (*WM* 426; *TM* 408). It is important to recognize that Gadamer does not dispute the fact that objective science knows things as they truly are, even though that implies that everything in the world of science is subject to human calculation and control. What he does contest is the supposition that being in itself is singular and, in particular, that being as science knows it comprehends all that in truth is. This monopolistic claim that the only real world is the world of science does seem endemic to centuries of thought about natural science. Perhaps the tenacity and significance of such universalism is best measured by what Gadamer is willing to sacrifice in order to combat it. If natural science—however rigorous its methods or extensive its research—will never comprehend the whole truth, that is ultimately because the whole truth does not and never will exist. This is the negative import of the historicity of truth; more positively, it implies that science cannot claim to be exhaustive, because truth keeps happening. We will need to return to this idea again.

Method is designed not only to the Faustian end of manipulating its objects, however. No less fundamentally, it consists in the self-control of the researcher, the cognitive subject. The correlate of its *Weltverhalten* is its *Sichverhalten*. Self-control is implied in the Baconian self-abasement of stooping to observation and experience, and also in the self-aggrandizement of refusing to stoop before the idols of the tribe, cave, market, and theater. For Descartes, as for Bacon, the rigor of method derives from the almost religious process of self-purification that eliminates all obstructions so that knowing occurs unimpeded. The fulfillment of this aim requires a consciousness maximally transparent to itself, one without any alien forces influencing it unawares toward a given conclusion or directing it outside its own control. For Descartes, dubitability is the index of what is alien to consciousness; what are immanent, on the other hand, are the structures it has itself erected upon indubitable foundations. These alone are worthy of being dignified as truth, and truth thus defined consists in the constructions of self-transparent consciousness.

If so, truth depends on the possibility that consciousness can be self-transparent and self-identical—that it does not vary in time, and that it contains nothing that is not its own, because it has constructed itself. It must be possible, then, to avoid the condition of (what Heidegger calls) "being thrown." Most simply, this phrase means that being is prior to consciousness: we are situated in a world before we begin to think for ourselves, even before we are conscious of ourselves. The question is whether and to what extent we can, by taking thought, ever escape this condition or build upon firmer foundations than those that are given to us and we merely accept. Descartes believes, indeed simply presumes, that such an escape and new beginning are possible. In the first meditation, he proposes to make a "clean sweep" of all that "I had accepted from my earliest years." Upon the methodological maxim that he "must withhold assent no less carefully from what is not plainly certain and indubitable than from what is obviously false," he suspends credit in what he had earlier accepted and proceeds to reconstruct truth within a consciousness purged of tradition (*Philosophical Writings*, p. 61). Even if we first find ourselves in the condition of being thrown, Descartes implies, it is possible to step out of it and begin anew, this time on our own.

What makes this possibility itself dubious, as Peirce observes, is the fact that "no one who follows the Cartesian method will ever be satisfied unless he has formally recovered all those beliefs which in form he has given up" (*Essential Writings*, p. 86). It is not by accident that in matters of faith, for example, however heretical the Cartesian method, its results were quite orthodox and traditional. The method itself seems a circular detour, less an exercise of self-sovereign reason than of rationalization. Descartes himself does not so much make a radical beginning as justify the beliefs that he had accepted as true from an early age.[15]

Modern science, Gadamer suggests, has adopted the Cartesian principle of doubt as its basis and thus begins by attempting to render tradition inert and eliminate the effects of prejudice (*WM* 255; *TM* 240). Prejudices are the elements most alien to consciousness because, paradoxically, they seem to belong to it and yet are not of its devising or under its control. Being thrown means that prejudice is not merely prior to consciousness but is its condition. We understand our world before we begin to think about it; such pre-understanding gives rise

15. This is one of Heidegger's conclusions about Descartes in *Being and Time*, p. 131.

to thought and always conditions it. This is not to say that this or that prejudice cannot be falsified and overcome—only that all prejudices cannot be simultaneously exorcised by the exertion of self-control, because the affirmation of some prejudices is always the condition of disaffirming others. Perfect doubt would render knowledge impossible. Thus the project of a radical beginning is doomed to failure. Instead of beginning, we are always in the midst of an ongoing process; if we can know more, that is because we understand something already, prereflectively. Being thrown is being always under way, and thus no method can pretend to be perfectly foundational or perfectly free of prejudices.

The pre- of prejudice indicates that it is prior to conscious judgment; and if prejudice, this alien element that precludes the self-transparency of consciousness, is not only ineluctable, but the very condition of consciousness, then the dominion of mind over its objects, and more especially over itself as an object, must necessarily be imperfect. Gadamer departs from Hegel as well as from Descartes in that he conceives self-consciousness as an unreachable goal and self-knowledge as an infinite task. He ascribes the finitude of self-consciousness to the fact that understanding (including self-understanding) is, and always remains, conditioned by its situation; and this situation cannot be objectified or taken into account in such a way that its effects could be subtracted from the process of cognition. "The concept of the situation is characterized by the fact that one does not find himself standing over against it and therefore can have no objective knowledge of it. One stands in it, finds himself already in a situation, the clarification of which is a task never to be perfectly completed. . . . The clarification of this situation, that is, effective-historical reflection on it, is not perfectable, but this imperfectability is not due to a deficiency in reflection, rather it is ascribable to the essence of the historical being that we are. Being historical means never dissolving into self-knowledge" (*WM* 285; *TM* 269).

The verb *aufgehen*, which I have here translated as "dissolving," also suggests division without remainder. It is as if historical being were a prime number which, however it is analyzed, leaves some excess, some remainder that exceeds self-knowledge and thus eludes prediction and methodological control. Above, we characterized this remainder as hap; here, we can say that hap is an aspect of historical being and (since all being is historical) of being generally. Just as our situation cannot be completely objectified because we are in it, so our own being cannot be perfectly known because we are. This is what calls into question the *possibility* of method considered as full self-control based on full self-knowledge. But Gadamer calls method into question as an *ideal* as well. The fact that we are—which precludes definitive self-knowledge—is precisely what also gives us those intimations of what we are that we do possess.[16] Refining ourselves out of time, out of our world, and out of existence, in the name of objective knowledge, turns out to be just as undesirable as it is impossible.

A total knowledge and control of the world requires a total knowledge and control of ourselves. That is the premise of method; but since we are situated in the world and belong to it, perfect self-knowledge and self-control require perfect knowledge and control of the world as well. The two are reciprocally necessary. The fact that we are, and thus understand what it means to be, makes each kind of knowledge possible to some degree but at the same time precludes its complete fulfillment. Precisely because we are, being is never wholly assimilated to consciousness. *Bewusstsein* (consciousness) is more *Sein* than *bewusst*, Gadamer writes, more being than conscious; and being is never fully manifest (*PH* 38). This remainder, being, is always *to be* understood and interpreted.

That the understanding of being remains a perpetually unfinished task renders suspect the certainty promised by methodical research. We have seen that, for science, experience is certified by being repeated and, if so, what cannot be repeated—namely history—must be disclaimed by the method of science. Thus the finality and certainty of method depend on the fact that method is not itself historical, any more than are its results. But there is in fact another certainty, one that requires no methodical validation and that is historical. ''The kind of certainty that yields the assurance attained by going through doubt is distinct from the immediate lived certainty with which all purposes and values enter human consciousness when they raise the claim to be unconditional. The certainty of science properly distinguishes itself from such certainty acquired in life. The certainty of science always has a Cartesian aspect. It is the result of a critical methodology that seeks to concede validity only to the indubitable. The certainty [of life, however,] does not grow out of doubts and overcoming them; rather it always precedes our being seized by doubt'' (*WM* 225; *TM* 211).

The certainty of beliefs that are taken over from a self-evident tradition and thus are prior to doubt, Gadamer suggests, is no less sure of itself than the methodologically verified certainty that is posterior to doubt. What is in fact not doubted because one lives it is, until it is doubted, just as certain as what cannot be doubted. Prejudices of which we are not conscious possess the notorious tenacity of the obvious. Nor is this certainty due merely to a misplaced or premature confidence. Prejudices can change, but not all prejudices are false;

---

16. As Alasdair MacIntyre explains, "If truth is hidden, it is not because it requires searching out by some device of method, but because it is so plainly before our eyes in our everyday activities and conversations that we cannot perceive it" ("Contexts of Interpretation," p. 42.).

some remain unaffected by the fires of doubt. These acquire no increment of certainty in the process of being methodically certified. I am no more certain of my existence now than before I read Descartes; and Gadamer, far from finding the Cartesian enthymeme indubitable, in fact considers it false. Thus we can ask whether the indubitable is itself a historical phenomenon. If what we *can* doubt changes as much as what we *do* doubt, and if even methodical verification rests on foundations that crumble though we cannot doubt their endurance, then all confidence in having finally arrived is premature. Even posteriority to doubt cannot preserve truth from temporality, raise it to the permanence of conceptual representation, or convert it into a possession of consciousness.

The fact that neither type of certainty is immutable suggests that the primordial understanding that derives merely from living in a historically particular world—merely from being—retains its force at the most advanced levels of consciousness. This prior understanding influences us in unpredictable and essentially uncontrollable ways. Through it, history affects and indeed effects consciousness; and consciousness so determined Gadamer calls "effective-historical consciousness." Rather than a law unto itself, consciousness—"even modern historical, and scientific consciousness—is governed by effective-historical determinations, and that beyond any possible knowledge of being so governed. The historically effected consciousness is finite in so radical a sense that our being, effected by the whole of our history, essentially far surpasses the knowledge of itself" (*WM* xxii; *TM* xxii). In brief, we are, more than we know.

The knowledge that we are more than we know—that the mind does not manage its own origins or destiny—sets us the task of becoming more aware of the preconscious determinants of consciousness, that is, of coming to know ourselves through the knowledge of our history. This task of unearthing the historical determinants of consciousness is infinite, because history extends indefinitely into the dark backward of time. Equally important, history extends indefinitely forward, and that not merely because there is no conceivable end of time. History, in the sense with which we are concerned here, does not move automatically with the clock hands. Rather it has to be made, even if unconsciously and involuntarily. History is made when our history affects us behind our backs. If our being more than we know means that this always happens, then the perfect objectification of history is impossible. Making history into an object depends on methodological sterility: the exemption of consciousness from influence by foreign forces and also therefore from the effects of its objects. Method is essentially general, rather than determined by any concrete object; thus it maximizes the dissociation of the subject from the object. In the attempt to objectify history, however, the putative object contaminates the methodological sterility of the subject. One such historical "object" is the artwork: "We see in the experience of art a genuine experience of the work, one that does not leave him who has it unaltered" (*WM* 95; *TM* 89). Like a photographer's attempt to capture a freight train at the moment it actually strikes his camera, making history into an object not only does not succeed, but in fact historicizes the subject. Art makes history when it changes those who experience it.

Objectification does not succeed for a second reason. The mutual autonomy of subject and object is the condition of objectivity: where I share nothing with what is to be known, it can be an object for me. By contrast, when (as in the case of historical knowledge) there is a shared mode of being between subject and object, what is to be known cannot be wholly set over against the knower. Thus, history cannot be fully objectified or fully known because, precisely to the extent that history is objectified, such knowledge must necessarily overlook the knower's share in making history. "In this objectivism," Gadamer writes, "the understander is seen . . . not in relationship to the hermeneutical situation and the constant operativeness of history in his own consciousness, but in such a way as to imply that his own understanding does not enter into the event" (*PH* 28). To the extent that the knowledge of history is objective, it is not complete, and vice versa. To be complete, one might object, we need only add the knowledge of ourselves—but acquiring that knowledge was the rationale for the study of history in the first place.

Objectivity, finally, requires a static object in addition to a static subject; and this returns us to the question of how history is made. Even if time is not finite, we tend to think of history—and especially historical events—as finished, over and done with, and thus object-like. We have already called that notion into question insofar as the force of history remains operative, but Gadamer suggests further that history itself also changes. The meaning of the past is not fixed and static. "By being actualized anew in understanding, texts are drawn into a genuine [process of] happening, exactly as are events themselves through their continuance" (*WM* 355; *TM* 336). The text is altered in its significance by understanding, as an event is altered by its consequences. Both texts and events change precisely because they continue and endure. But a text has no consequences except in its being continuously understood. Thus, just as an event is not finished, its meaning not complete, until it ceases to have consequences— and hence becomes inconsequential—so also the text is not a whole until it is no longer understood. The text is an unfinished process, one that is continually completed in the history of its being understood. We have seen that, in the case of art, understanding is effected and enlarged by the text; now we can see further that the text is continuously effected, brought about, and realized by understanding. The history of understanding is the effectuating history of the text. Understanding makes history, makes the past by belonging to it and adding itself to it. This is to say that the knowledge of history cannot be objective, because its "object" is expanded by the knowing. Objectivity always arrives too late.

Crucial to Gadamer's conception of method in general, as we have sketched it here, is that method is a response to the alienation of self and world, and also an attempt to overcome it. The schism of subject and object originates in such a breakdown, and both owe their existence to it. Hermeneutics, too, originates in this sense of rupture. Both it and method are "responses to the world as the *atopon* (the strange), that which does not 'fit' into the customary order of our expectations based on experience" (*PH* 25). What distinguishes method from hermeneutics, however, is that method responds to alienation with alienation. In objectifying the object by purifying the subject, method drives a wedge between them, and so itself prevents the reunion that is its goal. Instead of homecoming from the condition of *Fremdheit*, method strives for dominion over the world. It aims not to understand the world but to change it, to recreate it in the image of consciousness. This goal requires, above all, that consciousness come to know itself through reflection, to assert its sovereignty over itself, and to exercise its freedom to realize itself.

The universality of method, its claim to be the sole path to truth, depends on the totality of its control over itself. This is the point of maximum vulnerability in methodologism, and it is here that Gadamer asserts the counterclaim of history. If consciousness not only effects history (without being conscious of it) but also is itself historically effected, then self-consciousness, self-sovereignty, and the freedom of self-effectuation cannot be complete. Hap, historical being, persists as the remainder that eludes the web of method.

But hap functions not only negatively, as a lamentable imperfection in epistemology. Even if it escapes methodological manipulation, it is not for Gadamer merely a matter of chance. Rather, hap is a remainder of the primordial unity of self and world that method, however rigorous, is not entirely able to break up. For this reason, hap points the way home—or rather, is already there. When we happen upon something true, something that possesses an immediate certitude, though it cannot be methodically certified, then we already belong to and participate in the *Geschehen der Wahrheit*, the happening of truth. We belong to history.

METHOD AND TRUTH IN THE NATURAL SCIENCES

Having reviewed Gadamer's conception of method in general, and having considered in an introductory manner some of his objections to the universality of method so described, we need now to turn to the particulars of the method of natural science as Gadamer understands them, and in so doing to ask whether and to what extent his picture of science corresponds to that depicted since 1960, when *Truth and Method* was published. We need to inquire further whether specifiable aspects of the human sciences cannot in fact be correlated with those of the natural sciences.

In his afterword, Gadamer wrote, "As I finished the present book at the end of 1959, I was very uncertain whether it hadn't come 'too late,' that is, whether its attempt to restore the balance for traditional and historical thought was not almost superfluous by then. Signs of a new wave of the technological opposition to history were multiplying. Corresponding to that was the increasing acceptance of Anglo-Saxon epistemology and analytical philosophy. . . . A new 'positivistic' self-understanding, required by the acceptance of American and English methods and questions, pressed onward" (*WM* 313). As it turned out, Gadamer's fears that his book would appear too late to have any impact, because the final victory of positivism was imminent, were perfectly unfounded. The signs that the battle was turning were there to be read: in 1960 Gadamer mentions that "the problematic of logical, artificial language" characteristic of positivism had broken down and that "the anti-metaphysical passion of logical positivism has been dissolved with the recognition of the autonomous meaning of spoken language"—for which he cites Wittgenstein, and presumably means the *Investigations*. By 1975, John Wisdom can speak of positivism only as a "dead horse," but he dates the demise of its anti-metaphysicalism thirty years earlier. This animus against metaphysical meaninglessness, he writes in *Philosophy and Its Place*, "had very many eminent followers; but they had all given up these extreme positions at the latest by about 1945. I remember Hempel in the mid-30's reporting that it was customary in the Vienna Circle to interject 'metaphysical' if any member lapsed into a meaningless statement, and that this happened so often it had to be shortened to 'm.' By 1945, this was a thing of the past" (p. 41). With the cooling of this antimetaphysical passion and the discreditation of the verifiability criterion of meaning that was its support, not only a battle was lost, but the war. The consequence was hardly the triumph that Gadamer predicted. In fact the void that was left by the demise of positivism has apparently been filled with what, of all things, Gadamer least expected. Charles Taylor writes,

> Once we awaken from our positivist slumbers we realize that none of these features [absent from the human sciences] hold of natural science either. The two turn out to be methodologically at one, not for the positivist reason

that there is no rational place for hermeneutics; but for the radically opposed reason that all sciences are equally hermeneutic.

This is an extraordinary reversal. Old-guard Diltheyans, their shoulders hunched from years-long resistance against the encroaching pressure of positivist natural science, suddenly pitch forward on their faces as all opposition ceases to the reign of universal hermeneutics. ["Understanding in Human Science," p. 26]

"This is a pleasing fancy," Taylor goes on to say; but whether it is ultimately fanciful or not, he realizes that now, in the 1980s, those who would dispute the universal scope of hermeneutics find themselves on the defensive.[17] One result of this change is that, from the present point of view, Gadamer ironically seems very much like the old-guard Diltheyans Taylor mentions, despite Gadamer's telling and extensive critique of Dilthey.

The profundity of the reversal that had begun well before the publication of *Truth and Method*, though it became clear only thereafter, can best be appreciated by considering what has happened to the notion of truth in natural science. Nothing can be clearer than the fact that the focal aim of *Truth and Method* is to locate and preserve a domain of truth peculiar to the historical sciences, one that would deflate the universalist pretensions of the natural sciences, and thereby show that method is not the exclusive path to truth. With genuine fervor, Gadamer asks, "Is there no knowledge in art? Does not the experience of art possess a claim to truth that is, to be sure, distinct from that of science but just as certainly is not inferior to it? And does not the task of aesthetics consist in grounding precisely the fact that the experience of art is its own kind of knowledge, certainly distinct from sensory knowledge ... but yet knowledge, that is, the mediation of truth?" (*WM* 93; *TM* 87). Even supposing (what I think is the case) that Gadamer succeeds in grounding the truth claim of art, he fails to legitimate it in *opposition* to that of science—not because the truth claim of science proved exhaustive but because natural science has, to an astounding extent, simply forfeited its own claim to truth.

Evidence is not far to seek. In all the talk about models, theories, conjectures, hypotheses, paradigms, and research programs one finds that the rationale for using this kind of language to describe scientific research is precisely to avoid laying claim to truth. "No claim is made about the 'reality' of the model," Marshall Walker remarks in *The Nature of Scientific Thought*; "the sole criterion is successful prediction from the simplest, most convenient, or most satisfying

---

17. Contrary views, arguing that the scope of hermeneutics is limited, are offered by Habermas, "The Hermeneutic Claim to Universality," and Dreyfus, "Holism and Hermeneutics."

model'' (p. 5). Theories, as Larry Laudan observes in *Progress and Its Problems*, are just as modest as models. "One need not, and scientists generally do not, consider matters of truth and falsity when determining whether a theory does or does not solve a particular empirical problem" (p. 24). But, Laudan later says, even if scientists are not concerned with truth, philosophers have been: "The preoccupation of classical philosophers of science has been with showing that the methods of science are efficient instruments for producing truth, high probability, or even closer approximations to the truth. In this enterprise, they have failed dismally" (p. 223). Thus the criteria of science shift radically. Hypotheses are called not true but fruitful. With Stephen Toulmin, "we might ask 'Is Snell's *hypothesis* true or false?', meaning 'Have any limitations been found to the application of his formula?' But very soon—indeed, as soon as its fruitfulness has been established—the formula in our hypothesis comes to be treated as a *law*, i.e. as something of which we ask not 'Is it true?' but 'When does it hold?' " (*Philosophy of Science*, p. 79). Thomas Kuhn in *Structure of Scientific Revolutions* suggests that "we may . . . have to relinquish the notion, explicit or implicit, that changes of paradigm carry scientists and those who learn from them closer and closer to the truth" (p. 170). But given his well-known dispute with Kuhn, Karl Popper might be expected to retain a notion of truth, or at least of falsity, especially because his philosophy of science is popularly termed "falsificationism." Yet Popper too abandons truth.

> We need not say: "The prediction p is true provided the theory t and the basic statement b are true." We may say instead, that the statement p follows from the (non-contradictory) conjunction of t and b. The falsification of a theory may be described in a similar way. We need not say that the theory is "false," but we may say instead that it is contradicted by a certain set of accepted basic [observation] statements. Nor need we say of basic statements that they are "true" or "false," for we may interpret their acceptance as the result of a conventional decision, and the accepted statements as results of this decision. [*Logic of Scientific Discovery*, p. 274]

Indeed, almost the sole recent philosopher of science who feels no embarrassment about truth is Michael Polanyi.

How the sure and steady advance of science toward the truth suddenly degenerated into a rout is most clearly explained by Imre Lakatos.

> For centuries knowledge meant proven knowledge—proven either by the power of the intellect or by the evidence of the senses. . . . The proving power of the intellect or the senses was questioned by the sceptics more than

two thousand years ago; but they were browbeaten into confusion by the glory of Newtonian physics. Einstein's results again turned the tables and now very few philosophers or scientists still think that scientific knowledge is, or can be, proven knowledge. But few realize that with this the whole classical structure of intellectual values falls in ruins and has to be replaced: one cannot simply water down the ideal of proven truth. . . .

Popper's distinction lies primarily in his having grasped the full implications of the collapse of the best-corroborated scientific theory of all times: Newtonian mechanics and the Newtonian theory of gravitation. ["Falsification," p. 205]

Even though Lakatos overestimates Popper's uniqueness, nevertheless Popper marks a significant redirection in the course of philosophy of science. If Newton's, the best-corroborated of all scientific theories, turned out to be at best incomplete and at worst false, then either Newton was not scientific or else science does not stake its claims on the basis of evidence, proof, and all that goes by the name of verification. If Newton was no scientist, however, where is science to be found? Popper suggests that of course Newton was a scientist par excellence, though his theories were not true. Indeed, Newton's hypotheses exhibit precisely what makes science scientific: they could be, and in fact were "falsified," that is, "contradicted by a certain set of accepted basic statements."

If Einstein's hypotheses are not so contradicted, however, and even if they are corroborated by the basic statements, they should not therefore be called true. It remains the case (in the view of both Lakatos and Popper) that only what has been definitively verified and proved is worthy of being dignified with the name of truth; and if the fate of Newton is exemplary, nothing in science can be so thoroughly verified as to be exempt from suspicion. Nothing can be certainly true; and although that does not affect the scientific character of science, nevertheless Popper's falsificationism retains and in fact assumes the positivist thesis that verification is the exclusive access to truth. "One cannot simply water down the ideal of proven truth," Lakatos asserts. Rather than do so, like Popper and the many others we have cited, he simply refuses to claim truth for science. But again we must ask: If science offers no truth, where is truth to be found? The widespread abandonment of truth in the philosophy of science derives perhaps not so much from intellectual honesty as from the unwillingness to entertain the possibility that the positivist equation of truth with verification is not only inapplicable to science but may indeed be untrue.

Thus Gadamer's focal thesis retains its pertinence: truth cannot be equated with methodical proof. If *Truth and Method* did not arrive too late, as its author feared, that is neither because a new wave of positivism had already overwhelmed all opposition nor, conversely, because hermeneutics now reigns unchallenged.

The fact is that positivism did not die, though it did go underground; and hermeneutics has not exactly won the day. But if it were to move more conclusively into philosophy of science, one might predict that there would be a good deal less skepticism (as a good deal less circumlocution) about the truth claims of science than is now evident.

This is not to say, however, that *Truth and Method* remains untouched by recent developments in philosophy of science. In one respect, it doesn't matter what the specific character of scientific method is, because Gadamer's argument is directed against method as such. Nevertheless, some of his characterizations of the method of natural science are now no longer tenable. (So little elaborated or defended are these characterizations that they might more accurately be called assumptions.) Of these the most basic is that natural science has but one method, induction. *Truth and Method* opens with a brief critique of Mill's *Logic*, which includes a final book on the moral sciences. Mill's aim, Gadamer explains, was not "to recognize the unique logic of the human sciences but, quite the contrary, to show that the inductive methods fundamental to all experiential sciences are exclusively valid" in the human sciences as well (*WM* 1; *TM* 5). Gadamer takes issue with Dilthey on the question of induction as well: "Dilthey's conception of inductive procedure derived from the natural sciences is inadequate" to historical experience (*WM* 288; *TM* 213). Gadamer's critique of Mill and Dilthey centers on their assumption that the inductive method is universal and on their consequent misapplication of it to the human sciences. No more than Mill or Dilthey, however, does Gadamer doubt that induction is the key to the natural sciences. In this respect Gadamer's conception of method in the natural sciences (unlike that of Husserl and Heidegger) remains fundamentally Baconian, for he credits Bacon with developing the "theory of experience as the theory of a true induction. . . . His methods of induction aim to supersede the irregular and accidental way in which daily experience occurs" (*WM* 331; *TM* 312).[18] Induction may not be applicable to the human sciences, but Gadamer does not at all doubt that it is fundamental to natural science.

This is questionable on several counts. Even ignoring Kant and conceding what three centuries of scientific thought have so often asserted—that the edifice of science is erected upon the basis of induction—it does not follow that science has but one method. Mill in fact distinguishes five methods of induction. Nor

---

18. By contrast, Bacon's role in the development of natural science is now consistently downplayed. Whitehead wrote, "The Baconian method of induction . . . if consistently pursued, would have left natural science where it found it" (quoted in Danto, *Analytical Philosophy*, p. 7). In the same vein, Kuhn has more recently observed that "Bacon's naive and ambitious program was an impotent delusion from the start" (*Essential Tension*, p. 118).

is it self-evident that induction, taken as a whole, is the exclusive method of science. "Science has not one aim but many," Stephen Toulmin writes in *Foresight and Understanding*, "and its development has passed through many contrasted stages. It is therefore fruitless to look for a single, all-purpose 'scientific method': the growth and evolution of scientific ideas depends on no one method, and will always call for a broad range of different enquiries" (p. 17).

What makes Gadamer's conception of science most questionable, however, is that though science employs a variety of methods, it is doubtful whether induction is one of them and indeed whether induction is a method at all. The book that most forcefully raises these doubts is clearly Popper's *Logic of Scientific Discovery*, published in German twenty-six years before *Truth and Method*: "The theory to be developed in the following pages," Popper writes, "stands directly opposed to all attempts to operate with the ideas of inductive logic. It might be described as the theory of *the deductive method of testing*, or as the view that a hypothesis can only be empirically *tested*—and only *after* it has been advanced" (p. 30). Empirically *tested*, Popper emphasizes, not empirically *derived*. The theory of induction is a theory about the derivation of concepts, laws, and other generals, and about how their validity depends on their origins. By contrast, Popper argues that the origin of a hypothesis is irrelevant to its empirical (scientific) character and in fact not susceptible to logical analysis.

> There is no such thing as a logical method of having new ideas, or a logical reconstruction of this process. My view may be expressed by saying that every discovery contains "an irrational element," or "a creative intuition,"in Bergson's sense. In a similar way Einstein speaks of the "search for those highly universal laws . . . from which a picture of the world can be obtained by pure deduction. There is no logical path," he says "leading to these . . . laws. They can only be reached by intuition, based upon something like an intellectual love (*'Einfühlung'*) of the objects of experience."
> [*Logic of Scientific Discovery*, p. 32]

This, it must be admitted, sounds very much like Gadamer (*WM* 50; *TM* 50). There is no method of generating hypotheses. But to this absence there are two responses: Gadamer turns from method to tradition, whereas Popper turns from methodical genesis to methodical testing. Popper retains the primacy of method in testing, and Gadamer retains the primacy of induction in method.

Both men level their attack on Bacon, specifically on his thesis that science should entertain nothing of conjecture, anticipation, or prejudice. But whereas Gadamer assumes that the Baconian conception remains the norm, Popper argues that modern science, especially experimental physics, is founded on precisely the expectant guesses that Bacon expressly desired to prevent.

> Like Bacon, we might describe our own contemporary science—"the method of reasoning which men now ordinarily apply to nature"—as consisting of "anticipations, rash and premature" and of "prejudices."
> But these marvellously imaginative and bold conjectures or "anticipations" of ours are carefully and soberly controlled by systematic tests. . . . Using all the weapons of our logical, mathematical, and technical armoury, we try to prove that our anticipations were false—in order to put forward, in their stead, new unjustified and unjustifiable anticipations, new "rash and premature prejudices," as Bacon derisively called them. [pp. 278–79]

If so, the difference between the human sciences and the natural cannot be based on the function of prejudice in the former or of induction in the latter.

Yet this, as nearly as I can tell, seems to be Gadamer's general view of the matter. The problem seems to center in his idea of experiment, which he conceives as essentially the artificial reproduction of processes and the reining in of our haste to generalize (*WM* 331; *TM* 312). Experiment, in his view, consists in the careful building up of general laws from masses of concrete observations in order to predict future phenomena (*WM* 6; *TM* 6). What Popper suggests, however is that experiment consists rather in the priority of prediction over observation. The experimental scientist selects a hypothesis (no matter from where) and sets up a decisive experiment, one in which the observations will contradict the prediction or else corroborate (though not verify) it. "Bold ideas, unjustified anticipations, and speculative thought, are our only means for interpreting nature: our only organon, our only instrument, for grasping her. . . . We have to be active: we have to '*make*' our experiences. It is we who always formulate the questions to be put to nature; it is we who try again and again to put these questions so as to elicit a clear-cut 'yes' or 'no' (for nature does not give an answer unless pressed for it)" (p. 280).

Without questions of this kind, as Popper shows, there can be no answers, no experiments, no natural science; and yet Gadamer suggests that the logic of question and answer (which we will examine in detail later) is special to the hermeneutic sciences. They do not build generalizations from particulars in a linear, incremental, and inductive manner, but rather begin with the whole, the general, the prediction, and work toward the part and then return to the whole again. "Whenever someone wants to understand a text, he always formulates a projection. He projects before him a meaning of the whole as soon as the initial meaning is indicated. Such an intimation occurs only because one is already reading with certain expectations of a determinate meaning. In working out such a preliminary projection—which is, of course, continually revised as there is a further penetration into the meaning—consists the understanding of what is there. ... How do we come to accept a difference between our habitual linguistic customs and that of the text? One must say that it occurs in general in the experience of taking offense at a text—whether because it makes no sense or because its sense is irreconcilable with our expectations." (*WM* 252; *TM* 236–37). The preliminary projection of the whole meaning is then revised so as to accommodate the offensive part, and the circle keeps rotating. The hermeneutic circle is designed in part to replace the linear model of inductive understanding, because the latter is inapplicable to the human sciences. Thus, when Popper demonstrates that it is inapplicable to the natural sciences as well, it is not surprising that the alternative, "conjectural" model he proposes should involve something of the same process of anticipation, frustration, and renewed anticipation that comprises the hermeneutic circle of question and answer.[19]

This is obviously not to say that Gadamer is mistaken about the circularity of understanding, only that he overspecializes it by apparently confining it to the human sciences. The question, then, concerns the character of experience generally. When Popper says that "science is no more closely connected with 'our experience' " than any other means of knowledge (p. 100), we understand that he is combatting the empiricist and positivist description of science as specially based on experience. This is experience conceived as positive, confirmative, and cumulative—the conception that Gadamer attributes to the natural sciences generally: "Modern science only carries further in its methodical way what all experience always had striven for. All experience is valid so long as it confirms itself; to that extent its dignity rests on its fundamental repeatability" (*WM* 329–30; *TM* 311). The result of repetition is confirmation, and confirmation in this view is the end and goal of experience. Rather than revise this view, Popper affirms it and simply abandons experience as the basis of science. Gadamer, however, suggests that it is mistaken, and that its mistake derives from

---

19. E. D. Hirsch has noted the affinity of Gadamer's question-and-answer logic to the hypothetical method of natural science. But he overstates this affinity when he writes, "The doctrine of pre-understanding ... is no more or less than the doctrine of the logical priority of the hypothesis" (*Validity in Interpretation*, p. 261). A pre-understanding need not be and is usually not consciously thematized. For the contrast to hypothesis, see *DD* 33–34. See also Peters, "Nature and Role of Presupposition," pp. 210–11, and Linge's introduction to *PH*, p. xlvii. In the hermeneutic circle there is implied something like the ad hoc revision of unreliable hypotheses, such that the hypothesis is not disconfirmed in toto, but rather adapted in the way proscribed by Popper for the hypothetico-deductive sciences.

concentrating so exclusively on the *telos* of experience that the process of experience, which is not positive and confirmative at all, tends to be overlooked. "This process is essentially negative. It cannot be simply described as an uninterrupted cumulation of typical universals. This cumulation happens rather through false generalizations being continually contradicted by experience" (*WM* 335; *TM* 316). The similarity to Popper's description of the falsification process of experiment (not experience) is unmistakable. Had Popper revised and preserved the idea of experience, he would have come to much the same conclusion as Gadamer. In both the natural and human sciences, the process of understanding is the process of disillusionment.

Gadamer asks, "Does not the task of aesthetics consist in grounding precisely the fact that the experience of art is its own kind of knowledge, certainly distinct from sensory knowledge, the ultimate data from which science builds the knowledge of nature?" (*WM* 93; *TM* 87). We have so far been occupied in answering this question in the negative: the experience of art is not in this respect unique if we accept Popper's conclusions, for natural science does not erect its structure or rest its claims on the foundation of sensory data. This is not the only respect in which the human and natural sciences could be distinguished, however. Closely connected with the foundationalism Popper repudiates—namely the inductive, confirmative, cumulative view of science—is the idea of progress; and in retaining this idea while rejecting its basis, Popper's theory is noticeably strained:

> One may discern something like a general direction in the evolution of physics—a direction from theories of a lower level of universality to theories of a higher level. This is usually called the 'inductive' direction; and it might be thought that the fact that physics advances in this 'inductive' direction could be used as an argument in favour of the inductive method.
> Yet an advance in the inductive direction does not necessarily consist of a sequence of inductive inferences. . . . It may be better, therefore, to describe that trend—the advance towards theories of an ever higher level of universality—as 'quasi-inductive.' [p. 276]

Gadamer too identifies natural science with progress. Though he emphasizes depth of penetration into an object rather than (like Popper) breadth of generalization, perhaps these amount to the same thing. In any case, the law of scientific progress in Gadamer's view is to be contrasted with the law of history. "Modern historical research is not only research but the mediation of tradition. We do not see it only under the law of progress and its certified results. . . . What lies at the basis of this fact? Apparently one cannot speak of an identical object of research in the human sciences in the same sense as in the natural sciences where research penetrates ever more deeply into nature. . . . Historical research . . . cannot be conceived teleologically by reference to the object. Such an object in itself apparently does not exist. Just this distinguishes the human sciences from the natural sciences. While the object of the natural sciences can be defined ideally as what would be known in a complete knowledge of nature, it is senseless to speak of a complete knowledge of history" (*WM* 268–79; *TM* 253). This is a passage of unusual import for Gadamer's hermeneutics generally,[20] but we are interested only in the distinction it draws between the two sciences, a distinction here based on the teleological character of the natural sciences and the absence of that character in the *Geisteswissenschaften*.

Again, Gadamer does not demonstrate that natural science is progressive. He merely assumes it, and this thesis can now no longer be assumed without argument. Kuhn's *Structure of Scientific Revolutions*,[21] published two years after *Truth and Method*, has not won universal (or even general) assent; but the controversy it aroused has left its mark everywhere. Kuhn does not base his view of science on induction any more than Popper does. Just as Popper insists that all observation is theory-laden, so Kuhn asserts in the same Kantian vein that "a paradigm is prerequisite to perception itself" (p. 113). But since Kuhn rejects not only the verification model of positivism, but also Popper's falsification model, he does not adopt Popper's talk of a "quasi-inductive" scientific progress. Old paradigms are neither verified nor falsified but merely abandoned and replaced. The new paradigm does not contradict the old paradigm as a special case, nor can the new paradigm be said to represent an advance in universalization toward the whole truth or in penetration toward the thing in itself. The consequence is that science can no longer be explained by appeal to a telic conception of progress. Kuhn writes,

> The developmental process described in this essay has been a process of evolution *from* primitive beginnings—a process whose successive stages are characterized by an increasingly detailed and refined understanding of

20. Grondin explains the importance of Gadamer's nonteleological view of history when he writes, "In dialectic, thought continually takes on new forms without there being postulated unconditionally a process of successive approximation to the truth. In philosophical hermeneutics, this infinite process is designated as 'truth' " (*Hermeneutische Wahrheit*, p. 24).

21. Gadamer greeted the publication of Kuhn's book enthusiastically, because, he said, "it supported my view. The framework of theoretical assumptions which guide scientific investigation has a communicative side which in the final analysis is connected with language. That argument supports the universality of the hermeneutical approach" ("Hermeneutics and Social Science," p. 336). Bleicher notes the parallel in *Contemporary Hermeneutics*, p. 127.

nature. But nothing that has been or will be said makes it a process of evolution *toward* anything. Inevitably that lacuna will have disturbed many readers. We are all deeply accustomed to seeing science as the one enterprise that draws constantly nearer to some goal set by nature in advance.

But need there be any such goal? Can we not account for both science's existence and its success in terms of evolution from the community's state of knowledge at any given time? Does it really help to imagine that there is some one full, objective, true account of nature and that the proper measure of scientific achievement is the extent to which it brings us closer to that ultimate goal? [*Structure of Scientific Revolutions*, p. 170–71]

In that Gadamer differentiates the natural and human sciences on the basis of teleology, this distinction remains questionable—not because the human sciences are demonstrably progressive, though Gadamer denies it, but because the natural sciences may not be progressive, though he affirms it.

The dubiousness of the distinction framed in this way, however, does not vitiate the significance of Gadamer's argument. Gadamer makes so many unargued assumptions about natural science because his aim is more defensive than offensive. He intends not so much to attack science as to defend history, art, and humane knowledge generally. Gadamer adopts the teleological view of science because the correctness of this view, he suggests, is what has caused science to abandon its own history. History is what the onward march of progress has always superseded. The only real science is the science of the present, and from that standpoint the history of science is only a history of dim prefigurations of the present at best, and of outright errors at worst. "It is not simply historical naivete when the natural researcher writes the history of his science from out of the present condition of knowledge. Errors and deviations have for him only a historical interest, because the progress of research is the self-evident measure of his considerations. It is therefore of secondary interest to see how the advances of natural science or mathematics belong to their historical moment. The validity of scientific or mathematical knowledge is independent of this interest" (*WM* 267; *TM* 251–52).[22] This Whig interpretation of the history of science[23] has

---

22. Gadamer again emphasizes the nonhistorical nature of mathematics in "Historical Transformations of Reason," p. 3: "One of the excesses of modern historicism was the attempt to differentiate mathematics according to the historical conditions of its development and elaboration, and to hand it over to relativism. Mathematics is a pure science of reason." Misgeld is surely right to say that Gadamer "certainly has not taken much notice of those studies interpreting the development of scientific method and theory in terms of the traditions of criticism immanent to the development of natural science" ("Gadamer's Hermeneutics," p. 226). In this respect Gadamer and Kuhn are far apart.

23. See Kuhn, *Essential Tension*, pp. 131, 149.

indeed resulted from the notion of progress to which Gadamer attributes it. Though Kuhn does not himself embrace this notion, he is under no illusion that practitioners of science can view their history in any other way.

> Revolutions close with a total victory for one of the two opposing camps. Will that group ever say that the result of its victory has been something less than progress? That would be rather like admitting that they had been wrong and their opponents right. To them, at least, the outcome of revolution must be progress, and they are in an excellent position to make certain that future members of their community will see past history in the same way. . . .
>
> When it repudiates a past paradigm, a scientific community simultaneously renounces, as a fit subject for professional scrutiny, most of the books and articles in which that paradigm had been embodied. Scientific education makes use of no equivalent for the art museum or the library of classics. . . . Whitehead caught the unhistorical spirit of the scientific community when he wrote, "A science that hesitates to forget its founders is lost." [pp. 166–67, 138–39]

"The result," Kuhn adds, "is a persistent tendency to make the history of science look linear or cumulative," and it is this tendency alone that he attempts to rectify. Dropping the notion of verification or falsification or progress among paradigms, as Kuhn does, means that the history of science is not a process by which the past has been *superseded*; but the past is nonetheless, and perhaps more absolutely, abandoned in Kuhn's revolutionary view of science than in Gadamer's progressive view. The old paradigm is not comprehended in the new but simply dropped.

Kuhn is not only a logician of science like Popper but also a historian. He argues that it is necessary to understand the history of science in order to understand what it essentially is and has always been. Thus *The Structure of Scientific Revolutions* brings to the history of science something of the same freshness as did nineteenth-century historicism when it replaced the dogmatism characteristic of Enlightenment historiography. But, as Gadamer shows in *Truth and Method*, historicism concealed and in fact intensified the premises that it in fact shared with the Enlightenment. In one respect the same is true of Kuhn's revolutionism, for though in his view it is necessary to preserve the history of science in order to understand its essence, yet the essence of science, so understood, is that it abandons its history. Thus the old split between the historian and the practitioner of science is preserved, widened, and absolutized. The man who studies history is not the one who makes it. Thus the history of science is no less objectivized for the Kuhnian historian of science than are the objects of nature for the scientist himself. Exactly this, Gadamer argues throughout *Truth and Method*, is what distinguishes the human from the natural sciences. For research in the human sciences is characterized by its belonging to what is, by reason of this belonging, no object.

We have seen that, *pace* Gadamer, induction and progress can no longer be confidently identified as the *specifica differentia* of natural science; and if Gadamer assumes the same of objectivity, we need to ask whether this too must be contested. "The purpose of this book," Michael Polanyi writes of *Personal Knowledge* (1958), "is to show that complete objectivity as usually attributed to the exact sciences is a delusion and is in fact a false ideal" (p. 18). We have mentioned Polanyi only once in the preceding pages—as a philosopher of science, almost the only one, who is still willing to accredit science with truth. In light of the above quotation, this clearly implies that Polanyi does not equate truth with complete objectivity. Unlike Popper, Kuhn, and many others, Polanyi refuses to endorse the positivist conception of truth by declaring it irrelevant to natural science. Rather, he redefines truth as what cannot be objectified. This redefinition brings Polanyi into the closest proximity with Gadamer, for central to *Truth and Method* is the thesis that not all truth can be methodically derived and objectified. Is is not too great an exaggeration to say that what distinguishes Polanyi's philosophy of science from Gadamer's philosophical hermeneutics is what distinguishes Sartre's existentialism from Heidegger's. This is no small difference, to be sure, but the overlapping of Polanyi and Gadamer is nonetheless striking.

How close they are can be illustrated by contrasting them both with Popper. Of Popper's conception of intellectual honesty Lakatos writes, "*Belief* may be a regrettably unavoidable biological weakness to be kept under the control of criticism: but *commitment* is for Popper an outright crime" ("Falsification," p. 205). Gadamer certainly does not advocate commitment as a new method, but his disagreement with Popper on this score is patent: "If there is a practical consequence of the investigations here presented, it leads not to an unscientific 'commitment' [*Engagement*], but to the 'scientific' honesty of acknowledging the effectual commitment involved in all understanding" (*WM* xvi; *TM* xvi). Intellectual integrity consists in admitting what is in fact the case, and if commitment is in fact universally implicated in understanding, then it is dishonest to rely wholly on *the control of criticism* to eliminate it. Gadamer rarely uses the Sartrean language of engagement, however; he would never call knowledge personal as Polanyi does. Nevertheless, by comparison with Popper, Gadamer is fundamentally in agreement with Polanyi. "Commitment," Polanyi writes in *Personal Knowledge*, is "the only relation in which we can believe something to be true'' (p. 311). Popper admits in *Logic of Scientific Discovery* that ''the striving for knowledge and the search for truth are still the strongest motives of scientific discovery'' (p. 278). Polanyi adds only what is indeed difficult to deny: some truths have been discovered, some discoveries are believed, and these necessarily involve commitment. If this commitment undermines objectivity, then we must concede with Polanyi that the truthfulness of science depends on its not being objective in the sense of being detached from those who credit it.

''To accept commitment as the only relation in which we can believe something to be true,'' Polanyi continues, ''is to abandon all efforts to find strict criteria of truth and strict procedures for arriving at the truth'' (*Personal Knowledge*, p. 311). We need to remember that Polanyi is writing not specifically about hermeneutics (however like Gadamer this sounds) but rather about natural science. In abandoning the search for the strict rules and criteria that guarantee the objectivity of truth, Polanyi also abandons ''the vain pursuit of a formalized scientific method'' (p. 311). To put it simply, if we mean by the scientific method a fully explicit procedure for discovering or confirming natural truth, there has never been and never can be any such thing. The scientific method is not verification, nor even falsification, for there is no specifiable ''logic of scientific discovery'' at all.

The emphasis here is on *specifiable*. Methodization is formulation by reflection: we not only know the rules of a method but know that we know them. If science is to claim objectivity, it must itself be made objective in this way. Gadamer seems (from a post-positivist point of view) overly impressed by the extent to which Carnap and others have made explicit the presuppositions of science, but Polanyi is not impressed at all.

> The curious thing is that we have no clear knowledge of what our presuppositions are and when we try to formulate them they appear quite unconvincing. I have illustrated already in my chapter on probability how ambiguous and question-begging are all statements of the scientific method. I suggest now that [assertions of] the supposed pre-suppositions of science are so futile because the actual foundations of our scientific beliefs cannot be asserted at all. . . . As they are themselves our ultimate framework, they are essentially inarticulable. [pp. 59–60]

We do not know the presuppositions of science by reflection from the outside. We live in them. But we know them nonetheless. The existence and validity of this tacit knowledge, Polanyi argues, has been concealed by the dominant effort to make explicit and objectivize all knowledge. ''Objectivism has totally falsified our conception of truth, by exalting what we can know and prove, while covering up with ambiguous utterances all that we know and *cannot* prove, even though the latter knowledge underlies, and must ultimately set its seal to, all that we *can* prove" (p. 311). It is but a step further to identify the tacit knowledge that we know and cannot prove with tradition, and to say with Gadamer that "tradition retains a justification that is beyond reasons and to a great extent determines our institutions and attitudes." Customs "are freely taken over, but not at all created out of a free insight or grounded in their validity. Rather, that is what we mean by tradition: the ground of their validity" (*WM* 265; *TM* 249).

In explicating what he calls the "naivete of reflection," Gadamer clarifies the implications of traditionary knowledge: "By proceeding from the special case of the understanding of tradition, I have myself shown that understanding is always an event. The issue here is not simply that a nonobjectifying consciousness always accompanies the process of understanding but rather that understanding is not suitably conceived at all as a consciousness of something" (*PH* 125). The assumption of reflection is that all understanding is object-oriented, objective, and objectifying: but the understanding of tradition is an event that happens to understanding and to which understanding belongs. Thus traditionary knowledge cannot be conceived as consciousness of an object that stands over against a subject. In Heideggerian language, this is knowledge *of being* that comes *by being*—not *of objects* or *by objectifying consciousness*. Tradition is in one respect analogous to a tool—Heidegger's "ready-to-hand"— for the more effectual it is, the more it recedes from consciousness.[24]

Significantly, Polanyi employs Heidegger's favorite example of the ready-to-hand in elucidating the meaning of tacit knowledge.

> When we use a hammer to drive in a nail, we attend to both nail and hammer, *but in a different way*. We *watch* the effect of our strokes on the nail and try to wield the hammer so as to hit the nail most effectively. When we bring down the hammer we do not feel that its handle has struck our palm but that its head has struck the nail. Yet in a certain sense we are certainly alert to the feelings in our palm and the fingers that hold the hammer. . . . They are not watched in themselves; we watch something else while keeping intensely aware of them. I have a *subsidiary awareness* of

---

24. I do not mean to place too much weight on this analogy. As Gadamer writes, "Language [the bearer of tradition] is by no means simply an instrument, a tool. For it is in the nature of the tool that we master its use, which is to say we take it in hand and lay it aside when it has done its service" (*PH* 62); this is not the case with language. Yet what Heidegger says of the ready-to-hand can also be applied to language and to traditionary understanding generally: "The peculiarity of what is proximally ready-to-hand is that, in its readiness-to-hand, it must, as it were, withdraw in order to be ready-to-hand quite authentically" (*Being and Time*, p. 99).

the feeling in the palm of my hand which is merged into my *focal awareness* of my driving in the nail. [p. 55]

It is most of all language that exemplifies this subsidiary awareness. "Language is language," Gadamer writes, "when it is absorbed into making what is said visible, and has itself disappeared" (*PH* 126). In this sense language is transparent to consciousness; but precisely for this reason—namely, that we do not objectify language in the act of using it —it is also true that our language always remains to some degree necessarily opaque. As Polanyi says, "Just as, owing to the ultimately tacit character of all our knowledge, we remain ever unable to say all that we know, so also, in view of the tacit character of meaning, we can never quite know what is implied in what we say" (p. 95). If this is so of the natural (as of the human) sciences, the urge to methodize always runs up against an insuperable limit. But this limit cannot be conceived of only as an obstacle to rigor. That we always mean more than we are aware of is, as Polanyi suggests, the ground of objectivity rightly conceived: the objectivity of scientific discoveries "is manifested by the fact that their future implications extend indefinitely beyond the experience which they were originally known to control" (p. 37).

Objectivity in this sense is the excess of the future over the present in the mind of the scientist. Similarly, Gadamer denies that the *mens auctoris* is the locus of truth in art; and again, Polanyi helps us to understand what it might mean to say that truth, like objectivity, involves a dimension of knowledge that necessarily remains tacit to the scientist as it does to the artist. The question is whether it is possible to methodize the rules that govern the application of the phrase "is true." Of any true proposition p, we can say "p is true." But, Polanyi argues, "p is true" contains no more information than p alone. One might conclude therefore that "is true" is always redundant, and that there is thus no need to use the word *true* at all. We can simply eliminate it from our vocabulary, as so many philosophers of science have in fact done. Yet "is true" is redundant only because it is always silently implied in asserting p. Even if its explicit usage is abandoned, therefore, the tacit "is true" remains. This is what makes it possible to lie, and what makes the liar paradox possible without mentioning truth at all. Being tacit, the implied "is true" cannot be abandoned, eliminated, or avoided—because, Polanyi contends, it is the act of assertion itself. The proposition p can be tested, proved, and affirmed; but "p is true" cannot—except by going through the same tests, proofs, and affirmations that were needed for p alone. This is to say that "p is true" is at once redundant in its explicit form, unavoidable in its tacit form, and fundamentally indefinable in either. Polanyi does not conclude that the notion of truth is meaningless because the rules of its application cannot be methodized; rather, he reinterprets and preserves truth as what is at bottom always an a-critical act of affirmation, one that can never finally be an object of consciousness because we cannot avoid performing it, even in the very process of objectification. In Gadamer's words, "a nonobjectifying consciousness always accompanies the process of understanding" (*PH* 125).

To the extent that the tacit dimension is the definitive province of hermeneutics, Gadamer is able to say that "hermeneutical reflection . . . is universal in its possible application. As opposed to the sciences, it must also fight for self-enlightenment with regard to the methodology of science as such. Any science is based upon the special nature of that which it has made its object through its methods of objectifying. The method of modern science is characterized from the start by a refusal: namely, to include all that which actually eludes its own methodology and procedures. Precisely in this way it would prove to itself that it is without limits and never wanting for self-justification" (*PH* 93).

The putative universality of science is won by declaring off limits all that cannot be objectivized. What is beyond the limits established by its methods of objectifying is either unreal or merely outside the domain of the particular science. But this is only another way of saying either that science in general has no limits, or that the methods of the particular science cannot be criticized without undermining its objectivity. A science is its method. What makes it a science, in Gadamer's view, is that it cannot reflect on its own method without ceasing to be science—and becoming hermeneutics. This delimits all natural sciences to the field of their objectification, defines them as against hermeneutics, and demonstrates that hermeneutics is more basic than any particular science and indeed than natural science in general. Whereever we attempt to examine the ground we are standing on, there we are engaged in hermeneutical reflection—not natural science.

The most important question that Polanyi, as a philosopher of science, poses to Gadamer, then, is whether science, in examining its own foundations as Polanyi does, is any less scientific for engaging in hermeneutical self-reflection. Polanyi thinks it is more scientific. But perhaps that is what Gadamer means as well when he writes that his book is concerned with "the '*scientific*' honesty of acknowledging the effectual commitment involved in all understanding" (*WM* xvi; *TM* xvi). One must not forget that for Gadamer the hermeneutic sciences are indeed sciences, though it must also be admitted that he often encourages us to forget that the natural sciences are hermeneutic.[25]

_____

25. What confusion this causes can be seen by contrasting Misgeld and Hufnagel. Misgeld writes that Gadamer "makes it appear as if there were no continuum between hermeneutical reflection

We have, then, not yet discovered a criterion for distinguishing human from natural science. If human science is not inductive, neither is natural science, according to Popper; if human science is not progressive, Kuhn suggests that natural science is no more so; and if human science is not objective in the sense of being detached and impersonal, natural science in Polanyi's view is not in that sense objective either. Before consigning the distinction to Occam's razor, however, it is well to ask whether we may not have been looking for a criterion in the wrong place. Primarily we have been concerned with the *ground* of knowledge in the natural sciences, and how that ground is cultivated. Now we must turn to the fruit. "The difference that confronts us," Gadamer suggests, "is not in the method but in the objectives of knowledge" (*WM* xvii; *TM* xvii).

Gadamer calls application the fundamental problem of hermeneutics; correlatively, we need to examine not only the process of discovery in the natural sciences but the process of application as well—that is, the question of technology. It is here, I think, in the sphere of application, that Gadamer finds the firmest foundation upon which to differentiate the two sciences. "The special problem that the human sciences raise consists in the fact that one miscomprehends the essence of the human sciences when one measures them by the criteria of a progressive knowledge of lawfulness. The experience of the social-historical world cannot be raised to science by the inductive procedure of the natural sciences. Whatever science might mean here and even if the application of general experience to the current object of research is implied in all historical knowledge, nevertheless historical knowledge does not strive to comprehend the concrete phenomenon as the case of a general rule. The individual does not serve simply as a confirmation of a law from which in its application predictions become possible. Its ideal is much more to understand the phenomenon itself in its unique and historical concretion. However much general experience is operative, the aim is not to confirm and broaden these general experiences in order to achieve the knowledge of a law" (*WM* 2; *TM* 6). Centrally at issue in this passage are the general laws that are the fruit of natural science and the foresight they make possible. However these laws are generated or corroborated, they function to

---

and other forms of epistemological, logical, or methodological reflection, as if in fact, hermeneutical reflection might not frequently be developed in the context of the latter" ("Gadamer's Hermeneutics," p. 232). Hufnagel, by contrast, affirms that "hermeneutic philosophy, in brief, is reflection on the interdependence of science and its pre- or extra-scientific context" (*Einführung*, p. 65). These contradictory views result in part, as Jansen writes, from the fact that *Truth and Method* lacks "a plain, unitary conception of scientificity" whereby to unify the natural and human sciences ("Die hermeneutische Bestimmung," p. 370).

render intelligible the events that fall within their domain. Marshall Walker in *Nature of Scientific Thought* puts this most simply: "If a specific occurrence is predicted by a law that has predicted many such occurrences accurately, then the scientist says that he *understands* that occurrence" (p. 1). To understand an event, in this sense, is to subsume the instance under a general concept, rule, or law. What other sense of understanding is there? To understand something is to see it as an instance of a universal; however concrete, the instance is never unique, for a "unique instance" is a mere contradiction. Thus, if history consists of unique and unrepeatable events, there can be no scientific understanding of it at all.

In science, to understand a process is at the same time to know in general how it could be brought about again or prevented. Thus this knowledge is above all applicable: it has reference not only to past but also to future instances. Because these events are never more than instances, they will be repeated again and again as conditions allow. It is not difficult to understand why possession of this knowledge, so applicable, should be so desirable. On the other hand, even if there were a science of the historically unique, it is not clear why anyone would want to acquire it. Historical events will never be repeated; they are instances of no general laws. Knowledge of the historically unique enables no predictions, no command of the future. If the usefulness of knowledge consists in the application of generals to particulars, then such a science of history would be, of all sciences, most useless.

Yet if subsumption (the basis of technology) is not the only way knowledge can be applied, then it may be that history does possess cognitive value. The function of laws is to overcome and surpass the merely apparent variety of history[26] by recourse to the uniformity of nature; and knowledge of such general laws, once achieved, would obviate any further consideration of historical experience.[27] Yet for Gadamer, history names precisely what is not to be overcome, dominated, or obviated by human consciousness. By contrast to natural science, he says, the aim of historical research is not "to achieve knowledge of a law, for example, how men, peoples, states generally develop themselves but instead to understand how this man, this people, this state is what it has become—how it can have happened that it is so" (*WM* 2; *TM* 6). This knowledge is more immediate than that afforded by laws in that it is not (exclusively) mediated

---

26. For a positivist view, see Hempel, "Function of General Laws in History."

27. Cf. Comte: "One can say without any exaggeration that genuine science—far from consisting of simple facts—always aims as much as possible at freeing us from immediate [empirical] research by replacing the latter with rational foresight which represents in every respect the hallmark of the positive spirit" (quoted in Habermas, *Knowledge and Human Interests*, p. 77).

through conceptual universals. In explaining what something has become specifically by appeal to what it has been, historical understanding works from the concrete to the concrete, without subsuming temporal particularity into atemporal generality. It does not surpass the variety of the past because it does not surpass the past at all. History is not subject to concept or mind or consciousness. Historical understanding sees every moment of history, including its own, as ineluctably factical and particular, immersed in having been, and never finally determined as an instance of a general concept under which it could be conclusively subsumed, but rather always awaiting interpretation and always exceeding it.

We need not here elaborate further on Gadamer's view of historical understanding since it is fully explicated in the second part of *Truth and Method*, which we will consider in due course. What is of primary concern at this point is that in differentiating application in the historical sciences from the subsumption under laws that is typical of application in the natural sciences, Gadamer places the distinction between the two kinds of science on a firm foundation. It is unnecessary to deny that the nature and existence of laws in natural science are, or have been, beyond dispute. The nominalist controversy concerning the reality of generals comes to mind here—in particular, the objection that laws are merely convenient abbreviations for collections of particular experiences. But this position is no longer credited; and even if it were, it would remain the case that the convenience and utility of such abbreviations consisted in their generality, real or not.

Gadamer does not deny that the "the application of general experience to the current object of research is implied in all historical knowledge," but he does deny that history is, or can be, fully understood as an instance of a general rule applied to it. The understanding of history involves a form of application that is itself a way of knowing and not merely a way of subsuming a particular historical event under an already known general law. Such application derives from our being historical; thus it cannot be postponed until after knowledge is complete but instead is coincident with it. The human sciences are characterized by a practical knowledge that is itself knowledge, rather than merely the subsequent application of knowledge in practice. Technologism, the principle that we must first "know" and only afterwards "do," has not faded away with positivism. In Popper's view, and even in Kuhn's, self-conscious theory precedes practice, whether that practice is experimental or utilitarian. In the human sciences, by contrast, Gadamer argues that theory and practice are so intertwined that neither can be accorded priority.

On the basis of this distinction, it cannot be said that the natural sciences dissolve into hermeneutics; and yet, as we have seen, there is such a coincidence between them that the distinction cannot be absolutized. If *Truth and Method* does absolutize the difference between the two kinds of science, it is outdated. That Paul Feyerabend's exposition of the theory of science is titled *Against Method* itself suggests that to call method into question is no longer automatically to call science into question.[28] Yet absolutizing distinctions is not in fact characteristic of *Truth and Method*. We find almost nothing of the outworn dichotomies between the two kinds of science: of fact versus value, understanding versus explanation, or the human versus the natural. In the life-world to which both sciences ultimately belong, these dichotomies are unknown.

Like Heidegger, Gadamer considers hermeneutics so basic, so intimately implicated in the life-world, that it is universal: it comprehends the natural sciences as a special case in a way that modern philosophers of science too have come to understand. Yet at the same time the polemical thrust of *Truth and Method* derives from Gadamer's belief that the natural sciences still stand as an independent alternative, and therefore a threat, to the human sciences. It cannot be maintained, logically speaking, that the natural sciences are both a special instance of and an alternative to the human sciences. Yet logic is not the final arbiter here. Rather, history—the history of the centuries-long contest between the two sciences—impelled Gadamer to assume the assumptions that he intended to question, precisely in order to question them.

METHOD AGAINST ITSELF

"The title of *Truth and Method* never intended that the antithesis it implies should be mutually exclusive" (*PH* 26). What, one wonders, is an antithesis that is not mutually exclusive? It might be more accurate to say that, for Gadamer, truth and method—like human and natural science—form a contrast that is never raised to antithesis. He does not press the two toward mutual contradiction, or then go on to press either toward self-contradiction as a step toward synthesis.[29] Rather, they remain in an uneasy and unstable tension that is not finally resolved.

28. See also Whitehead: "The speculative Reason is in its essence untrammeled by method. Its function is to pierce into the general reasons beyond limited reasons, to understand all methods as coordinated in a nature of things only to be grasped by transcending all method" (*The Function of Reason*, p. 65).

29. "For Hegel the point of dialectic is that precisely by pushing a position to the point of self-contradiction it makes possible the transition to a higher truth which unites the sides of that contradiction: the power of spirit lies in synthesis as the mediation of all contradictions" (*HD* 105).

In this crucial instance, as in others less important, Gadamer does not pursue the method of Hegelian dialectic. The final synthesis, the omnicomprehensive system, the ultimate reconciliation is never achieved. "To explicate the totality of the determinations of thought, as was the aim of Hegel's *Logic*," Gadamer writes, "is at the same time to attempt to comprehend the continuum of meaning in the great monologue of modern 'method' " (*WM* 351; *TM* 332). Thus instead of Hegel's dialectical monologue, which fails to do justice to that continuum by reason of its teleology, Gadamer pursues an infinite dialogue "which never leads anywhere definitively and which differentiates us from that [Hegelian] ideal of an infinite spirit to which all that exists and all truth is present in a single vision" (*TM* 492). But does Gadamer's indefinite prolongation do justice to the fact that in dialogue we seek the finality of agreement and unity? "It is true that the claim of systematic unity appears even less redeemable today than it did in the age of Idealism. As a result an inner affinity for spellbinding multiplicity pulls upon us. . . . Nonetheless the exigence of reason for unity remains inexorable" (*RAS* 19). Whatever we may hear about the end of metaphysics from Heidegger and others, Gadamer says, "the tradition of metaphysics and especially its last great form, the speculative dialectic of Hegel, is continually near us. The task, the 'infinite relation' remains. But the way of demonstrating it seeks to withdraw from the grasp of the synthetic power of Hegelian dialectic" (*WM* xxiv; *TM* xxiv). "In this way," Gadamer suggests, "I became an advocate of the 'bad infinite' for which the end keeps on delaying its arrival" (*RAS* 40). Gadamer does justice to our urge for unity, but also to the frustration of not achieving it. There is in the bad infinite at once infinite hope and infinite deferral.

This double infinity is the consequence of the human finitude and historicity that preclude the consummation of self-consciousness in absolute spirit. "By absolute spirit, Hegel means a form of spirit that contains nothing more in itself that is alien, other, or in opposition" (*PH* 114). It is transparent to itself in that its knowledge is neither motivated nor mediated by anything of which it is not aware. This is part of what is meant by methodical knowledge: it has no inner limits. But absolute knowledge means having no outer limits either—no objects to which it must be opposed. For it recognizes everything as an expression of itself, and it knows itself completely. Thus, undefined from the outside as well as the inside, absolute spirit marks the universal monopoly of method. Within a perfected self-consciousness, everything (including consciousness itself) is known absolutely—in its whole truth—and the truth, for Hegel, is only the whole truth. Anything less is abstract, dependent, incomplete, and relative.

The extent to which Gadamer is indebted to Hegel cannot easily be overestimated.[30] By way of example, we need only mention that tradition, which plays so crucial a role in *Truth and Method*, is hardly to be distinguished from objective spirit in *The Phenomenology of Mind*. Yet no less important than Gadamer's rehabilitation of the Hegelian concept of objective spirit[31] is his repudiation of the possibility of absolute spirit. This is nothing new, to be sure. Like Nietzsche, Marx, Freud, and Heidegger, Gadamer denies the perfectability of self-consciousness; rather, he sees consciousness as a process always completing itself—continually overcoming itself, but always leaving something to be overcome. This is the bad infinite.

Gadamer focuses his objections to Hegel by exposing what Gadamer calls "the naivete of reflection" (*PH* 122). Reflective philosophy is erected on the fact, simply put, that if you know something, you also know that you know it. Consciousness of an object is simultaneously self-consciousness. The question that Gadamer asks, like others before him,[32] is whether knowing that you know is like knowing an object. He concludes that it is not: "The kind of knowledge in question here implies that not all reflection performs an objectifying function, that is, not all reflection makes what it is directed at into an object. . . . We have a nonobjectifying consciousness of our psychic acts" (*PH* 123). When we hear a bird's song, we hear the song not the hearing; though we are aware of our hearing, it is not thematized or objectivized. This is not to say that psychic acts cannot be objectivized: methodization is possible, but only subsequently to a nonthematic awareness, and then only by means of new intentional acts which are not themselves thematized. If consciousness means consciousness of an object, we always remain unconscious of our consciousness—never objectively self-conscious at all.[33]

30. "In trying to work out a systematic hermeneutics, [Gadamer] has come closer to that great moving force in German philosophy, Hegel. . . . Insofar as Gadamer moves away from Heidegger, he tends toward a rapprochement with Hegel" (Palmer, *Hermeneutics*, p. 215). Moreover, Grondin observes that "Hegel's concept of mediation already bears within it the germ of Gadamer's concept of effective history" (*Hermeneutische Wahrheit*, p. 44).

31. "The thrust of the theory of the objective spirit is that not the consciousness of the individual but a common and normative reality that surpasses the awareness of the individual is the foundation of our life in state and society" (*RAS* 31).

32. Notably Heidegger. Richardson explains Heidegger's thought on nonobjective awareness when he writes, "It is this manifestation (or accessibiity) of beings prior to objectivizing presentation and rendering such a presentation possible that Heidegger calls ontic truth. . . . The entire polemic against presentative thought . . . is based on the fact that . . . it forgets this pre-presentative openness" (*Heidegger*, p. 177).

33. Ricoeur, also influenced by Heidegger, comes to a similar conclusion: "It belongs to the essence of consciousness never to be entirely explicit, but always related to implicit consciousness" (*Conflict of Interpretations*, p. 102).

Language is not only the best example of this fact; for Gadamer it is its basis. Insofar as all consciousness is linguistic, the invisibility of language in speech necessitates the incompleteness of self-consciousness. However influential the work of grammarians, philologists, linguists, and philosophers of language, "unconsciousness of language has not ceased to be the real mode of being of speech" (*WM* 382; *TM* 366). The reason is that when we speak and listen, we are attentive to what is said; that "what" is thematized. But we are not focally aware of the manner of speaking or the rules of expression except when communication is for some reason impeded. In fact, the more we focus on the expression per se, the less we hear of what is said. That is, the invisibility of language is not only concomitant with, but the condition of, objectification. To be objectively conscious of language would mean that nothing would get said at all.

"It is part of the nature of language that it has a completely unfathomable unconsciousness of itself. To that extent, it is not an accident that the use of the concept 'language' is a recent development. The word *logos* means not only thought and language, but also concept and law. The appearance of the concept 'language' presupposes consciousness of language. But that is only the result of the reflective movement in which the one thinking has reflected out of the unconscious operation of speaking and stands at a distance from himself. The real enigma of language, however, is that we can never really do this completely" (*PH* 62). To be conscious of an object requires that we be unconscious of the conditions of that objectification. This is what Gilbert Ryle in *Concept of Mind* has finely called "the eternal penultimacy of consciousness" (p. 195). Gadamer calls it the bad infinite, the infinity that never leads to Hegel's absolute spirit. It is in this way that Gadamer interprets the ambiguity of *aletheia*: "The conflict between revealment and concealment is . . . the truth of every being, for as unhiddenness, truth is always . . . an *opposition of revealment and concealment*. The two necesarily belong together" (*PH* 226).[34] Every revelation is also a disguise: every consciousness of an object is made possible by a nonobjectivizing consciousness. However comprehensive the work that consciousness has already completed, there always remains something for it still to do. Since concealment belongs to revelation, one might say that revelation constantly increases its own task. Absolute knowledge thus becomes impossible.

"The more radically objectifying thought reflects upon itself and unfolds the experience of dialectic, the more clearly it points to what it is not. Dialectic

---

34. One implication of the dual nature of *aletheia* is that "there can be no statement that is absolutely true" (*KS* 1:53).

must retrieve itself in hermeneutics'' (*HD* 99). ''The task of philosophical hermeneutics can be thus characterized: it would have to retrace the way of Hegel's phenomenology of spirit backwards'' (*WM* 286; *TM* 268)—that is, from absolute to objective spirit, from subjectivity to substance, and from concept to language. The linguistic character ''of all thought continues to demand that thought, moving in the opposite direction, convert the concept back into the valid word'' (*HD* 99). Hermeneutic moves from dialectic to dialogue.

The unconsciousness of language in speech, we have seen, marks the essential incompleteness of self-consciousness. For this reason, the truth discovered in and by self-consciousness cannot be the whole truth, as Hegel contended it was. Moreover, language, history, and tradition—the conditions of truth—are not themselves whole. Perhaps the heart of Gadamer's dispute with Hegelian holism is summarized in this one sentence: ''Der Begriff des Ganzen ist selber nur relativ zu verstehen'' (The concept of the whole can itself be understood only relatively) (*WM* xxiii; *TM* xxiii). This holds macrocosmically for the whole of history and for the briefest moment, for the totality of tradition and for any particular text. No whole, of whatever magnitude, is complete, autonomous, self-enclosed, or self-identical. This fact alters the nature of the hermeneutic circle. ''Understanding is always a movement in such a circle, for which reason the repeated return from the whole to the parts and vice versa is essential. In addition, this circle continually expands itself in that the concept of the whole is relative and the inclusion in ever larger contexts alters the understanding of single parts'' (*WM* 178; *TM* 167). The universe of discourse, like the physical universe, is constantly expanding. Thus the hermeneutic circle, in which truth is understood as the conclusive reconciliation of whole and part, might better be conceived as a hermeneutic spiral, in which truth keeps expanding. That is, the whole truth never *is* but always *to be* achieved.

It follows that ''the truth that science tells us''—no less than any other truth— ''is relative to a specific attitude toward the world and cannot at all claim to be the whole'' (*WM* 425; *TM* 407). Similarly, from the necessary incompleteness of self-consciousness, it follows that the dominion of method cannot be universal. The absence of absolute knowledge clearly suggests that truth is relative. Though truth may be nonetheless true for all that, Gadamer must grapple with the specter of relativism[35]—particularly because one of the triumphs of

---

35. Hoy rightly considers the ''threat of relativism'' a ''major issue'' in *Truth and Method*, though he concludes that Gadamer's position is ''not properly called relativism because it is held by both relativists and nonrelativists'' (*Critical Circle* pp. 45, 69). Hoy's terminological solution does little to allay what remains a major threat. Hirsch brands Gadamer as a relativist in *The Aims of Interpretation*, p. 17; and by far the most detailed attack on Gadamer's relativism is found in Seung's *Structuralism and Hermeneutics*, pp. 183ff.

reflective philosophy is to have shown that all claims for the relativity of truth are self-defeating precisely to the extent that they claim absolute truth for themselves. How then can Gadamer assert that "it is no disproof of the acceptance of fundamental conditionedness that this acceptance itself claims to be absolutely and unconditionally true, and thus cannot be applied to itself without contradiction"? (*WM* 424; *TM* 406). It is precisely the reflexive argument that exposes the paradox of relativism. Thus Gadamer takes it as his task to exorcise the specter of relativism by exposing the naivete of reflection, and of the methodologism that is its expression.

But what if the naivete of method as the highest form of reflection could be demonstrated by the strictest of methods? We began this chapter with an analysis of Gadamer's central thesis: truth cannot be limited to what is confirmable by method. Then we suggested that the natural sciences are less methodical and more hermeneutic than Gadamer conceives them. Now we broach the question of whether method itself—in its most methodical form, mathematical logic—does not in fact bring us to the same conclusions as *Truth and Method*. What we are after is an absolute proof that the truths which can be derived with absolute rigor are either necessarily incomplete or else potentially paradoxical. In brief, we want to prove methodically that not everything that is in fact true can be methodically proved: truth exceeds method, as method itself compels us to admit.

To understand how this comes about, we need to cross what Gadamer calls "the greatest kind of philosophical gulf that exists today between peoples—the one between Anglo-Saxon nominalism on the one hand and the metaphysical tradition on the Continent on the other" (*PH* 75). Gadamer sees this gulf being narrowed in Wittgenstein's observation that our language "is in order, as it is. That is to say, we are not *striving after* an ideal" (quoted in *PH* 174).[36] We, however, need to go back to the time preceding the *Investigations* when that ideal—namely, of logical, artificial languages—was still in force; even then, we will be able to see, the gulf was narrower than it seemed.[37]

For the Greeks, for Gadamer, and even for us, science—not only natural science but *episteme*, the highest knowledge—"is represented by the example of mathematics, a knowledge of the immutable, a knowledge that rests on proof" (*WM* 297; *TM* 280). From this kind of knowledge, Gadamer implies, the human

36. The quotation is from *Philosophical Investigations* 1.98; curiously Wittgenstein says something very similar in the *Tractatus* 5.5563.

37. For a useful comparison of Gadamer and Wittgenstein, see Smith, "Gadamer's Hermeneutics and Ordinary Language Philosophy." On Heidegger and Wittgenstein, see Erickson, *Language and Being*.

sciences have nothing to learn. We know that in the work of Galileo and Newton natural science took a qualitative leap forward by being quantified. So too in Aristotle's development of syllogistic reasoning, and again in the axiomatic structure of Descartes' *Meditations* and "regulae," philosophy aimed to achieve the kind of compulsory agreement that is the special advantage of mathematics. Yet Plato's Socratic dialogues, Gadamer suggests, neither possess nor claim to possess this compulsion. "In particular, when the concern is with the postulation of ideas, it is repeatedly said to be a task of infinite difficulty to prove their validity to one who would contest them. As is so often the case in Plato, the discrepancy between what one sees and what one can defend against an opponent is emphasized specifically" (*DD* 96). Gadamer calls this "the discrepancy between an insight and its demonstrability" or between "a correct assertion and an irrefutable one."

"Aristotle's syllogisms or a deductive system, Euclid's geometry, for instance, can construct proofs which by virtue of their logical cogency compel everyone to recognize the truth, but this, according to Plato, is not to be achieved in the realm of the philosophy of ideas. And it seems important to him to make that fact clear from the start to anyone who wants to participate in the communal seeking and inquiry which lead to the ideas. Thus the question raised here implies philosophy's criticism of itself. Why does the possibility of compelling someone to understand in the way mathematics can, for example, not exist for philosophy?" (*DD* 99). One reason for this inability is that, however direct the original insight upon which it is based, philosophy is conducted in words—in natural, conventional languages—which do not present the idea itself but rather a substitute for it. Thus, instead of offering proofs with demonstrative compulsion by means of expository argument, the Platonic Socrates necessarily participates in communal seeking among a group of inquirers united by a common aim. The dialectic takes the form of dialogue.

Where Gadamer parts with Plato—or rather, where he sees Plato pointing beyond his own statements—is in the latter's distrust of dialogue and, more fundamentally, of natural language. "What Plato had in mind is obviously that this ambiguity of words allows a word to let something else be there instead of presenting the thing meant. In this age of artificial, logical languages this point needs no further elaboration. As we all know, the reason for the invention of mathematical symbol-languages and their perfection in the last hundred years was that conventional language entangles us in pseudo-problems; ergo logic's claim to have rid us of this kind of error by perfecting an artificial system of signs. Such a perfected sign language would accomplish what Plato argues natural languages could not" (*DD* 108). In that Plato continually points out the deficiency of natural language[38]—and thus accepts dialogue as merely second best—he implicitly invites the construction of artificial languages. Thus, to establish the primacy of dialogical over compulsory agreement, Gadamer seeks to strengthen the claim of natural language by weakening that of artificial language.[39] This tactic, I want to suggest, was unnecessary. For its was precisely in the process of strengthening the compulsory quality of mathematical logic that it was proved impossible to render that compulsion irresistible. This process indeed recapitulates many of the arguments that Gadamer himself draws from the phenomenological movement: specifically, the critique of Hegelian totalization, of reflection, and of method as the exclusive avenue to truth.

Here this process can be traced only in a very elliptical manner, but we can glimpse enough of it for our purposes by focusing on how paradox came to be such a central question in the mathematics of our century. If we take Euclidean geometry as our initial example of methodical proof, we can see immediately that its rigor depends on erecting an enormous structure upon very slender but very solid foundations. Its axioms express perfectly self-evident ideas about space, and the theorems derived from them are deduced by steps no less self-evident. One of Euclid's axioms, however—that through a point outside a line only one parallel can be drawn—seemed to the ancients less self-evident than the others; and thus they attempted to derive it from the other axioms that were more so. Despite repeated attempts, they failed. But this failure scarcely proved that such a derivation, given more ingenuity, was impossible. "It was not until the nineteenth century, chiefly through the work of Gauss, Bolyai, Lobachevsky, and Riemann, that the *impossibility* of deducing the parallel axiom from the others was demonstrated. This outcome was of the greatest intellectual importance. In the first place, it called attention in a most impressive way to the fact that a *proof* can be given of the impossibility of proving certain propositions within a given system."[40] In the course of our discussion we have already met with a similar notion in Popper's logic of falsification: the scientific character of scientific hypotheses resides in the fact that they can be conclusively disconfirmed. The via negativa is necessitated by the fact that certain propositions—

---

38. Elsewhere, however, Gadamer suggests that "there is a hint of irony present" in Plato's argument, for "in the end, the true being of things becomes accessible precisely in their linguistic appearance" (*PH* 77).

39. Cf. "In contrast to every artificially instituted system of signs, it appears to me that the life of language perfects and furthers itself without being detached from the living traditions in which historical humanity stands" (*KS* 1:175).

40. Nagel and Newman, *Gödel's Proof*, p. 10. Kleene traces this history in greater detail in *Mathematical Logic*, pp. 186ff.

the all-statements that would crown an infinite induction—cannot be confirmed short of infinity—that is, empirically, by experience. Thus, Popper argues, experience functions rather to disconfirm. The work of Gauss and his colleagues, however, was a nonempirical proof of the impossibility of proving a certain proposition.

The result was that the parallel axiom came to be seen as neither self-evident nor deducible from other axioms. Thus it became optional: one could employ it, replace it, or delete it. The assumption that *no* parallel can be drawn, for example, is basic to spherical geometry. One can supply a set of axioms for yet another space or for no known kind of space at all. In this way, mathematics was purified of all reference. As Nagel and Newman state in *Gödel's Proof*, "The postulates of any branch of demonstrative mathematics are not inherently about space, quantity, apples, angles, or budgets; and any special meaning that may be associated with the terms (or 'descriptive predicates') in the postulates plays no essential role in the process of deriving theorems" (p. 12). If by *true* we mean true of space, apples, or budgets, then Russell can say, "Pure mathematics is the subject in which we do do not know what we are talking about, or whether what we are saying is true" (cited in ibid., p. 13). But correspondence is not all that we mean by truth, and what the purification of reference from mathematics accomplished was the relocation of the truth of mathematics within the sphere of coherence.[41] The crucial problem of mathematics, then, was to demonstrate the internal consistency of nonreferential axiomatic systems, miniature languages that are both complete and unambiguous, because they refer to nothing but themselves. The demonstration of coherence in such a system again necessitates the via negativa. It is not enough to prove time and time again that such sets of axioms are mutually consistent, for the next time they may not be so. The stronger proof comes from demonstrating that they cannot possibly be inconsistent or self-contradictory. Thus, paradox assumed its centrality as the ultimate threat to mathematics (as to Gadamer's historicism), because if such axiomatic systems are not coherent, they are nothing.

The first solution proposed by Hilbert and others to the problem of proving the noncontradictoriness of axiom sets was "mapping"—that is, translating or interpreting one set in terms of another. "In [Hilbert's] interpretation, Euclid's axioms were simply transformed into algebraic truths" (*Gödel's Proof*, p. 20).

---

41. Japp notes that "the statement as apophansis [proposition] is defined precisely by its appeal to a logic of consistency or of noncontradiction" (*Hermeneutik*, p. 46). For the argument that apophansis is a secondary and derivative mode of understanding, see Heidegger, *Being and Time*, pp. 195ff.

Mapping, however, merely postpones the problem, in that the consistency of Euclidean geometry becomes dependent on whether algebra is consistent. It offers a relative, not absolute, proof of consistency. To construct an absolute proof, in Hilbert's view, required the complete formalization of the axioms. This process, also called axiomatization, involves emptying the primitive terms of all meaning and specifying, by means of explicit rules, how they may be combined. The calculus so formed delimits the permissible transformations of one string of terms into another, and each step in deriving a string or theorem can be regulated and scrutinized with perfect clarity. Everything is perfectly explicit. Axiomatization is the perfection of method.

Essential to a calculus, an axiomatized system, is first that it be self-contained. Thus one can make statements about the calculus that, by the very procedure of axiomatization, one can see do not belong to the calculus itself. Of such extrinsic statements, the most crucial is that the system is consistent or inconsistent. These are not mathematical but metamathematical statements. Second, the calculus cannot possess an infinite number of structural properties or an infinite number of rules. Both autonomy and finitude are required in order to construct an absolute proof of noncontradictoriness, one that is neither relative to another system nor requires an infinite series of steps.

Another development, associated with Boole and Frege, arose in response to the problem of consistency. "This new development sought to exhibit pure mathematics as a chapter of formal logic; and it received its classical embodiment in the *Principia Mathematica* of Whitehead and Russell in 1910" (ibid., p. 42). This reduction of mathematics to symbolic logic was not a case of the mapping we mentioned above. Rather, the thesis was that arithmetic fundamentally and essentially *is* logic, and thus no transformation from one independent system to another is involved. Yet in this reduction, no less than in mapping, the consistency of artihmetical axioms remains dependent on, and indeed equivalent to, the consistency of logic. It thus became necessary to eliminate all possible paradox from logic, and in particular from the logic of sets that was the basis of *Principia Mathematica*. Russell's attempt to do so resulted in his theory of types.

Whereas Hegel, and Gadamer after him,[42] take interest primarily in the motion paradoxes of Zeno, Russell is concerned with semantic paradoxes, of which the liar paradox of Epimenides is the prototype. These are most directly related to set theory. Russell's own variant of the liar paradox is as follows: there is a barber who shaves all and only those men in the town who do not

42. See *Hegel's Dialectic*, p. 13.

shave themselves. Does he shave himself? There can be no answer and no such barber. In all such contradictions, Russell says,

> there is a common characteristic, which we may describe as self-reference. The remark of Epimenides must include itself in its own scope. . . .
>
> When a man says "I am lying," we may interpret his statement as: "There is a proposition which I am affirming and which is false." All statements that "there is" so-and-so may be regarded as denying that the opposite is always true; thus "I am lying" becomes "It is not true of all propositions that either I am not affirming them or that they are true"; in other words, "It is not true for all propositions p that if I affirm p, p is true." The paradox results from regarding this statement as affirming a proposition, which must therefore come within the scope of the statement. This, however, makes it evident that the notion of "all propositions" is illegitimate; for otherwise, there must be propositions (such as the above) which are about all propositions and yet cannot, without contradiction, be included among the propositions they are about. Whatever we suppose to be the totality of propositions, statements about this totality generate new propositions which, on pain of contradiction, must lie outside the totality. It is useless to enlarge the totality, for that equally enlarges the scope of statements about the totality. Hence there must be no totality of propositions, and "all propositions" must be a meaningless phrase. ["Theory of Types," p. 154]

In the word *meaningless* we hear the ongoing positivist critique of metaphysics, the science of all beings. More specifically, if the whole truth consists in the totality of all true propositions, Russell shows that there is no such totality because it keeps expanding, and if it stops anywhere it contains contradictions. Because no whole can contain itself as one of its parts, any set is either incomplete or else inconsistent. Since a nonreferential logic, especially, cannot endure inconsistency, any given totality must be a part of some larger whole, and so on, ad infinitum.

Before going on to the theory of types itself, let us do Gadamer the unconscionable injustice of reducing *Truth and Method* to one proposition: all propositions are relative.[43] Since Russell has said that "all propositions" is a

---

43. It should be emphasized that this is indeed an unconscionable reduction. Gadamer's focus is neither on propositions nor the logic of propositions but rather on a prepropositional logic, which Hans Lipps calls "hermeneutic logic" and Gadamer calls the logic of question and answer. Furthermore I do not mean at all to assert here that Gadamer is in fact a relativist. I sympathize with Seung, who writes that although he has himself "given a relativistic account of [Gadamer's] position" in *Structuralism and Hermeneutics*, he has concluded that "It is clearly unjustifiable to level the charges of contextualism and relativism against Gadamer" (*Semiotics and Thematics in Hermeneutics*, pp. 174, 178).

meaningless phrase, we can assume that he would take the above proposition as meaningless. But that is so for the same reason that "all propositions are either true or false" is also meaningless; and if we throw out the latter, Russell states in "Theory of Types," then "all general accounts of deduction become impossible" (p. 156). We have already cited Gadamer's admission that his own argument cannot be applied to itself without contradiction (*WM* 424; *TM* 406). Yet he refuses to disavow it, and for precisely the same reason as Russell. "That the thesis of skepticism or relativism contradicts itself [sich aufhebt] is an irrefutable argument. But is anything achieved thereby? The argument of reflection boomerangs back on the arguers in that it renders suspect the truth value of reflection. It affects not the reality of skepticism or that of truth-dissolving relativism but rather the truth claim of formal argument in general" (*WM* 327; *TM* 308–09). It is worth emphasizing that, from either Gadamer's or Russell's perspective, the contradiction belongs to reflection; and thus to affirm the thesis of relativism despite its contradiction is to repudiate the absolute truth claim of reflection and therefore of formal argument—that is, of method. Here Gadamer and Russell separate. Gadamer concludes that "the formal refutability of a thesis does not unconditionally exclude its truth" (ibid.), whereas in Russell's logic there is no criterion of falsehood other than refutability. Russell aims above all to fortify and extend method, Gadamer to limit it.

Despite this difference in ends, however, the means by which Gadamer limits the province of method are strikingly similar to those by which Russell preserves it, namely the theory of types. Russell first makes the nominalistic proposal that we prevent the contradiction involved in a whole that contains itself as one of its parts by refusing to mention wholes—that is, by substituting "any" for "all." "All" cannot be dispensed with completely, however, since it is required for the definitions basic to set theory. Thus the problem remains, and Russell offers the hierarchy of types as its solution.

> The division of objects into types is necessitated by the reflexive fallacies which otherwise arise. These fallacies, as we say, are to be avoided by what may be called the "vicious-circle principle," that is, "no totality can contain members defined in terms of itself." This principle, in our technical language, becomes: "Whatever contains an apparent variable must not be a possible value of that variable." Thus whatever contains an apparent variable must be of a different type from the possible values of that variable; we will say that it is of a *higher* type. [p. 163][44]

44. Although I am intent here on finding similarities between Russell and Gadamer, it should not go unmentioned that this passage in particular represents the very antipodes to the logic of the hermeneutic circle, in which part and whole are reciprocally definitive.

In less technical language, any proposition containing the word *all* cannot be an instance of that all. We can meaningfully say, "All propositions are either true or false" (and thus preserve the possibility of deduction), but that proposition is not an instance of the propositions it describes.[45] Rather, it belongs to a higher logical type, and propositions about that proposition belong to a still higher type.

> Elementary propositions together with such as contain only individuals as apparent variables we will call *first-order propositions*. These form the second logical type.

> We have thus a new totality, that of *first-order propositions*. We can thus form new propositions in which first-order propositions occur as variables. These we will call *second-order propositions*; these form the third logical type. Thus, for example, if Epimenides asserts "all first-order propositions affirmed by me are false," he asserts a second-order proposition; he may assert this truly, without asserting truly any first-order proposition, and thus no contradiction arises. [p. 164]

For the fact that the elimination of contradiction in this way is not mere logical legerdemain, we may accept the testimony of St. Paul: "One of themselves, even a prophet of their own, said, The Cretians are always liars. . . . This witness is true. Wherefore rebuke them sharply" (Titus 1:12–13). As Gadamer argues, the self-contradiction of a reflexive proposition does not of itself demonstrate its falsity. On the other hand, Russell argues that a proposition need not and, if we are to prevent contradiction, cannot be interpreted reflexively. In either case the Cretan may assert truly that all Cretans are liars, and it could be truly asserted that all propositions are relative.

In defending himself, Gadamer tacitly appeals to Russell's hierarchy of types: "It belongs to the prejudices of reflexive philosophy that it understands as a relationship of propositions what does not at all lie on the same logical level" (*WM* 424; *TM* 407). Yet Gadamer is not, like Russell, fundamentally concerned to preserve logic but rather to limit its claims; and in Gadamer's view, the variety of levels is not merely logical. If we can conceive Russell's hierarchy of types more in Gadamer's manner, as a model of self-consciousness, it would seem that the higher logical type corresponds to a higher, because more inclusive, consciousness. Yet this higher consciousness at no level ever becomes fully self-conscious—that is, self-identically reflexive. It can affirm a proposition at the level below that of its own type; but the type, though higher in terms of logical

---

45. Wittgenstein summarizes as follows: "No proposition can say anything about itself, because the propositional sign cannot be contained in itself (that is the whole 'theory of types')" (*Tractatus* 3.332).

inclusiveness, is lower in terms of consciousness than the propositions the type contains. The heightened consciousness of what is objectified in the *proposition* asserted is achieved at the price of a lower consciousness of the type to which the *assertion* belongs. This belonging, Gadamer suggests, is not an *objective* knowledge of itself, whereas Russell would say (if he would say anything at all on the topic) that it is no knowledge of itself at all; yet both agree that belonging is the condition of objectification. Thus Gadamer arrives at the conclusion, by a route similar to Russell's, that "a nonobjectifying consciousness always accompanies the process of understanding" (*PH* 125).

Gadamer cannot keep contradictions out of *Truth and Method*; thus he denies, on plausible grounds, that a contradiction is either necessarily false or meaningless. He affirms that nonobjective, reflexive knowledge of ourselves can be true, however self-refuting. A perfect, exhaustive self-refutation would be possible only if self-consciousness knows itself as objectively as its objects. But if obliviousness of what we belong to is the condition of objectification, a self-refutation, however objective, always leaves some remainder which is not objective, though it may be true. Truth, then, cannot be equated with what is methodologically objectifiable.

This, clearly, is not Russell's conclusion; quite the contrary. But does Russell succeed where Gadamer fails—in keeping contradiction out of the *Principia Mathematica*? Does he, moreover, succeed in snatching up that last remainder so that from the principles of mathematics there elaborated can be exhaustively deduced all arithmetical truths? "It has always been known," Gadamer writes, "that the possibilities of rational proof and doctrine do not fully exhaust the sphere of knowledge" (*WM* 21; *TM* 23). This fact appears as early as Plato's seventh letter (*DD* 96). But the sphere of all knowledge is rather large; and it seems plausible that at least a small part of it, such as arithmetic, could be so rigorously and exhaustively axiomatized as to be complete beyond possible supplement, and consistent beyond rational doubt. This was the aim of *Principia Mathematica*. It is Kurt Gödel's achievement to have shown that this aim was not, and, much more important, could not possibly be, achieved without exceeding the confines of arithmetic.

The details of Gödel's argument are, because of their technical nature, inaccessible to all but professional mathematical logicians, but Gödel's summary of his results is clear enough.

> If to the Peano axioms we add the logic of *Principia mathematica* . . . we obtain a formal system S, for which the following theorems hold:

I. The system S is *not* complete; that is, it contains propositions A (and we can in fact exhibit such propositions) for which neither A nor $\underline{A}$ [i.e., neither A nor not A] is provable. . . .

II. Even if we admit all the logical devices of *Principia mathematica* . . . in mathematics, there does *not* exist a *consistency proof* for the system S (still less so if we restrict the means of proof in any way). Hence a consistency proof for the system S can be carried out only by means of modes of inference that are not formalized in the system S itself. . . .

III. Theorem I can be sharpened to the effect that, even if we add finitely many axioms to the system S . . . we do *not* obtain a complete system. . . .

IV. Theorem I still holds for all . . . extensions of the system S that are obtained by the addition of *infinitely many* axioms. . . . ["Some Mathematical Results," p. 595]

Fortunately, in Nagel and Newman's *Gödel's Proof*, there is available a nontechnical and thoroughly readable exposition of the argument itself, and I rely heavily on it in the summary that follows.

To catch even a glimpse of Gödel's demonstration, we need to recall, first, Hilbert's distinction between mathematics and metamathematics. The function of axiomatization is to render the vocabulary and syntax of an axiomatic system—the elements and their principles of combination—perfectly explicit. Whatever cannot be expressed in this language cannot be expressed at all within the calculus. This means that the language is perfectly self-enclosed in being neither referential nor relative to any other language. Anything that is said about the *whole* system, therefore, cannot belong to that system but lies essentially outside it. A statement that a given mathematical calculus is consistent thus belongs not to mathematics but to metamathematics. These must be kept rigorously distinct, for confusing them leads to the semantic paradoxes.

Second, we need to recall the function of mapping. To prove the consistency of calculus X, it is translated into the terms of calculus Y; if Y is consistent, then X is consistent. Whitehead and Russell reduce (not map) arithmetic to symbolic logic, for in this way they hope to provide a nonrelative proof of the consistency of arithmetic. Gödel's ingenuity consists primarily in mapping the *Principia*'s symbolic logic back onto arithmetic so that each symbol and each logical connective is assigned a number. Any axiom, theorem, or sentence of the calculus thus comes out as a multiple-digit number. For example (mine, not Gödel's), p $v\,q \supset q\,v\,p$ might be translated: 1, 234, 321. Thus every formula derivable from the system has a unique number, called a Gödel number; and moreover, this number can be read as the formula itself.

When you send someone to the supermarket for celery, you expect to get celery, not the word *celery*. If you number your shopping list and ask for number 17, you expect to get hamburger, say, not the number 17. But to go shopping with a Gödel-numbered shopping list in the market of arithmetic is to get back a number. What the Gödel numbers make possible is a metamathematical notation of mathematics within the confines of mathematics itself. Curiously, this is precisely what natural language can do without any difficulty. For example, the sentence you are now reading is composed of thirteen words. Or, the sentence you are now reading is false. As Gödel mentions, his argument is related to the liar paradox, though it is not itself paradoxical. There are many theses, of course that cannot be proved; and an argument might well conclude, "The conclusion of the argument you are now reading cannot be proved." This says nothing against the truth of this sentence; and it is in fact true precisely if the conclusion cannot be proved.

We thus come to the nucleus of Gödel's argument, and it is most prudent to leave its exposition to Nagel and Newman.

Gödel showed (i) how to construct an arithmetical formula G that represents the meta-mathematical statement: 'The formula G is not demonstrable.' This formula G thus ostensibly says of *itself* that it is not demonstrable. . . . In Gödel's argument, the formula G is also associated with a certain number *h*, and is so constructed that it corresponds to the statement: 'The formula with the associated number *h* is not demonstrable.' But (ii) Gödel also showed that G is demonstrable if, and only if, its formal negation ~G is demonstrable. . . . However, if a formula and its own negation are both formally demonstrable, the arithmetical calculus is not consistent. Accordingly, if the calculus is consistent, neither G nor ~G is formally derivable from the axioms of arithmetic. Therefore, if arithmetic is consistent, G is a formally undecidable [i.e., unprovable] formula. Gödel then proved (iii) that, though G is not formally demonstrable, it nevertheless is a *true* arithmetical formula. It is true in the sense that it asserts that every integer possesses a certain arithmetical property, which can be exactly defined and is exhibited by whatever integer is examined. (iv) Since G is both true and formally undecidable, the axioms of arithmetic are *incomplete*. In other words, we cannot deduce all arithmetical truths from the axioms. Moreover, Gödel established that arithmetic is *essentially* incomplete even if additional axioms were assumed so that the true formula G could be formally derived from the augmented set, another true but formally undecidable formula could be constructed. (v) Next, Gödel described how to construct an arithmetical formula A that represents the meta-mathematical statement: 'Arithmetic is consistent'; and he proved that the formula 'A⊃G' is formally demonstrable. Finally he showed that the formula A is not demonstrable.

> From this it follows that the consistency of arithmetic cannot be established by an argument that can be represented in the formal arithmetical calculus. [*Gödel's Proof*, pp. 85–86]

The implications of this argument are astounding, to laymen and professional mathematicians alike. First, G cannot be derived from the calculus of *Principia Mathematica*, but G is nevertheless true. Hence, some axioms must be missing from the calculus. We can, however, add axioms so that G could be so derived. We can even make G itself an axiom. But such additions make possible the construction of still other true but undeducible formulas. Thus the axioms never quite catch up with the truths that the calculus can express but not prove. Moreover, though Gödel proves neither that the calculus is consistent nor that it is inconsistent, he does prove that the system cannot be proved consistent from within. Thus paradox may await just around the corner. Gödel's via negativa shows that no absolute (finite and nonrelative) proof of the consistency of arithmetic is possible that can be represented by arithmetic. What a proof would look like that could not be represented by arithmetic, no one knows.

To the best of our knowledge then, mathematics cannot be exhaustively axiomatized. And if not mathematics, what can be axiomatized? Nagel and Newman write, "The discovery that there are mathematical truths which cannot be demonstrated formally does not mean that there are truths which are forever incapable of becoming known. . . . It does not mean, as a recent writer claims, that there are 'ineluctable limits to human reason.' It does mean that the resources of the human intellect have not been, and cannot be, fully formalized, and that new principles of demonstration forever await invention and discovery" (p. 101). It means that reason cannot finally be equated with systematic proof. "In short," Douglas Hofstadter summarizes, "Gödel showed that provability is a weaker notion than truth" (*Gödel, Escher, Bach*, p. 19). With the confidence that Gödel gives us, we may affirm with Gadamer that truth always and necessarily exceeds method, as method itself compels us to admit.

If absolute proof is no longer available as a criterion determining when we may justifiably call something true, the temptation is to abandon the word *true* altogether, and many have succumbed. But this is merely to affirm a notion of truth that one doesn't apply precisely because one knows that it is universally inapplicable. We have already seen that Popper was tempted in this direction in the *Logic of Scientific Discovery*. Many years later he explained,

> The reason for my uneasiness concerning the notion of truth was, of course, that this notion had been for some time attacked by some philosophers, and with good arguments. It was not so much the antinomy of the

liar which frightened me, but the difficulty of explaining the correspondence theory: what could the correspondence of a statement to the facts be? In addition, there was a view which, though I decidedly never held it, I felt unable to combat effectively. The view I am alluding to is that if we wish to speak about truth, we should be able to give a criterion of truth. . . .

The term 'positivism' has many meanings, but this (Wittgensteinian) thesis that 'a concept is vacuous if there is no criterion for its application' seems to me to express the very heart of positivistic tendencies. . . . If this interpretation of positivism is accepted, then positivism is refuted by the modern development of logic, and especially by Tarski's theory of truth, which contains the *theorem*: for sufficiently rich languages there can be no general criterion of truth. [*Objective Knowledge* pp. 320–21]

This theory of truth first appeared in English in 1944 when Tarski's essay "The Semantic Conception of Truth" was translated. It is constructed on the basis of Morris's distinction between syntactics, semantics, and pragmatics, Hilbert's distinction between mathematics and metamathematics, Russell's theory of types, and Gödel's proofs. Tarski shares with logical positivists generally the "hope that languages with specified structure could finally replace everyday language in scientific discourse" (p. 58). Gadamer's contention is that scientific discourse, thus methodized, cannot possibly replace everyday language. Thus Gadamer endeavors to undermine the claims of artificial language. Our object here is not to decide between these two perspectives but rather to determine whether and to what extent Gadamer's apparent opponents can be summoned to his aid. Specifically, we want to consider here how Tarski's theory of truth can be brought to support Gadamer's critique of absolute knowledge and his correlative affirmation of human finitude.

We have seen that Gadamer addresses, at least briefly, the problem of self-contradiction that, to all appearances, lies at the heart of *Truth and Method*: "One must ask himself whether the two propositions 'All knowledge is historically conditioned' and 'This knowledge [the previous proposition] is unconditionally true' lie on the same level so that they can contradict each other" (*WM* 504–05; *TM* 483). Gadamer here intimates that they do not lie on the same level and do not contradict each other. To affirm the blatancy of the contradiction, on the other hand, is to affirm with Hegel the possibility of transparent self-consciousness. Perfect self-contradiction is conditional on perfect self-knowledge. Thus the attacks on *Truth and Method* based on its self-contradictoriness are circular in that they assume that self-consciousness (method) is the final arbiter of truth, an assumption that Gadamer makes explicit and everywhere denies.

But what happens to truth, one may well wonder, once the levels are discriminated in such a way as to prevent both self-contradiction and self-knowledge? Here Tarski can be of assistance. The purposes of "The Semantic Conception of Truth" are to explain wherein the truth of any sentence consists and to stipulate the conditions under which it can be kept free of contradictions. Semantics deals with the relation between language and the objects to which it refers. The objects to which the word *true* refers are sentences. When we want to refer to a sentence, we place it in quotation marks. We want to know, then, when we would term the sentence "Snow is white" true. Clearly we would do so if snow is white. Thus, Tarski suggests, "Snow is white" is true if, and only if, snow is white. This is the form taken by every definition of a particular truth. Insofar as this form seems to be a tautology, the problem of truth is apparently left dead center, and the fact that it does seem so has led to the "redundancy" theory of truth (associated with Strawson—see his article entitled "Truth"— among others) and to the "affirmation" theory of Polanyi mentioned above.

Worse than tautology, the form is open to semantic paradoxes like that of the liar, which is also called the antinomy of truth. If, instead of "Snow is white," we substitute the sentence "The sentence you are now reading is not true," the above form forces us to assert that the sentence is true if, and only if, it is not true. To prevent paradoxes of this kind, Tarski says, we need to note the assumptions that make them possible:

> (I) We have implicitly assumed that the language in which the antinomy is constructed contains, in addition to its expressions, also the names of these expressions, as well as semantic terms such as the term *"true"* referring to sentences of this language; we have also assumed that all sentences which determine the adequate usage of this term can be asserted in the language. A language with these properties will be called *"semantically closed."*
>
> (II) We have assumed that in this language the ordinary laws of logic hold. ["The Semantic Conception of Truth," p. 59]

Ordinary language is clearly a closed language in Tarski's sense, though not necessarily the only one. It is closed in being capable of autoreference as well as heteroreference. Since the reflexivity of autoreference is what leads to paradox, Tarski implies that a paradox-free language would be exclusively heteroreferential; that is, the objects to which it refers would not include itself. To talk about this language itself, then, we would need another language logically distinct from the first language—though both might still be called English, say. The language talked about is the object-language, and that in which we talk about the object-language is the metalanguage.[46] This is a move reminiscent of Gödel's mapping of the symbolic logic of the *Principia* back onto arithmetic, but here the problem of how to keep metalanguage distinct from object-language is even more pronounced. These levels can be distinguished, in fact, only on the condition that the object-language has been axiomatized. One must know exhaustively its vocabulary, syntax, and the rules governing which of its sentences can be asserted. Only on this condition can one be sure that the object-language is heteroreferential: nothing asserted *about* the object-language can also be asserted *in* that language. Any language so formalized that true statements can be predicated of it which it cannot predicate of itself is an open language—that is, essentially incomplete, because there are some true propositions that it cannot assert. "The problem of the definition of truth," Tarski says, "obtains a precise meaning and can be solved in a rigorous way only for those languages whose structure has been exactly specified" (p. 58).

Given such a specification, the form we considered above is neither tautologous nor potentially paradoxical. " 'Snow is white' is true if, and only if, snow is white" is not tautologous, because the two halves of the form are composed of two essentially different languages. On the left side is the object-language; on the right side occurs the essentially richer metalanguage that thematizes and characterizes the object-language. The left half says something about snow, the right half something about a sentence. This form is not potentially paradoxical, moreover, because the axiomatized object-language is heteroreferential. If we again substitute "The sentence you are now reading is not true," so that it is true if, and only if, it is not true, the distinction of levels requires us to read it just as we read "Snow is not white" is true if, and only if, snow is not white. Thus Tarski specifies a paradox-free form for the definition of every particular truth.

We are now in a position to ask about the nature of truth implied in these conclusions. "It should be noticed," Tarski writes,

> that these terms "object-language" and "meta-language" have only a relative sense. If, for instance, we become interested in the notion of truth applying to sentences, not of our original object-language, but of its meta-language, the latter becomes automatically the object-language of our dis-

---

46. I have argued against applying the object-language/metalanguage distinction to literature and literary criticism in "The Heresy of Metaphrase." Habermas takes Gadamer to be arguing that "a given non-reconstructed everyday language remains the last metalanguage" ("The Hermeneutic Claim to Universality," p. 203). There is some truth in Habermas's contention; yet no everyday language can, with logical rigor, be called a metalanguage. As we will see below, the terminology of *object-* and *metalanguage* is applicable only to artificial languages.

cussion; and in order to define truth for this language, we have to go to a new meta-language—so to speak, to a meta-language of a higher level. In this way we arrive at a whole hierarchy of languages. [p. 60]

This hierarchy of languages clearly corresponds to Russell's hierarchy of types. The truth of any language requires a yet higher metalanguage to define it. Gadamer describes a process much like that indicated by Tarski when he writes, "The furtherance of research is no longer generally understood within the schema of broadening and penetration into new regions or materials but rather achieving a higher level of reflection in putting the question." This seems to describe *Truth and Method* as well; but Gadamer goes on to say, "Even where that happens, we are still thinking teleologically from the viewpoint of the progress of research, as appropriate to a researcher" (*WM* 269; *TM* 253). One wonders, though, whether Tarski is thinking teleologically. One point he is making about the whole hierarchy of languages necessary to define the whole hierarchy of truths is that it can never be whole. This fact becomes clear in his paraphrase of Gödel's conclusions about arithmetic, which, Tarski says, follow from his theory of truth: "*The notion of truth never coincides with that of provability*; for all provable sentences are true, but there are true sentences which are not provable. Hence it follows further that every such discipline is consistent, but incomplete" (p. 64). More precisely, if the discipline is consistent—and the hierarchy of languages guarantees consistency—it is incomplete. Just when truth becomes the whole truth, it becomes potentially inconsistent. Can we think of that as a form of progress which cannot possibly arrive at an end?

"The problem of a 'metalanguage,' " Gadamer writes, "may be unsolvable because it involves an iterative process. But the incompletability of this process says nothing against the fundamental recognition of the ideal to which it approaches" (*WM* 392; *TM* 375). True, this says nothing against the construction of artificial languages; but it says a great deal against the notion that artificial languages such as Tarski proposes can (or even claim to) arrive at what Gadamer calls "the totality of the knowable." They do not approach this ideal; they are constructed precisely so as to avoid it, for arriving at the whole truth would mean the collapse of the hierarchy into homogeneity. It would mean the possible reintroduction of paradox; and given even one paradox, all propositions in a logical system become true and trivial. The conclusion implied in Tarski's argument is that if any particular truth is to be meaningfully defined, neither it nor its definition can be the whole truth.

Gadamer does not avail himself of these means of bolstering his own denial of Hegelian totalization because they are tainted. His antipathy to artificial-language schemes blinds him to the coincidence of his views with those of the prominent mathematical logicians we have considered. The reasons for this antipathy are clear. Constructing an artificial language implies that language is a tool like any other. If a hammer doesn't tighten nuts very efficiently, we exchange it for another tool. If ordinary language is inappropriate for research, we devise a language more suitable.[47] This instrumentalism implies that we stand outside language. It is no less manipulable than the objects it makes manipulable. Artificial language thus exemplifies the dominion of subjectivity, which puts everything at our disposal and under our control.[48]

But this *everything* is, as we have seen, a serious oversimplification; and Gadamer knows that it is. Indeed, that method never exhausts truth is his thesis. What he does not acknowledge is that the advocates of method know this too. From Russell, Gödel, and Tarski, Gadamer would find no disagreement when he writes, "A physics that were to calculate itself and be its own calculation would be self-contradictory. . . . Biology researches what is exactly as does physics, and is not itself what it researches. The being in itself toward which its research is directed, whether in physics or biology, is relative to the positing of being that is the framework of its questions" (*WM* 428; *TM* 410). Relativity is implied in objectivity. All natural science, as objective, is not itself what it studies. Hence the object of no science is all that is, and thus the object of every science is relative to its own framework. Either an objective science is incomplete because it excludes itself from what it studies; or, if it claims to include itself, it is self-contradictory, since the science (as objective) provides its own exception. Either objective and incomplete, or complete and inconsistent—that is the

47. Smith shows that in the *Investigations*, Wittgenstein "sees that the ideal of an invented perfect language is somehow misconceived and that language should be 'in order' as it stands. Still, he wants man to prevail over language, to dispose over it, and that leads him to maintain the tool concept even if signs are now seen to be just one of many tools at man's disposal" ("Gadamer's Hermeneutics and Ordinary Language Philosophy," p. 308).

48. Gadamer would be in full agreement with Deely, that natural language "carries an entire tradition of perceptions and orientations distinguishing a people, even at intersections of enculturated social life, modifying this tradition in the present and extending it into the future through the individuality of its users who are cybernetically, as it were, both constituted by and constitutive of the linguistic and cultural tradition they express, in a kind of circular feedback relationship. Artificial languages, by contrast, reduce such linguistic and cultural tradition down to the state or 'size' of a purely current understanding, suppressing or making 'invisible' the questions of how this understanding was achieved and what it fails to bring into account (its *filtered* and *perspectival* qualities), if they are deployed without critical attention to their proper ground. Thus, while a natural language is expansive, an artificial language is restrictive and tends to close down the understanding of its users upon those elements that can be perfectly controlled—a kind of triumph of safety over life" (*Introducing Semiotic*, p. 90).

dilemma of natural science, whether from the point of view of hermeneutics or that of mathematical logic.

But are not the human sciences stretched on this same rack? In them, the researcher is himself what he studies. The human sciences are therefore not objective, but neither are they even potentially complete. For them, history is the medium of self-knowledge, and that medium is altered and extended by each act of knowing. Yet even if necessarily incomplete, even if more is always needed, self-knowledge is at least always possible in part.

Gadamer often alludes to a hierarchy of levels like that of Russell, Hilbert, Gödel, and Tarski, but he never quite embraces it; and there may be good reasons for not doing so. The hierarchy is designed to prevent self-contradiction by precluding reflexivity and self-reference;[49] but Gadamer's thesis is that self-knowledge is limited—not that it is impossible—and insofar as it *is* possible, and indeed achieved in the human sciences, to that extent self-knowledge is open to self-contradiction. We recall that Tarski's distinction between object-language and metalanguage is possible only on condition that the language has been axiomatized and rendered artificial. Only if "we decide not to use any language which is semantically closed" can paradox be precluded. "This restriction," Tarski continues, "would of course be unacceptable for those who, for reasons which are not clear to me, believe that there is only one 'genuine' language (or, at least, that all 'genuine' languages are mutually translatable)" (p. 59). Gadamer must be counted among these believers. Every linguistically constituted world view, he writes, "potentially contains in itself every other one, that is, each can expand itself into the other. It can understand and comprehend from itself the 'view' of the world offered by other languages" (*WM* 424; *TM* 406). But this universal commensurability implies that there is no hierarchy of higher and lower,

---

49. By contrast with artificial language, Habermas writes in *Knowledge and Human Interests*, "The specific character of ordinary language is this *reflexivity*" (p. 168). To this, Gadamer would undoubtedly agree; yet he does not follow Habermas in drawing Cartesian conclusions about the possibility of a full emancipation through self-reflection. The "self-consciousness" of language does not include consciousness of itself as an object. Language is, however, nonobjectively self-reflexive. Thus Gadamer would concur with Apel: "If we abstract from the pragmatic dimension of symbols, there can be no human subject of the reasoning process. Accordingly, there can be no reflexion upon the predetermined conditions of why reasoning is possible. What we do get is an infinite hierarchy of meta-languages, meta-theories, etc., containing (and concealing) the reflexive competence of man as a reasoning subject" (cited in Habermas, "Postscript," p. 158). Elsewhere Apel explains, "As is well known, Wittgenstein . . . declared that his own sentences about language and its depicting relationship to the world were meaningless [*Tractatus* 6.54 and 7]. . . . [Thus analytic] philosophy could not . . . reflect philosophically on its own method, since this would have been nonsensical metaphysics according to Wittgenstein" (*Analytic Philosophy*, pp. 7, 12).

of meta- and object-languages. There are no logical or linguistic levels wherein a being at all self-conscious can finally retreat from all self-contradiction.

If Gadamer does contradict himself, nothing needs to be said defending him in that regard. No one suggests that self-contradiction is a virtue, yet it is important to remember that, though symbolic logic is indeed nothing if not consistent, this is because it is nonreferential. It places such a premium, an exclusive premium, on formal consistency because it has nothing but form to offer. Outside its sphere, however, all is not lost with the appearance of paradox. "Thus the sun did not stop setting for us, even after the Copernican cosmology entered our knowledge" (*WM* 425; *TM* 407). And if it ever does stop—if the earth begins rising instead of the sun setting—it will not be because logical consistency demands it.

Gadamer's thesis is not that the assertion "All knowledge is historically conditioned" will "always be considered true, any more than that it has always been considered true. The historicism that takes itself seriously will rather count on the fact that one day people will no longer consider its thesis true, that is, will think 'unhistorically.' But certainly not because the unconditioned affirmation of the conditionedness of knowledge is not meaningful but rather contains a 'logical' contradiction" (*WM* 505; *TM* 483). If people begin thinking unhistorically, that too will happen for historical reasons. It is historical life, not logical consistency, which is the final arbiter and ground of truth. That is Gadamer's thesis.

A Reading of
Truth and Method

1

The Critique of Aesthetics

Gadamer describes the general intent of *Truth and Method* as follows: "It aims to seek out the experience of truth that transcends the realm of control of scientific methodology wherever it is met and to inquire into the legitimacy proper to it. Thus the *Geisteswissenschaften* merge with kinds of experience which lie outside science: with the experience of philosophy, with the experience of art, and with the experience of history itself. All these are kinds of experience in which truth that cannot be verified by the methodological means of science makes itself known" (xxviii / xii).[1] So far this exposition has endeavored to raise doubts about a very specific aspect of this general intent, namely the division Gadamer posits on the basis of method between what is inside and what is outside natural science. How the "scientific method" is to be defined has become so vexed a question during the last few decades that it is difficult to determine what belongs to science and what does not. It is now possible to doubt that some particular method makes certain inquiries scientific or indeed that science has any specifiable method at all. We have seen, moreover, that science no longer claims a monopoly on truth; quite the contrary, it seems to have come full circle and to

---

1. In this and the following chapters, all untitled parenthetical citations in the text refer to *Truth and Method*. The first page number refers to the fourth German edition, the second, following the slash, to the English translation.

have abandoned its truth claim entirely. This reversal occurred not because truth was suddenly discovered elsewhere, outside science, but rather because it became clear that if only the strictest criteria of proof can guarantee truth, then natural science has no more claim to it than has any other mode of inquiry. The changes that have transpired in our conception of natural science have rendered inconsequential one aspect of the critical thrust of *Truth and Method*—its attempt to legitimize an avenue to truth that lies outside and in opposition to the methodological control of the natural sciences. It now seems that by the time Gadamer had delivered the blow that was to puncture the universalist pretensions of natural science, the target had self-destructed. In certain respects at least, *Truth and Method* appeared, as its author feared, too late.

Too late, that is, to fulfill one part of Gadamer's aim. But, as Gadamer would be the first to admit, a book has a life of its own that is independent of the life of the author. The turn of events that blunted the impact of *Truth and Method* considered as a critique of natural science has, as it were, turned the book as well, exposing a somewhat different side to our attention. To contend, as I have done, that science's monopoly on truth no longer stands in need of critique from without (because the more severe critique is coming from within) is hardly to contend that the truth claim of philosophy, art, and history is automatically legitimated, as if by default. So far from being already legitimated, we scarcely understand what truth means in the Geisteswissenschaften. Gadamer's positive task has not been preempted—it has only lost the occasion for defensiveness vis-à-vis the natural sciences.

This positive task is to make sense of an elementary fact concerning the experience of interpreting tradition, especially the artistic tradition: "The fact that truth, achievable in no other way, is experienced in an artwork constitutes the philosophical significance of art, which asserts itself against all rationalization" (xxviii / xii).[2] Gadamer attempts to make sense of this fact; he does not attempt to prove it. The endeavor to prove that art in general exerts a truth claim or to demonstrate that this or that work is "demonstrably" true would be self-defeating because it would, by that very endeavor, imply that the truth of art is dependent on a demonstration extrinsic to the work, and superior to it. This absence of proof does not imply that Gadamer merely assumes as a fact what

---

2. Peter J. McCormick writes, "Whether artworks present truths at all is not at issue for the hermeneutic thinker" ("Problems with Literary Truths," in Kresic, ed., *Contemporary Literary Hermeneutics*, p. 71). This is not correct. Whether artworks present truths is at issue, but Gadamer does not attempt to prove this fact with the usual means. For the reemergence of the truth question in aesthetics prior to *TM*, see Heidegger's "Origin of the Work of Art" in *Poetry, Language, Thought* and Gadamer's introduction to the separate German edition of this essay.

other people would want to have proved. He does not assume the truth value of art; he admits it. There is a compulsory quality to the truth of art, which, despite its lack of proofs and reasons, cannot be reasoned away. Such truth cannot be merely entertained like a hypothetical assumption; it does not assert itself as a possibility that could be credited if only it could be verified. Rather it is true already in such a way that one can only admit it, and concede thereby that art is not somehow deficient, not in need of demonstration for its truth, but rather is itself a mode of truth that is prior to demonstration.

The positive task of *Truth and Method*, then, is to enable us to admit the truth of art and of tradition generally. This task involves, instead of proof, a clearing away of obstacles. What once prevented such admission were the universalist pretensions of science. Thus Gadamer writes, "The experience of art is the most important reminder to scientific consciousness to concede its limits" (xxviii / xii). This reminder, however, has always been ineffectual with those who needed most to heed it; and if natural science has conceded its limits, it was forced to do so rather by running up against them from the inside than by being reminded of them from without. The question now is what obstacle yet remains to impede our admission of the truth claim of tradition, or has Gadamer entered the field of battle to find it empty of all resistance?

He proceeds, "The following investigations begin . . . with a critique of aesthetic consciousness in order to defend the experience of truth endowed us by the artwork against the aesthetic theory that permits itself to be narrowed by the truth concept of science" (xxix / xiii). It is not merely natural science, then, that obscures the truth claim of art but also aesthetic theory itself, insofar as it lets itself be influenced by and confined to the kind of truth once anticipated by science. Though natural science itself no longer prevents our admitting the truth of art, scientific aesthetics does. Scientific aesthetics includes, but is not limited to, poetics and stylistics as they have been practiced during the last two decades. More broadly, it comprehends all theories of art that deny, ignore, or displace the truth claim of art, beginning with Kant's. Insofar as all specifically aesthetic theories of art do this, aesthetics is scientific aesthetics.

The first of the three main parts of *Truth and Method* is entitled "The Opening Up [or freeing up, *Freilegung*] of the Truth Question in the Experience of Art." The primary confinement that needs to be freed up, the main obstacle preventing openness to the truth of art, is to be found in Kant and his successors. And it is not the *Critique of Pure Reason* that Gadamer submits to analysis, as if Kant's scientific epistemology were directly responsible for concealing art's truth claim; instead it is the *Critique of Judgment*, Kant's aesthetics proper, in which Gadamer sees the problem. But the two critiques are indivisibly united, of course, and that is Gadamer's point. Aesthetics proper began, and has since remained, dependent on a theory of science. Kant's question "What can we know?" has already been answered before he treats of art, and thus the truth question is already closed before the question of the beautiful is opened. This closure is in fact the condition of aesthetics proper. The autonomy of the aesthetic consists in its negative definition: it is not science, not knowledge, not truth. The first step then in the "Freilegung der Wahrheitsfrage an der Erfahrung der Kunst" is "Die Transzendierung der ästhetischen Dimension." *Truth and Method* begins not where I began the exposition of it—that is, with the critique of scientific universalism, which I culled from scattered pages throughout. Aesthetics is its first target. Gadamer's aim here is not to break up the grand monopoly of science but to break open the cramped and tiny autonomy of aesthetics so that it can admit the truth of art.

Gadamer transcends aesthetics, as we shall see, in several interdependent ways: he shows, first, that aesthetic consciousness (*Bewusstsein*) *is* more than it knows of itself; second, that this "more" that it *is* is intimately connected with the way a work of art is (its *Seinsweise*); and third, that the being (*Sein*) of art and of aesthetic consciousness can best be understood by means of humanistic concepts from which aesthetics proper derived but which were artificially narrowed in the process. Aesthetics never completely escaped its humanistic heritage, though it did forget it; and Gadamer overcomes aesthetics proper by recalling it to its origins. To transcend the confines of aesthetics proper in these ways not only opens up the question of truth in the experience of art but also prepares for the extension of the truth question to the Geisteswissenschaften in general in the second part of *Truth and Method*. In the later chapters of the book the truth claim of art becomes merely a special instance—an exemplary instance—of the truth claim of historical tradition in general.

Truth and Method is itself an interpretation of historical tradition. What that means, it is the aim of the book itself to disclose. We turn then to a detailed examination of it.

THE PRODIGAL AS PARADIGM

(1.1.1.A) By way of introducing his analysis of aesthetics, Gadamer discusses "the problem of methods." This phrase refers not to the dubiousness of methodologism in general but rather to the more local difficulty common to the nineteenth and twentieth centuries of defining the method specific to the Geisteswissenschaften. Exemplifying this difficulty is a speech of Hermann Helmholtz, the German physicist best known for formulating the law of the conservation of heat. In this speech Helmholtz differentiates the natural from the human sciences by distinguishing logical from artistic induction. Gadamer finds it significant that a natural scientist would recognize such a distinction rather than altogether banishing the humanities from the realm of science. There is something different about them, Helmholtz affirms, and yet they remain sciences.

The Geisteswissenschaften are sciences, he argues, because, like the natural sciences, their method is inductive. In this assumption Helmholtz seems to have been influenced by Mill's *Logic*, which universalized and refined induction as the method basic to all science, and which also gave rise to the word Geisteswissenschaften—a translation of Mill's phrase "moral sciences." But if, under the influence of Mill, Helmholtz suggests that induction defines the genus of the method of Geisteswissenschaften, it is apparently under the influence of Kant that he suggests its species. He calls this method "artistic-instinctive" induction—an adjectival pairing that would have been unthinkable before the aesthetics of genius. As opposed to the self-conscious reasonings typical of logical induction in the natural sciences, the human sciences arrive unconsciously at their conclusions. Their induction requires an instinctive psychological tact, and they rely on memory and on the authority of others, whereas the natural scientist utilizes his own reason alone.

Gadamer affirms that there is much that is right in Helmholtz's distinctions and even asserts that Dilthey (who had given so much more thought to the question) did not progress much beyond Helmholtz's formulations. There is indeed something which could be called tact that is necessary for interpreting traditional materials; something like artistry is necessary for interpreting art. But can this something be classified as a species of induction, or of another method? As long as we assume so, the human sciences must resign themselves to being poor relatives of the exact, natural sciences.

(1.1.1.B) Even if we made that assumption, however, we would need to ask how interpretive tact is acquired. As the first and most important of four ways of answering this question, Gadamer offers the concept of *Bildung*, which, he says, "was the greatest idea of the eighteenth century, and precisely this concept indicates the element in which the nineteenth-century Geisteswissenschaften lived, even if they did not know how to justify it epistemologically" (7 / 10). Instead, such philosophers as Dilthey attempted to understand the Geisteswissenschaften within the framework which they could justify, namely that of the natural sciences. No more can Gadamer justify Bildung epistemologically, yet he contends that this humanistic concept is what makes the human sciences into sciences, for in Bildung they find their own source of truth (18 / 15).[3]

If the word *Bildung* can be left untranslated, that is first because its meaning is familiar enough in English. We call *Tom Jones* a *Bildungsroman*, still more Goethe's *Wilhelm Meister*. Hegel's *Phenomenology* is often termed the Bildungsroman of the spirit, for reasons that we will recall in a moment. But it is also important to leave the word *Bildung* untranslated because, given the crucial role of the concept in the Geisteswissenschaften, Gadamer structures the first third of *Truth and Method* around Bildung and its linguistic cognates: *Bild* (form, image, picture), *Nachbild* (reproduction), *Vorbild* (exemplar), *Gebilde* (structure), *Urbild* (original), *Abbild* (copy), and *Einbildungskraft* (imagination). What Gadamer writes of the word *Spiel* (another key word) also applies to Bildung: "Language has accomplished in advance the abstraction which is the task of conceptual analysis as such. Now thought needs only to utilize this advance accomplishment" (98 / 92).[4] In a manner admittedly reminiscent of Heidegger, Gadamer lets his conceptual analysis be guided by the forethought of language. The result is that a word such as Bildung remains a sound as well as a meaning, and as such it preserves the echoes of all its cognates. Unlike a technical term, it sacrifices definition to resonance, and thus retains the breadth and depth it has acquired along the way, in its history and in *Truth and Method* itself.[5]

This manner of proceeding is less method than anamnesis—disforgetting, or remembering what was forgotten. It does not begin with self-consciousness but proceeds toward it through the medium of history. The conceptual language of philosophy does not consist in mere tools, neutral in their import, but rather it has a historical life of its own which the philosopher ignores at the price of naivete. "The conceptual framework in which philosophy develops has always already captivated us in the same way the language we live in determines us. Thus conscientious thought must become conscious of this captivation. A new critical consciousness must now accompany all responsible philosophy and place before the forum of historical tradition to which we all belong the habits of speech and thought which are formed [*bilden*] in the individual's communication

---

3. Rorty suggests that Gadamer substitutes "the notion of *Bildung* (education, self-formation) for that of 'knowledge' as the goal of thinking" (*Philosophy and the Mirror of Nature*, p. 359). In fact, it is Rorty who wants to contrast Bildung and knowledge; for Gadamer, to the contrary, Bildung is both a way of knowing and of being.

4. See also Gadamer's *Die Aktualität des Schönen*, pp. 15 and 54: "The word is the advance achievement of thought which is performed prior to us," and "One must sharpen his ear for words if one wants to think."

5. "The concept-historical provenance of a concept belongs to the concept no less than the overtones belong to a tone" (*KS* 4:5).

with his environment. The following investigation endeavors to fulfill this demand by combining as closely as possible an inquiry into the history of concepts with the substantive exposition of its theme'' (xxxi / xv). Listening to such a word as Bildung and being guided by it are ways of listening to history, and history in turn is requisite to self-critical philosophy. It is as if the philosopher must lose the self in history in order to gain it; and that, as Gadamer shows, belongs to what Bildung itself is.

Originating in medieval mysticism, Bildung first suggests cultivating the image (*Bild*) of God in man; and the post-Renaissance usage of the term retains the sense of full, almost supernatural, realization of human potential. During the period from Herder to Hegel, Bildung explicitly acquires the sense of ''rising up [*Emporbildung*] to humanity'' that Gadamer finds at the basis of the human sciences, for at this stage Bildung means the specifically human way of coming into one's own (*ausbilden*) through enculturation. Bildung is distinct from cultivation in that it is more the acquisition of potencies than the development of latencies. Whereas ''cultivation of a talent is the development of something given, so that its practice and maintenance is a mere means to an end'' (9 / 12), in Bildung, by contrast, the cultural tradition which one assimilates is not disposed of, used up like a means. It is appropriated and becomes one's own in the process of self-formation, but it does not disappear or cease functioning. Bildung does not supersede culture but preserves it.

Hegel associates Bildung with a progress away from immediacy and particularity toward universality. The man who must have everything now, who succumbs to immediate desires and circumstances, is ungebildet. Work, on the other hand, is restrained desire; it sacrifices the present to the future and subordinates the particular needs of the moment to the broader situation. ''In that working consciousness forms the object, acts selflessly, and considers the universal, it rises above the immediacy of its existence to the universal—or, as Hegel expresses it, 'indem es das Ding bildet, bildet es sich selbst' '' (10 / 13). In that consciousness forms the thing, it forms itself. When a man gives himself over to his work so wholly that it becomes distanced from his personal needs and private desires, he not only allows what he makes to assume its own form but does the same to himself. In the selflessness of serving, he becomes himself more fully.

Entering the world of trade can be part of the process of Bildung, but Hegel suggests that the world and language of the ancients are specially appropriate for self-formation. Understanding this world, given its remoteness from ours, necessitates the self-alienation that is the initial movement of Bildung; yet ancient art, literature, and philosophy also offer the possibility of returning to ourselves with a better self-understanding. Bildung, as the basis of the human sciences, always has this structure of alienation and return, excursion and reunion. The primal story of Bildung is that of the prodigal son, and it is no accident that a Bildungsroman such as *Great Expectations* should make explicit use of that biblical paradigm. In Bildung one leaves the all-too-familiar and learns to allow for what is different from oneself, and that means not only to tolerate it but to live in it. It is oneself that one finds in the alien, even while feeding with the swine. There is always this sense of chastening and deflation when we discover that there is something more, something other than ourselves. But even in the humiliation of recognizing oneself in the other, there is also a sense of elation and expansion, of coming into one's own that Scripture depicts as homecoming and coming into one's inheritance.

The structure of Bildung is so crucial to Gadamer's understanding of the Geisteswissenschaften that it deserves special attention. "To find one's own in the alien, to become at home in it," Gadamer writes, "is the fundamental movement of spirit, whose being is only return to itself from being otherwise" (11 / 15). In this structure of excursion and return we discern the circular structure of hermeneutic understanding.[6] Already we can see why it is not a vicious circle in which the mind just spins its wheels. The spirit consists in movement—first in its departure from its home into the strange and unfamiliar, the otherwise. If the move is complete, the spirit finds a home, makes itself at home in the other, so that its new home is no longer alien. But at this point, the elsewhere that had once seemed so foreign proves to be not only a new home but its real home; we discover that the movement which before had seemed to be an exile was in fact a homecoming, and what had seemed to be home when we set out was in fact merely a way station. The initial alienness of the other was a mirage produced by self-alienation.

The being of spirit, Gadamer writes, is only return: that means, it can *only* come back to itself—without, as it were, setting out. Its self is only at the end, not at the beginning. To be only in return means that the traveler, recalling Heraclitus, is different from and more than when he set out. But, to reverse the Heraclitean maxim, he can *only* go home again: the "more" that he is upon return is that he is more fully himself. There is, in ontological terms, an access of being. Further, to *be* only in return means that the spirit *is* only insofar as it

6. Ricoeur succinctly explains the circular structure of Bildung: "It is thus the growth of [the interpreter's] own understanding of himself that he pursues through his understanding of the other. Every hermeneutics is thus, explicitly or implicitly, self-understanding by means of understanding others" (*Conflict of Interpretations*, p. 17).

keeps returning—that is, keeps on the move. Gadamer departs from Hegel in that he envisions no end point where the movement of alienation and return can cease in a total self-appropriation. For Gadamer the spirit is at home only elsewhere; and though this does not mean that it is a homeless vagabond, nevertheless spirit remains perpetually on the way home: it exists as a movement toward being more fully what it is.

Only *Dasein* can say to itself in Heidegger's simplest formulation, "Become what you are" (*Being and Time*, p. 186). Bildung is fundamental to this continuing process, and Heidegger shows how it derives from the fact that Dasein is understanding. "As projecting, understanding is the kind of Being of Dasein in which it *is* its possibilities. . . . Dasein is constantly 'more' than it factically is, . . . that is to say, it *is* existentially that which, in its potentiality-for-being, it is *not yet*" (pp. 185–86). Moreover, "the projecting of the understanding has its own possibility—that of developing itself [*sich auszubilden*]. This development of the understanding we call 'Interpretation' [*Auslegung*]. In it the understanding appropriates understandingly that which is understood by it. In interpretation, understanding does not become something different. It becomes itself. Such interpretation is grounded in understanding; the latter does not arise from the former. Nor is interpretation the acquiring of information about what is understood; it is rather the working-out of possibilities projected in the understanding" (p. 188–89).

In these passages Bildung is given an ontological formulation that is basic to understanding why Gadamer begins with this concept in justifying the human sciences. Heidegger says that *Auslegung* (interpretation) is the *Ausbildung* of the understanding. In this process something happens to what understanding *is* (and therefore to what Dasein is, since Dasein is understanding). What the interpreter is—not just what he thinks and does—changes in interpreting: it is an event of being that occurs. But this event changes what he is in such a way that he becomes not something different but rather himself.

Heidegger's description of interpretation, however, seems rather to pertain to the self-indulgence that explains not understanding but misunderstanding. Understanding does not arise from interpretation, Heidegger asserts; instead, we can interpret only because understanding has already projected possible interpretations. To say that the interpreter finds himself in interpretation, therefore, seems to mean that, like Narcissus, he has understood nothing other than himself. This assumes, though, that in the process the interpreter remains self-identical; and indeed Heidegger writes that "in interpretation, understanding does not become something different." Yet he goes on to say that "it becomes itself." This kind of coming into one's own suggests that the interpreter who finds himself in interpretation does not find merely himself but rather finds himself as if for the first time—that is, he becomes more truly what he is. Interpretation is not merely something a subject or consciousness does to an object but, more fundamentally, something that happens to what the interpreter is. The development of and into what one is, Heidegger calls Ausbildung. It is an ontological event, not merely a cognitive or epistemological act.

"Not what we do, not what we ought to do, but what happens to us above and beyond our wanting and doing" (xvi / xvi) is Gadamer's theme throughout *Truth and Method* and also here in the introductory discussion of Bildung. Bildung prepares the sensitivity and receptiveness to otherness that Helmholtz calls tact. This openness is a way of knowing what is appropriate or inappropriate in certain social circumstances. Tact is a social sense, but it is also closely allied to a sense of the beautiful and to the historical sense that knows what is appropriate in interpreting a past age because it can distance itself from itself in order to sense the difference of the past from the present. Like the five senses, the sense of tact offers a kind of immediate knowledge that does not judge on the basis of general principles and cannot give reasons for its conclusions. In this respect it is like the intuitive or artistic feeling Helmholtz mentions; yet tact, unlike a sense, is not merely a natural capacity for feeling. It must be acquired, and thus presupposes Bildung. Tactful interpretation involves, therefore, "not merely a question of procedure or behavior but rather of what has come into being. . . . The tact that is effective in the human sciences is not exhausted by the fact that it is a feeling and unconscious; instead it is at the same time a way of knowing and a way of being" (14 / 17). Against those who maintain that tact is mere feeling without cognitive import, Gadamer argues that tact acquired through Bildung is a way of knowing; and against those who contend that tact is merely a means of knowledge (and therefore reducible to a procedure or method), Gadamer asserts that it is also a way of being.

Tact involves keeping oneself open to what is other than oneself, and it is therefore open to what is more than oneself—to the universal. Yet this universal is not a fixed concept or general rule applied to a particular situation. Tact does not operate by the conceptual subsumption typical of the natural sciences.[7] Rather the universal viewpoints to which it is open consist in the viewpoints of possible others. Tact is a sense for the social and communal.

Thus tact leads Gadamer to common sense, the second element of the

7. Method is, strictly speaking, tactless insofar as a method consists of universal rules that, by definition, require no tact in their application, no concern with whether they are applicable, because they are universally applicable.

humanistic tradition[8] whose significance he stresses. "There is something obvious about grounding philosophical-historical studies and the way they work on this concept of sensus communis because their object, the moral and historical existence of man as it takes shape in his deeds and works, is itself decisively determined by the sensus communis" (20 / 22).[9] What was produced by common sense must be understood by common sense, though not necessarily the same one. Common sense is not a fixed body of maxims. It is historical, first of all, because it changes. A person with common sense has *phronesis,* to employ Aristotle's term; he has practical wisdom as opposed to purely theoretical, abstractly conceptual knowledge. The practical man, possessed of common sense, knows what to do in particular circumstances. What common sense dictates changes as circumstances alter because it is relative to them. By contrast, what Edmund Burke calls "metaphysical abstraction" remains irrelative and therefore irrelevant to understanding the vicissitudes of common, political life. Although Gadamer does not mention him at this point, Burke's comments in *Reflections* are perfectly apropos: "I cannot . . . give praise or blame to any thing which relates to human concerns, on a simple view of the object, as it stands stripped of every relation, in all the nakedness and solitude of metaphysical abstraction. Circumstances (which with some gentlemen pass for nothing) give in reality to every political principle its distinguishing colour, and discriminating effect. The circumstances are what render every civil and political scheme beneficial or noxious to mankind" (pp. 89–90). For common sense, as Gadamer too says, "the conclusion based on the universal and the proof on the basis of axioms cannot suffice because everything decisively depends on the circumstances" (20 / 23).

Common sense is a knowledge of the concrete, and it is also concrete knowledge because it is a sense acquired by living in a concrete community and determined by upholding the value of communal traditions. Common sense is therefore historical in this second way, in that it preserves tradition—and not just as a datum of knowledge but as a principle of action. Traditional sense, as

8. This section of *TM,* "The Significance of the Humanist Tradition for the Human Sciences," can be read as a reply to Heidegger's "Letter on Humanism." It affirms Heidegger's critique of humanism as correct in principle but also shows that historical humanism was less "humanistic" than Heidegger thought.

9. Habermas comments, "Gadamer poses the question: 'Is the phenomenon of understanding adequately defined when I state that to understand is to avoid misunderstanding? Is it not, rather, the case that something like a "supporting consensus" precedes all misunderstanding.' We can agree on the answer, which is to be given in the affirmative, but not on how to define this preceding consensus" ("The Hermeneutic Claim to Universality," in Bleicher, ed., *Contemporary Hermeneutics,* p. 203).

Burke writes, "is of ready application in the emergency; it previously engages the mind in a steady course of wisdom and virtue, and does not leave the man hesitating in the moment of decision, sceptical, puzzled, and unresolved" (p. 183). The readiness or immediacy of applicability Burke speaks of here indicates that common sense is a kind of knowledge that motivates. It combines *is* and *ought* in such a way that its applicability is built in. So too according to Vico, Gadamer explains, "what gives the human will its direction is not the abstract universality of reason but instead the concrete universality, representing the community of a group, a people, a nation, or the whole human race" (18 / 21). The concrete principles upon which common sense acts without reasoning and deliberation are of ready application in the service of the commonweal because they derive from common life. They are rightly called general principles in the same sense as we speak of the general good and the commonweal.

Helmholtz, we recall, suggests that the natural scientist relies entirely on his own reason whereas the human scientist depends on memory and the authority of others. Burke reverses the value Helmholtz assigns to these two modes: "We are afraid to put men to live and trade each on his own private stock of reason; because we suspect that this stock in each man is small and that the individuals would do better to avail themselves of the general bank and capital of nations, and of ages" (p. 183). Because it acknowledges the finitude of reason, common sense draws from the bank of common tradition. It is acquired by example more than from precepts, so also it learns from eloquence more than from demonstration. Gadamer aligns Vico's discussion of common sense with the pre-Ramistic rhetorical tradition in which eloquence is more than "mere rhetoric."[10] "It means saying something right, that is, something true and not just the art of discourse, the art of saying something well" (16 / 19).[11] "Youth," Vico says "requires pictures [*Bilder*] for imagination and for the development [*Ausbildung*] of their memory. This function cannot be performed by critical research, and so Vico supplements the critica of Cartesian rhetoric with the old topica. This is the art of finding arguments and serves the development [*Ausbildung*] of a sense of the convincing that works instinctively and ex tempore and therefore cannot be replaced by science" (18 / 20).

In this connection Gadamer mentions the "anti-rhetorical methodologism of modernity," and it is certainly true that many formulations of scientific

10. Klaus Dockhorn offers extended commentary on Gadamer in the context of the history of rhetoric in "Hans-Georg Gadamer's *Truth and Method*."

11. So also Ricoeur writes, "An argument that can properly be called rhetorical takes into account both the degree to which the matter under discussion seems to be true and the persuasive effectiveness it has" (*Rule of Metaphor*, p. 29).

methodology from Descartes and Locke onward have been explicitly anti-rhetorical. Helmholtz, as we have seen, talks about the reliance of the natural
scientist exclusively on his own reason. But since Peirce, at least, we have come
to recognize that natural science is a communal enterprise, a project of the
"interpretive community."[12] And if such communities are the condition of scientific knowledge, then communication (which includes rhetoric and the sense
of the convincing) is the condition of that knowledge as well. Science cannot
replace the ground it stands on, the sense that founds community, the sense of
the common ground—that is, common sense.

We can see how the concept of common sense was thinned and narrowed
during the nineteenth century (the century of the Geisteswissenschaften) by
turning to an analogue of common sense, namely judgment, the third concept
from the humanistic tradition that underlies the human sciences without their
acknowledging it. Common sense considered as sound judgment brings us closer
to the *Critique of Judgment*. It prepares for the detailed discussion of Kantian
and post-Kantian aesthetics that follows in Gadamer's next major section, and
it recalls Helmholtz's suggestion that the human sciences are distinguished by
a specifically aesthetic element.

Judgment is like common sense in that it too cannot be logically certified.
If we understand judgment as merely the faculty that guides us in subsuming a
particular under a universal, then it would seem less like a sense than a rule—
a rule for the application of rules. Yet it cannot be that; for if judgment were
itself a rule, it would require yet another, higher faculty of judgment to guide
its own application.[13] If this regress is to be avoided, judgment cannot be conceived as a rule or *concept* belonging to conscious reflection. Rather it is appropriate to speak of the *sense* of judgment by analogy with sensory judgments
(of heat, light, and so on) that are made with a certainty that is not the result
of logical demonstration. Such judgment can be learned—but not in the abstract
since it is not an abstract rule. It can be learned only in the concrete by being
practiced from case to case.

Because judgment is not a general concept, Kant ranks it among the lower

12. Apel's critique of "methodological solipsism" is strongly influenced by Peirce: "If one
really hopes to objectify the whole world, including the dimension of communication, by a language
of a unified science, then one must, strictly speaking, cling to the a priori of methodological solipsism,
for the totalization of the idea of scientific objectivity implies that the subject of the objectifying
science could, in principle, practice science without being a member of a communication community"
("The A Priori of Communication," p. 299). Since such solipsism is impossible, in Apel's view,
the communication community is prior to (and cannot be made an object of) science. In a similar
vein, see Habermas, "The Hermeneutic Claim to Universality," pp. 186–87.

13. See Kant, *Critique of Pure Judgment*, pp. 177–78.

powers of the mind in the first *Critique*. Common judgment for Kant is common in the sense of average and ordinary; everyone of ordinary intelligence is able to subsume *grass* under *green*, and the judgment that is common in this sense has nothing to do with community. So also when Kant avoids the above regress in his transcendental doctrine of judgment, the ideas there treated apply to their objects a priori, and not because they have been so applied by a community. In Kant's exposition of pure reason, judgment as a cognitive faculty has lost its relation to common sense as the sense of what is common among men.

Likewise in the *Critique of Practical Reason*, common sense gets flattened out as a basis of moral judgment. The "moral sense" philosophy of ethics developed by Shaftesbury and his successors had been intertwined with common sense; moral judgment included not merely correct subsumption but a concern for the commonweal necessitated by common life. Kant, by contrast, contends that moral judgment has a higher legitimacy than can be afforded by the community and defends it against the "empiricism of practical reason"—the idea that the good is what people in fact want or feel. "Kant requires that our will be directed solely by the impulses founded on the self-legislation of pure practical reason" (30 / 32). Rather than deriving from communal life, the concern for general welfare implicit in the categorical imperative derives from this self-legislation. Hence, in Kant's view, moral judgment supersedes the sensus communis.

In the third *Critique*, however, Kant makes room for common sense. Baumgarten had suggested that judgment decides on the perfection or imperfection of the individual as such and not as a subsumed instance of a universal. This is not conceptual judgment, then, but rather judgment that decides on perfection immanently, that is, according to an internal agreement within the individual sensible object. This becomes Kant's "reflective judgment"; and he writes, "A sensible judgment of perfection is called taste" (28 / 30). "Here," Gadamer elaborates, Kant "can speak of a real common sense. . . . In aesthetic taste is understood the necessity of common agreement, even if it is sensible and not conceptual. The true common sense, therefore, says Kant, is taste" (31 / 33).

"So for Kant," Gadamer concludes, "only the aesthetic judgment of taste is left over from the full breadth of what could be called the sensible capacity of judgment" (31 / 33). As taste, the common sense has lost its connection to the political and social tradition of humanism. Within that tradition, "the sensus communis is an element of civic and moral being" (29 / 31). Since the time of Kant, however, common sense has been confined to the universal communicability of aesthetic judgment alone.

With respect to taste, this fourth and final humanistic concept, what concerns

Gadamer is not merely that Kant confines common sense to taste but that he also confines taste to the aesthetic. Gadamer adduces Gracian and even Aristotle to suggest that, contrary to Kant's artificial narrowing, taste is a moral and social—and not merely an aesthetic—idea. Taste is most obviously like a sense: even in primarily non-sensory contexts there remains an allusion to the tongue which judges the tasty and the tasteless, like all sense organs, without having or needing reasons. So too is aesthetic taste a sensible judgment which possesses a decisive sureness even though it employs no general rules. To dress by abstract rules, for example, is almost by definition to dress tastelessly (one thinks of Swift's Lagadans whose clothes are geometrical); and yet dressing according to one's private predilections scarcely guarantees good taste either. Nor is taste-fulness insured by following the more social laws of fashion. These laws are indeed general and communal; the penalty for breaking them is ostracism. But taste can break the laws of fashion and yet remain good taste. "In contrast to fashion it becomes clear that the generality which belongs to taste is grounded quite otherwise than is fashion and does not merely mean empirical generality" (34 / 35). Taste is a communal sense, but this community is ideal rather than empirical. The man of taste does not believe that everyone does or even will agree with his judgments but rather that an *ideal* community *would* do so.

Gadamer does not at all dispute these basic Kantian conclusions. Taste is a communal sense, a sense of the whole, and therefore a hermeneutic sense. It judges the particular in relation to a whole according to whether the particular is fitting and appropriate, even though that whole (like the ideal community) is not empirically given. Where Gadamer does take issue with Kant is in the latter's narrowing of taste to the aesthetic. Something like a sense of taste, Gadamer asserts, "is required everywhere a whole is intended but is not given as a whole" (35 / 36). A moral or legal code intends a whole because, first, it is intended to be complete in itself (for example, there is no need for additions to the Decalogue or the Constitution); and, second, such a code is whole because it intends to cover life completely—there are to be no legal loopholes, no moral holidays. Yet this whole is not given. Whether legal or moral, laws seem never to apply exactly and unequivocally to the individual case; and if life does not prove for that reason to be one long series of exceptions, that is because the code is constantly supplemented and developed by being applied to concrete cases.

Insofar as a particular case is merely an instance, it can merely be subsumed under the general rule by common judgment. But what of the special case? If it is to be a case at all, and not merely evidence of a loophole or an exception that breaks the rule, then precisely here common, subsumptive judgment does not suffice, for we need to judge the case by a rule that is not given. This is the function of taste: to judge by unformulated and unformulable rules. But what kind of rule is it that is not given and therefore seems no rule at all? What is meant here is a rule that is not given as a whole but is always to be made whole. There is nothing peculiar about such laws, Gadamer suggests; all the laws that govern our civic and moral life are precisely of this kind. They are intended— but not given—as wholes. Tritely and falsely put, such laws are elastic. Less tritely and more truly, they are always *to be* formulated "through the productivity of the individual case" (35 / 37).

Taste offers a special avenue of knowledge in that it is judgment of the "individual case." If this phrase is not to be a mere contradiction, we must say that taste attends to the uniqueness of the individual and yet has an eye to the not-yet-given whole. Gadamer contends that aesthetic judgment, conceived as what first makes the individual a case, surpasses the bounds of the aesthetic proper because it is necessary to the moral and legal life of mankind as well as to its aesthetic life. Taste is necessary wherever subsumption does not suffice— and that, Gadamer adds, is true even in the training of pure reason. In the first *Critique*, Kant mentions that examples sharpen the judgment, but he adds a caveat: "Very seldom do they fulfill the conditions of the rule" (36 / 37). The other side of what Kant sees as a deficiency in examples is what Gadamer sees as the deficiency of rules and concepts. Very seldom, even by Kant's reckoning, do precepts exactly fit the examples. The concrete is not exhaustively understood as an instance of a formulable concept; and thus not only our moral and legal life, but cognition generally, if it is to understand the individual case, must involve taste and aesthetic judgment.

But does Gadamer really want us to begin talking about someone's "good taste in ethics" or "good taste in knowledge" as we would his "good taste in music"? Did anyone ever talk this way? If Gadamer is right about Greek ethics, for instance—that it is "in a deep and comprehensive sense an ethics of good taste"—people once did in fact talk this way; and the fact that we ourselves do not is one measure of Kant's abiding influence. Not only does Kant limit common sense to taste, and taste to the aesthetic, he limits the aesthetic itself to judgment of the beautiful and sublime. The very trichotomy that established the autonomy of aesthetic judgment also repressed its role in cognitive and ethical judgment. "What Kant legitimated and wanted to legitimate in his critique of aesthetic judgment was the subjective universality of aesthetic taste in which there is no longer knowledge of the object." But this refusal to admit that taste is a way of knowing "blocked the way to recognizing the truth claim that tradition possesses" (38 / 38). By demonstrating the autonomy of the aesthetic, Kant opened up a special place for the human sciences, but at the same time he deprived them of the name of sciences by disenfranchising their object, art, as a source of knowledge and forced them to look to something other than their object in order to reclaim the name of sciences. Gadamer concurs with Kant that aesthetic judgment is distinct (though not absolutely) from conceptual knowledge. "But," he asks, "will it do to reserve the concept of truth for conceptual knowledge? Don't we need to recognize too that the artwork possesses truth?" (39 / 39). Our reluctance to speak of "good taste in knowledge" is merely the other side of our reluctance to admit the truth claim of art. If reasserting the role of aesthetic judgment in ethics and cognition makes them too subjective, that is in large part due to Kant's subjectification of aesthetics—the analysis of which occupies the next section of *Truth and Method*.

Before turning to it, we need to sum up what Gadamer has accomplished thus far. Bildung, common sense, judgment, taste—these are concepts belonging to a tradition that pre-dates aesthetics proper (if we date that from Kant). Yet Kantian aesthetics did not originate ex nihilo but rather was built on the foundation of precisely this tradition. Therefore, if the human sciences, having developed on the foundation of Kantian aesthetics, now find themselves largely without self-justification, it is not necessary or even desirable to refute Kant. What we need to do instead is to learn to listen to the earlier tradition that still lives in Kant, just as Kant still lives in the present. If it is aesthetics proper that blocks us from admitting the truth claim of art, opening up the way does not necessitate "getting around" aesthetics because, as part of the tradition in which we live, its own claims cannot be superseded and should not be ignored. A concept such as taste retains its earlier moral and social, as well as aesthetic, resonances even though Kant concentrates exclusively on the latter. The prehistory of aesthetics survives in it, haunts it like a ghost that is not to be exorcised. So also the Kantian echoes are not to be silenced in current discussions of aesthetics. And Gadamer does not wish to silence them. He does not aim to refute but rather to listen the more closely to Kant in order to hear not only what Kant says but what more gets said in the process.

This "more" is that precisely within aesthetics there is still to be found a mode of knowledge and a source of truth that can legitimate the human sciences as sciences. Indeed this legitimacy had already been conceptualized by the humanistic tradition. Considered together, Bildung, common sense, judgment, and taste involve a mode of knowing that is like a sense in that it judges immediately, without recourse to formulated or indeed formulable criteria and without submitting its conclusions to the "higher" court of demonstration. Its judgments are final: there are no superior criteria of truth by which to judge them. Yet this mode of knowing is unlike an innate sense and is more like a consciousness in that it is educable. It is formed in Bildung, and such education occurs not only in studying a foreign culture but in living in one's own. Common sense is a sense for the common that is acquired in communal life. To live outside oneself in the community is to come into one's own; the second nature acquired through custom and tradition is actually the first insofar as through the latter one becomes more fully what one is. Bildung, common sense, judgment, and taste, are not only ways of knowing but ways of being, and in this unity of knowing and being Gadamer discerns the significance of the humanist tradition.

WHAT IS MORE THAN ART?

(1.1.2.A) If Gadamer's presentation of the humanistic tradition seems a thinly disguised preparation for an all-out attack on Kant, it is worth emphasizing that this onslaught never comes. Gadamer does not refute Kant: he interprets him. Yet there are refutations, we know, that refute by interpretation, so that the opponent's arguments, even as they become intelligible, are reduced to transparent thinness and topple as if of their own accord. But Gadamer creates no straw man in this interpretation. Far from it, there is typically a general agreement with and even a strengthening of Kant's positions as Gadamer interprets them. Whenever Gadamer seems to have finally opened up a chink in Kant's armor (for example, "The recognition of art seems impossible for an aesthetics grounded in the pure judgment of taste"), he immediately closes it again ("Yet if one looks more closely, such a conception corresponds neither to Kant's words nor to what he has in mind"). "Kant seems," says Goethe in an often quoted remark, "to have woven a certain element of irony into his method. For, while at one time he seemed to be bent on limiting our faculties of knowledge in the narrowest way, at another time he pointed, as it were with a side gesture, beyond the limits which he himself had drawn."[14] Gadamer, I think, focuses on such ironic gestures as are found in the *Critique of Judgment* so that in his own appropriation, Kant sounds noticeably like Gadamer but is truly Kant nonetheless. And of course the reverse is true as well. Our expectations to the contrary notwithstanding, Gadamer's hermeneutics is in significant respects, undeniably Kantian. We saw that Gadamer cites Helmholtz's appeal to the artistic moment of the human sciences as an example of Kant's influence. But the far more significant example of that influence is *Truth and Method* itself insofar as it attempts to legitimate the human sciences independently from and in opposition to the natural sciences.

---

14. Cited by Bernard in his introduction to the *Critique of Judgment*, p. xxxiii.

None of the above should be taken to imply, however, that Gadamer actually celebrates Kant's "subjectification of aesthetics." Quite the contrary, it is this subjectification that necessitates Gadamer's "transcending of the aesthetic dimension"; this is because Kantian aesthetics knocked the foundations from under the human-sciences-to-be in the very act of establishing their independence. While preserving this independence, Gadamer aims to reassert those ontological foundations; and in attempting to do both at once he is profoundly un-Kantian.

We should be clear regarding what *subjective* means in the context of aesthetic judgment. Most important is that taste offers no knowledge of its object, and its judgments are thus subjective in the privative sense of being not-objective. Moreover, to say "That flower is beautiful" is to say nothing about the flower but rather about a subjective feeling, namely the feeling of pleasure which I have in response to it. The aesthetic judgment is called "aesthetic" because it is judgment by feeling; and its opposite, therefore, might better be conceived as anaesthetic than unartistic. Feelings are subjective in the further sense that no one else can have them for us. As we do not learn pain from the pin or from seeing someone else pricked, so flowers do not teach us beauty nor can aesthetic judgment be acquired by imitating others. Taste, Kant says, must be a *selbst-eigenes* faculty, one's very own.

The feeling of beauty, however, is unlike that of pain and even of sensory pleasure in that it is not merely agreeable to the senses, like the taste of sweetness. Instead the taste for beauty registers the pleasure involved when the cognitive faculties themselves play. If knowing is the work of the imagination and understanding, then aesthetic judgment (in which nothing is known of the object) is their play. The cognitive faculties dally and linger with the object without coming to the point of making a determination about it. Moreover, although the pleasure of beauty is a subjective feeling that must be one's very own, yet it is not private. When I say, "I feel dizzy," I do not expect you to feel dizzy too; but when I say, "That flower is beautiful," I not only expect you and everyone else to understand this judgment but also to agree with and share it. And even if in fact no one agrees, I will still think that everyone ought to agree.

The aesthetic judgment's claim to universal validity, despite its empirical non-universality, is very much like a truth claim, even in Kant's view and all the more in Gadamer's. Though subjective, an aesthetic judgment is like an objective judgment in that both are intended as binding on everyone. Taste presupposes a sensus communis. But for Kant taste is common because it has been abstracted from the private rather than because it is grounded in the communal; and it is certainly not grounded in actual communities, for the empirical non-universality of aesthetic judgments (even within individual societies) is patent. Can Gadamer retain the moral and political foundations of the older tradition of sensus communis without losing the aesthetic judgment's claim to universality; or does Kant himself retain them insofar as he refuses to decide whether common sense is innate or acquired—that is, whether common sense is a historical condition of taste or a creation from what is one's very own? (*Critique of Judgment*, para. 22).

What specially interests Gadamer in Kant's exposition is the definitive indeterminacy of aesthetic judgments. They are definitive in that they are certain and cannot be appealed or refuted, just as they cannot be proved; and yet their certainty is intended as binding for all men and not just for the individual judge, even though that whole, the totality of all men, is never empirically given. Moreover aesthetic judgments are indeterminate in several senses. They come to no conclusions, make no final determinations about the object such that one could have done with it and move on to something else. Aesthetic judgment never reaches conceptual determination of the object but, in tarrying, is always on the way toward it. It never reaches the end because it does not begin with, or judge by means of, determinate concepts. Universal concepts are not given in advance of aesthetic judgment as the criteria of the beautiful. But no more does taste judge the beautiful on the basis of previously given examples of beautiful objects or tasteful judgments. The ground upon which taste judges is definitively non-given. Just as aesthetic judgment never ends in a conceptual or communal universality, so also it does not begin there. If aesthetic judgment is nevertheless grounded in an actual political and moral community, as Gadamer wishes to affirm, then that community cannot be conceived as an empirically given or conceptually determinate universality. The empirical non-universality of aesthetic judgments says nothing against their being grounded in a community if that community is not an empirical universal. But neither is it a conceptual universal. We are left, then, with the question of how to understand common sense, how to explain what makes possible the universal communicability of the aesthetic judgment. What is it that Gadamer means when he refers to "what grounds commonality and founds community" (41 / 41)?

"It is a subjective principle to which Kant reduces common sense," Gadamer observes; "he denies that taste has cognitive significance" (40 / 40). Gadamer endeavors to reassert that cognitive significance, and he does so by reexamining the role of the cognitive faculties in aesthetic judgment. Kant does say, after all, that the object of aesthetic judgment is *zweckmässig* to our cognitive faculties—that is, so well suited as almost to seem purposely designed to encourage the free play of imagination and understanding. What kind of object is this? In one sense Kant is not concerned to give an answer because he is interested in the pure judgment of taste, where *pure* means without regard to the object in any respect but its beauty, and hence without regard to whether it is an object of nature or of art.

Yet, in his discussion of free and dependent beauty, Kant seems to suggest that natural objects have at least a methodological precedence over artistic objects in that they occasion pure, as opposed to intellectualized, aesthetic judgments. As an example of free beauty, a flower does not seem to exist for any particular reason, and so judgments of it are free of the conceptual trappings of purpose. On the other hand, wherever a concept intervenes—and that happens not only in poetry but in all the representational arts—there is only dependent beauty. The concept hinders and circumscribes the free play of imagination. If Kant means to say that, of all kinds of art, only non-representational, non-conceptual formalism occasions a purely aesthetic judgment, then it is clear that an aesthetics based on the pure judgment of taste fails to do justice to art.

This, Gadamer infers, is exactly what Kant means to say: free beauty, as in the flower or arabesque carpet, is *not* beauty proper; or if it is, then art is more than beautiful. An aesthetics that would be more adequate to the full scope of art must surpass the pure aesthetic judgment—in Gadamer's view *and* Kant's. We begin to see that Gadamer does not transcend aesthetics by viewing it from above; rather, in his interpretation of Kant, aesthetics transcends itself. There can be no free play of imagination if understanding restricts imagination to exemplifying given concepts or fulfilling set purposes, but just as certainly there can be no harmony of imagination with understanding if the understanding is banished and inert. Concept and purpose (the impulse toward unity) are thus reaffirmed as the surplus by which art exceeds pure aesthetic judgment. But if we are not to slip straight back into aesthetic rationalism and utilitarianism, we need to see that the understanding's impulse toward unity does not ideally inhibit the imagination's spontaneous productivity (*das Bilden der Einbildungskraft*).

Kant's exposition of the ideal of beauty makes clearer the harmony of imagination and understanding. It is the human form alone that can embody ideal beauty, because in it there is an expression of the moral, without which, Kant says, nothing can be universally pleasing. With respect to the pure judgment of taste, this seems to be a reversal on Kant's part since he says here that a house, tree, or garden cannot embody ideal beauty because their purposes are not sufficiently conceptually determined (whereas before he had said that the presence of concepts diminishes the pure sense of beauty). But if the human form is alone capable of embodying ideal beauty because of its expression of the moral, then Kant's aesthetics cannot be a merely formalist aesthetics based on pure taste alone.

The nature of art, Gadamer says, following Hegel, is to present man with himself. And if Kant is to be understood as doing justice to the beautiful in art as well as in nature, his exposition of the ideal of beauty must be read with special reference to art. In art, objects other than man can present the human and the moral—but only by reason of their representation. A stunted tree does not of itself express misery, but a picture of it can do so. By contrast, a picture of a crippled human body expresses the same misery as does the body itself. In such a case no personification is involved, and hence there is no split of the representation from the represented. ''Only in the representation of the human form does the whole content of the artwork speak to us as the expression of its object as well'' (45 / 45). This is the autonomy of art within the autonomy of aesthetic judgment generally: art is no longer charged with presenting the ideals of nature, for they cannot of themselves be universally pleasing. Precisely because they are not themselves determined by moral life and purpose, they do not embody the ideal beauty. Only what is in itself meaningful can do so. Though it is true, then, that the beautiful in general pleases without a concept, yet Kant himself suggests that ''only the beautiful that speaks to us meaningfully evokes our total interest. It is precisely the knowledge that taste is conceptless that leads beyond an aesthetics of mere taste'' (46 / 46).

At this point, we again witness an apparent reversal on Kant's part (or is it Gadamer's?). For what speaks to us most significantly, in Kant's view, is not art but the beauty of nature. Natural beauty has no significance of content: it does not mean anything and seems beautiful to no end. Yet because it is so amenable, so well suited to us without being purposely so, natural beauty points to us as to the ultimate purpose of its creation and calls us to our own moral destiny. Although nature is meaningless, ''yet it has something to say to us. In respect to the idea of mankind's intelligible destination, nature as beautiful nature achieves a *language* which brings it to *us*'' (48 / 47). We find our own fullest intelligibility, then, in the meaningless otherness of nature; because art is designed for us, on the other hand, it does not offer confirmation by an other. Only what is not designed for us (nature) can tell us what we are designed for.

Yet if natural beauty achieves a language which we can understand, nevertheless what it says remains rather vague. The advantage of art is its greater specificity and definiteness; its language, though indeterminate by comparison with the language of concepts, is yet *anspruchsvoll*: it speaks to us (*uns anspricht*) in such a way as to make a determinate claim (*bestimmter Anspruch*). We have to take seriously the artwork's significance; it is important to "get it right."[15] And yet this claim on us does not impede the play of our cognitive faculties as would their being bounded by a given concept. The criterion of getting it right is not given or definable by anything outside the artwork, but neither is it right to say that there is not the impulse toward unity and determinacy typical of the understanding. Saying that would be to ignore the demand of the artwork: there is something we must understand, something always to be understood. If taste implies a denial of this binding and compelling quality, then we need more than pure taste to do justice to art.

When Kant himself surpasses the pure judgment of taste, it is in the direction of genius. Through the concept of genius Kant assigns a special place to art because, whereas taste judges both natural and artistic beauty, the productivity of genius pertains to art alone. Yet before we conclude that Kant has finally driven a wedge between nature and art, we should recall what Gadamer reminds us throughout this section: "The 'critique of aesthetic judgment' does not try to be a philosophy of art" (41 / 41); it "basically does not permit a philosophical aesthetics in the sense of a philosophy of art" (52 / 51). Genius in Kant's aesthetics defines art as such, but it does so in a way that reclaims art from its apparent autonomy and brings it back into the sphere of the naturally beautiful. "Through genius, nature gives the rule to art," Kant says (51 / 51). Art has no unique identity as opposed to nature. Thus for Kant, "the beautiful in nature or art has one and the same a priori principle, which lies wholly within subjectivity. The autonomy of aesthetic judgment provides no basis for an autonomous sphere of validity for beautiful objects" (52 / 51).

It is precisely this validity, however, the validity of the beautiful object, that Gadamer is seeking; and it is to be found, he intimates, in the Anspruch of art. If Kant himself does not finally do full justice to this claim, it does not follow that Gadamer must finally reject Kantian aesthetics. Rather he points out that philosophy of art per se lay outside Kant's purview. The priority of nature to art in Kant's discussion of taste and genius results from the fact that the "critique of aesthetic judgment" lays the groundwork for the "critique of teleological judgment" that forms the second and concluding part of the *Critique*. Here in this second part, judgments of *natural* purpose are Kant's sole interest. Thus the priority he assigns to nature in aesthetic judgment is merely a methodological priority required by the direction of his argument. Kant leaves space for a philosophy of art, but he does not himself fill it; and thus if we follow the

15. It should be stressed that in Gadamer's view the motive to correctness derives from the work, the importance of what it has to say and its claim on us, not from the subjectivity of the interpreter—e.g., his integrity or rigor.

direction of Gadamer's own argument, the way leads *through* Kant, not around him. Anspruch means to Gadamer within the realm of art what *Urteil* means to Kant within the realm of the beautiful generally. It is the bridge between the understanding's conceptual knowledge of what something is and the practical reason's moral knowledge of what something ought to be. But unlike Urteil, Anspruch is less something we do than something that first happens to us.[16] *Das Kunstwerk spricht uns an.*

(1.1.2.B) It seems then that if we are to do justice to the beautiful in art per se (and not just as a species of the beautiful generally), we need to locate a standpoint from which art can be viewed as art. To this end the concept of genius was found most promising by Kant's successors—notably Schiller, Fichte, and Schelling. If art is essentially the art of genius, as Kant had said, then from the standpoint of art per se, taste and hence natural beauty lose their methodological priority. Especially if taste for Kant ideally takes on a "determinate unchangable form" (52 / 52) that will be "invariant against the mutability of time" (54 / 53), then genius seems more appropriate than taste to that eternality. Nothing is clearer in history than the fact that taste changes, whereas genius is apparently permanent though time. Pope and Chaucer, for instance, may be said to have been equally possessed of genius. But taste, by contrast, is always wanting to pick and choose, to prefer and reject, even among the best, as if its criteria are not quite pure but have some determinate content. Genius, on the other hand, is loose and broad enough to accommodate everything of quality. Be this as it may (Gadamer picks up on it later), when genius becomes the standard of art, the moral significance Kant ascribes to nature and thus to the alien medium is minimized, since art becomes the unmediated subjective and introspective encounter of man with himself. Art is further subjectivized when Kant's privative definition of taste (that is, its freedom from the concept) develops into the more aggressive anti-rationalism of genius, considered as unconscious production. The art of genius, then, takes its origin not from consciousness but from life. It sharpens the *Lebensgefühl* (feeling of life) because, as post-Kantian aesthetics was to argue, the art of genius stems from *Erlebnis*.

As Gadamer sketches the history of the word *Erlebnis*, he shows that the kind of experience it signifies comes from being alive. Erlebnis means the experience of having lived through something (not necessarily painful). As dis-

---

16. Jauss argues that Gadamer is mistaken in contending that the work first speaks to us before we interrogate it. For Jauss, the work does not speak at all prior to the interpreter's question. See his "Literary History as a Challenge to Literary Theory," reprinted in *Toward an Aesthetic of Reception*, esp. pp. 30ff.

tinct from *Erfahrung*, a knowledge which can be gathered also from others, *das Erlebte* is always first-hand, always *das Selbsterlebte* (57 / 55). Erlebnis signifies not only the process of acquisition, moreover, but also the residual content of what is so acquired—that is, both the immediacy of the origin of an experience and its lasting significance. The meaning of Erlebnis becomes especially clear in such works as Dilthey's biographical essay on Goethe in *Das Erlebnis und die Dichtung*. Goethe himself had said that his poetry was like a great confession, and Dilthey reads the works from the life as if both were Erlebnisse. The works are the lasting significance (*Erlebnis*) produced from the immediacy of experience (*Erlebnis*) that is the fundamental material of poetry.

In Dilthey's later work on the theory of the human sciences, the concept of Erlebnis takes on special epistemological significance. Das Erlebnis is the fundamental datum upon which all humane knowledge is uniquely based: "The primary givens to which the interpretation of historical objects returns are not the data of experiment and measurement but rather units of meaning" (61 / 59). These are primary in being indecomposable into more elemental psychic units such as sensations which are in themselves meaningless. This irreducibility signifies for Dilthey's life philosophy that, at bottom, experience is the experience of meaning. So too in Husserl's phenomenology, unless something is intended and meant in an experience, nothing is experienced. Lived experience is necessarily meaningful experience.

Yet life here means primarily an ultimate datum, a given which, as the basis of knowledge, is of purely epistemological significance. Life has become an object of research. Though Dilthey's concept of life was developed in opposition to the mechanization of the mind characteristic of positivist psychology, yet, just as the age of mechanics felt alienated from the natural world, so also we find an alienation from the historical world when historical life becomes an object of research. Dilthey had written of William Scherer that "he was a modern man, and the world of our forefathers was no longer the home of his spirit and heart but instead his historical object" (4 / 8). The same is true of Dilthey himself. For him, Gadamer writes, "the spiritual creations of the past, art and history, no longer belong to the self-evident content of the present, but instead are objects relinquished [*aufgegebene*] to research, data [*Gegebenheiten*] from which a past can be made present again" (61 / 58). As the German makes clear, the given of research is what has been given up.

Gadamer emphasizes the hermeneutic rather than the epistemological significance of Erlebnis. What he hears in this word is not only the sense of temporal rupture, the break with the past that is both the cause and effect of Dilthey's epistemological alienation, but also a sense of connection with a temporal whole.

In English, as in German, not everything is "an experience." Rather, an experience is an event, or series of events, that stands out as a unified whole from the background of the everyday when nothing much is experienced. By reason of its rounded completeness, an experience disrupts the usual episodic course of things when one thing just follows another. Time as mere sequence is broken off—punctuated—by the advent of coherence and meaning. What an experience means is immediate, in the sense of not mediated by a concept; but for that very reason its meaning is not (in another sense) immediately apparent. Rather it constitutes itself in memory and reflection. It takes time to determine the meaning of an experience because this meaning is not exhausted by what was initially given, what it initially meant. An experience is something the meaning of which accompanies one through life, determining that life and being determined by it. It remains fused with the whole movement of life. The meaning of an experience, then, is emphatically not given; and thus experience cannot serve as the datum of research. Its meaning is not given but always to be given. It takes time, and this time—the lifetime necessary to understand the meaning of an experience— is precisely the episodic time that the experience interrupted. The wholeness of an experience ruptures the everyday seriality of time, and yet its unity of meaning is such that it needs that continuing flow to explicate it. An experience gives wholeness to, and acquires meaning from, that seriality. What Gadamer understands by Erlebnis, then, has the circular, hermeneutic structure of excursion and reunion: from the exceptional to the quotidian, from the extraordinary to the ordinary, from discontinuity to continuity, and back again.

In this respect, Gadamer affirms that art is Erlebniskunst—that is, produced from and received as experience. Art is not merely one thing among others to be experienced in one way among others. Rather, the experience of art, in its structure of exile and reunion, represents the essence of experience as such. "At one blow, the power of the artwork rips the person experiencing it (den Erlebenden) out of the context of his life (seines Lebens) and yet at the same time relates him back to the whole of his existence. . . . An aesthetic experience (Erlebnis) always contains the experience of an unending whole" (66 / 63).

But what does it mean to talk about an "unending whole"? Isn't a whole precisely what ends? And even if that phrase is not merely a self-contradiction, what does it mean to talk about an infinite whole as something that is experienced? For the Greeks, and later for Goethe and nineteenth-century aesthetics, one way— perhaps the only way—of experiencing the infinite is through the symbol. What Gadamer had before considered under the historically grounded rubric of Erlebnis and adventure, he now considers as symbol, a concept no less historically significant. In that the mind, in its free symbol-making capacity, was the foundation of the post-Kantian aesthetics of genius, Gadamer is still concerned with the subjectivization of aesthetics. The question he addresses in his discussion of the symbol is whether art is in fact adequately understood in Dilthey's way as experience—as confession and expression of the artist's experience or as object of experience for the beholder. He does not doubt that it is such, but he asks whether it is also something more. If so, aesthetic experience (even if it is an experience of the infinite) is itself limited; and insofar as the symbol is such an experience, it is no less true that there are limits set to the freedom of the mind's symbol-making activity. Given such limits, art cannot be adequately understood as subjective production.

That art is something more than the object or product of experience is already clear to us, for the aesthetics of genius is now largely defunct. Romantic art is no longer the universal standard—as witnessed, for instance, by the revival of interest in Donne and Pope, in whose poetry the criteria of value are not sincerity and intensity of experience but rhetorical ingenuity, wit, and the play of convention. Nor are we ready to depreciate non-symbolic art. It is no longer appropriate to say of Bunyan and Spenser that their poetry is not symbolic but "at best" allegorical.[17] The superiority which the nineteenth century assigned to the symbol and the corollary demotion of allegory are no longer self-evident, and the dubiousness of that dichotomy enables us to see that the freedom of symbol making is unlimited only if the symbol can be ultimately distinguished from allegory.

It is worth recalling that symbol and allegory—like imagination and fancy— were for centuries used as synonyms, and that in antiquity they were not antithetical but simply unrelated. "Allegory originally belongs to the sphere of discourse, of logos, and is thus a rhetorical or hermeneutic figure. Instead of what is really meant, something else, something readier to hand, is said, and yet in such a way as to let the other be understood. Symbols, on the other hand, are not limited to the sphere of logos because a symbol has its meaning not by relation to another meaning; rather its own perceptible being has meaning. It is as a thing shown that the symbol lets something else be recognized" (68 / 65). In both allegory and symbol, one thing stands for another. But allegory is something said, a symbol something shown. Allegory involves a relation of meaning to meaning, symbol a relation of being to meaning. One way of posing the question of the limits of the symbol, then, is to ask whether something that

17. For a modern rehabilitation of allegory, see Paul de Man, "Rhetoric of Temporality" and *Allegories of Reading*.

is shown must not also be said—that is, whether there is any direct route from being to meaning that does not detour through language.

The special advantage of the symbol is its directness and immediacy. It participates in, and indeed is, what it means. As is especially clear in the religious sphere, this immediacy of meaning presupposes a metaphysical unity of the finite symbol with the infinity it represents. The rationale for the indirectness of allegory, by contrast, is that no such coincidence between the visible and invisible, finite and infinite, can be assumed as already existing. But this correlation can nevertheless be instituted. "The rhetorical element in the concept of allegory . . . remains active in that allegory presupposes not the primal metaphysical relatedness [to the invisible] that the symbol claims but rather a coordination instituted by convention and inculcation which allows it to employ imagistic representations for the imageless" (70 / 67). In allegory the relation of the finite to the infinite is made possible only through convention, and that means not only through language but through rhetoric and dialogue. As a relation of meaning to meaning, allegory is a relation among participants in dialogue. Allegorical conventions are not created immediately, moreover; they evolve through time, in dialogue with one's forebears as well as one's contemporaries. Tradition is the condition of allegorical representation; and to preserve tradition is one function of allegorical interpretation, of Homer or of Scripture.[18] Whether as representation or as interpretation, allegory registers the need for tradition;[19] and when, in the Enlightenment, tradition came to be conceived as the locus of all that was questionable, the way was prepared for the Romantic demotion of allegory and promotion of symbol.

As symbol, art is the unity of idea and appearance. It is what it means, whereas allegory means something other than it is. Art as symbol is inexhaustibly interpretable, whereas allegory for the Romantics means something definite and determinable—and, worse, something conceptual and therefore inartistic. As symbol, art is private revelation, not communal wisdom. It is instantaneous whereas allegory is historical, and eternal whereas allegory is temporal. All these aspects of the dichotomy depend on the premise that in symbolic art, being is

18. Susan Sontag argues, just the opposite, that allegorical interpretation was a means of eliminating offensive elements from tradition (*Against Interpretation*, p. 10). Even if that is so, however, we might suggest that the need to revise tradition was a function of the need to preserve tradition.

19. Gadamer allies allegory to the sensus communis when he writes, "Such an artform [as allegory] is possible and is poetic only where there has been preserved a communality of the interpretive horizon to which allegory belongs" (*KS* 2:13).

wholly subsumed into meaning and substance into significance, so that there is nothing left over, no remainder still to be understood.

Yet it is doubtful that the symbol, even the religious symbol, achieves an equation or identity of the finite and infinite. A symbol always means more, even infinitely more, than what it physically is; and this "more" marks the tension of representation—that is, the disproportion between form and essence or image and meaning. Like an allegory, the symbol means more than it seems to mean. This excess of meaning allows Hegel in the *Aesthetics* to call "symbolic" precisely what we would call "allegorical." The important point here is that if the symbol is able to mean more than it is, it is able to do so only on the basis of the same institution of meaning that makes possible allegorical representation.

If during the nineteenth century the symbolic was opposed to the allegorical as art to non-art, the absoluteness of that dichotomy has now become dubious, and the distinction between symbol and allegory has become relative. Such a relativization does not leave intact the opposition of art and non-art. This dichotomy too is a product of the nineteenth-century elevation of the mind's symbol-making power to perfect freedom; but if that freedom is in fact limited by the continuing life of an allegorical tradition, then "the concept of aesthetic consciousness becomes itself doubtful—and with it the standpoint of art to which it belongs" (77 / 72). The question Gadamer poses, then, is this: Can we understand art solely as the object or product of aesthetic experience? Can we do justice to art as long as we consider it exclusively *as art*?

No doubt art is symbol, and thus Gadamer can learn from those who have explicated the symbol that art is a coincidence of form and meaning that cannot be reduced to a concept. So also art is experience, and, like experience, it has the structure of excursion and return. And, too, art is a function of subjectivity, of genius and aesthetic judgment, as Kant showed. But if it is more than this, if art is more than art, then that "more" is not to be explained by constructing a philosophy of art. The very fact that the *Critique of Judgment*, while providing a foundation for aesthetics, does not permit a philosophy of art turns out to be a positive merit, and one that Gadamer takes advantage of. Gadamer does not intend to propose a new aesthetics. Those we now have, he seems to imply, are already sufficient to understand art as art. It is art conceived only as art that is insufficient.

THE TRUTH ABOUT ART

(1.1.3.A.) There is indeed something compellingly self-evident about conceiving art as art. Yet this truistic phrase was never meant merely as an appeal to the obvious. Rather its embattled defensiveness indicates that art had somehow been lost in non-art, from which it had to be retrieved and purified. As long as art and nature were conceived as complementary, as in Kant and before him, there was no need for aesthetic protectionism; yet in the *Critiques* the seeds of division are no less evident than the impulse toward synthesis. Insofar as Kant limits the province of knowledge to pure natural science, art lies outside that realm and therefore offers no access to reality. But this means too that artistic reactions against mechanized nature are also reactions against mechanized reality. Non-art, from which art must be differentiated, comes to be equated with the real. "Where art rules, the laws of beauty are in force and the boundaries of reality are transcended. It is 'the ideal realm' which is to be defended against all encroachment and even against the patronizing moralism of state and society" (78 / 74). When Schiller urges the readers of the *Letters on Aesthetic Education* to comport themselves aesthetically, he proposes not only that they educate themselves *through* art but also *for* art—for inhabiting this ideal realm, not for the real community in which they live. But since reality, moral, social, and scientific, has now been ceded to the un-ideal realm of non-art, art itself undergoes a corresponding change. It comes to be seen as artifice, appearance, and unreality.

Insofar as aesthetics as such grounds the autonomy of art in this contrast to reality, it must be called the aesthetics of disappointment. The reign of art conceived as illusion, magic, or dream is temporary; for illusion becomes transparent, magic becomes a mere trick, and from dreams we finally awaken. When our visions all are ended, the un-ideal realm reasserts its dominion all the more oppressively. If art imitates a reality that art itself is not—that is, if the autonomy of art consists in its dichotomy from the real—then art is always headed for disappointment. But do we in fact experience such disappointments? Does art ever actually get falsified by some more genuine, more real reality? And if not, does art then really need protection and insulation, or does it make sense to define the inviting appearances of art by contrast to harsh reality?

Schiller thought so at any rate. The ideal of aesthetic Bildung he advocates involves only half the circular structure that we have discussed before: he urges abstraction, alienation, adventure, and escape—but not return. Like judgment and common sense, taste too abstracts from immediate desire and personal preference, and thus it too contains an element of alienation. Yet taste involves a communally determined criterion of content that makes even good taste local and sometimes provincial. But whereas taste always excludes something, Schiller's ideal of aesthetic *Bildung* aims to embrace everything of quality, from all cultures and all times. It achieves this universality first by abstracting the aesthetically trained consciousness from its community so that all definite criteria of judgment are nullified; and, second, having thus divorced itself from its world, it divorces the artwork from its world also. "By disregarding everything in which a work was rooted as its original life context, all religious or profane functions in which it possessed its meaning, the 'pure artwork' becomes manifest" (81 / 76).

This double abstraction Gadamer calls aesthetic differentiation. It differentiates the aesthetic consciousness of the beholder and of the producer from their respective worlds; and from each of these worlds it also abstracts the artwork per se, the purely aesthetic, art as art. But through the same process by which aesthetic differentiation attempts to make the artwork immediately available to the beholder as pure consciousness to pure consciousness, so also it renders the two worlds inaccessible to each other, for the purity and immediacy of the aesthetic are achieved by abstracting from the media which permit accessibility between worlds. On the one side, such media include the elements of content that require us to take a moral, religious, or philosophical stand with respect to the work. Whatever hits home, and so points to our particularity, is differentiated from the artwork proper. On the other hand, the media of accessibility also include interpretation and performance, and these too are distinguished from the artwork itself. Aesthetic differentiation, in sum, consists in the double differentiation of the work from its world and from ours.

The immediacy with which the purified artwork is present to purified aesthetic consciousness implies the co-presence of all times in the mind of the beholder. Whereas taste is temporally localized, so that a person has a taste for the art of his own time or some other, purely aesthetic appreciation brings all times into simultaneity. Nineteenth-century medievalism—in Scott's novels, for instance, or Bavarian King Ludwig's castles—was not a flair for archaism. Quite the contrary, simultaneity makes archaism impossible. Reconciling the art of diverse ages requires no effort of integration: art is eternal since the artworks of all times are co-present in abstracted aesthetic consciousness. The embodiment of this simultaneity—one might almost say the monument erected to aesthetic consciousness—is the universal museum or library. What begins as a private collection based on a specialized taste becomes expanded, comprehensive, and in a strict sense tasteless. Aesthetic differentiation makes amends for the relativity of taste and the difference of times by abstraction and in a strict sense by indifference.

As the artwork is abstracted from its world, so also is the artist abstracted from the community. In the nineteenth century, patronage becomes merely patronizing, and art patrons become customers, consumers. The artist takes on the character of a gypsy or some other kind of social pariah who is, paradoxically, nonetheless sought out as a social savior. "The experimental search for new symbols or a new all-encompassing 'word' may, to be sure, gather a public and create a community. But since every artist finds his own community, the formation of merely particular communities only testifies to the disintegration that is taking place" (84 / 79). In fact, the sense of the common never gets formed in purely aesthetic Bildung because the aesthetic proper—in its purity—is premised on alienation and abstraction without reunion.

(1.1.3.B.) "To do justice to art, aesthetics must go beyond itself and abandon the 'purity' of the aesthetic," Gadamer writes (88 / 83), for purification is a process of exclusion. Art in itself, art as art, is always art as not something else or as not anything at all. The process of purification whereby art becomes nothing (but art) finally refines art itself out of existence. Hamann's *Aesthetics*, Gadamer says, takes aesthetic differentiation to its limit: it abstracts even from art, for in Hamann's view, beyond pure aesthetic experience lies pure perception. It is at this point that Gadamer calls a halt and reasserts the non-transparency of *as*. *As* is not equation. It presupposes difference and negation, and it strikes a cleft in self-identity.[20] Art as art is, by reason of the difference implied in *as*, also non-art.

Gadamer draws on Aristotle, Gestalt psychology, and phenomenology to show that perception, even aesthetic perception, is not naturally or originally pure. It is "impure" in being always meaningful: we do not hear pure sounds but always a car in the street, a baby crying; we do not see pure colors and shapes but always a face, a knife, a wreath of smoke. Perception is instinct with meaning. Perception understands, and understanding involves the construal of something *as* something. "Every construal-as articulates what is there in that it looks away from, looks at, sees together as" (86 / 81). Gadamer's analysis of the *as*-structure of perceptual understanding suggests that the now familiar circle of excursion and return operates at the heart of perception.[21]

20. Cf. "The logos is of such a nature that whenever anything is meant by it, that thing is meant as identical to itself and, at the same time, as different from other things. Thus Selfsameness and Difference are always present in anything which is and is recognized as what it is. Only the interweaving of Selfsameness and Difference makes an assertion (logos) possible. In any assertion something which, in *being* what it is, is *identical* to itself, is linked to something *different* from itself. But it does not thereby lose its selfsameness" (*DD* 143; see also 168).

21. "Heidegger's great merit," Gadamer writes in "Philosophie und Literatur" (p. 19), "is to have shown that this abstraction from the full concretion of life as it is lived [i.e., pure perception] is a basic presupposition of the 'objectivity' of scientific research and that behind it there is an 'ontological' prejudice." See *Being and Time*, pp. 187–203.

The circle can be broken, however. It is possible to look at something in such a way that it is "just there," so that we see just what is there. It is possible to abstract conception or intellect from perception, but the point is that this process requires abstraction from a more primary cohesion. The resulting un-understanding perception—perception of what Heidegger calls the present-at-hand—indicates, by the effort of abstraction it requires, that it is derived and secondary; and even if it were not, that is not the way we look at art. We do not rush toward a concept, it is true. We do not say, "Oh, that's a portrait of the artist's mother," and then pass on. We do not hurry past but rather linger; and yet we do say, "That's Whistler's mother," without such conceptualization being a reason for having done with the painting on the one hand, or reducing it to pure form and color on the other. Even with respect to aesthetic perception, then, "mere seeing and mere hearing are dogmatic abstractions. Perception always includes meaning" (87 / 82). Non-representational, non-conceptual, for-malist, abstract art is therefore simply that: abstract.[22] It is the product of ab-straction, not the result of or opportunity for a more pure, more primordial perception. Perception is rather primordially impure in that it is imbued with meaning from the outset.[23] It already understands, and this implies that perception construes or interprets something *as* something (else). Art, perceived purely *as* art, is already more than art. Even pure art means.

Interpretation, therefore, is not something alien imposed on an artwork. Art is itself already interpretation,[24] and that fact suggests one of the ways of tran-scending aesthetic purism. When Kant himself points beyond the pure judgment of taste, we recall, he directs us to the concept of genius. For Kant, genius differentiates the artist from the craftsman in that the products of the artist are complete in themselves, not by reference to a purpose; thus they are inexhaustibly interpretable because their interpretation does not stop when they have fulfilled some purpose. But whereas the use of the concept of genius declined as a credible way of explaining the distinctive character of the artist and the completeness of

22. In *Truth and Method*, Gadamer's emphasis falls naturally, though perhaps reductively, on representational art. He has however attempted to redress the balance in a number of essays in *Kleine Schriften* 2: "Kunst und Nachahmung," "Begriffene Malerei?", "Bild und Gebäude," and "Vom Verstummen des Bildes."

23. That there is nothing purer than or prior to meaning is a crucial premise in Gadamer's argument because, as Apel writes, "hermeneutic analysis commences from the fact that intelligible human behavioural reactions, as linguistically-related intentional forms, themselves possess the quality of understanding" (*Transformation of Philosophy*, p. 55).

24. In " 'London' and the Fundamental Problem of Hermeneutics," I have developed in greater detail the implications of the fact that both art and criticism are interpretive activities.

the artwork, the inexhaustibility of interpretation remained as a problem to be explained—by Gadamer as well as his predecessors.

Valéry suggests that art is endlessly interpretable because, if it serves no purpose by means of which its completion can be determined, is itself essentially incomplete. It is as if Valéry conceives all works of literature as fragments, which require the reader to finish them. If the reader can in fact complete a poem, however, that implies he is in possession of precisely the power, the authority, and indeed the genius that the author lacked. But it seems clear that if we want to deny genius to the author, it will not do to transfer it to the reader. Yet even if we hold the reader down to the proportions of an ordinary person, it would remain the case that the work conceived as a fragment offers no standard of appropriate reaction. "One way of understanding a form is no less legitimate than the other. There is no measure of appropriateness. . . . Rather every encounter with the work has the rank and rights of a new production.—That appears to me," Gadamer concludes, "an untenable hermeneutic nihilism" (90 / 85).[25]

Such flatly negative pronouncements are rare in *Truth and Method*, and it seems that Gadamer is reminding himself as well as his readers of something not to forget. First, it is a fact to be explained that a work of art is anspruchsvoll. It makes demands on us, and one of these demands is to get it right. It is characteristic of artworks themselves that they invite us to interpret them appropriately. What they have to say is too important not to do so. Second and more fundamentally, the fact that interpretation is possible must be explained before addressing the problem of the multiplicity of interpretations. If every interpretation must count as a new production, that can be true only because no *interpretation* occurred or could occur. There is merely one work, then another unrelated to the former. This implied impossibility of interpretation Gadamer calls hermeneutic nihilism. His second point is related to the first in that, if interpretation is to be possible, it must be an interpretation of the work, appropriate to the work, and the work therefore cannot be fragmentary—that is, lacking in integrity and identity. Appropriate interpretation and appropriateness of the work to itself are correlative concepts.

Gadamer also discerns the aporia of hermeneutic nihilism—the same inability to explain the possibility of interpretation—in Lukács' argument that the artwork is an empty form, a mere locus of a multiplicity of possible aesthetic experiences. Its emptiness and lack of self-identity imply the discontinuity of

25. This discussion of nihilism in the context of aesthetic interpretation anticipates similar discussions in the second part of *Truth and Method* concerning historicism. Cf. "The epistemological climax [of historicism] is relativism, its consequence nihilism" (*KS* 1:40).

those experiences, since they now have in common only a relation to an empty form. Lukács does justice to the sense that experiencing an artwork is entering a self-contained world, that experiencing it is adventuresome and exceptional in that it stands out from the everyday. Yet by exclusively stressing the exceptional nature of aesthetic experience, he disintegrates aesthetic time into a series of discrete points unrelated to each other. It seems, then, that whether we conceive the artwork as essentially incomplete (Valéry), or as essentially empty and the experience of it as self-contained (Lukács), we reach the same result as we would if we conceived it as full, complete, and self-identical: namely, discontinuity and distintegration. Either there is one monadic experience after another, or one monadic artwork after another—with nothing inbetween.

Gadamer invokes Kierkegaard's critique of aesthetics from the viewpoint of ethics to show that this kind of disintegral, pointillist existence is not only intellectually untenable but humanly unendurable. Once we have learned to comport ourselves aesthetically, as Schiller urged, we have not finished but only just begun. "The phenomenon of art sets a task for existence: the task, namely, in view of the demanding and insistent present of the particular aesthetic impression, still to achieve the continuity of self-understanding that alone can make human existence bearable" (91 / 86). For Gadamer, as for Kierkegaard, the absurdity of aesthetic existence, lived moment to moment, points up the need to transcend the aesthetic dimension, even while preserving it. To do so is the function of interpretation, and thus interpretation is the task that the phenomenon of art sets for existence. Hermeneutics is what makes continuity out of discontinuity.

On the one hand, Gadamer affirms that discontinuity (of artwork from artwork, and of art from the everyday) is real. Thus the pantheon of art is not a totality timelessly present to pure aesthetic consciousness. Discontinuity disrupts simultaneity. And yet art is more than pure art. More than symbol, art is rhetoric and allegory, the work of mind gathering and assembling itself from and in history. Art is historical interpretation; and it is to be understood, if at all, only historically. Because it is not immediately intelligible or timelessly present to itself, it is not so to us either; art requires interpretation. But the opacity of art implies a corresponding opacity in aesthetic consciousness. The consciousness of the interpreter is no more pure, no more transparent to itself, than is the artwork. We too are historical and in need of interpretation. We too need to understand ourselves. Just as art is more than art, so also is the experience of art more than pure aesthetic experience: it is a mode of self-understanding. "But all self-understanding takes place through something other that is understood, and includes the unity and sameness of this other" (92 / 86). When we interpret art, we interpret ourselves. Correlatively, in order to interpret ourselves, we need to interpret art, for not being present to ourselves, we need an other through which to understand ourselves; and art, as exceptional and extraordinary, provides the alterity necessary for self-understanding. Such understanding can therefore itself be charged with preserving the integrity and otherness of the artwork because it needs that otherness. Yet if we are to understand the work, the world of the artwork cannot remain alien to our world, a foreign universe in which we are merely exiles. "Rather we learn to understand ourselves in it, and that means we sublate the discontinuity and pointillism of experience in the continuity of our own existence" (92 / 86).

Gadamer does not hesitate to employ the Hegelian notion of sublation (*Aufhebung*) to explain the hermeneutic activity that makes continuity out of discontinuity. Yet hermeneutics remains a response to irremediable indigence, a perpetual need for which there is no final Hegelian fulfillment. Hermeneutics is an eternal task (in neo-Kantian terms), a historical task (in Gadamer's), that foresees no end. Gadamer does not underestimate the double bind that the hermeneutic circle involves—that is, the fundamental contradiction which results when Cartesian self-identity, self-presence, and self-certainty are abandoned as the basis and criterion of interpretation. In this un-Cartesian world without reflection, without a mirror in which I can see myself immediately with my own eyes, the dark glass of art is a source of knowledge and of truth—the truth of self-knowledge. That art is a source of truth is the motive for understanding it, and understanding it correctly. Yet to understand it correctly I must already have understood myself, and can do so only through art.

This is a vicious circle, wheel-spinning, or mere self-contradiction, however, only if we assume precisely the Cartesian self-identity the denial of which necessitates moving in the circle in the first place. If it is not always the same self that understands because the self is a product as well as a condition of understanding, then the hermeneutic circle becomes a spiral, though no less without end. The infinite fecundity of the work as it is interpreted again and again is motivated by human finitude and indigence, the hollowness at the center, and the cleft in self-presence that is marked by the hermeneutic *as*. Yet for the same reason that the historical multiplicity of interpretations—and history itself—is a figure of human impossibility, the impossibility of wholeness and fullness, of being something finally and definitively, so also is it a figure of what we can be and *that* we can be—that is, of human possibility.

It is as if Gadamer reads Kant through Hegel, Hegel through Kant, and both through Heidegger. With Hegel, Gadamer affirms that art, as both created and received, is inseparable from history. Though Kant had denied any truth claim to art, Hegel's aesthetics is a "history of worldviews, that is, a history of truth" (93 / 87). As truth, art for Hegel has exceeded the sphere of the subjective, and this represents an advance over Kantian subjectivism that is not to be denied. Yet Hegel's very acknowledgment of the truth claim of art is mitigated by the fact that the inclusive knowledge of philosophy, the claim of the concept, surpasses the claim of art. And this superiority of the concept Kant did well to deny. Art is not a form of pre-philosophical thought. As far as we know, the history of art is not pre-anything; it points to no destination, even its own. The historical multiplicity of world views it offers represents no progress toward "true" art, still less toward "true" philosophy. When we interpret art in all its variety, we do not try to get above or beyond or behind that multiplicity. The very fact that we cannot transcend art into some more true realm is one mark of its truth. We do not expect the truth to be found somewhere else but precisely there, in the works themselves and in their unsurpassable plurality.

Recognizing the truth claim of art already represents a step in the direction of de-subjectivizing the experience of art; but as long as we think of truth as an act, achievement, or possession of consciousness or understanding, it is necessary to transcend the subjectivism which that implies. To this end Gadamer adopts Heidegger's philosophical question, "What is the being of self-understanding? With this question [philosophical thought] fundamentally transcends the horizon of self-understanding" (95 / 89). Gadamer phrases this question in terms of his own project: "We ask what the experience [*Erfahrung*] of art . . . is in truth and what its truth is. . . . We see in the experience of art a genuine experience of the work, which does not leave him who has it unaltered, and we ask about the kind of being of what is experienced in this way" (95 / 89). The genuineness of the experience of art is indicated by the fact that it alters the one who experiences it; it alters the understanding subject. But what must art be that it alters our self-understanding, and what is the being of the interpreter if it alters in the process of understanding art? What kind of truth is not a possession of an experiencing subject because it changes that subject? By addressing these questions Gadamer hopes to understand the kind of truth to be found in art. The truth of art does not belong to consciousness; rather consciousness belongs to the truth of art. That, precisely that, if it can be made intelligible, is the truth of art: the truth about art is that it is true, and the truth of art is a truth about truth, namely that truth is not a possession of consciousness.

This negative insight, positively expressed, Gadamer places in italics: "*Alle Begegnung mit der Sprache der Kunst [ist] Begegnung mit einem unabgeschlossenen Geschehen und selbst ein Teil dieses Geschehen*" (94 / 88). The sentence beggars translation. Experiencing and interpreting art Gadamer calls *Begegnung*:

coming up against something, confronting it, something happening to us, or our happening onto something. What we confront in art is *Sprache*: language, discourse, speaking. And to do so is to come up against *Geschehen*: event, happening, an occurrence of *Geschichte* (history) and of *Geschick* (fate), what happens to us. The event that happens to us in an encounter with the language of art is *unabgeschlossen*: unlocked, unclosed, open, disclosed, unconcluded, inconclusive, inclusive (the connotations are negative, double negative, and positive). What the *unabgeschlossene Geschehen* is open to and includes is the event that is the language of art. The encounter belongs to the event of language and is caught up in it—for which reason the event is unconcluded. It does not stop happening.

"It is this," Gadamer writes, "which must be validated in the face of aesthetic consciousness and its neutralization of the truth question" (94 / 88). Clearly in the above, then, he means to have said something about truth. The experience of art is an experience of truth, but the experience of truth is not something we *have*; truth is not what we *acquire* or come to *possess* in a process of methodological certification. The truth of art is not an object that belongs to the subject but rather something the subject belongs to and does not control. This something is an event, an event of truth that we keep getting caught up in, in such a way that we belong to it; and precisely because our experience of art belongs to and is part of art, the event of truth in the language of art does not cease. Art keeps on meaning. If aesthetic differentiation divorces the work from the interpretation and both from the truth, what Gadamer anticipates here and explicates in the next section is a way of reuniting them, a way of thinking about art, truth, and interpretation that will explain, first, the fact of multiple interpretations; second, that multiple interpretations can all be true to the work; and third, that the work can be multiply interpreted, multiply true, without disintegrating into fragments or degenerating into an empty form. It is a formidable task.

THE PLAYER IN TRUTH IS BEING PLAYED

(1.2.1.A) It is not art as art that Gadamer takes as his clue to the mode of being of art; for art as art entails, as we have seen, not a truism but an exclusion of and differentiation from non-art. Common to the many forms that aesthetic differentiation assumes is the fission of the art object from the interpreting subject and his world. This opposition, Gadamer believes, explains nothing that needs explanation. Most of all it fails to account for the truth of art and, correlatively, for the *inter* of interpretation—that is, the possibility of what we have been calling reunion. The subject / object dichotomy suggests that truth is *in* or belongs *to* subjectivity. Aesthetic understanding, in this conception, is a science of art that would produce the truth *about* art but could not acknowledge the truth *of* art because then the truth would belong to the object as well, and the subject / object dichotomy would collapse. Thus, in order to admit the truth of art, it is necessary to insure just this collapse—or, more positively, to provide for the reunion of subject and object that is interpretation. Gadamer's conception of art as play serves these destructive and constructive functions.

Play is the way of being of the work of art, Gadamer affirms. But before we conclude that he is about to construct another aesthetics (indeed, yet another aesthetics of play), we should recall first that, even if he is, it is an aesthetics preparatory to a discussion of concerns germane to the human sciences at large and that it cannot therefore be an autonomous aesthetics. Second, and related to the first point, is that, as Gadamer has already intimated, to describe the way of being of art is at the same time to describe the way of being of self-understanding, historical experience, representation, language, and *truth*, all of which are developed with increasing focus in the chapters that follow and none of which are the concerns of an aesthetics proper.

I underscore the last item in the series, truth, because while it is radical enough, given the history of aesthetics or epistemology, to open an explication of truth with an explication of art, it is yet more radical, even scandalous, to embark on an explication of truth by beginning with an explication of play. More remarkable still is that Gadamer does so without a hint of scandal, posturing, or melodrama. We have long been familiar with the relevance of play to aesthetics, especially in Kant and Schiller. But there, play is a state of mind, a free play of faculties, and thus a property of subjectivity. In the nineteenth century, moreover, play is a virtue designed to serve as a substitute for truth, a compensation allotted to what lacks the virtue of truth, namely art. So too, outside aesthetics, in Nietzsche, Wittgenstein, and (problematically) Derrida,[26] it is arguable that play and game are employed to avoid raising the question of truth or else explicitly to subvert the claim of truth. Thus from both standpoints, within

26. Derrida writes, "There are thus two interpretations of interpretation, of structure, of sign, of play. The one seeks to decipher, dreams of deciphering a truth or an origin which escapes play. . . . The other, which is no longer turned toward the origin, affirms play and tries to pass beyond man and humanism. . . . For my part, although these two interpretations must acknowledge and accentuate their difference and define their irreducibility, I do not believe that today there is any question of *choosing*" (*Writing and Difference*, pp. 292–93). Excepting Derrida's accentuation of the difference between play and truth, Gadamer would find much to agree with here. For more on Gadamer and Derrida, see Hoy, *Critical Circle*, pp. 77–100, and James S. Hans, "Hermeneutics, Play, Deconstruction."

and without aesthetics, Gadamer's triunion of art, play, and truth can be considered either reactionary or post-modern.

While the relevance to truth becomes evident later on, Gadamer is first concerned to explicate the work of art as play. Play seems a particularly unwise choice of a starting point if one of Gadamer's aims is to transcend subjectivist aesthetics, because it seems apparent that playing is a subjective behavior, and playfulness a subjective attitude. Above all, we would say, people play. And thus it comes as some surprise when Gadamer writes, "When we speak of play in the context of the experience of art, play does not mean the behavior or even the disposition of the creators or the enjoyers of art, and not at all the freedom of a subjectivity that dabbles in play, but rather the way of being of the artwork itself" (97 / 91). The artwork is play. But even so, isn't it we who play, we who experience art?

An experience—a fortiori, an experience of art—changes the one who experiences it. If so, how? Gadamer asks, and who then is the subject of the experience? To answer these questions, he asks a related one: How is it possible to understand the work of art otherwise than as an object that stands over against a subject existing in itself? How can we conceive the way an experiencing subject changes when it no longer exists in itself by opposition to an object? What happens to us in the experience of art, Gadamer suggests, is very much like what happens to us in play: we lose ourselves. We lose, first of all, our relation to the world of earnest, of serious purpose; but we do so by acquiring a different, even deadly, seriousness. For a game to be genuine it must be taken seriously. "The mode of being of the game does not permit the player to behave toward the game as to an object" (97 / 92). One cannot toy with or play at a game if it is to be a real game. One cannot behave *as if* it were serious; it must be so. There is nothing at all fictive about the tension of a chess game or the humiliation of being mated. A boxer in the Olympic Games does not act *as if* he wanted to knock out his opponent; he actually tries to do so. Are these young men naturally brutal? If not, what comes over them that they can act in this way? What comes over everyone who plays?

What takes over is the game, Gadamer contends. What we see here is the "primacy of the play over the consciousness of the players." "The subject of the game is not the player; rather the players are merely the way the play comes into presentation" (98 / 92) In a game the subject is changed: as a player, I no longer "act naturally," as myself. In a sense it is someone else who imposes the pain, suffers the humiliation of defeat, or crows in disproportionate exultation at victory. This change results from the fact that since the subject is not allowed to act toward the game as an object in itself, the subject does not remain itself either. The player loses self-control and cedes control to the game. Baseball coaches are fond of saying, "Don't let the ball play you!" But it is not possible, ultimately, to avoid being played, and Gadamer suggests that we don't really want to avoid it. The idea of the game is that the subject should take leave of itself and that the game should take over. Thus Gadamer writes that "all playing is a being played." "The charm of play, the fascination it exercises, consists precisely in the fact that the game becomes master over the players. . . . The one who tries is in truth the one who is tried. The real subject of the game is not the player . . . but the game itself" (101–102/95–96).

In this way too "the 'subject' of the experience of art, what remains and persists, is not the subjectivity of those who experience it, but rather the artwork itself" (98 / 92). Gadamer places *subject* in quotation marks here because, of course, neither the artwork nor the game is a subject. The important point is that a painting or poem or fugue does not exist in the consciousness of a subject. Its way of being is not as a subject. But neither is the artwork an object, and it is important to stress this fact because Gadamer's phrase "the artwork itself" summons up Kantian or positivist or other connotations of a *Ding an sich*, an artwork-as-opposed-to-the-experience-of-it, which is precisely what Gadamer is trying to avoid. To say that the game takes over, or plays, the player is not to imply that an object takes over where the subject leaves off. Quite the contrary, the subject loses itself precisely when it does not stand over against an object in itself, when it no longer treats the game as an object but as something it joins, gets caught up in, and finally belongs to. By game, then, Gadamer does not mean an object. A Monopoly game is not what is in the box, nor is soccer to be found in a book of rules. So too a poem is not what is in a poetry book. The game properly exists only when it is played—that is, when object and subject coalesce so that object is no longer object and subject no longer subject. As we cannot know the dancers from the dance, as Gadamer might say with Yeats, so also dance comes to be only through the dancers. Dance is the dancing of it, the game itself is the playing of it, and the artwork itself exists only in its working, only in its being experienced. The experience of art is not experience by a subject, for the subject is not itself. It is altered in experience. And it is not experience of an object, because the subject is altered, has an experience, only if it does not objectify the artwork. Play is the mode of being of the work itself. That means: the artwork is first itself when it is no longer an object for a subject, but rather when the two are reunited. The work of art is the playing of it. This ambiguous phrase has the proper circularity. The work is what is played by the players it plays.

When Gadamer stresses that the game is something that happens to us, when our participation appears as subjection as the game becomes master, and when play does not at all mean the freedom of subjectivity, it may well seem that instead of free play Gadamer is explicating a kind of determinism. Within the wider context of *Truth and Method*, we cannot even say that we are free *not* to play or be played. But even in the narrower context of games, it is important that no game whatever lets one do just what one wants. There is always some obstacle that prevents immediate success, some opponent, some rule, some boundary of time or space, or just unpredictability—the bounce of the ball, the roll of the dice—that overrules personal preference and limits freedom. Even with respect to a game that one freely chooses, in that no play is perfectly free play, all playing is being played. When an artwork plays (as we would say that a record or film is playing), this is not free play: to play is to sacrifice freedom and accept limits. These limits, however, are not something we would want to surpass even if we could—as if hockey would be a better game if we could just get rid of the goalie, or would be better still if there were no opponents at all. Football would hardly be improved if we dropped the offside rule that causes so much trouble, nor would jacks be more fun if we could just pick them up without the bother of bouncing the ball. Being limited, being played, is a condition of playing at all. If I am going to play chess, I am not permitted to move the king first, the rook diagonally, or a pawn backward. And if I am going to play *Rhapsody in Blue* or *Blue Boy*, I am no less restricted.

But no more so either. To experience a work of art, to play it, is not to indulge in free play because to experience the work is also to be played by it and to be governed by the limits it imposes. Yet, though no game ever lets one do just what one wants, it is also true that no game (if it is to be a game) ever determines exactly how it will be played. In this sense there must in fact be free play. Though there can be play only within limits and restrictions, it is also true that the limits imposed are themselves restricted by the need for play. Too little play in a gearbox is just as bad as too much. But though it is possible to imagine a gearbox seized up, a game that permitted no play is simply no longer a game.

Essential to play is the freedom of movement to and fro, back and forth, up and down the field—the repeated circular movement of excursion and return that is under control of neither the individual players nor referees but belongs to the playing of the game. Every move is prescribed in advance—by the task to be performed, by the game plan, by the moves of the opponent, and by the rules. Yet there is such freedom that no game is ever played twice identically, and for all this variety it is still the one game. To every game there belongs an element of unpredictability that one no more wishes to get rid of than one does its boundaries and restrictions. This freedom for variety of interpretation belongs to the artwork as well. That an artwork can be understood means that it can be understood in a number of ways without these understandings being either misunderstandings or understandings of another work. An artwork, even conceived as a rule book, cannot determine a single correct understanding of it; and furthermore an artwork is not a rule book but rather the playing of it, and the playing necessarily includes the freedom for infinite variety even within finite limits. This is to say that the fact of multiple understandings does not of itself imply misunderstanding, although this too is a real possibility. When I play golf, sometimes my score is high, sometimes low; sometimes I drive straight onto the fairway, sometimes into the rough; sometimes I slice, sometimes I hook. In all this variety I am still playing golf. But when I bat the golf ball, even with a club, I have ceased.

When we play, we choose not only not to work but choose to play some particular game: marbles, or table tennis, or basketball. Each has a specific spirit and a field of play that is set aside and closed off from exit and intrusion. When we assume this spirit and take the field of play—that is, when we play something, we take on a task that transforms our own aims into the ends of the game. Our aim may be scoring points or even winning, but these too serve the game. One must want to win precisely for the ends of the game—that is, in order to play the game well. The task of the game is finally just to play the game, to play it for no end other than playing it, and thus to play it without end. The purpose of the game is merely to be played.

But to play something is also to represent it. The autotelic character of games Gadamer calls self-presentation. This means that the game presents itself, plays itself; but it also means that we present ourselves in it. When we play something, the game assigns us a task and a role to play in performing it. In tag, someone must be "it"; in football, someone must play quarterback, someone offense, and someone defense. Whenever we play something there is already self-representation as this or that; and when children dress up to play house, such role playing merely makes evident the self-representation-*as* that is involved in all games.

Where the task of the game is representation itself, there is also the potential for representation to someone else who is not himself playing. When children play house, their world is closed: an adult who wants to watch must peek, must absent himself, for his presence would break the spell of the game or turn it into a show. Professional sports, too, maintain this sense of closure even though the spectators are obviously present. A baseball player who plays specifically to the stands we call a "hotdog." He discredits the game by turning it into a show. Neither are religious rituals or plays in a theatre shows, although they too are representations for a congregation or an audience. They are at once closed off from those in attendance and yet exist completely for them as well. "A play too remains play, that is, it has the structure of play in being a world closed in on itself. But the cultic or profane play, however completely the world it presents is closed in on itself, is as if open on the side of the spectator. In him it first comes to achieve its full significance. The players play their roles as in any game, and so the game comes to be presented, but the play itself is the whole consisting of players and spectators. Indeed, it is most geniunely experienced by and presented as it is 'meant' not for the player but for the spectator. . . . A total change happens to play as play when it becomes a play. It puts the spectator in place of the player" (104–105 / 98–99).

Play, as we have seen, is representation-of; *a* play is also representation-for. As Gadamer at this point begins his discussion of drama, it is important to remember that just as he offers play as a symbol or figure of art in general, so also he discusses plays not for the purpose of providing a theory of drama per se but to clarify the general character of art. The artwork is not only play but also *a* play, not only representational but also a representation-for—that is, for a listener, viewer, or understander who is neither the playwright nor the player. The mode of being of the artwork includes this *for* essentially. It is not an empty form nor a mere fragment because a closed, self-contained world is presented in a play, full and whole. Yet it is also true that a wall has been let down on the stage: the closed world of the stage is also open, is for an audience, even though the open space between auditorium and stage is impregnable. The play is gone and the moment that openness is transgressed. The closure of the play is curiously the condition of the play's possibility and accessibility, its being a play for us. In a game, a boundary is set, a limit fixed, and freedom restricted; but so also if there is to be play, there must be freedom of movement to and fro without constriction. In *a* play, openness to an audience, representation-for, is the analogue of the freedom of play, the inability and unwillingness to rule out and close off possibilities.

This becomes clearer if we recognize that the correlate of representation-for is meaning. We do not ask what a game or a move in it means. Rather, only *a* play, only what is representation for us, has the possibility of meaning. The "for us" that is necessary if there is to be meaning at all, Gadamer calls openness; and this openness of meaning—that it is always for us—is precisely what precludes keeping "us" out of the meaning. We too belong to the meaning. Thus Gadamer writes, "The play is the whole consisting of players and spectators" (104 / 98). The game, the artwork, we have seen, is the playing of it; and the playing of a play—that is, the play itself—includes the audience. It cannot close out the audience if it is to be a play. If representation-for is necessarily open to an audience and open to interpretation, it is also open to contingency, circumstance, and to the concrete occasion when it is presented. No one can predict how a game will be played; no one can predict what a play will mean.

(1.2.1.B) When play becomes a play, Gadamer suggests, a complete change, a metamorphosis, occurs that puts the spectator in the place of the player. We need to be careful here not to conceive of a play as something to be found in the consciousness of the spectator, any more than it is to be found in that of the actor. That a play must be performed in order to be a play implies that what it means is not a possession of the playwright; likewise, that a performance must be open to an audience implies that its meaning is not a possession of the players. But it does not therefore belong to the audience. Rather the spectators, as Gadamer says, belong to the full meaning of the play. They belong to it, not it to them. The detachability of the play from any particular subject (whether playwright, player, or spectator) Gadamer calls the metamorphosis into Gebilde—that is, structure, form. This word echoes and recalls Gadamer's initial discussion of Bildung. When a person undergoes Bildung, he is gebildet; he learns to detach himself from his immediate desires and purposes. And this process is for Gadamer a figure of the change that occurs when play becomes a play—that is, when it becomes Gebilde.

The Super Bowl—say, the classic meeting of the Jets and Colts—is a game. However like a ritual or a play, it is unlike them in that it happens only once. You must be there to appreciate it; it must be broadcast live. Even on videotape it loses its savor, and still less can we have Warren Beatty play Joe Namath or Charleton Heston play Y. A. Tittle. The game cannot be detached from its *initial* occasion—there are no others—or from the behavior of the particular players. No one else can play them because the game cannot be played again at all; but if it is, then there occurs a total metamorphosis of the game. It becomes *a* play, a Gebilde.[27] This means that, as a play, it is essentially open. Anyone can play it, and it can be played at any time. It becomes repeatable. The form (*Gebilde*) of a play is not a structure to be found somewhere inside it like the girders inside a building. Form is no more or less than the repeatability[28] of a play: it is what

---

27. Gadamer elsewhere explains, "This word '*Gebilde*' suggests that the appearance [of the work] has left the process of its origination behind it. . . . The *Gebilde* does not so much point back to the process of its formation as require to be perceived as a pure appearance in itself" (*KS* 4:260). Whereas Derrida more conservatively allies truth with an origin (see n. 26 above), Gadamer allies truth with what is not limited to or validated by its origin: Gebilde, appearance, disclosure, *aletheia*.

28. Compare Derrida on iterability in "Signature Event Context," p. 180.

allows the players and spectators to keep changing while the play is still the same play. The play is not in them; they are in the play, and it merely comes to be presented, performed, and embodied in them.

No one doubts that when a football game, Olympic Game, or card game is turned into a play, a work of art, the game is transformed utterly. In becoming repeatable and permanent, it is simply not a game anymore. "So the transformation into form means that what was previously is no more. But it also means that what presents itself in the play of art is the lastingly true" (106 / 100). There was once, for example, a real card game played in 1711 between a certain Miss Arabella Fermor and her would-be suitors that ended ignominiously in one of Miss Fermor's curls being cut off. When that game is transformed into Pope's *Rape of the Lock*, with all its machinery of sylphs and gnomes, with its Homeric grandeur and Virgilian pathos, it is, to be sure, no longer the real game. It is placed within a whole history of games—from the *Iliad* to the *Aeneid* to *Paradise Lost*—games that anyone can play, and does. The game has become repeatable, permanent; but the curious thing is that the real game played in 1711 does not become less real for being no game in the poem. It becomes more so. The truth of the game played in that drawing room is to be found in the poem, not in the consciousness of the players, now centuries dead, for the poem reveals that they were counters in a game being played with them. And that game is true because it does not cease. Ever new players are played. The *Rape* is performed repeatedly in ever new situations, and that repetition is the poem's truth. "The Rape of the Lock" is the name of a game that is played with us when we play it, and who can fail to do so?

No one can say that such games are fiction. There is not even comparison, let alone contrast, with any reality. Even *art* is too patronizing a word to describe what such games are. When play becomes no play but rather a play, what is transformed into form is the very truth. "It is not enchantment in the sense of a bewitchment that waits for a word to break the spell and transform everything back, but quite the opposite it is itself the spell-breaking transformation back into true being. From its re-presentation in a play emerges what is" (107 / 101). As they are replayed in the artwork, the days of our lives are won back from alienation and unintelligibility into meaning and being what they truly are. We say of the work, "Yes, that's the way it really is."

This response Gadamer calls not pleasure but the joy of recognition, which may be quite the opposite of pleasurable. Recognition marks the cognitive import of the work.[29] When we say yes in this way, it means that we recognize something as familiar. We are seeing something again that is a repetition of what we have always known. But in the surprised double take of recognition we do not merely cognize something again. It is defamiliarized, because to recognize is to know what we have always known as if we had never really known it before. To re-know in this way is to know for the first time what something truly is, to know it in its essence. Through knowing it *as* something, it is refamiliarized. Imitation, representation in the artwork, is original presentation, for there what is imitated first comes into its own. It becomes more truly what it is. It is "raised as it were through representation to its valid truth. With respect to recognition of the true, the being of the representation is more than the being of the material represented, the Homeric Achilles more than his original" (109 / 103). More what? we might ask. Gadamer continues, "The fundamental imitative relationship consists not only in the fact that what is placed there is there, but rather also that it has come into the there more like itself" (Das mimische Urverhaltnis . . . enthält nicht nur, dass das Dargestellte da ist, sondern auch, dass es eigentlicher ins Da gekommen ist). Less literally, the fact that an imitation imitates something means not only that what is imitated exists in the artwork too, but that it exists there more genuinely than before. It is more fully itself and is more accessible for being imitated. When something is imitated, when it is represented and recognized *as* something (else), it becomes something more than what it was, and that "more" is that it becomes itself more fully. This, we recall, is the result of Bildung; and Gadamer suggests that the same happens when anything is transformed into a Gebilde—that is, when it becomes repeatable by being repeated (other-wise) in an artwork. It is not only or even primarily human beings that are gebildet; any being can come more fully into its own through the process Gadamer calls *Darstellung*: being placed there, presented, represented, and performed. What he is describing is not just how people are educated but how worlds are created.

We see more clearly now why Gadamer begins his ontology with an ontology of the work of art as play and, specifically, plays. Quite simply, a play is not there—it does not exist, it is not fully itself—until it is performed. Performance is not something ancillary, accidental, or superfluous that can be distinguished from the play proper. The play proper exists first and only when it is played.

29. Grondin rightly calls attention to the influence of Plato on Gadamer here: "Imitation is understood in its cognitive import as remembrance. The platonic *anamnesis* is joined with *mimesis*" (*Hermeneutische Wahrheit*, p. 117).

Performance brings the play into existence, and the playing of the play is the play itself. An artwork is: to be represented. Representation is its mode of being. Thus the work cannot be differentiated from the representations of it since it exists only *there*, only in the flesh. It comes to be in representation and in all the contingency and particularity of the occasions of its appearance.[30]

Isn't this relativism with a vengeance? Not merely the meaning but the very existence of the work is relative to interpretation? Initially, the answer is yes. It is absolute relativism, and in that absoluteness lies its interest. Yet in being absolute this relativism turns out to be not what we usually call relativism at all. If by relativism we mean that the artwork exists in the mind of the author, actor, or spectator, that it consists therefore in a discontinuous series of experiences, or that it is an empty schema waiting to be filled with meaning by an experiencing subject, then Gadamer is no relativist.[31] Moreover, if we mean by relativism that the work is one thing and the interpretation of it another, and that the meaning of the work is relative to the interpretation, then it is also clear that Gadamer is no relativist, for these are precisely the theses he is intent on subverting.

Absolute relativism, as I employ this phrase,[32] means, first, that the work exists nowhere but in its representations and, second, that these representations are not to be found in any individual consciousness. When I go to the theater, what I see there is an interpretation of, say, *Macbeth*; but I also see *Macbeth* itself. There is nowhere I could go to find the uninterpreted *Macbeth* because interpretation brings it into existence. But I do not *also* see *Macbeth*, as if seeing the play itself were distinct from seeing the interpretation. The interpretation is *Macbeth* itself and vice versa. There are not, then, two separate things, such that one could be relative to the other. The only way to experience the work itself is in an interpretation that is not differentiated from the work. The differentiation of work from interpretation is an index of the inadequacy of the interpretation. And that implies either that the uninterpreted work exists and is knowable (which Gadamer denies since the interpretation brings the work into existence) or else that there is at least one interpretation that cannot be differentiated from the work. There are in principle, then, true and adequate interpretations, whose

30. The thesis that the work of art is tied to the specific conditions obtaining when it is represented pre-figures Gadamer's later argument that historical works generally exist most fully when they are applied—that is, linked—to particular circumstances or a particular case.

31. P. D. Juhl mistakenly infers that "it follows [from Gadamer's hermeneutic] that a statement about the meaning of a work is a statement about a particular critic's subjective understanding" (*Interpretation*, p. 8). Quite the contrary, as we have seen, play cannot be understood by appeal to the subjectivity of the players.

32. Naumann too employs this phrase, but to quite different ends, in *Gesellschaft, Literatur, Lesen*, p. 110.

truth consists in the fact that they are not distinguishable from the work itself. True interpretations are interpretations *of the work itself*. They are to be explained therefore by reference not to the meaning-conferring acts of the interpreter but to the work itself.

Yet though there are, in principle and in fact, interpretations indistinguishable from the work, it is nevertheless possible and indeed easy to distinguish among a variety of interpretations themselves indistinguishable from the work. Johnson's *Macbeth* is clearly different from Coleridge's, and both from G. Wilson Knight's. This variety "does not involve merely a merely subjective variety of conceptions but instead the possibilities of what the work itself can be, as it interprets itself, so to speak, in the variety of its aspects" (112 / 106). If the variety of interpretations is not subjective, if there is a variety of true interpretations, then it is a variety of the work's own possibilities for being interpreted in this way and that. And since the being of the artwork is to be interpreted—that is, it exists only in interpretation—the work's being interpreted in this way and that is also the work's being this way and that. The work is the multiple possibilities of its interpretation. It is open to interpretation.

There can therefore be no determinate criterion of correct interpretation nor any single, correct, canonical interpretation. Yet it is also the case that every interpretation strives to be true. Many succeed, many fail. But how is it possible to make or recognize a true interpretation when the criterion of truth is not and cannot be given? Decision on the basis of a non-given rule is the function of taste, judgment, and common sense as Gadamer has explicated them, as we saw earlier. They operate precisely where no determinate rule of operation can be adduced, where procedures cannot be programmed, and where common sense is required to make judgments that cannot be decided by reasons alone. Whether an interpretation is true is a matter of taste. If this seems to denigrate truth, that is only because we have denigrated taste as a cognitive capacity able to arrive at the truth. It is only because we have thought truth is exclusively something that has been or can be proven. Since Gödel and Gadamer, that conception is no longer tenable.

What taste decides is that an interpretation is of the work. If we think of *Macbeth* as the name of a rule by which to judge interpretations, not only is it an extremely complex rule but one that is given nowhere outside the changing applications and interpretations of it. As a law, this rule is common and unwritten rather than statutory, but it is hardly empty or less binding for being common. It prescribes what interpretations fall under it, and these are indefinitely many, and yet it is not so indefinite as to be open to all. Some interpretations are always excluded, and the offense against taste that is aroused by misinterpretation registers the integrity of the work. As Gebilde, the artwork is repeatable. It can be played and replayed, with new actors before new audiences with new, correct interpretations. And if the work is repeatable, that means—despite the multiplicity of its true interpretations—it is nevertheless one work that is many. There is only one *Macbeth*, for us as for the court of King James. Taste is the capacity that enables us to know the sameness of a work that changes, whose identity and continuity are open to the future.

There are, then, two theses Gadamer wishes to maintain: first, there are true interpretations—that is, interpretations which belong to the work and not just to us. In them the interpretation, representation, or medium is undifferentiable from the work itself. This means "that the medium as medium cancels itself out. In other words, reproduction [for example, a reading, performance, or piece of criticism] . . . as such does not become thematic" (114 / 108). When the medium *does* become thematic, the attention paid to the interpretation itself is a sign of some critical failure—that is, such attention is the index of an interpretation that does not belong to the work and which must therefore be explained by appeal to an interpreting mind. In true interpretation, by contrast, "the being of art cannot be determined as the object of an aesthetic consciousness because, just the opposite, aesthetic demeanor is more than it knows of itself" (111 / 105). There is more than it is conscious of.

But isn't the artwork, defined as the object of an aesthetic unconsciousness, even more subjective than it is when defined as an object of aesthetic consciousness? What Gadamer suggests is that we are still trapped in romantic subjectivism as long as we take the artwork as an object in either of these two ways. When he writes that aesthetic consciousness *is* more than it knows, he is addressing the ontological question about what consciousness (or unconsciousness) *is*. It *is* more than it knows because "it is part of the event of being that occurs in representation and belongs essentially to the play as play" (111 / 104). The true interpretation is part of the play; and that, as it were, is the joke that the artwork plays on consciousness—namely that what aesthetic consciousness had taken as its object is what that consciousness itself belongs to. When consciousness plays, it is being played. This is the second thesis Gadamer wishes to defend: when an interpreter interprets, he is being interpreted and himself belongs to the continuing life of the artwork that embodies itself, its own possibilities, in the variety of its interpretations. The artwork *is* differently as it is interpreted differently. Interpretation is an advent of being in that the play comes into existence as it is represented on the stage.

But it is not just a play that comes into existence in being represented. There is here a double mimesis: as the player presents the play, so also the playwright presents something by the play. And just as we do not differentiate between what the actors represent and the play itself, so also we do not differentiate what the author represents in the play from the real and very thing represented. "To the double distinction between a dramatic poem and its material and between poem and performance corresponds a double non-distinction as the unity of truth that one recognizes in the play of art" (112 / 105). True interpretation is not just true to the play; it is interpretation of the play's truth. It is not only the play that comes to exist in the interpretation but the thing that the play represents. What Gadamer is describing is the process by which worlds come to be, an event of being and truth. The event of truth is the unabgeschlossenes Geschehen, the unconcluded event, in which we are always caught up, even and especially when we are playing. The player in truth is being played.

(1.2.1.C) We have seen that Gebilde (form) is Gadamer's term for the repeatability of the artwork. The work does not have form but rather *is* form, and that means that the whole of the work, not some element of structure in it, is permanent. However this whole changes, it does not disintegrate into a multiplicity of aspects that would have to be added up somehow. No summing of partial views is either necessary or possible, for the work is wholly there in each. Yet Gebilde suggests something that just stays the same; and it accounts for neither the fact that the artwork is not in continuous existence because it is not always being interpreted nor the fact that, when it is interpreted, it is interpreted differently at different times. What Gebilde does not sufficiently express, then, is the kind of temporality specific to art. Gebilde tends to imply something eternal and timeless—as if form persisted when it is not embodied, or as if the artwork existed disembodied, in the abstract, when it does not exist in concrete interpretations.

Since it does not, the principle of permanence in change requires a description that is more temporal than the Platonic-sounding Gebilde. Gadamer therefore offers *Fest* as more apposite. The German noun Fest can be heard in the English *festival* and *feast*; and in its adjectival and prefix form, it is akin to *fast* in the sense of "held fast" or "fastened." The *feste Burg* in Martin Luther's hymn is "mighty," as the translation goes, because God stands fast in time. But the permanence of a periodic festival is not the continuous resistance to time of an embattled citadel; its fastness is discontinuous because it derives from repetition, disappearance and return. The festival does not return from somewhere. It exists only in being celebrated, just as a play exists only in being performed; and the very fact that it exists temporally accounts for its peculiar way of being.

The festival changes from time to time because it is celebrated by different celebrants under different circumstances—that is, because it is contemporaneous with different times. Yet the changes that transpire as the festival is repeated do not imply that some other festival is now celebrated. We cannot say, "Originally it was celebrated in such and such a way, and then differently, and then differently again" (117 / 110). The original festival does not suffer change. It does not suffer difference—though, to be sure, it is not always celebrated identically. But neither was there initially a "genuine" festival from which the others degenerated, nor is the original to be contradistinguished from its belated imitations. The differences does not come after the origin, in other words, but belongs to it originally.[33] The "first annual" celebration of a festival is merely the first, not the authentic or real celebration. In a sense the original already includes the difference from itself insofar as it is inaugural—that is, to be repeated. "According to its own original essence, it is in such a way as to be continually something different. . . . An entity that is only insofar as it is continually another, is temporal in a more radical sense than everything that belongs to history. It has its being only in becoming and in return" (117 / 110).[34]

If the artwork like a festival exists only in repetition (interpretation, representation), then it too is radically temporal. If ordinary temporality is the mode of being of what suffers change and difference, the radical temporality of the artwork approximates a kind of eternal permanence. It does not suffer difference at all—but only because it is and always was different from the very beginning. An artwork's way of being is: to be different; and only thus does it remain itself. Its first appearance, its first publication, its first presentation on the stage, or first interpretation is, like that of a festival, merely the inaugural repetition of something to be continually repeated, and is no more authentic or genuine than the second or any subsequent repetition to follow. We celebrate the festival itself, not the first festival.

However remote its origin, the artwork is wholly contemporary[35] with each

---

33. Cf. Derrida: "'Ritual' is not a possible occurrence [*eventualité*], but rather, *as* iterability, a structural characteristic of every mark" ("Signature Event Context," p. 189). Hoy is surely right when he observes that "Derrida's philosophy is not as complete a break with the history of philosophy as many would like us to believe. On the contrary, he is best understood as the latest development of a tradition going back to Kant and Hegel, a tradition which includes contemporary hermeneutics as well" ("Must We Say What We Mean?" in Kresic, ed., *Contemporary Literary Hermeneutics*, p. 105).

34. Compare Hegel's remark that could almost stand as the epigraph to *Truth and Method*: "To find one's own in the alien, to become at home in it, is the fundamental movement of spirit, whose being is only return to itself from being otherwise" (11 / 15).

35. Gadamer differentiates contemporaneity from simultaneity. Whereas contemporaneity fuses times, simultaneity takes all times as equally given, equally present. Festivals illustrate con-

age in which it is understood. It does not transport the interpreter into another time, another world. "It is the truth of his own world, the religious and moral world in which he lives, that presents itself to him and in which he recognizes himself" (122 / 113). Yet this recognition is indirect: we recognize our world in something we have returned from or returned to. There has been a route traversed, an excursion undertaken, and a task accomplished. That such a route must be traveled indicates first that the contemporaneity of the artwork is not the simultaneity of the interpreter's consciousness to all ages. The presence of the artwork to the interpreter is not an immediacy that is given but one that is achieved: a work must be performed. The task of performance is to mediate the work in such a way that medium is not differentiated from what is mediated. The past must be *made* manifest to the present because its presence and immediacy are not given. The work of art history is necessary precisely because we are not simultaneous with all ages.

To understand another age takes work, and yet it is this same work that allows us to understand our own age. As Gadamer says, we celebrate the festival itself, not the first festival; the artwork transports us not to another world but to our own. However, the fact that we do indeed need to be transported to our own world, that our world is cognizable only in recognition and repetition, suggests that we are no more present to our own world than to any other. That immediacy too is a task to be achieved through mediation. It too takes work, an artwork. There must be an *ecstasis* out of ourselves, an excursion into another, past world, but an excursion such that, when we arrive, we discover that this other world and time is our very own. As time thus becomes continuous, we come to recognize that the festival itself, our very own festival, is not merely our own. It is a repetition. To come into our very own requires an excursion into the alien that is also a return to ourselves because our identity is not a given but a task, not the unity of a self-presence but a reunion with the past. When we interpret the artwork, we interpret ourselves; and as the work comes to be in interpretation, so we come to be also.

(1.2.1.D) There is joy in homecoming and reunion. Gadamer calls it the joy of recognition, and it is in this recognition that he discerns the cognitive import of art. But just as this joy cannot be identified with (aesthetic) pleasure, so also it is not to be equated with happiness alone. Indeed Gadamer emphasizes

---

temporaneity in that there "memory are present are one" (*KS* 2:171). Moreover the function of the theater as a mediation between times becomes especially clear when, in the eighteenth century and after, there is the performance not only of newly written plays but also those of a classical repertoire.

haplessness rather than happiness. It is above all tragic joy that comes from recognizing the game that is played with us.

In tragedy Gadamer locates the truth of play, of the artwork as play, and the working of art on the spectator. What the work does to the spectator, its *Wirkung*, has been included since Aristotle in the definition of the tragic play. That a tragedy works on, plays, the spectators is not incidental but essential to its being a tragedy, and the same is true of the work of art in general. It works on the audience. Yet is is also true that the play is performed with utter disregard for the audience and at an absolute distance from it. The wall that has been let down permitting the play to be seen is nevertheless an insuperable barrier. What transpires on stage admits no intervention, no amelioration, for there is no rescuing Desdemona, no warning Oedipus. We can only watch the tragedy to its inevitable end without being able to do anything about it. That is the meaning of aesthetic distance, and it is in tragedy that the impotence of that distance is thematized. "What is understood as tragic can only be accepted" (123 / 115). The autonomy of the aesthetic, as evidenced in the meta-aesthetic genre of tragedy, consists in the fact that we cannot do anything about the play.

Yet it does something to us. Aristotle calls its effects *eleos* and *phobos*, and the catharsis of them. The words eleos and phobos, as Gadamer understands them, refer not to subjective emotions but to a state of being of the tragic hero and of the audience interchangeably. They are conditions of ecstasis that occur when one is overwhelmed, torn apart, and ripped out of oneself by the power of what is happening. "Being overcome by misery and terror presents a painful schism. In it there is a disunion with what is happening, a not wanting it to be true, a refusal to acknowledge the horrible event. Just this however is the effect [*Wirkung*] of the tragic catastrophe, that the schism from what is, is dissolved" (124–125 / 116). Catharsis is the spectator's return to himself from ecstasis by a return to face what in truth is; and that truth is admitted, accepted, even affirmed in tragic joy.

This truth is scarcely the justice of a moral world order. Quite the opposite, where there is justice, where the debt of guilt is paid in full, there is no tragedy. Guilt is real, no doubt, but the tragedy consists in the excess of punishment even beyond desert. The power of tragic fate is manifest precisely in the disproportion of guilt and fate, a disproportion between will and consequence, intent and meaning, from which even the mighty are not exempt. The great ones of the earth are, like us, caught up in events that are larger than they, events that expose the littleness of knowing, feeling, doing—the littleness of subjectivity—in the face of the frightful immensity of what happens. In tragedy the insistence of history on and in consciousness is dramatized. The truth of tragedy, of the game that is played with us, protagonist and spectator alike, cannot be proved, still less evaded, but only admitted. For the truth is something we can do nothing about.

Nor can the playwright. Gadamer calls tragedy a ground phenomenon of the aesthetic, and he places it at the turning point of his discussion of the aesthetic because it is tragedy that best shows the inability of aesthetics to comprehend art. Tragedy, itself art, is more than art. It is access to "a metaphysical order of being valid for all. The affirmation 'This is how it is' is a kind of self-knowledge for the spectator who returns with insight from the illusions in which he, like everyone else, lives" (126 / 117). That "everyone" includes the artist as well as the interpreter. No more than Oedipus is Sophocles free from the insistence of history, and this recognition marks the limit of the aesthetics of freedom—the bohemian artist's free genius and, what is finally the same, the genial interpreter's free bestowal of meaning. "For the poet free invention is always only one side of an intercession bound by a previously given validity. He does not freely invent his plot, however much he still imagines he does. Rather even today there remains something insistent about the old fundamental mimesis theory. The free invention of the poet is the presentation of a common truth that is binding on the poet as well" (127 / 118).[36] As is especially manifest in tragedy, which reveals the insistence of history as the common fate, the artist, like his audience, is bound to and by the common. His freedom is not a freedom from history but rather a freedom to recognize the common bond and the common historical world that binds him as well. The world of art is "never only a foreign world of magic, hallucination, or dream to which the player [playwright, or spectator] is transported; instead it is always still their own world with which they are more genuinely at one in that they recognize themselves more profoundly in it. There remains a continuity of meaning which unites the artwork with the existent world and from which the alienated consciousness of a cultured society never completely sunders itself" (127 / 118). Even as it accept the finitude of consciousness (the fact that consciousness cannot completely free itself from the continuity of meaning), tragic joy affirms the sense of the common, of community and a communal history.

36. Ricoeur comes to much the same conclusion when he writes that "*mimesis* serves as an index of the discourse situation; it reminds us that no discourse ever suspends our belonging to a world" (*Rule of Metaphor*, p. 43).

ART AS HISTORY

(1.2.2.A) Tragedy marks the return of art from eternity to history. If art is not to be understood as an object present to a conscious subject, that is at least in part because consciousness is itself subject to a past. Until the turning point in his discussion of tragedy, Gadamer's exposition has been (at least apparently) future-oriented. His endeavor to transcend aesthetics has required a reunion of what aesthetics differentiates; and that is first the artwork and the interpretation of it. Thus Gadamer begins with art as play, for the game is the playing of it. So too plays do not exist apart from their representation and interpretation on the stage. In being dependent on interpretation for their existence and meaning, plays are themselves open to interpretation; and that means in part open to a future, to our own world. With the tragic, however, comes the *peripeteia*—and the *anagnoresis*: art is also open to its own world, to the past, and no less essentially so.

We recall that aesthetics consists in a double differentiation—not only of the work from the representation of it, but also of the work from what it represents. It is on this second relation that Gadamer now focuses: the relation of the work to what it represents—that is, its world, its original, its past. If art is to be understood wholly as representation, Gadamer must show not only that it is *to be* represented but also that it represents something. Against aesthetic differentiation he reaffirms mimesis; or more precisely, against double differentiation, double mimesis. Gadamer may be right that there is something insistent about the old mimesis theory of art, but in Gadamer's as in all attempts to resuscitate it, Plato's indictment of mimetic art must be taken into account; and Gadamer's notion of double mimesis leaves art especially vulnerable to the charge of being at a double remove from the truth.

The Platonic schema of imitative degeneration begins with the truth, the original, the idea of the bed, then proceeds to the actual bed, and finally to the painting of the bed. Gadamer's exposition, however, reverses this order. We might be tempted to say that he begins with the reproduction (the performance), proceeds to the representation (the play), and only now arrives at the original. But this is not the case, and if it were, it would be no reversal of Plato at all. It only replaces the schema of imitative descent with the no less Platonic schema of cognitive ascent —in which truth is what is achieved at the climax, the pinnacle, or merely the end of the line. And the line, for Gadamer, emphatically does not end. More precisely we can say of Gadamer's expository structure that it begins with the differentiation of reproduction from representation and collapses it, and now proceeds to do the same for the differentiation of representation and original. Double mimesis offers a genuine response to Plato in that it corresponds, as Gadamer says, to a double non-differentiation. It is worth emphasizing that for Gadamer truth appears neither at the beginning nor at the end but in the interim, in the process of representation.

Since the original is purportedly both the beginning from which all representations derive and the end to which they return, a paradise always lost and always to be regained, it marks a crux in any theory of representation. The original is precisely what is not a representation, and thus it threatens to block any attempt to universalize representation. Yet the reverse is also true. Representation marks a crux in any theory of originality, for how is it possible that an original, itself not a representation, can be represented? If we answer that it cannot be represented at all, then we find ourselves saddled with something like Kantian noumena and Hegel's critique of this notion. If, on the other hand, we answer that the original can be represented only imperfectly, then we are again saddled with Plato's conception of art as degenerate *eidos*; and the question remains how eidos, even if degenerate, can be represented at all.

Gadamer addresses this question in the discussion of the picture that follows. If we recall that Bild (picture, image) is sometimes used to translate eidos, we can appreciate the directness of Plato's relevance to this discussion, though he is mentioned only in passing. Just as important is that Bild and the *bildenen Künste*—sculpture and architecture, as well as painting—resonate with the associations that accrue to them from Gebilde, Einbildungskraft, and Bildung, discussed earlier. Abbild (copy) and Urbild (original) also belong to this family. In *Truth and Method*, as in a poem, sound does the work of structure. It collects what exposition distributes. For philosophy too is language, not merely *logos*. In his reliance on language Gadamer displays his resistance to Platonism no less than in his explicit arguments. His argument here, in terms of the question raised in the previous paragraph, is that the Urbild can be represented because it is already a Bild as the German language insists.

Despite its advantages, conceiving art in general as play, plays, and a specific kind of play—namely tragedy—presents the danger of a reductive synecdoche. It is clear that not all arts are—like drama, music, and dance—performing arts. Those arts that are not performed we call plastic, formed (*bildene*). But though it is plausible that a play exists only in the representation of it, a statue does not exist at all in the reproductions of it, still less *only* there. So also copies of a painting are to be distinguished from the painting itself. In that the painting itself is immediately present to us when we look at it, we can dispense with media of accessibility such as copies, even though we could not dispense with the reproduction of a drama on stage. Destroying all the copies of a painting leaves the painting itself. Here in the non-performing arts, then, aesthetic differentiation—the distinction of a representation from its reproductions—reasserts its rights, as is especially clear in the case of a framed picture.

The frame, a symbol of aesthetic differentiation and of aesthetics itself, announces first the dividing line between art and non-art. The frame makes the painting a picture, and this involves distinguishing between the picture and its world, so that the picture is freely transportable into any world, as accords with the simultaneity of aesthetic consciousness to all worlds. Second, the frame marks the difference of the picture itself from copies of it, or more generally from the particular conditions of our approach to it. In both respects the integrity, autonomy, and immediate presence of the framed picture apparently obviate the work of historical mediation. It is already present, and thus neither historical investigation nor reproduction is necessary to represent it to us.

Gadamer does not contend that the picture is to be found only in the reproductions, the copies of it. Quite the contrary, he is concerned to show that the picture cannot be copied because it is itself not a copy. The picture (*Bild*) is related to an original (*Urbild*), but not in the same way that a copy (*Abbild*) is. Thus the fact that the picture cannot be copied nor is a copy does not authorize us to detach it from its original world. But this implies too that the world cannot be detached from the picture of it.

A copy fulfills its function to the extent that it is self-effacing, that it points away from itself and instead toward the original. The virtual image in a mirror (*Spiegelbild*) is in one sense an ideal copy because it not only conveys a perfect image but in being virtual it is self-effacing to the point of being non-existent. Yet precisely for this reason, that it does not exist, what we see in a mirror is an image, not a copy or a picture. A copy has a being of its own and is useful because it does not depend, like a mirror, on the presence of the original. It would not do to improve the accuracy of passport photos by replacing them with mirrors. A copy necessarily exists in its own right, and yet that existence best serves its function by canceling itself out and ceding its rights to the original. When a copy asserts itself in contradistinction to the original, its very existence is merely a flaw in its functioning. Yet it is also correct to say that what we want from a copy, as from a mirror, is the very image of the original, its own image, not that of the copy. Copy and original can always be differentiated, even though for most purposes—for the purposes of the copy itself—there is no differentiation of representation from represented.

Like a copy, a picture exists in its own right. It is not self-effacing like a copy, however, because it serves no purpose. We do not look "through" the picture, or by means of it, at something else. It is not a means but rather itself

what is meant. What the picture means is the picture. "The representation remains
. . . essentially combined with what is represented, even belongs to it" (132 /
123). But if what is represented in the picture can be found only in the picture,
the situation is analogous to a play that exists only in the representation of it.
What is represented in the picture (*Bild*) is the original (*Urbild*); and if what is
represented in the picture exists nowhere but in the picture, that means that the
Urbild exists nowhere but in the Bild of it. The original cannot be differentiated,
divorced, or detached from its representation because representation belongs to
the original essentially and *originally*. "Non-differentiation remains an essential
element of all experience of pictures" (132 / 123). If we do not look "through"
a picture at its original, that is because in the picture we see the original itself.
As the play is the playing of it—its own playing—so the picture is the repre-
sentat' n of the original itself, the original's own representation, its self-representation. In the picture, the original represents itself.

The transition and reversal here hinges on the double meaning of the gen-
itive, so that the mimesis *of* the original is something the original is doing by
itself. What we see in the picture is the original's self-representation; and thus
in a sense the picture disappears, just like a copy. Clearly Gadamer does want
to assert the non-differentiation of picture and original, yet just as clearly his
intent is to distinguish the picture from the copy. Both involve non-differentiation
from the original; both, unlike the mirror image, exist in their own right. But
whereas the copy effaces itself before the original, the picture asserts its own
independent being. But given the independence of picture from original, are we
not forced to concede the validity of aesthetic differentiation? On the contrary,
Gadamer contends, the autonomy of the picture means not that it does not
represent something but that the picture is indispensable: it discloses something
in the original that cannot be discovered except by looking at the picture. The
picture "represents something which, without it, would not represent itself in
this way" (133 / 124). The consequence of the unsurpassability of the picture
is that if the original is to present itself in this way, if it is to *be* (present) in
this way, it cannot do so without the picture. "This does not necessarily mean,"
Gadamer continues, "that it is dependent on just this representation to appear.
It can also represent itself as what it is in another way" (133 / 124). That the
original has alternative possibilities of self-presentation constitutes its autonomy
and independence from the picture; yet insofar as the original always presents
itself *as something*, it is always dependent on some picture, just as the picture,
if it is to represent something, is dependent on some original. This interdependence with the picture implies that the original can present itself in this way
too, as this picture represents it, as well as in other ways. The original is more

because of the picture; it exists more fully. It now exists *as* it is represented in the picture; and if the picture has an independent existence, that implies that there has been a proliferation of being. Being happens as art when the fecund original emanates the autonomous being of the picture. The original originates.

But the reverse side of the original's fecundity is dearth and need. The original needs the picture to come more fully into its own. "The picture has its own independence which affects the original. For strictly speaking, it is first through the picture [*Bild*] that the original becomes original [*Ur-bild*]" (135 / 125). There is a kind of backward origination by which the original comes to exist ex post facto. If art imitates nature, then nature is: what art imitates. A scene becomes picturesque by having been pictured. The statesman presents himself to the citizenry and thus becomes available for representation—in pictures, or in the statehouse. But in either case he no longer belongs to himself, for he must conform to the picture people have of him. As is especially evident in the age of television campaigning, the ruler is himself ruled by his picture. He is its creature, and yet the picture is nothing but the appearance of the original.

If the original can be represented, there must be a rift in its self-identity. That it does not belong wholly to itself is the condition of its belonging to something else as well. Nature can in truth be what art imitates. If the original can be represented, the original can be what the picture represents, and that is the original's own possibility of being. It can represent itself as what is depicted in the picture and thus come into its own. *As* here means what it always does—something like "is / not."[37] To say that the hermeneutic *as* marks the rift in self-identity implies that the original is / not itself. The original too undergoes a movement of alienation and return: it represents itself as something it is not, and yet in that self-alienation comes into its own. The Urbild undergoes a process of Bildung when it becomes a Bild. Picturing is an ontological process, the very process by which a world originally comes into being. Thus the frame is breached and aesthetic differentiation fails. "The picture contains an indissoluble relation to its world" (137 / 127). The picture is nothing but the appearance of the original, of the original as something, and of the original *as*.[38]

(1.2.2.B) It may seem like the long way round to go through hermeneutic ontology to reach a conclusion that every art historian takes for granted—namely, that it is impossible to separate the work of art from its original world. But this circuitous route is necessitated by the fact that aesthetics has defined itself partly

---

37. Ricoeur makes this point in *The Rule of Metaphor*, p. 214.
38. "In this 'as,' " Gadamer writes, "lies the whole riddle" (*KS* 2:22).

in contradistinction to art history. The work of art as pure art is precisely what is divorced from its world and time, and thus the object of pure aesthetics is divorced from art history. Yet aesthetics, we recall, consists in a double differentiation, not only of the work from *its* world but from ours as well. In this respect, art history appears as a sub-species of aesthetics[39] insofar as it attempts to replace the artwork in its own world by withdrawing it from ours—that is, by distinguishing the original interpretation from current or intermediary interpretations. However, if the artwork does in fact need to be put back into its world by the art historian, then the necessity for his own activity itself testifies to the very divorce of work and original world that the art historian assumes to be impossible. Art history cannot be conceived subjectively, as something the historian does *to* the work as object. Either the artwork itself retains its original world even in our world, or else art history is impossible.

If the artwork does *not* exist disembodied and in the abstract, as pure aesthetics claims, then the indissoluble relation of art to its world implies a relation to its original world no less than to any subsequent one.[40] Moreover these two worlds can never be set in opposition to one another, for all relating of the artwork to its original world is performed by the historian in his own world. His is the mediation that corresponds to representation in the performing arts. The historian performs even non-performing arts in representing them in their world to us in ours. The artwork's original concretization, performance, or creation is not exhaustively definitive of the artwork but neither is it irrelevant. In every case, including the first, an artwork exists in the concrete, in performance and interpretation. Just as Gadamer has shown that the one who plays is being played and that the "subject" of the play is the play itself, so in respect to art history too, the artwork, not the historian, is the performing subject. If art history is not something that the historian does to the work, then the work itself performs its original world and belongs to it. That the work belongs temporally to its world Gadamer calls the occasionality of the work; that it belongs spatially he calls its decorativeness.

Every artwork is occasional in that it betrays the age in which it was created, whether it means to do so or not. The historian can focus on those elements of style or content that locate the work in a particular time without paying regard to the meaning of the work. Thus he discerns a meaning that the work does not

39. On the unwitting collusion between aesthetics and historicism, see Palmer, *Hermeneutics*, pp. 181–82.

40. For Gadamer, as Janet Wolff rightly says, "works of art are at the same time contemporary with every present, *and* placed in their historical origin and function" (*Hermeneutic Philosophy*, p. 110).

itself intend. Such interpretation is to that extent distinguishable from the work; and that distinction implies that the historian is a subject who makes the work historical, a historical object. Since Gadamer, by contrast, is concerned to show that the work makes the historian by making history, he defines occasionality not by reference to those elements of a work that betray the time of its creation but rather by appeal to artistic phenomena in which time is part of what the work itself intends, "phenomena such as the portrait, the dedicated poem, or contemporary allusions in comedy" (137 / 127). Not all pictures of people are portraits, but those that are have a relation to the original that exists quite apart from whether a historian or anyone else is aware of it. The portrait itself means the person portrayed; it means the original, and what it means cannot be fully understood without understanding the original as well. The historian does not place or re-place the portrait in its world when he tells us who is portrayed, for that world is already there. A picture may betray the identity of models not meant to be recognized; a portrait, however, does not betray, but rather portrays, a person. The person, the original, the occasion of the work's creation is part of what it means. Works that are occasional in this way have their meaning determined in part by their initial occasion, and the historian who explicates the meaning as determined by that occasion does what the work itself is already doing.

Few historians, I suspect, would really want to quarrel with this conclusion. They too want to read with the grain of the work, not against it. Perhaps they would not resist either the idea that, in doing what the artwork itself is already doing, their work is ideally an extension of the working of the artwork. Yet there may be some uneasiness here because the next step is to suggest that the historian's interpretation belongs to the work itself and ideally cannot be differentiated from it. The work means the interpretation, and if so, the work cannot be differentiated from the variety of interpretations produced on a variety of occasions. That way lies relativism, the idea that the work experiences a continued determination of its meaning by the occasions of its continued interpretation; and from relativism defined in this way art history seeks safe harbor and sure anchor in the artwork's original occasion.

Art history too involves a relativism, of course: the meaning of the work, according to the historical view, is relative to the occasion of the work's creation, and exclusively to that occasion—that is, exclusive of its relation to every other occasion. One question that must be addressed to art history, then, is how a meaning initially occasional, inextricably contexted in a world, later becomes what the historian takes it to be: unoccasional and ideally extricable from his own world insofar as he sees his own task as precisely that extrication. Can we call the meaning determined by the initial occasion the true meaning, and yet consider the meaning determined by subsequent occasions falsehood, error, and misinterpretation? Isn't the historian's own interpretation a meaning determined by a subsequent occasion? If the historian's meaning is determined exclusively by the artist's original occasion and not the historian's own, how is it that the artist labors under the burden of an occasionality that the historian has escaped?

These are far-reaching questions that receive extended discussion in the second major part of *Truth and Method*, on history. Suffice it to say here that Gadamer is willing neither to ignore the original occasion in the name of aesthetic timelessness, nor to inflate the initial occasion at the price of disenfranchizing all subsequent occasions in the name of art history. It is either all or nothing. Either the meaning of art is determined by every occasion of interpretation or by none at all; and since we can now see that even the eternality of art was an idea occasioned by nineteenth-century interpretation, Gadamer finds universal occasionality the more credible position. His may seem to be a relativistic position, no doubt; but it should already be obvious that, even if so, it is not a subjective relativism. What the work means is not dependent on what anyone— whether historian or non-historian, interpreter or artist—wants it to mean or tries to make it mean. Universal occasionality implies that occasions, not just intentional acts, determine meanings. These meanings, moreover, are the working of the work and inseparable from it. "It is not as if the artwork were 'in itself' and only the working [*Wirkung*] differed—it is the work itself that offers itself under different conditions. The observer of today not only sees differently, he sees different things" (141 / 130). It is a different work in a different world. Every interpretation, whether the original interpretation of the author, which the historian wants to call the work itself, or any subsequent interpretation, such as that of the historian, which Gadamer calls the work itself too—every interpretation is bound up with an entire temporal world. If a world determines the meaning and the very existence of every interpretation, we are forced to admit that the work at all times is an interpretation not only *of* a world but *by* one.

The question is how these many worlds, many works, can yet be one. For us it is always easier to discern the effects of alienation, dissemination, and dispersion than those of reunion. But the hermeneutic question concerns both excursion and return. Thus the medium of art, which mediates by self-assertion rather than self-effacement and returns by excursion, is fundamental to hermeneutics because it addresses at once both sides of the question. That performing arts such as drama and dance mediate between worlds and times is clear enough, since it is evident that such performance belongs to its present time as much as to the times of former performances, including the first. This mediative function is much less evident in the plastic arts that Gadamer is concerned with in this section. Yet in these non-performing arts too, as he is able to show, the work's original world is preserved by being related to and mediated by the present. Thus the non-performing arts, like all art, are more than pure art.

"A work of architecture is never primarily an artwork" (149 / 139). We can certainly view it as such and appreciate the exclusively aesthetic merits of design as if it were a particularly large statue or monument. But this is a reductive abstraction that ignores the context of life and the world of purposes by reason of which the work of architecture is never pure art. When that context alters during the passage of time, the building does not retain its "purposefulness" while losing its "purpose" and thus become an object of merely aesthetic pleasure. People still live and work in it, adapting and renovating it to new purposes in a new world. In time, nothing can be preserved without being altered; there can be no staying at home and no return without alienation. In that the new world preserves something of the old by altering it, the work of architecture, like the performing arts, is a locus of mediation between past and present. It gives people a history that is not simply bygone; it is their own history, for they are still living in it, adding to it, and changing it. And as the present alters, so must the work of architecture—not because it is exclusively present, still less because it is past, but rather because it is a mediation of past and present and must change in order to continue to perform that mediation. Architecture too is occasional. It exists and persists in renovation and reproduction.

The work of architecture is, moreover, a world not only of time but of space. It creates space and gives a place to all other arts—to statuary, painting, music, and drama. For this reason, architecture is an omnicomprehensive art that assimilates all other arts to itself and converts them, as it were, into its own decorations. Although a picture asserts its self-identity by a frame and a statue by the pedestal on which it is erected, architecture comprehends even the frame and the pedestal, and thus reintegrates even closed artworks by opening their self-reference onto a larger context of life. They too are decorations and must be decorous—that is, suited to a greater whole and subject to a judgment of taste.

Like the occasional, the decorative must be understood in terms of mediation. Architecture exhibits this function most clearly in that, like the performing arts, in which double mimesis is evident, it too involves a double mediation. As a decoration, a work of architecture must draw the attention and admiration of the viewer to itself. Yet it cannot be a blot on the landscape, however admirable in itself, but rather must fit into the unity of its surroundings, and not by becoming invisible but precisely by reason of what it adds of its own to this unity. It must ornament, enhance, and increase the whole of which it is a part. Architecture decorates, then, but it is also to be decorated, and this is the second aspect of mediation. What decorates a work of architecture cannot be so insistent as to be an end in itself, and yet an ornament that is entirely self-effacing does not possess the requisite enlivening effect, and thus is no ornament at all. Works of art too, as we have noted, always ornament some work of architecture. Even if aesthetic differentiation would deny it, the artwork too is a decoration and thus performs a mediating function despite all attempts to frame it: "It draws the attention of the observer to itself, satisfies his taste, and then again redirects him away from itself to the larger whole of the life context which it accompanies" (150 / 140).

This larger whole is initially the work of architecture to which the artwork must be suited and which serves as the criterion of its decorum; yet, as we have said architecture itself decorates as well as is decorated. It decorates the still larger context of life to which it itself belongs, and this ultimate whole, this world that is the ultimate criterion of taste, is definitively not given. Thus decorum at every stage requires a judgment of taste, which is judgment by appeal to a definitively non-given whole—definitive not merely because the whole is so large and diverse as to be unmanageable in any form that it might be given, but because it is subject to historical variation.

But this means that the judgment of taste is itself occasional and essentially ad hoc. We can put this problem in more emphatic terms: though context determines meaning, context itself is essentially indeterminable and must be terminated arbitrarily if there is to be determinate meaning. If we do not conceive this arbitrariness subjectively, as a matter of will or desire, does this imply that meaning is itself an effect of the finitude of consciousness? And must the same be said of truth—that there is truth only *because* we see a part and never the whole truth?

(1.2.2.C) This is a disturbing question, one that Gadamer does not address nor even formulate here. But it awaits an answer even as Gadamer turns to the last of the arts he discusses, *Literatur*. Since at the outset Gadamer speaks of the experience of art as an encounter with language, it may seem odd that literature is afforded only scant and passing treatment. Plays in the previous discussion are *Dichtung* not *Literatur*. Plays are to be found not in the script but in the playing of them; so too, lyric and epic are reproductive arts, as manifest in oral interpretation. Yet novels, for instance, are written, book-dependent forms of art. They are bound to script and hence are scripture in the general sense of what is written, literature. Given the general thrust of Gadamer's argument thus far, and especially given the immense body of reader-response criticism that has developed in the last twenty years, partly under Gadamer's influence,[41] it does not come as a surprise that in this section literature, too, proves to be among the interpretive arts that exist only in the representation of representation. If what Gadamer has to say about literature has not been superannuated, however, that is because in denying that the literary work is a self-identical object, he does not make the complementary mistake of asserting that it is the possession of a self-identical subject, namely the reader. In contradistinction to what might be called the Deweyan branch of literary theory,[42] Gadamer insists that literature can be understood only as an ontological event—that is, the process of something's coming to be in representation—and not as the experience of a reader.

"Reading," Gadamer writes, "belongs essentially to the literary artwork" (153 / 143). Note the syntax: reading belongs to the work, not vice versa. Reading is the work's reading, the work reading, and the reader's being read. The work, moreover, is a reading of a world, a world's reading, and the work's being read. As the "subject" of play is the game rather than the player, so the "subject" of double mimesis is the world and the work. The work is read by what is not just a consciousness but another world.[43] At both ends, as it were, the work of literature belongs not to a writer or reader but to a world. It mediates between worlds; it presents the past and the past's claim on the present. Literature that belongs to a world—world literature—discloses not merely what once was thought but what still is to be thought. It is not simply material to be learned or written about in literary histories but to be understood and learned from, even in worlds remote from that of the work's origin.

This mediative function belongs especially to what is written—world literature, great books. Even architecture, like other remnants and relicts of the past, suffers time and decay in a way that literature does not. A book can be erased, defaced, or destroyed, but it can also be copied; and it is no less the

---

41. This influence is clearest in the *Rezeptionsgeschichte* of Jauss. Warning points out that "Jauss's application of Gadamer's a-methodical hermeneutics to literary theory has taken effect precisely as the offering of a method" (*Rezeptionsästhetik*, p. 24). The very fact that the a-methodical notion of *Wirkungsgeschichte* in Gadamer becomes a reception-historical method in Jauss, however, may suggest that Grimm is correct to write that Gadamer's "position is in no way that of reception aesthetics" (*Rezeptionsgeschichte*, p. 128). Yet Bohler argues that Gadamer himself did not know what he was about: "Gadamer cannot conceive what he does himself, . . . namely to develop the framework for a method of explicative historical interpretation" (Fuhrmann et al., ed., *Text und Applikation*, p. 500).

42. I am thinking in particular of Dewey's *Art as Experience*.

43. MacIntyre explains, "Gadamer is involved in an argument against a view of aesthetic experience which has haunted us for nearly two hundred years: the isolated self reading the isolated text" ("Contexts of Interpretation," p. 43).

same book in the ten-thousandth copy than in the holograph, because every word in the original is itself a copy, otherwise it is not a word. Writing shows most clearly that "reproduction is in truth the *original* mode of being of all transitory arts" (153 / 143).[44] The very directness of written tradition, the immediacy and permanence of what the written past says to the present, depends on the fact that the immediacy of comprehension through voice and gesture has been broken, interrupted, and diverted into an alien medium that in itself is incomprehensible and meaningless.[45] An old building suffers decay; but an old book is quite meaningless, dead, indeed not a book at all, until it is revitalized in interpretation. Yet that very alienation of voice into the meaninglessness of writing is the indispensable condition of the fact that the past returns more present to us in literature than in the architecture that survives uninterrupted from the same period. In great books the past does not live still but rather again, and the more fully for being interrupted. Books are not a direct expression of mind then, but an indirect one. Indirection is the condition of our most direct access to history, as death is the price of resurrection.

Once we have begun to think of great books, however, we have already gone beyond the boundaries of what can properly be called art. As a work of architecture is not primarily a work of art, still less is the greatness of a great book confined to its aesthetic qualities or even to its being an artwork. The canon of great books, however defined, includes religious, historical, philosophical, economic, political books, and books of many other kinds that can be called art only if we concur with Gadamer that art is itself more than art. If art is knowledge as well, then it will seem less aberrant to speak of the literature on photosynthesis or quasars, for literature is the place where art and science meet and merge.

Though literature comprehends everything written, however, not all literature is world literature certainly, and not all books are great books. Yet a book of world literature is great quite regardless of whether it is otherwise classed as art or knowledge, and it cannot be denied its greatness even if it presents knowledge about art. Johnson's *Lives of the Poets* is a great book no less, and often more, than the books of the very poets he writes about. Given the comprehensiveness of literature, even of world literature, it becomes difficult, and ultimately impossible, to distinguish categorically between literary art and the history, the science, the literature of it. But if we cannot differentiate great books from the

44. For a similar thesis, see Derrida, "The Supplement of (at) the Origin," in *Of Grammatology*, pp. 313–16.

45. In privileging the immediate comprehensibility of voice over the mediate comprehensibility of writing, Gadamer clearly is most liable to the charge of what Derrida calls logocentrism.

great books written about them, then in this respect too aesthetic differentiation breaks down. Art and the knowledge of it are reunited in that art is more than art, and that "more" is knowledge. Art history is not merely knowledge *about* art, then; it is also knowledge *of* art when art's own knowledge is presented in it.

Art's own history, whether it is the history of literary art or not, is conveyed in great books and small. All history of art, and all history generally, is literature; and though in this section literature is discussed only briefly and in passing, that is because the remainder of *Truth and Method* is concerned with understanding it.

(1.2.2.D) "The classical discipline that has to do with the art of understanding texts is hermeneutics" (157 / 146). But if hermeneutics was once an ancillary discipline concerned with facilitating the understanding of religious and literary texts, it is in Gadamer's conception neither ancillary nor limited to books. Understanding belongs essentially to every kind of art in that all art exists in and as interpretation. The original, the work, and the reproduction are representations, and representations represent something only insofar as they are again represented and interpreted. The artwork is an understanding that, like all understanding, exists only in being understood; and insofar as hermeneutics is especially concerned with understanding, it is a discipline ancillary neither to literary aesthetics nor to aesthetics in general. Rather, quite the opposite, "aesthetics must dissolve into hermeneutics" (157 / 146).

This assertion is not merely a polemical proposal for rearranging the hierarchy of disciplines by redefining their domains or absorbing one into another. There is clearly a kind of global imperialism, a Hegelian ambition to universality, built into hermeneutics, which is evident in the way it appropriates other disciplines. But though we need to acknowledge the impulse to appropriation and thus be on the watch for flattening and homogenization, yet too it is important to recognize that such appropriation is not merely a by-product of hermeneutics, as it is of semiotics, another pretender to the throne vacated by philosophy as queen of disciplines. Assimilation and integration are not merely side effects of hermeneutics but its raison d'être. Hermeneutics exists precisely to appropriate aesthetics. The given of hermeneutics is a "consciousness of loss and alienation with respect to tradition" (158 / 147), a sense that one's own history and consequently one's own self-identity have been ruptured; and in response to this sense of disintegration and fragmentation, hermeneutics endeavors to reintegrate and assimilate. With respect to the tradition of art, aesthetic differentiation— the differentiation of art from non-art, from the world, from time, and from us, that creates aesthetics itself—is one symptom of the loss and disintegration that hermeneutics exists to repair. The assimilation of difference—of aesthetic difference, as of any other—is not just the purpose of hermeneutics, but its essence as well.

"Yet hermeneutics, conversely, must be so determined as a whole that it does justice to the experience of art" (157 / 147). One element of that experience, and one essential to it, is that art can be framed: it can be estranged from its world, and has been. "For art and literature which are handed down to us from the past are torn from their original world" (158 / 148). They are already self-estranged, different from what they were; and the question is whether hermeneutic assimilation means that the difference vanishes, ideally at least, with the dissolution of aesthetics, or whether that disappearance would actually be an affirmation of aesthetics and of what Gadamer calls aesthetic indifference—that is, the simultaneity of aesthetic consciousness to all times and the ability to look at anything aesthetically, without regard to its truth.

Schleiermacher takes the position that if a tradition has become unintelligible because it is estranged from its original context, the task of hermeneutics is to reconstruct that context and reestablish that world. It is necessary to amass historical knowledge about the artist, the original audience, and the situation to which the work was tailored. In this way Schleiermacher hopes to recreate the circumstances and processes of its creation, and thus return directly to the past as it originally was. Is this the return we have long been considering? Gadamer calls it the explication of the unintelligible by appeal to the dead. Times change, Gadamer insists; death is real, and the historical reconstruction of a once living world gives it only a conceptual, imaginary life. The reconstructed original is no longer original, and reconstruction itself embodies the alienation it was meant to overcome. The ability to view everything aesthetically (as simultaneous) or historically (by a return to the past) is an indifference to time; yet time and difference are not to be denied. What is lost to the past is permanently lost, and the passing of time opens up a fissure that precludes any direct return.

The advantage of Hegel's hermeneutics over Schleiermacher's in this respect is that Hegel affirms difference as the condition of, rather than the obstacle to, assimilation and appropriation. The artwork or other work of tradition has been irremediably torn from its original world as fruit plucked from a tree. It is no longer part of that organic unity as it once was, and it cannot be replaced on the tree by historical reconstruction. Unless we are to let it rot, there is nothing to do but to eat the fruit, and its difference and separation from what it once was is just what makes possible its assimilation, its becoming part of us. For Hegel, this process involves integration to a more comprehensive unity, ultimately that of philosophy as a form of absolute mind that discovers in its own thought the truth of aesthetics, even while surpassing it. For philosophy, "the historical attitude of imaginative projection changes into a thinking attitude to the past" (161 / 150). Even if Gadamer does not conceive hermeneutics as progressing toward the higher unity of philosophy, even if no ultimate synthesis is possible because of the finitude of mind and the reality of time and difference, yet Gadamer affirms that "Hegel states a decisive truth in that the essence of historical spirit consists not in the restitution of the past but rather in thoughtful mediation with present life" (161 / 150).

Mediation between past and present preserves the difference even as the two are assimilated to each other, for mediation implies that there is no immediate access, no direct return, and no turning back time. There is return, however, through the indirection of representation. Torn from its original world, tradition now differs from itself and only represents what it once was. Yet it is its own self-representation; and this self-representation based on self-difference is what now makes the past immediately accessible to us. The past lives only in the life of the present; the past exists only *as* present and *as* it is represented. It is / not what it was. The media of accessibility are our own representations, no doubt, but they are nonetheless a continuation of the *self*-representations of tradition that is occasioned by difference from the original context. Our representations repeat that difference and affirm that distance, and yet since it is the past's own difference that we repeat and continue, we are already at one with it. If the past lives at all, it lives in our own self-representations.

Insofar as historicism from Schleiermacher to Dilthey and beyond can be described as the endeavor to keep ourselves out of the past or to separate the past from the present so as to understand it objectively, as it once was, historicism too is a mode of differentiation and alienation. No less than aesthetics, it too is in need of hermeneutic assimilation. Thus to the critique of historicism Gadamer now turns.

2

The Critique of Historicism

"I am absolutely convinced, quite simply, that we have something to learn from the classics" (512 / 490). This, in brief, is the first and last principle of Gadamer's hermeneutics. It is the fundamental presupposition of *Truth and Method*, and toward its legitimation all Gadamer's arguments tend. That we have something to learn means plainly that we have not yet achieved full knowledge, of either our world or ourselves. There is something outstanding still to be disclosed. And that we have something to learn specifically from the classics means that advancing into the future in order to remedy the deficiencies of the present will necessitate turning to the past. We do not get over the classics or beyond them, because what we have to learn from the past is not merely what someone once thought and did. It is not something that once was but rather still is true. We have something true to learn from history, and any theory of historical interpretation that tends to ignore, repress, or repudiate that truth arouses Gadamer's suspicion. Repudiation of the truth claim of the past constitutes explicit or implicit self-aggrandizement, and it explains not how interpretation is rightly to be performed but rather why it need not be undertaken at all.

That the present has something true to learn from the past involves the tripartite structure of mediation. Past and present are mediated and integrated by what is true. This implies that there is no access to the past that does not presuppose its truth claim. It does not imply that truth is located in the past, for

133

the truth claim of the past is that what it has to say concerns and addresses the present too. If it does not, it is simply not true. Moreover, if the truth of the past is not located in the past, the historian, in searching for it, does not leave the present in order to reconstruct history as it once was. For if the truth that we have to learn from the past is necessarily something that concerns the present too—if in fact it is something *we* have to learn—then any suspension or repression of the present is finally a denial of the past's claim to be true. The surprising conclusion that Gadamer draws is that historical reconstruction of the past as past—that is, reconstruction as opposed to mediation with the present—is the falsification of history. More positively formulated: we have access to the past only as mediated by its truth claim, and since that claim is a claim on us as well, our sole access to the past is through what the present shares or can share with it. Our present, our difference from the past, is not the obstacle but the very condition of understanding the past in its truth, and this truth is at least in part that the past to which we have access is always our own past by reason of our belonging to it.

HOW HISTORY BECAME ART

(2.1.1.A) In this and the following sections (2.1–3), we should keep in mind that in reviewing the history of hermeneutics, Gadamer is himself writing a history, namely his own. As he considers the rise of hermeneutics and its application to history from the Reformation to the twentieth century, he is guided by this salient prejudice, that the present has something true to learn from the past. Just as the critique of aesthetics is grounded on the premise that art can be true as well as beautiful, so also the cutting edge of Gadamer's critique of historicism is to be found in the premise that not just art history but history in general is a source of truth.

Since Gadamer follows Hegel rather than Schleiermacher and thus emphasizes mediation rather than reconstruction, Gadamer's history of hermeneutics looks somewhat different from Dilthey's. As we will see in detail below, Gadamer shows that historical hermeneutics, despite its rebellion against Hegel, was not finally able to escape his influence. More immediately relevant is that Gadamer is not able or willing to plot the history of hermeneutics in Dilthey's way, as the gradual emancipation of interpretation from dogma. Gadamer's disagreement with Dilthey consists not simply in the fact that such an emancipation never occurred in his view, nor even in the fact that it never could occur. Rather, Gadamer suggests that even if interpretation had in fact been liberated from dogma, it would not have been the climactic emancipation that Dilthey thought but rather the crippling of interpretation itself.

Dogmatic interpretation in the pejorative sense is forced interpretation, and insofar as this means false interpretation Gadamer is hardly concerned to defend it. Yet if *forced* implies that we are compelled to accept an interpretation, this actually says nothing about whether the interpretation is right or wrong. And even if dogmatic interpretation were always wrong, we would still need to ask what we are forced by. By what are we compelled to give a particular interpretation to a particular text? By a tradition of interpretation, a dogma, we can answer. It is not at all clear, however, that traditional interpretations are ipso facto mistaken, nor is it even clear that their force is extrinsic to the text. But perhaps dogmatic interpretation implies not so much that we are forced into an interpretation as that we force an interpretation onto the text. Again we need to ask, what drives us to do so? This force is the pressure to understand the text as true—that is, as commensurate with truth as we know it. We integrate the text with our beliefs and our dogmas, with our traditions of interpretation. For better or worse (and it is not always for worse), dogmatic interpretation is a process of integration because it accepts the truth claim of the text; and even when such interpretation rejects what the text says as false, its truth *claim* is thereby vindicated.[1]

Indeed only by forcing our dogmas on the text can our dogmas themselves be tested and, when necessary, be falsified. The attempt to emancipate interpretation obstructs the work of integration that is the raison d'être of interpretation and the condition of our access to the past. It divorces past from present by dividing the truth of the interpretation from the truth of what it interprets, and in the name of adequacy it strips interpretation of its rationale. By contrast, dogmatic interpretation is the endeavor to understand the past as still true, still in force, and such interpretation automatically gives rise to false interpretations only if the past is itself false, no longer in force, a dead relict from which we have nothing to learn. Strange as it may sound, Gadamer considers dogmatic interpretation in certain respects unavoidably necessary and even desirable.[2]

When Luther defends the principle of *sola scriptura* against the Tridentine theologians' insistence on the necessity of tradition to understanding, he disavows dogmatic interpretation in the first sense—that is, being forced into an interpre-

---

1. Gadamer makes this explicit in *Rhetorik und Hermeneutik*, p. 12.
2. I do not mean to deny that in other respects Gadamer considers dogmatic interpretation as very nearly the cardinal sin of interpretation, in that it attempts to fix the meaning of a text or event, render it static, and remove it from history.

tation by a dogmatic tradition, namely that of the church fathers. Yet he resists their authority precisely because he affirms dogmatic interpretation in the second sense, for he certainly aims to understand Scripture as true. The question is whether these two can be separated. Luther's principle is that Scripture is to be interpreted of and through itself according to its literal sense. But this sense is not immediately accessible in every part; and thus to arrive at it, the part must be understood in terms of the meaning of the whole. Such a procedure of understanding assumes that the Bible is itself a whole, however; and this assumption derives its legitimacy solely from the same patristic tradition that Luther otherwise means to abandon. In this and other respects, it was not difficult for Dilthey to show that Reformation hermeneutics did not entirely emancipate itself from tradition and dogmatic bias, and that was no doubt the case.

In Dilthey's view, it is not enough that the part be read in terms of the whole. The emancipation of interpretation from the dogma of the unity of Scripture requires that Scripture, like any other text, be read within the larger historical context of its composition. Not the individual text, then, but rather the totality of history is for Dilthey the whole relative to which each element finds its meaning. Thus he conceives the historian as a kind of omnicomprehensive philologist who deciphers the great book of history, whereas others, more specialized, see only a part and not the whole. We must ask, however, what guarantees the wholeness of history? Is it clear that history itself comprises a unity more integral than any text? And is it possible that Dilthey is himself dogmatically guided by unacknowledged (Hegelian) traditions in his unitary conception of history?

In any case, it is evident that for Dilthey hermeneutics comes into its own only when it frees itself from bondage to dogma and emerges as a historical organon, a prejudice-free method. For theology, this liberation from the truth claim of the past means that interpretation of Scripture is no longer proclamation of the kerygma; and for philology, it means that interpretation of the classics is no longer imitation and emulation, for the classics have lost their significance as exemplary models. In ceasing to serve dogma and becoming a universal organon of interpretation, hermeneutics exceeds it former function as a mere guide to understanding, one that helps it over occasional problems and obstacles. The increasing generality of hermeneutics implies that not just particular passages or texts but understanding itself has become problematical; and thus hermeneutic theory, beginning with Schleiermacher, set itself the task of determining what makes understanding possible in general, regardless of the sphere in which it is to operate.

Schleiermacher seeks the basis of understanding in something that is common to both theology and classical philology, and he locates it not where the

Christian humanists did, in the shared content of classical and Christian culture. Rather he locates it in a shared procedure of understanding, apart from any content.[3] This procedure or method comes into play whenever the possibility of misunderstanding arises, and for Schleiermacher the possibility of misunderstanding is universal. The distance and alienation that prevent immediate understanding and foster misunderstanding are not confined to written texts composed in the distant past; they obtain in conversation as well. The alienation of historical distance in Schleiermacher's view is merely a special instance of the more general, indeed universal, alienation of I and Thou.[4] The rationale for constructing a universal theory of understanding is the universal possibility of misunderstanding that is the consequence of human individuality. In emphasizing the alienation brought about by individuality, Schleiermacher manifests his rejection of the idea that human beings share a common nature. So too common sense and common belief cannot guide understanding or provide the foundation of its possibility. For Schleiermacher, then, understanding does not mean finding a common sense or sharable content; understanding consists rather in determining how the other has arrived at his opinion by reconstructing its genesis.

In this respect, Gadamer suggests, Schleiermacher has misunderstood understanding from the ground up. "We begin with this proposition: understanding means, first of all, understanding one another. Understanding is first of all having come to a mutual understanding. People understand one another immediately for the most part, or they communicate until they reach unity and agreement. Understanding, then, is always coming to an understanding about something" (168 / 158). For Schleiermacher, by contrast, understanding is not understanding one another: it is one's understanding the other—unilaterally. It is not coming to an understanding regarding a topic of common concern, but rather understanding the other regardless of what he is concerned with. This describes what understanding must be like when misunderstanding is taken as a basic premise.

---

3. Habermas's own program is not far removed from Schleiermacher's content-free hermeneutics. Habermas writes, "The task of universal pragmatics is to identify and reconstruct universal conditions of possible understanding" ("What is Universal Pragmatics?" in *Communication and the Evolution of Society*, p. 1). "Habermas, in his universal pragmatics," Misgeld writes, "wants to determine apriori what discourse is to be without attending to what may be topical in it [i.e., what the discourse is about]. The latter is for him a contingent matter. Ordinary language communication is construed to be *theoretic* from the beginning" ("Discourse and Conversation," p. 328).

4. Compare Betti: "In short, whenever something from the mind of an Other approaches us there is a call on our ability to understand" ("Hermeneutics as the General Methodology of the *Geisteswissenschaften*," in Bleicher, ed., *Contemporary Hermeneutics*, p. 53.)

Put simply, when after repeated attempts, you and I fail to come to an understanding concerning a common topic, then it is no longer a shared concern: what you are saying will come to seem merely your opinion. In trying to understand your opinion as such, I do not endeavor to understand it by reference to the subject matter being discussed, the common object that concerns me too. Instead I try to determine how you could have arrived at such an opinion. I attempt to discover the process by which you have come to believe such an idea or your motivation for expressing it.[5] I am no longer concerned with content but with genesis and motivation—not with what you mean but instead with the fact that you mean it. Even if I succeed in reconstructing the psychological process and motives that led you to this opinion, however, I may have understood you, but I still will not have come to an understanding concerning the subject matter. Reconstruction of the other in his otherness and apart from what he means is not the procedure of understanding that Schleiermacher thought; quite the contrary, it is in Gadamer's view the abandonment of the attempt to come to an understanding, to reach a shared meaning on a topic of common concern.[6] Positing the alterity of the other is a symptom of the failure of understanding,

5. Similarly R. D. Laing concludes, "If one is listening to another person talking, one may either (a) be studying verbal behaviour in terms of neural processes and the whole apparatus of vocalizing, or (b) be trying to understand what he is saying. In the latter case, an explanation of verbal behaviour in terms of the general nexus of organic changes . . . is no contribution to a possible understanding of what the individual is saying. Conversely, an understanding of what the individual is saying does not contribute to a knowledge of how his brain cells are metabolizing oxygen" (*The Divided Self*, p. 20). What Laing says of physiological understanding, that it does not help us to understand what the individual is saying, could also be argued for psychological understanding.

6. Baumann recalls one of Popper's anecdotes that is perfectly apropos here: "On one occasion Sir Karl Popper told his audience a story which had obviously shaken him. It concerned an anthropologist invited to join some other first-class brains in discussing an important matter in the methodology of science. At the end of long and heated argument, to which the anthropologist listened in silence, he was asked to express his view. Much to the dismay of everybody present, the anthropologist replied that he paid little attention to the actual content of the dispute. The content was, he thought, the least interesting of what he saw and heard. Of incomparably greater interest were other things: how the debate was launched, how it developed, how one intervention triggered off another and how they fell into sequences, how the contributors determined whether they were in disagreement, etc. Our anthropologist, presumably, viewed the topic which aroused so much passion as just one of those 'native beliefs' whose truth or falsity is largely irrelevant for a scholarly study. This was why he was not particularly interested in the topic. Instead, he recorded with genuine interest the interaction in which the learned experts engaged and which the declared topic of the discussion 'occasioned.'

"Sir Karl was, of course, indignant. For him statements are about something, and are to be judged, in this way or another, by being tested against this something. Whatever importance they may have arises from the degree of exactitude and veracity with which they grasp the subject of

not the principle of its success. For Gadamer, understanding is com-munication: it is either the expression of a common sense regarding a common concern or else the attempt to reach such a commonality.

Schleiermacher's hermeneutic theory, based on individuality, itself displays the very disintegration and alienation that understanding is constantly in the process of overcoming. Schleiermacher ignores the fact that understanding does indeed overcome alienation because his theory ultimately denies both the final purpose of understanding and the condition of its possibility—namely the formation and existence of communal traditions. Schleiermacher looks rather to method.

Spinoza seems to anticipate Schleiermacher in that he too suggests that in order to comprehend unintelligible passages in Scripture we need to understand the mind of the author. We do not use our own reason but rather empty our minds of prejudice in order to understand what the author, not we, had in mind. Whether the author's meaning corresponds with our own opinion does not matter since we are concerned only to determine the sense of his statements, not their truth. Yet clearly for Spinoza not all passages of Scripture are unintelligible, and the method he describes is local, not universal as it is for Schleiermacher. It comes into play only where immediate understanding breaks down; only where Scripture cannot immediately be understood as true does one proceed via history. So too for Chladenius interpretation is an occasional rather than a universal necessity. One interprets historical works only when one does not understand them—that is, interpretation and understanding are not the same; and interpretation remains an exceptional activity. When we do interpret, however, our criterion, according to Chladenius, is not the author's meaning "but instead the books themselves in their true significance, that is with respect to their content" (172 / 162). The books can mean more than their authors intended and it requires the interpretive occasion to bring out this surplus. But even where he limits meaning to the author's intention, Chladenius does not differentiate that intention from the truth.[7]

---

which they speak. When confronted with a statement, Sir Karl would presumably consider the 'immanent interpretation' the only worthy way of dealing with it. He would try to extract from the sentence the message it contained, and then attempt to put the truth of the message to the test.

"Sir Karl perhaps was not aware that the odd behaviour of this unnamed anthropologist would soon become the paramount rule of a powerful school of sociological theory and research" (*Hermeneutics and Social Science*, p. 172).

7. Currently, the reliance on authorial intention as the criterion of correct interpretation is not at all limited to Betti and Hirsch, its most notable proponents. See also the items listed in the bibliography by Juhl, Altieri, Skinner, and Cavell.

How radical a break Schleiermacher made with the pre-history of hermeneutics can be appreciated by considering the ways in which he differs from Spinoza and Chladenius. Whereas unintelligibility for Spinoza is an occasional problem that motivates an excursion into the historical and for Chladenius one that requires renewed attention to the object being discussed, Schleiermacher considers unintelligibility as the norm, and the detour into the historical as a permanent necessity. This detour, moreover, is directed not to the object of joint concern but rather to the subjectivity of the speaker or writer. Since for Schleiermacher misunderstanding is the norm and since the possibility of misunderstanding is what necessitates interpretation, understanding and interpretation are indivisible. They are not two acts but one. Interpretation is the art of avoiding the misunderstanding that follows automatically from every unregulated attempt to understand, for understanding fails naturally and of its own. Thus it needs assistance from a canon of interpretive regulations. These rules apply regardless of whether the content of what one interprets is true or false, profound or trivial, for they apply regardless of whether it is intelligible. They apply universally.

Schleiermacher develops a universal hermeneutics by isolating the process of understanding from what is understood and by dividing the understanding of others' meanings from dialectic, the understanding of the things, topics of discourse. Thus for him, what is to be understood is conceived not as a truth but as part of another's life, an expression of the individuality of the author, which requires psychological (as well as grammatical) reconstruction and explication in order to ascertain how this one utterance, this one part of the author's life, is integrated with the whole. Psychological interpretation "is ultimately a divinatory procedure, a placing oneself inside the whole outlook of the author, a comprehension of the 'inner emergence' of the composition of a work, a re-creation of the creative act" (175 / 164).[8]

Schleiermacher's hermeneutic is directed toward reproducing the production of an expression and not to what the expression means—its content—because he considers expression as an aesthetic form. In this respect Schleiermacher follows Kant's suggestion that the work of art is a free construction of subjec-

---

8. Collingwood seems close to Schleiermacher when he writes, "It is peculiar to history that the historian re-enacts in his own mind the thoughts and motives of the agents whose actions he is narrating." Yet the difference becomes clear when Collingwood explains what that reenactment involves: "The historian not only re-enacts past thought, he re-enacts it in the context of his own knowledge and therefore, in re-enacting it, criticizes it, forms his own judgment of its value, corrects whatever errors he can discern in it. This criticism of the thought whose history he traces is not something secondary to tracing the history of it. It is an indispensable condition of the historical knowledge itself" (*Idea of History*, pp. 115, 215).

tivity, unlimited by the object it represents. All expressions in Schleiermacher's view possess this aesthetic quality, and thus they are to be understood by reference not to what is thought in them but to the free subjectivity of the speaker or writer. That is, they are to be understood by psychological analysis. The cognitive value of aesthetic expressions is minimal, and so the criterion for interpreting them is not agreement between author and interpreter concerning a common object but rather psychological reconstruction of the genius of the author, whose individuality is conceived as being opposed to that of the interpreter. The interpreter is not attempting to understand himself or his world, or even both his own life and that of the author, but solely what the author had in mind and how it came to be there. Even if such reconstruction succeeds, however, the interpreter has already given up trying to understand any truth that pertains to him as well. In that respect, psychological understanding always fails.

Schleiermacher applies the part–whole principle not only to grammatical but also to psychological interpretation. Not only must every grammatical unit be understood in terms of the context of the whole utterance, but the utterance too must be understood against the backdrop of the author's whole mental life. If the whole is not to be prescribed beforehand by some dogmatically imposed limit, the process of interpretation will be infinite—that is, at any given moment, provisional. Yet Schleiermacher does envision a state of complete understanding made possible by the miracle of divination, when the individuality of the author becomes wholly clear because the interpreter has transposed himself into the author's horizon. Although the genius of the author is unique and cannot be subsumed under any other framework, yet it becomes intelligible by reason of the corresponding genius of the interpreter. His is the genius of divination, of the sudden insight that permits transposition into the mind of the author. Interpretive divination is the art that makes accessible the otherness of the author without assimilation to the interpreter—that is, without comparison or appeal to any common nature that unites them.

Although divination involves the reproduction of a production, these two—creation and re-creation—are not identical. How far they are different is apparent in Schleiermacher's formula: the end of interpretation is to understand the author better than he understood himself (180 / 169). Since expression is the creation of genius, it is primarily unconscious production; and because re-creation depends on the principles of the initial production being rendered explicit to the interpreter, the process of reproduction will be more conscious—and in that sense "better" understood—than was the original production.

To a certain extent Gadamer concurs: "The doctrine of genial production performs an important theoretical task in that it abolishes the difference between interpreter and originator'' (181 / 170). The author, conceived as an unconscious genius, does not understand himself at all, and thus his self-understanding cannot be the criterion of correct interpretation. He is merely one among many interpreters, all of whom are on a par. Yet for Gadamer precisely this equality of authority precludes any talk of "better" understanding on the part of the interpreter, just as it does on the part of the author.[9] The superiority of the interpreter claimed by Schleiermacher seems to Gadamer an unwarranted self-aggrandizement, and one that is quite new to hermeneutics, even though the formula had appeared before Schleiermacher. Humanists had always tried to imitate, emulate and even surpass the classics; but they did so because they conceived these works as exemplary models, as paradigms of content as well as form—that is, as purveyors of the truth of things. The self-confidence displayed in Schleiermacher's formula, however, derives from the fact that his hermeneutics was to be applied not only to the classics and Scripture with their normative claims but also to everything else—to expressions that possessed no claim to truth nor even to meaning. In becoming universal, hermeneutics became a method—that is, independent of content. Not even Schleiermacher would have claimed the superiority of the interpreter's understanding with respect to a content, the matter being discussed; but since, if hermeneutics is to be universal, it must ignore content and focus on free unconscious production not limited by the truth of the object discussed, it was easy for Schleiermacher to be betrayed into the smugness his formula expresses.

How immense was the significance of Schleiermacher's move from a local and occasional hermeneutics to a universal one can be seen in the fact that in liberating interpretation from dogma and tradition and converting it into an independent procedure, Schleiermacher aims at an undogmatic interpretation of scriptural dogma and an untraditional interpretation of classical tradition. But this means that the truth of dogma and of tradition is denied by the very procedure that is designed to promote their correct interpretation. "Neither the saving truth of holy scripture nor the exemplariness of the classics should influence a procedure that could grasp the expression of life in every text and leave undecided

---

9. On the question of "better" understanding, Ricoeur writes, "This link between disclosure and appropriation is, to my mind, the cornerstone of a hermeneutic which would claim both to overcome the shortcomings of historicism and to remain faithful to the original intention of Schleiermacher's hermeneutics. To understand an author better than he could understand himself is to display the power of disclosure implied in his discourse beyond the limited horizon of his own existential situation" ("The Model of the Text," *Social Research* 38 (1971): 558). If "better" is defined in this way, Gadamer and Ricoeur are not far apart, though Gadamer resists the implications of progress connoted by any notion of "better understanding."

the truth of what it said" (185 / 173). But isn't it this truth that motivates interpretation in the first place? Is it really necessary to make hermeneutics so universal that it is possible to conceive of its highest achievement as the true interpretation of falsehoods and the sensible interpretation of nonsense? This certainly is what the notion of "better understanding" leads to. But just as certainly that is not how Schleiermacher, himself a theologian, conceived of biblical interpretation. It is much more plausible to infer that he is willing to leave undecided the truth of Scripture precisely because he takes this truth as a given, as a dogma or tradition prior to interpretation and directing it. And that, Gadamer suggests, is the case with any interpreter. No text can be understood in itself and apart from tradition. Even Scripture may not be true, of course, but the irony is that Schleiermacher's theory actually falsifies in practice what it would understand because it suspends, as a matter of methodological principle, not just the truth of the text but its truth claim. This, ultimately, is the effect of psychological interpretation.

(2.1.1.B) Schleiermacher's hermeneutics is designed to understand particular texts and focuses on them. It brings in the larger historical context only to serve that end, and this fact points up the limits of its universality. The situation of the historian is reversed relative to that of the philologist, for to him history is not a means to the understanding of individual texts but rather the text is a means to the understanding of history as a whole and has no value in itself. In this respect Schleiermacher's hermeneutic was too limited to serve as the basis for constructing a universal history.

Yet there is nonetheless a continuity between the romantic hermeneutics of Schleiermacher and the historical school. The particular text can be used to construct the whole of history because it is part of that whole, just as a sentence is part of a text. This means, as Dilthey saw, that universal history is a realizable ideal because "not only are the sources encountered as texts, but history itself is a text to be understood" (186 / 174). History is textualized by historicism. The resistance of the historical school to Hegel's teleological view of history in terms of an end, climax, or fullness of history involved the premise that, contrary to Hegelian thought, there is no standpoint outside history from which to understand it. History, the historians insisted, can be understood only from within. But this is the premise of philological hermeneutics as well: a text becomes intelligible only in the oscillating attention between its whole and its parts—that is, only intrinsically and not by reference to anything outside it.[10] The resistance

10. Cf. Betti's "canon of the hermeneutical autonomy of the object" (in Bleicher, ed., *Contemporary Hermeneutics*, p. 58).

of universal world history to Hegelian philosophy thus drove hermeneutics into the wake of philology (186 / 175).[11]

Yet if history is a text writ large, what kind of wholeness does it have? A novel or a poem has a beginning and an end, a biography starts with a birth and concludes with a death, and the history of a bygone civilization also has a stopping place. But what marks the unity and completeness of universal history such that it could be meaningful or intelligible in itself? Is there any whole of history within the context of which a part could be definitively understood? Hegel could answer these questions because he conceived of history as coming to an end and fruition in the realization of the Idea in history, in the transparency of spirit to itself. But if in fact history ever did come to such an end, that would put the historians out of business as it were. There would no longer be any reason to study history because the Hegelian fruition of history consists in the fact that its ''lessons'' have already been learned. Thus the resistance to Hegel left historians in somewhat of a quandary: insofar as the truths of history are still to be learned, history is necessarily incomplete; yet only insofar as it is whole can any part of it be ultimately understood. Thus the crucial problem for non-Hegelian universal history is how understanding is possible on the basis of a whole that is not given.

In rejecting Hegel's view of history as philosophy, as the realization of the Idea, Ranke, Droysen, and Dilthey argue that the Idea is never fully or perfectly represented in history. It achieves no final conceptual clarity of expression and thus no independence from the circumstances in which it was expressed. Rather it remains inextricably bound to its context so that there is no understanding any idea without understanding its history—that is, without historical research.

There are, to be sure, ways of conceiving history teleologically other than Hegel's. Hegel sees history as a progress with the fullness of time coming at the end, but it is also possible to think of history as a regress and fall from a fullness located at the beginning. Winckelmann, in particular, employed the exemplariness of classical antiquity as a critique of the present which had fallen from ancient grandeur. But because in history he aimed to discover the particular character of Greek art and the causes of that particularity he came to see classical art not only as a standard but also as unique and unrepeatable, and hence discontinuous with the present. The present could not therefore duplicate the classical achievement even if it might want to. In that sense Winckelmann's classicism, like Hegel's idealism, invokes a standard for understanding history which lies

---

11. For evidence of the continuing influence of literary theory on theory of history, see Hayden White's *Metahistory* and *Tropics of Discourse*.

outside history—except that this standard is embodied "before" history rather than "after" it, as in Hegel.

Both exemplary and unrepeatable—this was Winckelmann's view of the classical heritage, and that of many after him. But to move beyond the humanist prejudice that favored the classics, it was necessary to conceive, as Herder did, of all epochs as "classical"—each with its own perfection. This democratization of excellence implies that history is plotted as neither rise nor fall. No period can be criticized by appeal to a standard embodied in its predecessors or successors, for each has its own unique value. "It is the fullness and multiplicity of the human which is increasingly realized in the ceaseless change of human fates. This basically is the way the fundamental premise of the historical school can be formulated" (189 / 178).

Yet there are two problems here. First, the idea of uniform excellence really empties excellence of any content. It is no longer excellence of quality but rather of quantity, for "at its basis lies the formal idea of the greatest multiplicity" (190 / 178). Between variety and value there is no necessary connection. Indeed the leveling of excellence is its elimination. Moreover, the emptiness of the formal ideal of plurality is evident in the fact that nothing can count against it, for everything counts as an instance of variety. The second problem is that whereas the universalization of history requires that every period be accorded a distinct value, yet this very insistence on variety renders problematic the unity of history. It seems that the price to be paid for universal history is its fragmentation into a multiplicity of discrete units.

Ranke addresses the problem of the coherence and continuity of history in this way: "Every truly world-historical deed . . . never consists solely in mere annihilation but rather, in the fleeting moment of the present, engenders something for the future" (190 / 178). That such deeds are future-oriented indicates that Ranke did not in fact stray far from Hegel, for both conceive the unity of history teleologically. But in Ranke's case, it is not an idea that is working itself out in history, and, moreover, his teleology is without a telos. The future that the world-historical deed engenders is not any particular point in time; rather this deed in a sense makes time. It is history-making in that it has a lasting effect (*Wirkung*) which both constitutes the deed's meaning and significance and allows the historian to understand an entire series of events as belonging to the history of that deed and hence as unified. Deeds which truly belong to world history are not merely historical but historic. The historic deed is consequential in both senses: it is significant and creates the unity of a sequence. It makes history and, what is the same, makes history coherent.

Even here Ranke is close to Hegel, for Hegel too speaks of historic individuals whose freely chosen actions determine the course of history. Ranke terms world-historical deeds "scenes of freedom," because freedom consists in power, and such deeds are of world-historical significance in that freedom is expressed in them as germinal power. But whose power is this? Ranke writes that "at the side of freedom stands necessity. It consists in what has already been formed, what cannot be overruled, and on this foundation all new activity arises. What has been constitutes the continuity with what will be" (192 / 180). Personal freedom is limited by necessity—that is, by the persistence and continuing effect of the past as it determines the situation and direction in which freedom is to be exercised. So also, if freedom is the power to engender a future, it will be limited by what is yet to come, for the future too is a form of necessity in that it necessitates changing one's plans and views. For Ranke, and Gadamer too, the fact that a deed is historic does not mean that it expresses the force of individual will, desire, and intention. It is not subjectivity that is the power in history. Thus we must ask again, what is the locus of this power? Hegel locates it in *Geist* (Mind, Spirit), but Ranke was not able to accept this proposal. For him the powers of history are political states: he calls them "real spiritual beings" and "thoughts of God" to show that they are not creatures of merely human design (194 / 182).

It is not at all clear how far Ranke really departs from Hegel even in this respect, however. What is clear is that the attempt to sidestep Hegel's reduction of history to a speculative concept drives anti-Hegelian historians into a self-conception that is at once theological and aesthetic. We have already touched on the first of these attributes. In that the historian is the one who thinks of states, it is he who thinks "the thoughts of God." This theological self-interpretation is confirmed when Ranke writes, "I think of the deity, . . . for whom there exists no time, as surveying all historical humanity in its totality and finding everything equally valuable" (198 / 185). Thus God himself is a historian—or is it the reverse? The historian too gazes over the whole of things and pronounces it good. "Thus the consciousness of the historian represents the perfection of human self-consciousness" (198 / 185). What history makes possible, what it awaits and prepares for, is the advent of the historian. Schleiermacher had spoken only of better understanding, but the understanding of Ranke's apotheosized historian is divine.

At the same time it is aesthetic. The consciousness of the historian to whom all times are equally good approximates the aesthetic consciousness that brings the art of all periods into simultaneity, so that it understands all works with equal facility and values them with equal magnanimity. As the aesthetic consciousness abstracts itself from its time, so also the historian tries, as Ranke said, to extinguish himself and to view all from above, impartially and *sub specie aeternitatis*. Thus Ranke conceives of the historian not only as god but also as an artist, a detached epic poet who sings the tale of world history omnisciently, from above—as if he himself were not an actor in it. This mixture of theology and aesthetics was the result of Ranke's attempt to escape Hegelian idealism. But, Gadamer asks, is not such a mixture precisely what Hegel called the religion of art, itself a form of absolute spirit?

Droysen sharpens and clarifies Ranke's position. Whereas Ranke's pantheism sees God as immediately present in all historical life and the historian as sharing by means of empathy directly in that life, Droysen discerns that such sharing is achieved not directly, through empathy, but indirectly, through research. And it is a sharing less with an omnipresent deity than with other egos, autonomous individuals. What makes these otherwise autonomous egos intelligible to a historian is that they express themselves—in language and in other forms of communal life such as family and community, church and state. As communal, such expressions are what make historical understanding possible because they are also the way in which the individual ego itself participates in history. Conceived of as private desire and intellect, the ego as such has not yet become historical. Thus specifically historical understanding requires neither an empathic understanding of individuals (Ranke) nor psychological interpretation (Schleiermacher), for the individual as such becomes an element in history only when he expresses himself, becomes active in the pursuit of the great common goals, and thus participates in what Droysen calls the moral powers of history. There are in a sense, then, no historic individuals since the individual does not become historic until he is no longer an individual. It is the attempt to understand the moral powers, the spheres of ethical commonality, that makes a historian, not an attention to other egos in their isolation.

Expression is intelligible first because it is already communal. But communal life is not merely the object of the historian: he must himself also participate in it. As the others whom he would understand become historical by their participation in common life, so must the historian raise himself above his own individuality. He achieves impartiality not by epic detachment, aesthetic abstraction, or self-extinction; rather he transcends his own particularity only by involving himself in the communal life of his own time and place—that is, in his own traditions. "By belonging to determinate spheres, of custom, of his native country, and of his political and religious convictions, the historian is defined and limited. But on just this insuperable one-sidedness depends his participation [in history]. His task of impartiality is set within the concrete conditions of his historical existence—not in being suspended above things" (202 / 190). Participation in, not suspension of, his own traditions is what makes understanding possible for the historian, not only because he thus rises above his own particularity but because these traditions, ultimately those of Western civilization, are in the last analysis one with those of the other egos that are to be understood. But even so, only *ultimately* are they one. Droysen stresses the infinity of research that is necessary for understanding. As Gadamer writes, ''The historian is divided from his object by the infinite mediation of tradition'' (204 / 191). The mediation that makes understanding possible also prevents it from being immediate.

But for Droysen, understanding always succeeds in the end. It succeeds because the historical is expression. As such, history makes sense; it is meaningful and intelligible. Moreover, hermeneutics, conceived of in Droysen's way, comes to dominate historical research. Droysen adopts Schleiermacher's maxim that the individual utterance is to be understood in terms of the whole, and the whole from the individual. And he does so because he shares Schleiermacher's assumption that history is as thoroughly understandable and intrinsically meaningful as a text, and that texts are the very symbol of intelligibility. In this respect Droysen too conceives of history only in terms of an aesthetic hermeneutics: the aim of the historian is to understand expression—the communal and communicable expressions of historical communities—but not things, not truth.

(2.1.2.A) In the work of Dilthey, the tension between this kind of aesthetic hermeneutics and Hegelian philosophy of history reaches its climax. Here it appears as a tension between experience and thought, empiricism and idealism, or most simply between life and truth. Just as Kant had provided a *Critique of Pure Reason*, so Dilthey wanted to provide a corollary critique of historical reason. Kant's purpose had been double: first to destroy the claim of metaphysics to a purely rational construction of nature (that is, without the aid of experience), and second to demonstrate the extent to which nature could be rationally understood—for example, in the mathematical constructions fundamental to natural science. Correlatively, Dilthey's positive intent was to defend and legitimate the claim of history to be a science. His critical intent was directed against Hegel, whom he conceived as the last in the long line of metaphysicians. In that Hegel discerned reason in everything, including history, he affirmed the universal commensurability of thought and thing, idea and being. The world is rational, and world history is the history of reason, the history of philosophy. History is intelligible to mind because it is a manifestation of mind. Against this purely rational construction of world history, then, Dilthey reasserted the necessity of experience. But this very reassertion rendered the intelligibility of history as problematical as the intelligibility of nature for natural science. ''If history is considered just as little a manifestation of mind as nature, then it is just as much a problem how the human mind is to know history as it had been to know nature through the constructions of the mathematical method'' (208 / 195). Thus the question that Dilthey needed to address was how experience could be the basis of a historical science—that is, how experience renders history intelligible.

Making history intelligible requires making it coherent. In Kantian terms, this is the requirement of synthesis and the application of unifying categories. But unlike Kant, Dilthey finds the commensurability of such categories with the historical world basically unproblematical. The synthetic understanding of history, as opposed to that of nature, is facilitated for two reasons. First, there is a coherence between the subject and object of history, and second, there is a coherence within the object of history—namely historical experience itself. For the first, Dilthey finds support in Vico's thesis that history is more intelligible than nature because it is man-made. As Dilthey writes, ''The first condition for the possibility of historical science consists in the fact that I myself am a historical being, that the one who studies history is the same as the one who makes history'' (208 / 196). This sentence is ambiguous. On the one hand, it means that the historian has the same kind of nature as the people he studies. This homogeneity of the subject and object of history makes historical science possible without necessitating the imposition of alien categories on the object. On the other hand, the sentence also means that the historian is himself historical, that he is himself making history whether or not he is making histories; and, as Gadamer later shows, the historian's own historicality renders Dilthey's science of history problematic at the same stroke with which it becomes possible.

The second coherence which in Dilthey's view allows the understanding of history is the intrinsic continuity within the object of historical study—that is, within experience. If the historian does not impose an alien unity on his material, that is because it is already unified. Dilthey takes the experience of the single individual as the basic object of historical investigation. If he can show that this experience is coherent, then the foundation of historical science will have been laid. This foundation consists not, as with the natural sciences, in atomic facts which must then be related, assembled, and so converted into meanings. Experience from the outset is the experience of meaning and connection. The continuity of an individual's life is not a causal sequence but rather a structure. It organizes itself around particularly significant experiences as a melody is organized around its motifs. An individual experiences the integrity and unity of his life not as a mere series of events in succession that must await its conclusion before it is whole. Rather he experiences it as a whole present in each part, as each part (like a symbol) belongs to the whole. It is the individual's own experience of this coherence that invites and permits the historian's application of the part–whole principle of exegesis. The meaning of the individual's life for him is also its meaning for the historian, for the historian "only thinks further what is already thought in the experience of life" (208 / 196). This continuity of thought is the basis of historical knowledge.

The problem with Dilthey's formulation in this respect is that the foundation thus constructed for historical science is too narrow. Though it may be true that the individual himself experiences meaning and that the historian can also experience that meaning, yet to make this meaningfulness the basis of history in general places a disproportionate emphasis on autobiography and biography. The historian is more than a biographer in that he is concerned with units larger than the individual life—with peoples and social institutions. Though these too may be wholes, their wholeness, coherence, and meaning are not experienced as such by anyone living in them. Only the historian can see the whole—but his special privilege in this respect breaks the continuity between the experience of the historian and the lived experience of the people he is writing about, and it was this continuity that was to legitimate historical knowledge epistemologically in the first place. The problem here is the transition from a psychological to a historical hermeneutic. To combat Hegel, Dilthey needed to assert that there was no transcendent subject experiencing history, only historical individuals. But now in order to explain the possibility of understanding the larger wholes that no historical individual can understand, Dilthey is forced to posit a "logical" subject of experience instead of actual individual subjects; and with that step he is forced back into speculative idealism. Indeed he had always been there, for the foundation of his historical theory is the identity of subject and object, which is the premise of idealism.

Dilthey found a confirmation and clarification of his views in Husserl's *Logical Investigations*. Husserl showed that consciousness itself is a relation in that it is always conscious of something. What Dilthey had before called structure, he now with Husserl calls significance. To say that experience is intrinsically significant is to say that it is not composed of atomic sense data subsequently integrated; rather relation is prior to the elements it relates and thus is not decomposable into them. For Dilthey, it followed from Husserl's *Investigations* that "life itself, this flowing temporality, is aimed at the formation of enduring units of significance" (212 / 199). Life makes meaning, and it makes thought. Thus he speaks of the "thought-forming work of life" (214 / 201). Yet insofar as the end of history is the production of ideas and concepts, he again embraces Hegelian history—that is, history conceived of as the emergence of mind. "Today we must begin with the reality of life," Dilthey insists in contrast to Hegel.

But when he comes to specify this reality as language, custom, family, and state, what Dilthey lists are precisely the institutions that for Hegel constitute objective mind.[12]

But, more, Dilthey includes art, religion, and philosophy among the products of life. For Hegel these are forms not of objective but of absolute spirit; and that means, most importantly, that they are forms of immediate truth. By bringing philosophy, along with art and religion, back into real life, Dilthey brings philosophy back under the aegis of history. It is not philosophy, then, that is the climactic form of absolute mind, but rather historicism. It is in the mind of the historian that the fullness and meaning of history is realized and embodied. "Even philosophy is considered only as an expression of life" (216 / 202). It is not knowledge but expression, and what it expresses is life. So too art and religion are conceived merely as especially transparent, especially expressive forms of life which are understood when they are translated back into the mental life from which they sprang. They are especially useful means for understanding life, and it is life that is to be understood. But who is it that understands life? Does not the reduction of philosophy, art, and religion to expressions of life mean that they are reduced to grist for the mill of the historian? They are means to an end that is the historian himself. What has raised the historian to this spurious eminence is the fact that he equates meaning with life but divorces life from truth. To return an idea to its origins, to reconstruct its genesis, is to deny its truth claim, which is also its claim to address the historian— at the very least at his own level, and perhaps above it.

But this is to imply that Hegel was essentially right: the only way to understand a historical expression truly is by leaving its truth claim intact, not by reconstructing its past, re-placing it in its original context, in the manner of Schleiermacher and Dilthey. It can be understood only if it is understood not only as an expression of life but also as an expression of truth; and to do so it must also be integrated with one's own thought, with the present and the future. In the attempt to escape Hegel's speculative metaphysics, which endeavored to view all history as history of thought, historicism viewed all thought as a form of history. But in elevating history above philosophy, the historicists succeeded only in turning history into art, specifically neo-Kantian art. Whereas Hegel had

---

12. Baumann quotes Mannheim to the same effect: "You may start with subjective motivations or personal intentions of a quite peculiar kind, but as soon as you take over a function in a given system of division of labor, or you act as a member of a family or a club, you will probably tend to act according to certain traditional patterns or rationally established rules" (*Hermeneutics and Social Science*, p. 98).

seen art too as a form of absolute spirit and hence as a form of truth, historicism sees history as expression and meaning but not as knowledge and truth. This is what neo-Kantian aesthetics says art is: the expression of life as divorced from truth. In rising above philosophy, history is reduced to aesthetics.

Even assuming (what Gadamer finds fundamentally incorrect) that the artwork is a free creation of the human mind, can history be understood in this way? Dilthey and Vico seem, in fact, to be seriously mistaken in their contention that history is man-made, that men make history in the way that an artist makes an artifact. It seems clear that history creates men as much as the reverse. But this idea too is included in Dilthey's principle that the historian is able to understand because he is himself historical. But isn't this historicality also a hindrance to objectivity? In Gadamer's words, "Must not the historical conditioning of consciousness present an insuperable limitation for the perfectability of historical knowledge? . . . Must not the constant change in the context of historical significance preclude a knowledge that attains objectivity?" (217 / 204).

(2.1.2.B) Dilthey thought not. His appeal to the notion of structure, as explicated above, implies, first, that historical experience can be understood in terms of itself and not by reference to some extrinsic standard and, second, that the part–whole schema can be universalized to apply to all historical study. The first of these possibilities implies that history does not keep changing and that the historian is not himself part of this change; the second implies (what is much the same) that the whole to be understood is fixed and determinate. It must be possible then for the historian to overcome the limits of his own historical situation; and in fact, according to Dilthey, it is precisely the historical sense that enables him to do so—to overcome his prejudices, to escape his particularity, and to understand everything, historically. Dilthey knew, of course, that historical understanding is in fact finite, yet he considered it in principle infinite. It is in principle possible for a historian of any time to understand any past whatsoever, because the limitations imposed on him by his own traditions, customs, and institutions are of a subjective nature only. That is, it is fundamentally possible to escape them and attain to a knowledge of the historical object in itself. The finitude of the historian is not a function of the kind of being he is but rather an accident of history, and a remediable one.

Finitude, according to Dilthey, is to be remedied by perfecting the historical sense, not by speculative philosophy. Whereas for Hegel, absolute knowledge comprehended the whole truth of history in a present self-consciousness, for any theory that would explain the necessity for study of the past, this infinity of the present must be denied. "The reason why it is necessary to learn from history is that human consciousness is no infinite intellect for which everything is equally contemporaneous and equally present (221 / 207). But the very fact that history is indispensable implies that "absolute identity of consciousness and object [that is, totally objective knowledge] is in principle unattainable for finite historical consciousness" (221 / 207). With respect to Hegel, Dilthey's quandary is this: insofar as human consciousness is infinite, the study of history is objective but unnecessary;[13] and insofar as consciousness is finite, the study of history is necessary but not objective.

In the end Dilthey does not solve this problem. His abiding concern with legitimating the objectivity of historical knowledge against the charge of relativism, specifically by showing how it is possible for the historian to escape his own history, could not ultimately lead anywhere but to a demonstration that history in general is escapable and its study therefore at some point dispensable. What makes historical objectivity possible in Dilthey's view is that histories are no longer a direct expression of history. They do not merely appropriate the past in the naive assimilation to the present typical of pre-historicist times. They do not simply carry on and hand down tradition. Rather the historian adopts a reflective, distanced attitude toward both his own traditions and those he studies. He is not only conscious but self-conscious, for historical objectivity both requires and makes possible the self-knowledge that makes objectivity possible.

If this reflective distance, the objective distance, is not to be an attitude that the historian merely imposes on history, Dilthey must show that reflection and historical self-consciousness arise in historical life itself. Like everything else, he argues, the objectivity that makes history a science is itself a product of history. Its beginnings can be glimpsed in proverbs and legends. In them wisdom has been given a fixed form, and they live a life independent of, and detached from, the minds of their creators. Here life objectivizes itself, makes itself objective. So too "in language, in custom, and in the forms of law, the individual has already raised himself above his particularity" (222 / 208). In these ways human life transcends itself as it strives for permanence, objectivity, certainty, and truth. Life strives toward science and self-detachment. Thus in detaching himself from life, the historical scientist is doing no more than life itself does.

It is clear that for Dilthey it is life itself that gives rise to truth. With this premise Gadamer is in profound agreement. Life overcomes its own relativity continually. But the fact that Dilthey keeps worrying about the problem of

---

13. Baumann comes to the same conclusion in *Hermeneutics and Social Science*, p. 231.

relativism indicates that he cannot ultimately accept the consequences of his own life philosophy in contrast to those of idealism; and that is partly because he remains committed to an earlier form of idealism, namely that of Descartes. On the one hand, as we have seen, life gives rise to certainty and truth; on the other, and this is no less central to Dilthey's thought, life must somehow get over itself to attain certain truth. The problem lies in this second premise. What certainty means here is what Descartes meant by it. The problem is not just that life leads to reflection, as in Gadamer's view as well, but that for Dilthey reflection leads everywhere to doubt.

Certainly some doubts arise of their own accord. But the universal reflectiveness of the historian amounts to universal doubt—that is, to the same suspension of the truth of history that we find in Descartes' first meditation. This kind of omnicomprehensive doubt is not a product of life but of method. For Descartes certainty results from suspending through doubt all that has been believed and from reconstructing the truth as what cannot be doubted. What is being suspended here? For the historian, "it is no longer philosophical prejudices which are to be overcome through epistemological grounding in the style of Descartes; instead it is the realities of life, the traditions of custom, religion, and positive law, which are destroyed by reflection and necessitate a new ordering" (224 / 210). The certainty of the historian, then, is not a certainty that arises from life but rather one established in opposition to it. The condition of the historian's objectivity is that he no longer considers history but only historicism as a source of truth.[14] The truth of historicism is established in opposition to the truth of the past, and the truth about historicism is that it destroys the past. It denies and falsifies what historical experience—the experience of the historian and of those he studies—really is: an experience of truth.

Dilthey turns from historical experience to historicist method for an understanding of the past, and this method remains not only that of Descartes but of romantic aesthetics. "He availed himself of romantic hermeneutics, [which] . . . took no account at all of the historical nature of experience. It presupposed that the object of understanding is a text to be deciphered and in that sense understood" (227 / 212). Deciphering by the part–whole procedure is not an

14. Apel explains historicism's abstraction from the truth value of history in this way: "Is there a *methodological abstraction* through which a scientific investigation of intended or expressed meaning is possible at the level of intersubjective agreement between human subjects? The philosophical founders of hermeneutics in the nineteenth century (Schleiermacher and Dilthey) answered this question in the affirmative and in fact replied in the following manner: By means of abstraction from the question of the truth or normative claim of the expression of meaning to be understood (e.g., the text that has been handed down), a progressive, universally valid objectivation of meaning is possible" (*Towards a Transformation of Philosophy*, p. 61).

experience insofar as it presumes a whole of which the understander is not a part. It is a method, an anonymous procedure, a formalism of understanding applicable to everything by anyone under any circumstances. It is applicable to history in that history is pure meaning, no less readable than a book because no less transparent an expression of mind. In this way Dilthey embraces Hegel, however unwillingly and unawares. But even if history is an expression of mind, Gadamer insists, it is not an expression of method. "Certainly general rules of experience [for example, commonsense proverbs] can be derived from it, but their methodological value is not like that of a knowledge of law under which every case can be unequivocally subsumed. Rules of experience rather require that one be experienced in their use and are basically what they are only in such use" (228 / 213). Method by contrast is the rule divorced from experience— that is, separated from the conditions of its use and promoted to universality. Method is what denies that historical experience is necessary.

Dilthey looks finally to historical method for the ground of truth—not to historical experience, not to the finite, conditioned experience of men who by reason of that finitude are permanently in need of history in order to understand themselves and the truth. Insofar as one sees human finitude as an obstacle to the truth, one will already have missed it, for the truth is: men are historical, conditioned, finite. Method is the attempt to deny that truth, and also the truth about truth which it implies—namely, that truth arises precisely in finite, historical experience. This is not relative but absolute truth in the sense that there is no truth more absolute to which it is relative. But it is not absolute in the sense of being infinite. It is finite in that there is always something else to be known, something more history has to offer. For history, even conceived of as the past, does not stop. It keeps influencing the present and being integrated with it. The historian is himself part of what history has come to mean. Any attempt to keep himself out of his history by means of method leads ultimately to the misunderstanding of history; for if he is indeed part of what history means, then the attempt to be objective by excluding that part which he himself is will render his history itself partial, incomplete, and in that sense subjective. If the truth is that we belong to history, then the only way to be objective about history is not to objectify it, not to stand over against it as a subject against an object. The only way to understand history is to belong to history. That is what historical experience is, and that is why such experience is a source of truth. There is no method of reconstructing or returning to the past, and none is needed. We already belong to history.

(2.1.3.A) The central problem in Dilthey, as Gadamer understands it, is epistemological: Dilthey wants to justify epistemologically the particular methodology of the human sciences and thus raise them to equality with the natural sciences. Thus he addresses the relation between objectivity and life. Life itself gives rise to objectivity, certainty, and fixity in Dilthey's view; but this emergence of fixed, permanent validity is also a resistance to life, which is growth and movement—history. On the one hand, Dilthey puts purportedly independent philosophical concepts back into history; on the other, he locates the basis of the historian's objectivity outside history, in a historical method not itself historical but rather supra-historical: speculative, absolute, and Hegelian.

Husserl takes one step toward overcoming this complex epistemological problem when he steps outside epistemology itself into phenomenology. "In the concept of intentionality, the dogmatically posited split between the immanence of self-consciousness and the transcendence of one's knowledge of the world, which lay at the root of the notion of epistemology and its theoretic constructions, was fundamentally overcome" (*RAS* 154). For phenomenology, there is no object that is not already correlated to, and constituted by, a subject. Nature is not such an object, the object of the natural sciences, for it too is a construct of mind; nor is mind an object, the object of psychology, for what a consciousness means or intends is not something contained in it, not a psychic content. Consciousness rather is a correlation of subject and object: it is always consciousness of something. When I am talking or writing or thinking about something, "what I have in mind" is not in fact in my mind in any way that could be determined by even a total psychological analysis. What I have in mind, what I mean and intend, is never just what is in my mind but is also "out there," for everyone else. I mean to be telling the truth. This fact is crucial for Gadamer as well as for Husserl: analysis of the author's mind per se always misses precisely what the author had in mind. Psychological analysis, apart from the truth of what is meant, is necessarily incomplete. That consciousness is intentional means that it intends an object. What consciousness intends, what it is conscious of, is not a psychological entity but an ideal unity of all possible experiences. It is meant as objective. The author's intention, therefore, is not to be confined within the parameters of the author's mind.

When by means of the transcendental reduction Husserl turns his attention from the object to the subject, he discovers that there are phenomena, modes of appearance or givenness, that are not objects of intentional acts. "Every experience has implicit horizons of before and after, and fuses finally with the continuum of experiences that are present before and after into the unity of the flow of experience" (231 / 216).[15] To employ an analogy with sight: along with the

---

15. It should be noted that the notion of the fusion of horizons so important to Gadamer is, as he is fully aware, implicit in Husserl's *Phenomenology of Internal Time Consciousness*.

object of attention, the focus of vision, there is also a field of vision, a horizon. The object is included within a horizon that comprehends not only the focus of attention (or intention) but also what is not the focus, a periphery of what is not objectified but could nevertheless become an intentional object, inside a different horizon. Where this visual analogy breaks down is that the horizon Husserl describes is not spatial but rather temporal; the fringes of every experience, everything present to us, shade off into before and after—that is, they merge into past and future experiences, themselves likewise merging into the unity of all experience, the continuum of time.

From Husserl's analysis of time-consciousness Gadamer derives several inferences. Single experiences, even the combined experiences of a single individual, are not the ultimate phenomenological data. They always involve a temporal horizon more comprehensive than what is intended (that is, presented) in them. "Every intentional experience . . . always implies a twofold open-ended horizon of what is not really intended in it but to which for that reason an actual intention can at any time be directed" (232 / 216). For example, it is always possible for me to call something to your attention that you hadn't noticed even though it lay within your field of vision. Because you hadn't noticed it, it will seem that you now see it for the first time: and yet because it lay within your field of vision, it will also seem familiar. You recognize it. The same applies to interpretation of historical documents and artworks: it is possible to interpret them in ways that are correct even though not in accord with what the author intended (in the usual sense). The concept of horizon implies that the artwork, like every experience, always means more than the author consciously intended. When an interpreter points out this surplus, he does not prove his superiority to the author. The surplus is in principle recognizable by the author himself, and the interpreter too means more than he intends. His interpretation too has a horizon and is therefore open to interpretation, to integration with the before and after.

Horizon is another way of describing context. It includes everything of which one is not immediately aware and of which one must in fact remain unaware if there is to be a focus of attention; but one's horizon is also the context in terms of which the object of attention is understood. This horizon can be called life or world—but must always be conceived of as mobile, fluid, and temporal. As opposed to the objective world of natural science, the life world is "the world in which we live in the natural attitude which never as such becomes objective for us but on the contrary represents the pregiven ground of all experience" (233 / 218). The life world too, in Husserl's view, is constituted by transcendental subjectivity; but no one in particular constitutes the life world, nor is it even consciously intended. Rather this world is anonymous, implicit, and prior to all acts of consciousness.

Here several problems arise. The life world is the whole in which we live as historical beings. It is a historical world; but in what sense, then, if there is a history of such worlds, is it a whole? The idea of a totality of such worlds does not make sense insofar as they are continually constituted by subjectivity, and thus the specter of relativism arises once more. And there is a paradox implicit in the idea of constitution as well. Phenomenological reduction is supposed to remove all givenness prior to the act of constitution, and this reduction includes the pre-givenness of the life world. But this implies either that the reduction eliminates subjectivity itself insofar as it is indivisibly integrated in the life world, or else that the life world is not in fact the basis of all acts of constitution. Husserl adopts the second alternative. He aims to be more Cartesian than Descartes. By the phenomenological reduction it is not just philosophical prejudices that are eliminated but the entirety of the pre-given world. Not the Cartesian ego but the ur-ego of transcendental subjectivity is the absolute to which all else is relative. In transcending Descartes, Husserl finds himself in the embrace of Hegel. And that, however undesirable for Husserl, is not for Gadamer an entirely bad place to be.

Husserl was himself aware of his proximity to idealism. He too refuses to oppose object to subject, conceiving them rather as always correlative, implying each other reciprocally. Despite this proximity, however, Husserl does not do justice to the concept of life as it had been developed in speculative idealism, even in his analysis of the life world. That Husserl still opposes self-consciousness to world can be seen quite clearly in the difficulty he has in showing how transcendental subjectivity constitutes other subjects, themselves an integral part of the life world. The Thou is an entirely Cartesian problem, as Husserl well knew. But insofar as he, like Descartes, begins with other people as objects of perception which only subsequently become other subjects like oneself, Husserl to that extent assumes the alterity of others—that is, the alterity of the world to life and consciousness.

Yet life is not an object of self-consciousness, as Husserl's own investigations had shown. How life can be nonetheless known—non-objectively—by self-consciousness appears with greater clarity in the papers of Count Yorck, Dilthey's friend and correspondent.[16] Life, as Yorck understands it, comprehends

---

16. Although Gadamer does not mention it here, his critique of historicism as limiting itself to a merely aesthetic view of history is clearly indebted to Yorck. See especially the citations from Yorck's correspondence with Dilthey in *Being and Time*, pp. 448–51.

both biological life and the life of self-consciousness, for both consist in *Urteil-ung*, the structure of life. Urteilung can be translated as primal division, but it is also related to Urteil, conscious judgment. In the sphere of biological life, Urteilung is self-assertion, the Darwinian struggle of all against all for survival; it is a division, then, but also productive of the one common life achieved in adaptation. In the life of consciousness, there is also a division into what is self and what is other. Self-conscious judgment abstracts the self from that of which it is conscious and so divides them. But what it abstracts from is their unity, for prior to abstraction is a projection of the self onto the world and from the world. What Yorck implies is that self-consciousness has the same structure as biological life because self-consciousness, like the biological, is a form of life.

In this respect, Yorck confirms one of Hegel's fundamental insights in the *Phenomenology of Spirit*, and one that is central to *Truth and Method* as well. "Life is defined by the fact that what is alive differentiates itself from the world in which it lives and to which it is bound, and preserves itself in such self-differentiation. The self-preservation of what is alive occurs in that it takes into itself things that are outside it. The fundamental fact of being alive is assimilation. Differentiation is thus at the same time non-differentiation. The alien is appropriated" (238 / 223). The same is true of self-knowledge. "Its being consists in the fact that it knows how to make anything and everything the object of its knowledge, and yet in anything and everything it knows, it knows itself. As knowledge it differentiates itself from itself, and as self-consciousness it is at the same time a comprehension that unites itself with itself" (238–9 / 223).[17] All of life, the meanest bacterium like the greatest intellect, lives only insofar as it embodies the circular structure of forage and assimilation, excursion and reunion, alienation and appropriation, self-differentiation and self-integration.

Gadamer's conclusion: "Hegel is completely in the right when he derives self-consciousness dialectically from life. What is alive is never really knowable by objective consciousness. . . . What is alive is not the kind of thing that one could ever from the outside succeed in having an insight into the quality of its being alive. The only way to comprehend the quality of being alive is from within. . . . From within one's own sense of life alone is life to be experienced" (239 / 223–24). In sum, no historian is objective insofar as he understands history, for it is only from his own life that the life of the past is intelligible. The condition of understanding is assimilation and integration.

17. Note how closely Hegel's description of life parallels his description of Bildung, cited above.

Hegel is completely right in this respect, Gadamer asserts; and he has often implied as much before. We need to pause for a moment and consider Hegel's role in Gadamer's history of hermeneutics before proceeding to the climax of that history in *Being and Time*. As the outset of his historical review, Gadamer plainly states that he plans to chart the rise of hermeneutics from the point of view of Hegelian integration, not that of the reconstruction advocated by Schleiermacher. Hegel therefore represents the standard by which Gadamer judges the historical school from Ranke to Dilthey and also the phenomenology of Husserl. Since none of them did justice to the concept of life that Hegel had already developed (in part because the historical school arose in conscious reaction to Hegelian history-as-philosophy), life came to be divided from truth. History, no longer viewed as philosophy, came to be viewed as art, an aesthetic object without a truth claim; and this happened by the same process by which historiography came to be science of history. Whatever his deficiencies, Hegel was not guilty of this reduction: for Hegel, history is the history of truth, of the homecoming of spirit as it progresses toward absolute self-consciousness in religion, art, and philosophy.

Yet Hegel is by no means a club with which Gadamer beats the anti-Hegelians into submission. That is because, first, the historical school had in fact a very ambivalent attitude toward Hegel and, second, because Gadamer does as well.[18] Gadamer is able to show again and again that the rebellion against Hegel never succeeded because the historians and methodologists of history were drawn to Hegel as much as repelled by him. When history became a text and thus was conceived of as a pure expression of mind, it was also conceived of as Hegelian history of mind. Moreover, when history was seen to climax in the birth of the self-conscious historian to whom all times are present, it was no less Hegelian. For Hegel too charted history as the rise of a self-consciousness to which all history is omnipresent. Husserlian phenomenology makes transcendental self-consciousness the absolute irrelative, as did Hegel as well. But though neither historicism nor phenomenology was able to carry through the critique of speculative idealism because they were implicated in it, both were aware that it

---

18. Pannenberg faults Gadamer for being hoist on his own petard: "Strangely the phenomena described by Gadamer always tend in the direction of a conception of universal history which he—with Hegel before his eyes—precisely wants to avoid" ("Hermeneutik und Universal Geschichte," in *Grundfragen Systematischer Theologie*, p. 116). On the other hand, Palmer argues that "the Hegelianism of Gadamer's basically Heideggerian hermeneutics is probably an improvement over Heidegger's conception" (*Hermeneutics*, p. 216). Whether for good or ill, there can be no doubt that, along with Kant and Heidegger, Hegel is a dominant influence on *Truth and Method*.

was in need of critique. The sole and fundamental rationale for all study of the past is the deficiency of the present, of self-presence, and of self-consciousness. And insofar as Hegel considered absolute self-consciousness as already or soon to be achieved, insofar as even his opponents glorified self-consciousness as historical or phenomenological method, all have equally forgotten history. For Gadamer, history, including the history of hermeneutics, does not climax in the perfection of self-consciousness; rather history is precisely what limits self-consciousness. That mind is not present to itself explains its need to understand itself through the medium of the past, yet this very deficiency of self-presence shows that history is not merely a means that we use to the end of increasing self-consciousness: the reason for our lack of self-presence is that we ourselves are creatures of history, historical beings. History is a way not only of knowing but of being. It is a way of knowing by being that is both the ground of all self-consciousness and the limit of the attempt through self-consciousness to divorce what we know from what we are.

(2.1.3.B) Fundamental to Heidegger's *Being and Time*[19] is that knowledge of the world cannot be detached from being in the world, nor subject from object. Dasein, human existence, is being-there; and where its being is, one might say, is in a world. But the world is not an enclosure, and Dasein is not in the world as a chair is in a room but rather as a train is in motion or someone is in love. As someone is in love by being loving, so being-in-the-world is, more precisely, not where Dasein is but what it is, its being. The world is not an essence, idea, or object of consciousness but rather a fact; and that Dasein exists as being-in-the-world, that it cannot transcend the world to become a pure consciousness, is called the facticity of Dasein. The interpretation of Dasein is a hermeneutics of facticity.[20] This facticity, the situatedness of knowledge in a world, is not a subjective limit on knowledge that could be finally overcome by increased self-consciousness. Rather it is a way of being, and it is not a limit that needs to be overcome, because facticity is not a burden on knowledge but its condition. Simply put, human being is ineluctably finite; and though that fact is no

19. For an extended comparison and differentiation of Heidegger and Gadamer, see Grondin, *Hermeneutische Wahrheit*, ch. 3.

20. Palmer explains the hermeneutics of facticity as follows: "This approach is based not on the way that the world belongs to a human subject but on the way in which the human subject belongs to the world. This belongingness occurs through the process of 'understanding' " (*Hermeneutics*, p. 180). Gadamer enters the necessary caveat, however: "We need to keep in mind that [the hermeneutics of facticity] is like a square circle, for facticity means precisely the irremovable resistance of the factical against all conceiving and understanding" (*KS* 4:210).

cause for jubilation, it is certainly no occasion for shock, despair, or lamentation either.

Heidegger's hermeneutics of facticity at once affirms Hegel's thesis that self-consciousness arises out of historical life and denies his thesis that the history of life can be conceived as a progress toward the fulfillment or perfection of self-consciousness. History does not chart the growth of reasonableness or of freedom; nor does it trace the emerging independence of mind. History does not overcome itself or render itself superfluous. Thus Heidegger confirms and radically extends not only one aspect of Hegel but also a premise fundamental to the anti-Hegelian historical school—namely the primacy of life over consciousness. History cannot be transcended because it is not merely something that we ought to study. We are historical whether we study history or not, and our being historical is not only the rationale for but the condition of, historical research. History is what we understand already, before conscious historical research comes on the scene. The primordial understanding of history that comes merely from being makes self-conscious research possible and precedes it. Because of this priority, Heidegger asserts, in contradistinction to Hegel, the historical school, and even Husserlian phenomenology, that absolute mind, universal historical method, and the transcendental reduction of being are fundamentally unrealizable.

Heidegger's phenomenology is not an epistemology because it does not attempt to firm up the foundation of understanding; nor is it a form of research because it does not attempt to ascertain the facts upon which an understanding could be erected. Rather it is a hermeneutic in that it takes understanding as primary and seeks to understand it, to interpret what Dasein already understands. Dasein is the being for which being is an issue. It is possible in principle to arrive at the meaning of being hermeneutically (and indeed only hermeneutically) only because Dasein already understands what it means to be. What it understands is not an object but a meaning. When Dasein understands the meaning of its own being, it understands itself not as an object, something that is; rather it understands what it means *to be*, what Dasein can be. It understands itself as potentiality for being—that is, as possibility and as history. Again, these possibilities are not independent objects but rather Dasein's own possibilities, its projects and projections: it understands its own understandings. Dasein interprets itself; and its extended understanding, the coming to be of what it can be, is its history. An understanding in this sense is what Dasein can itself be. Understanding is not a faculty of apprehension, nor an activity of the conscious subject, but a mode of being, specifically that of Dasein—which never is but is always to be. That it never is (self-present) means that it is always to be interpreted, is always open to interpretation and to a future.[21]

This, for Heidegger, is what understanding always is. Regardless of whether it is an understanding of history or of nature, it is an understanding of itself, of its own projections and possibilities for being. Thus it is clear that understanding so conceived cannot be the special method of the human sciences sought by Dilthey, for example. It is neither a method nor special to the human sciences. Yet insofar as Heidegger shows that the meaning of being is time and that understanding is oriented to the past and the future as well as the present, his thought gives historical understanding a new dimension. It is no longer necessary to appeal to empathy, historical sympathy, or psychological transposition as what makes historical understanding possible. Nor is it necessary to posit a common nature as what unites past and present. What is common to knower and known, present and past, is rather that both exist historically and thus belong to history.[22] What belongs to history in this sense has no nature, no permanent underlying essence that resists history or escapes it. It exists as what it can be, as possibility, and as future. But being unable to escape history means also, and no less fundamentally, that it exists as what has been.

This *Gewesenheit* (having been) marks the special significance of facticity for Gadamer. Dasein is thrown into a preexistent world that is not of its creating, and all the projections of its own understanding are projections of and from the tradition into which it is thrown. On the one hand, to say with Heidegger that thrownness belongs together with projection is to imply that we have understood history when we understand it not as a present that has passed but as our own possibility, our own future. Correlatively, to say with Gadamer that projection belongs with thrownness implies that understanding belongs to traditions.[23] These

21. Ricoeur is closely aligned with Heidegger and Gadamer on this question: "The subject that interprets himself while interpreting signs is no longer the *cogito*: rather, he is a being who discovers, by the exegesis of his own life, that he is placed in being before he places and possesses himself. In this way, hermeneutics would discover a manner of existing which would remain from start to finish a *being-interpreted*" (*Conflict of Interpretations*, p. 11).

22. Gadamer explains, "Fusing the horizon of the present with that of the past is the business of the historical human sciences. But they thereby do only what we always already do in that we are" (*KS* 1:57).

23. "Habermas," How emphasizes, "does not contend Gadamer's critique of correspondence theories of truth, but disputes that truth is to be found in the clarification, or uncovering of what is already in being; where for him, being is essentially the socially constructed historical being of distorted communicative relations, e.g., class relations" ("Dialogue as Productive Limitation," p. 135).

traditions are not a subjective factor extrinsic to understanding and distorting it, so that understanding would need to become more objective by becoming less traditional. Understanding belongs to tradition. It is what tradition itself can be. Tradition too has its possibilities: what tradition can be, its own possibilities, are its understandings. Tradition exists as its historical interpretations.

PREJUDICE AS A CONDITION OF TRUTH

(2.2.1.A) Just as Gadamer does not propose a new aesthetics, so also he does not offer a new hermeneutics in the sense of a new, more reliable method of understanding. The methods we already have, he implies, are already sufficient as far as they go; and if none has methodized understanding completely, that is because full methodization is impossible. There is ultimately no method of understanding, no formalizable system of universal rules which if rigorously applied could prevent misunderstanding, guarantee objectivity, or obviate the ad hoc guesses, premonitions, and projections of meaning that continue to mark the historicity of understanding. Nor is this merely a deficiency. The process of understanding has not only achieved all the regularization of which it is capable; it was already in good order prior to methodization. But if Gadamer offers no new and improved method of understanding because none is necessary, the question arises as to what he does offer and what purpose *Truth and Method* is meant to fulfill.[24]

The consequence of acknowledging the historicity of understanding, Gadamer writes, consists in correcting "the self-understanding of understanding as it is continually practiced" (250 / 235). Gadamer intends to correct not the ongoing practice of understanding, which is already in good order, but only the way we understand understanding. This is extremely problematical. On the one hand, as we have said, Gadamer makes and intends to make no methodological proposals because he sees no need to alter the practice of understanding. But what then is the need for *Truth and Method*? On the other hand, it is not just that there is no need but also that there is no possibility for methodizing understanding. But this means that *Truth and Method*, however valid its insights, can have no practical consequences even if that were desirable. Insofar as it is a book about what we can do nothing about—that is, insofar as it concerns itself

---

24. Hirsch emphasizes this problem: "If we cannot enunciate a principle for distinguishing between an interpretation that is valid and one that is not, there is little point in writing books about texts or about hermeneutics" (*Validity in Interpretation*, p. 251).

with what happens to us beyond our wanting and doing—*Truth and Method* is, if correct, also inconsequential. Precisely to the extent that it is right, there is nothing to be done.

Yet this, Gadamer implies, pertains only to understanding. By contrast, there is something to be done and there are corrections to be made in the way we understand understanding, the way we conceive what we are doing when we interpret. It is not interpretation but instead our conception of interpretation that requires alteration. But can Gadamer really want to divide understanding from self-understanding?[25] If it is possible to alter the interpreter's self-understanding without altering his practice, that can only be because self-consciousness does not govern interpretive practice. This, indeed, is one of Gadamer's central theses: to say that the methodization of understanding is ultimately impossible is another way of saying that self-consciousness does not finally control it. But if, right or wrong, our conception of what we are doing does not substantially influence interpretive practice, there is no need to correct that conception, even if it is mistaken and correction is possible.[26]

Yet the fact is that self-understanding is inevitably involved in understanding even though it does not govern the process.[27] "The only scientific thing," writes Gadamer in reply to Betti, "is *to recognize what is*"—even if we cannot control it (484 / 466). What we must recognize in the case at hand is that understanding is not directed by self-understanding, and that this is because self-understanding is not exterior or superior to understanding, in the position of control, but intrinsic to it. "All understanding is ultimately self-understanding," Gadamer emphasizes. "In every case the fact is that whoever understands understands himself, projects himself on his own possibilities" (246 / 231). Understanding always involves projecting oneself. What we understand therefore is ourselves, and thus

25. This remains an open question. On the one hand, MacIntyre objects, "Between practice, even intellectual practice, so [Gadamer] asserts, and the understanding of practice there is so clear a distinction to be drawn that the understanding of practice is not itself part of the transformation of practice. . . . Here I stand with Betti in holding that Gadamer partially misunderstands his own book" ("Contexts of Interpretation," p. 46). On the other hand, it is the non-differentiation of practical and theoretical understanding that Habermas finds central to Gadamer's achievement: "I find Gadamer's real achievement in the demonstration that hermeneutic understanding is linked with transcendental necessity to the articulation of an action-orienting self-understanding" (review of *TM* in Dallmayr and McCarthy, ed., *Understanding and Social Inquiry*, p. 351).

26. For a thorough review of this question, and one of the best essay-length introductions to *TM*, see Lawrence M. Hinman, "Quid Facti or Quid Juris."

27. Gadamer makes this clear when he writes, "Heightened theoretic awareness about the experience of understanding and the practice of understanding, like philosophical hermeneutics and one's own self-understanding, are inseparable" (*RAS* 112).

how we understand ourselves has an effect on everything else we understand. Thus the alteration of our self-understanding proposed in *Truth and Method* is at least potentially far from inconsequential.

All understanding is self-understanding—this is Heidegger's version of the hermeneutic circle, and it is Gadamer's as well. It describes not what interpretation should be, still less what it should not be, but instead what interpretation always is. "Anyone who wants to understand a text always performs an act of projection. He projects in advance a sense of the whole as soon as an initial sense appears. Likewise the initial sense appears only because one is already reading with certain expectations of a definite meaning. In working out such a fore-projection, which is of course continually revised, consists the understanding of what is there" (251 / 236).

Understanding is projection, and what it projects are expectations that precede the text. They "jump the gun," as it were, because they anticipate a meaning for the whole before arriving at it. What the interpreter projects in advance is what he understands already—that is, before beginning. He tries out a meaning already familiar to him and proposes it as a possibility. This projected meaning is his own possibility in that he has projected it; it is part of the world in which he already knows his way around, and it is something he can and does understand. What the interpreter projects, then, is himself, his own possibility for understanding. But the meaning so projected is also projected as the text's possibility, something the text could mean; and if it does, he will have understood it. That is, if the interpreter merely waits passively for meaning without anticipating it, none will appear. Understanding is like those races which begin only when the racers are already under way.

In understanding, unlike a race, however, it is possible to begin by proceeding in quite the wrong direction by projecting a sense inappropriate to the text. Nevertheless, it is not possible to avoid misdirection by proceeding in no direction at all, for that precludes understanding entirely. Objectivity in interpretation consists not in the avoidance of preconception but its confirmation; and arbitrary, inappropriate preconceptions are characterized not by the fact that they are preconceptions but only by the fact that they do not work out. Confirmation by the text is also self-confirmation, and thus the critical question is how it is possible for the text to break the spell of our inappropriate projections and make room for more suitable ones.

We always begin with the assumption of familiarity. Schleiermacher notwithstanding, we assume automatically that the text will be intelligible, not the reverse; and thus we do not begin by guarding against misunderstanding, but rather we make our projections on the basis of a presumed community of meaning. With respect to language, for instance, we anticipate normal usage until we have reason to believe it abnormal. Such reasons consist in "the experience of taking offense at a text—whether because it yields no meaning or because its meaning is irreconcilable with our expectation" (252 / 237). Given such experiences we have the option of deciding that the text is garbled or revising our expectations.

What is true with respect to language is also true with respect to what is meant. But here the task is made more difficult because when we try to understand a text, we do so because one of the expectations we project is that the text has something to say to us, something we do not already know and which is not already familiar. Still we must begin by projecting the familiar. We do not extinguish ourselves (as Ranke advocated) or suspend our beliefs about the thing that is meant. Yet, since we are prepared for the text to say something new, we read with an openness to the unexpected. Rather than stubbornly persisting in our preconceptions, we stand ready to revise them—and not because we are prepared to believe anything, nor because we merely want to know what the author has to say on the topic, but instead because we too want to know and learn about it. "The hermeneutical task becomes of itself a questioning of things" and not just a survey of opinions (253 / 238). We hold our own opinions open to disconfirmation and place them at risk not because we are neutral but, quite the opposite, because we too are interested. The hermeneutic task is to understand the text in terms of its subject matter because it is something that concerns us too.

For just this reason, our openness does not mean that we present ourselves as a blank slate ready to be inscribed. Because we are concerned and interested, our receptivity implies that we are willing to integrate the meaning of the text with our previous preconceptions by making them conscious, bringing them into view, and assimilating them to what the text reveals. Only if we are not disinterested can we take—and the text give—offense, so that our prejudices emerge into the open, and we thereby become able to understand the things themselves.

Yet the thing itself is understood only in the light of a suitable projection, an appropriate prejudice. If it seems that no prejudice can be appropriate precisely insofar as it is a prejudice, if it seems in other words that the whole task of understanding is the elimination of prejudices and not at all their projection, that is because we ourselves still share the prejudices of the Enlightenment, and especially the essential one: "This fundamental prejudice of the enlightenment is the prejudice against prejudice itself, which is the crippling of tradition" (255 / 239–40).[28] Tradition is always prejudicial because it operates in advance of any

---

28. Habermas, by contrast, argues that "Gadamer's prejudice for the rights of prejudices certified by tradition denies the power of reflection. The latter proves itself, however, in being able to reject the claim of tradition. Reflection dissolves substantiality because it not only confirms, but

investigation and prior to methodological legitimation of its results. But the fact that a prejudice, a pre-judgment, has this kind of precedence actually says nothing about whether it is right or wrong, or about whether it accords with the facts or not. A prejudice may be quite correct, but the Enlightenment considered all prejudices (that is, all pre-judgments predetermined by tradition) as false because it was willing to call true only those judgments that had received the imprimatur of method. The only certainty derived from methodological certification, and any certainty that had not passed the test of doubt was deemed not only uncertain but at least provisionally false.

This equation of truth with method left historians in a quandary, for either the historical study of traditions must be considered as a study of mere opinions or outright falsehoods, or else the historian must suspend his prejudices and thereby break with his own traditions precisely in order to understand them. In either case, objective historiography denies that history itself is a source of truth. The problem is not limited to the Enlightenment, however; it persists through the romantic period into our own time. Whereas the Enlightenment conceived history as the progressive freeing of reason from dogma and superstition—as the conquest of *mythos* by *logos*—romanticism found value in myth and wisdom in superstition; and it cherished the past simply because it was past. Precisely because romanticism reversed the Enlightenment's evaluation of past and present, it did not doubt that the basic Enlightenment schema was correct, that history had indeed moved from mythos to logos; yet the romantics conceived that movement not as a progress but as a regress and fall from primeval perfection.

Thus arose the romantic attempt to turn back time, to reconstruct the past and return to days of yore. But this very attempt merely perpetuated the sanguine contrast of myth and reason typical of the Enlightenment.[29] The primeval wisdom sought by the romantics was merely the reverse image of the primeval stupidity shunned by the Enlightenment. Even the romantic contrasts between authentic

---

also breaks up, dogmatic forces. Authority and knowledge do not converge" (review of *TM* in Dallmayr and McCarthy, ed., *Understanding and Social Inquiry*, p. 358). For the clearest, most fruitful summaries of the issues between Gadamer and Habermas that revolve around the role of tradition and prejudice in thought, see Theodore Kisiel, "Ideology Critique and Phenomenology," and Paul Ricoeur, "Ethics and Culture."

29. Rorty too raises doubts about the abstract antithesis between reason and tradition: "Much of the seventeenth century's notion of what it was to be a 'philosopher,' and much of the Enlightenment's notion of what it was to be 'rational,' turns on Galileo's being absolutely right and the church absolutely wrong. To suggest that there is room for rational disagreement here—not simply for a black-and-white struggle between reason and superstition—is to endanger the very notion of 'philosophy.' For it endangers the notion of finding 'a method for finding truth' which takes Galilean and Newtonian mechanics as paradigmatic" (*Philosophy and the Mirror of Nature*, p. 328).

myth and poetic myth, between the communal unconscious of our ancestors and the free creation of the modern genius, or between the state of nature and the state of civilization retained the Enlightenment's optimism about the division of reason and myth. Yet, though the romantics were certainly right that history charts no progress from myth to reason, it charts no regress either. No such rise and no such fall—indeed no such split at all—has ever occurred. In the past, as in the present, tradition and reason are, as they always have been, indissolubly joined.

Although the historical sciences of the nineteenth century grew out of the romantic reaction to the Enlightenment, they were premised on an assumption common to both periods—namely that, for better or worse, a split had opened up between reason and tradition. "If the enlightenment had determined that all tradition which reason pronounced to be impossible, that is nonsense, could be understood only historically, by a return to past ways of imagining things, then the historical consciousness that emerges with romanticism signals a radicalization of the enlightenment. For what was the exceptional case of unreasonable tradition has become for historical consciousness the rule. . . . [Tradition] is so little believed that the whole past, and finally even all the thought of one's contemporaries is understood only 'historically' " (260 / 244).

But if tradition did not in fact become impotent sometime in the Renaissance, that is because reason is, as it always has been, still prejudiced by tradition. It means too that the methodological demand of Enlightenment rationalism, that we free ourselves from all prejudice, was not and cannot be fulfilled, for that rationalist demand was itself a prejudice, and a false one. Reason is not absolute and infinite. It is not its own master. Rather reason is historical; and it cannot wholly free itself from prejudice, tradition, and the concrete conditions in which it operates because it cannot escape its history. Thus we cannot understand history as Dilthey did, as if it were composed of free, man-made events and subjective experiences as its elementary units. History is prior to individual experience and has a pre-determinant influence on it. "In truth history does not belong to us but instead we belong to it. Long before we understand ourselves reflectively, we understand ourselves in a self-evident way through the family, society, and state in which we live. . . . The self-consciousness of the individual is only a flickering in the closed circuits of historical life. For this reason the prejudices of the single individual, far more than his judgments, constitute the historical reality of his being" (261 / 245).[30]

---

30. Gadamer elsewhere elaborates this insight in Heideggerian language: "This darkness [the 'Da' of Dasein] is not only the darkness that is opposed to the world of light. We are dark to ourselves, and that means that we are. It co-constitutes the being of our Dasein" (KS 4:82).

(2.2.1.B) The startling consequence Gadamer draws is this: prejudices, which from the viewpoint of Enlightenment rationalism appear as obstacles to understanding, are historical reality itself and the condition of understanding it. Thus the elimination of prejudice, were it to succeed, would ultimately be the elimination of history—precisely the history which the historian exists to understand. But the historian cannot purify himself of prejudice because he, like those he studies, belongs to and is a creature of history. Nor is this fact to be lamented, for it is history itself that prejudices the historian; and his prejudices, therefore, are the media by which history becomes accessible to him. Knowing and being are here united. We can know history because we are historical.

History is what prejudices us, and if there is any knowledge produced by history, it is prejudiced knowledge. But if this conjunction of knowledge and prejudice is not to be a mere contradiction, there must be legitimate, justified, appropriate prejudices produced by history. That is to say, history must be productive of truth. Thus Gadamer reexamines prejudice in order to determine the ground of its legitimacy. Descartes distinguishes two kinds of prejudices: those that arise from haste and those from reliance on authority. Haste gives rise to errors in the use of reason, but authority, in Descartes' view, is responsible for not using one's reason at all. We have seen above that the projective nature of understanding means in part that it is always necessary to "jump to conclusions," and for just this reason one's conclusions, though initially "hasty," are constantly modified as understanding proceeds. But authority, the second source, is productive of less tentative and more lasting prejudice, and for that reason it interests Gadamer here.

For Descartes, faith in authority does not pervert the use of one's own reason but precludes its use entirely; and the question for Gadamer is whether this abstract antithesis of reason and authority is tenable. Is the recognition of authority a limit placed on the freedom of reason, or is it rather its expression? Is all obedience to authority blind? Gadamer finds that such obedience at least *can* be clear-sighted, and certainly more so than blind, universal revolt. Although it is no doubt a source of prejudice, authority "has its ultimate ground not in an act of subjection and the abdication of reason, but instead in an act of recognition and knowledge—the knowledge namely that the other is superior to oneself in judgment and insight and that his judgment therefore takes precedence, that is, it takes priority over one's own judgment. . . . [The acknowledgment of authority] depends on knowledge and is to that extent an act of reason itself which, recognizing its limits, trusts to the better insight of the other" (264–5 / 248). Obedience to authority, then, is not always irrational; indeed it is possible to see it in some cases as a highly rational recognition of the finitude of one's own reason.

Not everything can be constructed or even reconstructed by reason, and it seems most rational to acknowledge that fact—as Descartes himself did when he excluded morality from his total reconstruction of all truths by reason. The truths of morality depend on authority, but it is the anonymous authority of tradition, not that of any person or group. Moral principles are prejudices no doubt, but they are not therefore falsehoods.[31] What then is the ground of their legitimacy? "The real validity of morals is and remains to a great extent derivative from tradition. They are freely adopted but not at all created from a free insight or grounded on reasons. Rather that is just what tradition is: the ground of their validity" (265 / 249). Morals receive their legitimacy from tradition. Moral principles are not rationally grounded then; but neither is it irrational to accept them, for there is no absolute antithesis between tradition and reason. Nor are tradition and freedom antithetical. Traditions do not persist out of sheer inertia or force themselves on us whether we will or no. Instead they are preserved. Even the most violent revolution preserves far more than it alters, and the traditions so maintained are preserved not because they are overlooked in the rush of innovation but because they are remembered, affirmed, embraced, and cultivated. Acts of preservation are no less free than acts of revolution, even if they are less conspicuous.

If we can see in this way that tradition cannot finally be opposed to freedom or reason, perhaps we will be better prepared to acknowledge the role of tradition in historical research without conceiving it as something always and everywhere to be eradicated in the name of objectivity and method. No one doubts that tradition gives rise to false prejudices; but if it also gives rise to true ones, then the total emancipation from prejudice necessarily means that these truths will be suppressed. And if tradition is productive of true prejudices, it is also productive of real knowledge. "At the beginning of all historical hermeneutics,

---

31. Gadamer mentions Burke as one who escaped the Enlightenment prejudice against prejudice. The following passage from *Reflections* shows how far Burke was from equating prejudice with falsehood: "I am bold enough to confess that instead of casting away all our old prejudices, we cherish them to a very considerable degree, and to take more shame to ourselves, we cherish them because they are prejudices; and the longer they have lasted, and the more generally they have prevailed, the more we cherish them. . . . Many of our men of speculation, instead of exploding general prejudices, employ their sagacity to discover the latent wisdom which prevails in them. If they find what they seek, and they seldom fail, they think it more wise to continue the prejudice, with the reason involved, than to cast away the coat of prejudice, and to leave nothing but the naked reason" (p. 183). See also my essay "Burke's *Reflections*: On Imitation as Prejudice."

therefore, stands the dissolution of the abstract antithesis of tradition and historiography, history and knowledge" (267 / 251).[32] This implies that we know history as we know tradition—not as an object which is, or needs to be, alienated from us. We know it unobjectively, unselfconsciously, even naively, but know it nonetheless. Historical research too participates in this naivete in which traditions live on and the past persists unreflectively; even where the historian is self-conscious, he is still prepared, even anxious, to be addressed by tradition. He wants to let it say something to him which he in turn will address to his readers. Thus he passes down and carries on the tradition as determined by the new light he has shed on it.

"Modern historical research is not only research but the mediation of tradition" (268 / 253). It mediates tradition in the sense that historiography is the medium, the vehicle, by which tradition is handed down. But what historical research conveys is not something else, some object the vehicle contains. Historiography itself belongs to the tradition it hands down. This implies that historical research mediates tradition in a second sense. There is not only the tradition into which research inquires but also the tradition that directs historical inquiry and motivates it. This latter is the tradition of the historian's own time, and historical research mediates in the sense that it mediates between times and traditions and integrates them.

In retrospect it is no more difficult to see that Gibbon's history of Rome was written in the eighteenth century than it is to date a medieval Nativity painting from the clothes of the Holy Family. But why is it, then, that anyone still reads Gibbon? Certainly modern historians have more, and more accurate, facts at their disposal; but why does not the accumulation of such facts render the *Decline and Fall* superfluous and dispensable? In fact we recognize numerous histories which, however obviously they are dated, nevertheless do not become outdated by the progress of knowledge about the objects into which they were inquiring. The reason for this phenomenon, Gadamer suggests, is that the object itself is not the end and purpose of inquiry. With such books, "obviously one cannot simply base the criterion [of their value] on the object, as we would measure the value and importance of research. Rather the object appears truly significant only in the light of him who is able rightly to delineate it. Certainly we are interested in the object, but the object achieves its life only through the

32. Kermode, perhaps influenced by Gadamer, comes to this conclusion with respect to biblical interpretation: "There is a genuine continuity between the operations performed on the material by the evangelists, and the work of exegetes who, for almost two millennia, have continued their labors" (*Genesis of Secrecy*, p. 99).

aspects in which it is shown to us. . . . These aspects are not superseded during the progress of research'' (263 / 252). The *Decline and Fall* does not become dispensable because the aspect in which Gibbon presented the empire is part of what we want and need to know, for that Enlightenment aspect in which he placed it is, for better or worse, an aspect of Rome itself.

What we are here discussing is obviously not a peculiar merit or defect of eighteenth-century historiography. Historical study of tradition is always motivated by the present and its interests. No one really doubts this, even if he resists it. But if the study of the past is indeed always motivated by and thus mediated by the present, then historiography can never be understood in terms of progress toward or deviation from a self-identical object. "Such an object in itself," Gadamer concludes, "clearly does not exist at all" (269 / 253). We need to be careful here: what Gadamer writes is not that the object of history does not exist, but that it does not exist in itself. It *does* exist in relation and mediation, and only there. The past exists always and only in relation to its future. For this reason, there is no object in itself to which historical research is directed or in terms of which it could be evaluated.

Our very best histories, those we cherish and continue to read, reveal aspects of past events that became visible only in relation to and by the light of times quite removed from those events, indeed the times of the historian himself.[33] And if we continue to read such histories, it is not because the aspects thus revealed are false. Quite the contrary, Gadamer suggests, it is because they are aspects of the past itself no less than of the historian's time in which they became manifest. Can it be right to say that Gibbon would have been a better historian had he been less a man of his time, less prejudiced by the Enlightenment suspicion of Christianity, or less motivated by that prejudice in writing the *Decline and Fall*? It seems rather that if he had been completely objective, he would have been entirely unmotivated to undertake such a project, and he would have written not a better history but no history at all.

The object of history, then, is not what once was, but rather what once was in relation to what now is. For better or worse, such mediation describes how history is actually written, not how it should be. But are these necessarily antithetical? Though to historicism the mobile relation of past to present seems

---

33. Scripture, Kermode writes, "is an oracle that comes true only in circumstances quite unforeseeable, to be heard by later ears and divined by a later magic. And every text may be treated thus. It may have some sense that can be sought only at some long temporal remove" (p. 20). Shelley's "Defense of Poetry" first enunciates the positive function of temporal distance as a general principle of interpretation.

to preclude knowledge of the past, Gadamer encourages us to view mediation not as a defect to be remedied or accepted in resignation but as something in fact positive and productive of knowledge, albeit not objective knowledge.[34]

A history like Gibbon's that endures through time we call a classic. In terming such books *classical*, we imply at least implicitly that they share some quality with the classics of antiquity. Yet this quality is clearly unrelated to when they were written. The question, then, is also whether the ancient classics are classical because they were written in ancient times. For Hegel, the classical is a period concept and a descriptive term denoting the stylistic perfection of "classical" art that occurred between the phases of "symbolic" rigidity and "romantic" dissolution. The fact that the classic period of art is past suggests to Hegel that the period of art itself is past and the period of philosophy coming to maturity. If this conclusion, even when properly qualified, seems overhasty that is partly because for us and even for Hegel the classical, while it does name a historical period, does not name only that; and whereas it does describe certain stylistic features, it describes more than these.

The classical is a normative concept. Although the ideal of historicism was to have subjected the normative claim of the past to that of historical reason, *classical* remains an evaluative term implying a value judgment and indeed the positive value of the classics. It is not just descriptive of a style or a period. The value of a classic is not the value of a time now past and lost, nor is it the value of a time so perfect that it has become supra-historical and eternal. The classical suggests not so much a characteristic of certain historical phenomena but a specific way of being historical (271 / 255). Historical being is that which exists in preservation (*Bewahrung*). This kind of preservation is not mere storage but a constant putting to the test (*Bewährung*) of what, in thus proving itself, brings into being something true (*ein Wahres*). The normative value of the classic consists in its being a source of truth, historical truth. Historical research does not finally succeed in getting "behind" the classic or in explaining it from "above," because the truth that comes into being in the classic precedes historical research and persists through and in that research itself. A history of the classic is not merely research because it is also a testing, proving, and thus a participation in the truth of the classic. So also the classic does not exist in itself; its truth does not persist of itself but only through this historical participation, the constant mediation with the present of the historian. For this reason, what the classic says to us is not merely a statement about the past but a truth addressed to the present

34. For Betti's contrary view, see his remarks in "Hermeneutics," p. 73.

"The classic is certainly 'timeless'," Gadamer concludes, "but this time-lessness is a mode of historical being" (274 / 257). Being historical means that the classic exists in those representations of it which are its own representations and belong to it.[35] When in interpretation the classic says something to us out of its world, we understand that our world still belongs to that world, and it to ours. The question, then, is whether this fusion of worlds and times characterizes what happens in all historical interpretation and not just in that of the classical. If so, we will not be able to conceive of historical movement as the movement of events alone while the understanding of them remains fixed and static. Rather understanding, the valid knowledge gained from and in history, changes too; and such change is not the result of remediable accidents due to the subjectivity of the historian. It results rather from his mode of being—from his own being historical and belonging to tradition. "Understanding itself is not to be considered as an act of subjectivity but as joining in with an event of tradition in which past and present are constantly mediated" (274–75 / 258).

Though the historian belongs to a tradition, however, there is no reason to suppose that he belongs to the tradition that he is endeavoring to understand, so that he can merely give full sway to his prejudices and thus come automatically to a correct understanding. Quite the contrary, we must suppose a difference between traditions—yet without supposing, on the one hand, that misunderstanding follows automatically from that difference, or on the other, that the difference automatically renders the interpreter objective and the tradition to be understood an object. The interpreter is not objective since the tradition to which he belongs prejudices him; and thus if misunderstanding is not in fact automatic, there remains the problem of sorting out the true prejudices, those productive of genuine understanding, from the false ones.

But isn't this the whole idea of method? Not at all, if method means the suppression of prejudices, for the problem we are considering here involves discrimination among prejudices, not their elimination. Yet there is also a method that makes use of prejudices and sorts them out not beforehand in a whole-scale exorcism, but in the process of interpretation itself. This is the part–whole method of exegesis, the circular method most often associated with hermeneutics. By this method, the interpreter projects an expectation about the whole before he has arrived at the whole—which expectation is therefore a prejudice. But his anticipation of the whole is continually revised as more parts come into view

---

35. Jauss criticizes Gadamer's idea of the classic and its "illusion of a self-activating tradition" in *Toward an Aesthetic of Reception*, pp. 63ff.

until all the parts are integrated. At this point the circle is closed, interpretation is complete, and the real whole is understood, without prejudice, in terms of itself. By this method, if we do not begin in an unprejudiced state, at least we end in one.

But this means that the circular method finds its perfection in the elimination of prejudices no less than the Cartesian method that suspends them at the outset. Thus the method supposed to be typical of hermeneutics ultimately denies the historicity of the interpreter no less than the method supposedly typical of the natural sciences. Both assume that there are no true prejudices, that prejudices are subjective accidents, that they are finally or at least ideally remediable, that objectivity is therefore possible, and that it is certainly desirable.

All this Gadamer is concerned to deny. He denies first that the hermeneutic method, so described, is indeed a method. It is not a procedure which one can choose to apply or not, or for which there are either better or worse alternatives. One does not decide to understand circularly. There is no other way. It is not a method applied to understanding, then, but understanding itself. One cannot choose not to project a whole. Thus the act of projection is not subjective. Nor is the content so projected subjectively determined. We do not choose our prejudices, for we discover them in ourselves as things that exist prior to conscious choice. Yet this priority to consciousness does not make them subjective either, for prejudices derive not from a private subconscious but from a communal tradition. Thus hermeneutic understanding is not a method.

Nor can understanding be adequately explained in terms of parts and wholes. This kind of explanation is far too Euclidean, too geometrical, and too formal. What we are trying to understand is not just forms—not just parts and wholes— but content and meaning.[36] Yet even this is inadequate, for the content we are trying to understand is not merely the author's meaning, as if it were contained in the author. It is, above all, the truth that we are trying to understand. "It is only the breakdown of the attempt to understand what is said as true that leads to the endeavor to understand the text, psychologically or historically, as the meaning of another" (278 / 262). What is false or unintelligible is the other's meaning, but the truth pertains to us as well; and thus not only the other's meaning but the interpreter's own is necessarily involved when truth is at issue. Our projections derive from our prior relation not to a form but to what is being

36. "The hermeneutic circle is in truth a circle filled with content, which gathers not so much the components of the text as the interpreter and his 'text' into the unity of a processual whole" (KS 4:145).

said, to a topic that concerns us too and about which we hope to understand the truth. Thus we certainly project a whole, yet this is not a formal whole but rather a whole truth.

Still, we need to ask what kind of a whole truth is projected in understanding. For Gadamer, we recall, understanding is primarily the attempt to reach an understanding. The wholeness anticipated in all understanding, then, is the making whole, the unification, of two parties when they come to agreement on a given topic. Historical understanding is the endeavor to bring about a meaningful agreement, an agreement in substance, between two traditions, one past, the other present. This whole, therefore, is emphatically not the wholeness of the past tradition in itself. The whole that is projected is not the autonomy of an object that is to stand over against the interpreting subject, for that would be at the outset both to defeat the purpose of understanding, which is the unification of the two parties; and to deny that what is being said concerns the interpreter too. The past is not understood as a closed circle in the sense of a thing in itself that could be understood intrinsically. It is understood only in relation, for understanding it means reaching an understanding between the past and the present.[37]

For hermeneutics conceived as a method, projecting a whole also means anticipating a limit. This is the whole which, when finally filled in, marks the completion and cessation of interpretation and also the final overcoming of our prejudices. Certainly we do have experiences of enlightenment when we say, "Now I finally understand." Yet our own understandings, like those of our predecessors, however apparently definitive, never seem to be the last word. This lack of finality does not necessarily imply that we have overlooked some part or failed to understand the whole. On the contrary, it is in principle possible to have overlooked nothing whatever, and yet the total comprehension so achieved will not be only an understanding of the whole per se but a coming to an understanding with the whole—a joint understanding and a joining of traditions. In arriving at mutual understanding, then, our traditions and our prejudices are necessarily still in force. Understanding does not mean the elimination of expectation but its satisfaction and its appropriateness to the whole. However, the fact that the whole has been understood does not imply that interpretation ceases. The circle does not close in such a way that understanding thereafter merely goes around in circles or follows the beaten track,

---

37. In Horst Turk's words, "The circle is not between a part and whole of a text, nor between a text and its author or its times, but between the thing itself and the understanding of it" ("Wahrheit oder Methode," p. 139).

for the whole that has fulfilled and modified our expectations is also capable of fulfilling others. Even if an age is capable of an exhaustive understanding of its traditions, that does not at all exhaust what its traditions can be as they come to be understood in succeeding ages.

"Such a concept of understanding breaks entirely out of the circle drawn by romantic hermeneutics" (279 / 264). If understanding always means coming to an understanding, then it always involves two—and two different—participants. The ideal is not that one party should understand the other but rather that they should reach an understanding between them. "This between," Gadamer writes, "is the true locus of hermeneutics" (279 / 263). In understanding a text, as in political diplomacy or collective bargaining, psychic transposition is not the goal. The criterion of textual understanding is not recovery of the author's meaning but discovery of a common meaning, one that is shared with the interpreter. Such a meaning never depends exclusively on the author, any more than it does on the interpreter. "Not only occasionally but always the sense of the text exceeds its author. Thus understanding is not only reproductive but always also a productive activity" (280 / 264). We do not try to reproduce the author's opinion, moreover, because we are trying to understand what he says as the truth, not as the expression of his opinion, for the truth always concerns us too. Understanding means coming to an understanding of the truth about the matter under discussion. The fact that the truth so understood is never identical with the author's meaning does not imply, however, that the interpreter has a better understanding than the author. "It suffices to say that he understands differently if he understands at all" (280 / 264).[38]

Understanding is a productive activity because coming to an understanding involves mediation, integration, and assimilation—and assimilation requires difference. Historical difference accounts for the fact that understanding is pro-

---

38. Hirsch has paraphrased this assertion as, "One understands only when one does not understand" (*Validity in Interpretation*, p. 253). But Gadamer's assertion is not so paradoxical as Hirsch would make it seem. By the phrase "we understand differently," Gadamer contrasts his position with two alternatives, both represented by Hirsch: that we understand identically and that we understand better. Compare Hirsch: "When . . . I say that a verbal meaning is determinate I mean that it is an entity which is self-identical. Furthermore, I also mean that it is an entity which always remains the same from one moment to the next—that it is changeless" (p. 46). And also, "It is altogether possible, for example, that Lucan was better understood by Houseman than by many of Lucan's contemporary readers, and it is even more probable that Blake is better understood by scholars today than he was understood by any of his contemporaries" (p. 43). I have discussed this aspect of the debate in " 'London' and the Fundamental Problem of Hermeneutics," pp. 319–20. For Gadamer's argument on the unity of sameness and difference, as drawn from Hegel, see *HD* 23 and 58.

ductive, not merely reproductive. Just as the goal of understanding is not psychic transposition, so it is not temporal transposition into bygone times. Temporal distance is not a vast emptiness; it is filled with the continuity of custom and tradition, the ground of our projections and prejudices. Temporal distance is not an obstacle to be overcome, moreover, because it is the ground of the productivity of understanding.[39] What understanding produces is knowledge, and temporal difference assists knowledge in ways that are negative as well as positive.

First, it remedies the defects of what we have called the Cartesian method. If we could in fact eliminate beforehand all our prejudices and the errors consequent upon them, we could in one sense understand everything objectively; but we would then not need to understand anything, being already error-free. But in another sense we could understand nothing whatever, because the condition of understanding is projection, and projection is prejudice in operation. Temporal distance assists in this respect because it filters out local and limited prejudices. We recall the ancient principle that the true value of a work of art cannot be understood before the deaths of the author and the generation whom he addressed. The initial audience, then, is no more the criterion of correct understanding than the author, because that audience is disposed toward or against a work by special prejudices of which it is not aware and over which it has no control. Temporal distance has the effect of eliminating those temporary prejudices and of letting the character and value of the work emerge as they truly are. But can this effect be brought to perfection in the elimination of all prejudices? The death of the original audience, however interested and partial, cannot be ideally generalized as the death of all interest in the work or the disinterestedness of later generations. Historical understanding does not reach its fulfillment only when the work has become a curiosity, so dead as to be devoid of all but historical interest.

If historical interest is more than pure curiosity, it too is interested. Temporal distance certainly has the effect of excising the prejudices and errors of immediacy that obscure the past, but this work is never finished. Moreover, if the ideal distance is never that in which all interest in the work is extinguished, then temporal distance "not only lets those prejudices die off that are of a particular nature but also lets those emerge that bring about a true understanding" (282 / 266). Time does not eliminate all prejudices, then, but rather sorts out the true

---

39. Despite his roots in a very different tradition from Gadamer's, Danto comes to a quite similar conclusion: "It is just because we do not have direct access to the past that we have history to begin with: history owes its *existence* to this fact: [temporal distance] makes history possible rather than impossible or unnecessary" (*Analytical Philosophy of History*, p. 95).

from the false ones; and it is not the interpreter who does so, by means of a method, but rather time and temporal distance that make this discrimination.[40]

The interpreter certainly participates in this process. Gadamer hardly suggests that we are merely to ignore our prejudices, leaving them unconscious to control us unawares. However much he contends that prejudice in general is the condition of understanding and that some prejudices are the condition of correct, genuine, and true understanding, it is nevertheless to be emphasized that Gadamer has no doubt at all that some prejudices are also the cause of misunderstanding; and these it is certainly the duty of conscientious understanding to avoid.

Before false prejudices can be avoided, however, they must be made conscious, and that happens when they are provoked and irritated. Now, if we do not care what the other person is saying, if we think of him as only airing his opinions which we (like an analyst with his patient) want merely to understand, then nothing he can say will provoke us. By contrast, only if we too care about what is being said, only if we have acknowledged the other's truth claim and think of him as concerned with something that concerns us too—only if in fact he is addressing us—can we become irritated and our prejudices be aroused into consciousness. That a prejudice has become conscious does not mean it is false, nor is it for that reason simply set aside. The point is that if we trust to method and maintain a disinterested aloofness, we have not at all eliminated our prejudices but rather universally affirmed them, for we have rendered them immune to provocation and placed them out of jeopardy. Thus we keep safe even our false prejudices. Only if we are interested can our prejudices be challenged, and what interests us above all is truth. For this reason, we cannot divorce true (that is, correct) interpretation from interpretation of the truth. It is fundamentally impossible to arouse our prejudices, to distinguish true prejudices from false ones, and thus to come to a correct understanding of the past without admitting its truth claim.

These two, then, are indivisible: the historian cannot admit the truth claim of the other without bringing his own prejudices into play, and he cannot put his own prejudices at risk without admitting the truth claim of the other. The truth *about* the past, how it truly was, cannot be divorced from the truth *of* the past, what it says truly to us; and both are neither more nor less than what is truly understood through the medium of a true prejudice. Thus all understanding, the true as well as the false, is prejudiced. The subject of history (the historian)

---

40. Palmer (*Hermeneutics*, p. 185) interestingly allies temporal distance with aesthetic distance, as we have already seen in ch. 1.

is not a subject in itself, not a pure consciousness, because he is prejudiced by history; but neither is the object of history an object in itself because it is what is known by a true prejudice. History is the union of the one and the other, for history exists in the history of it and exists only in true history. *Die Wirklichkeit der Geschichte*, the reality of history, is the unity of history with the understanding of it, which Gadamer calls *Wirkungsgeschichte*.

Wirkung is related to *wirken* (knit, weave, integrate), to *verwirklichen* (realize, make real), and to *Wirklichkeit* (reality, actuality). *Wirkungsgeschichte* is the reality of history in that it is the history of realization. What is real works— that is, in realizing itself it works itself out. The history of how something works out, or history in its working out, is Wirkungsgeschichte. Wirkung, then, means work in the transitive sense. History is Wirkungsgeschichte in that it works something or works on something: it effects and has an effect. The effect of history—its realization, its reality—is history itself. Precisely for this reason history itself always exists in relation: to its effects and hence to subsequent history, the course of events.[41] The history of an event's consequences and effects is not something different from the history of the event but is rather the history of the event itself, its own history. Because history is a process of realization, an event can be understood as it really is only when its effects are understood. Among the effects of history are those on understanding, namely prejudices. For historical understanding, it follows that true prejudices can be defined as those which are themselves effects of precisely that history which one wants to understand. The ideal of understanding is also its reality: not to be objective but rather to be prejudiced—by history itself. Historical understanding is made possible by its belonging to and being part of the Wirkungsgeschichte it understands.

This conclusion holds in Gadamer's view, but it is also in his view too simple. It assumes that history is a pure, unbroken continuity such that the effect of every past prejudices every present; any time can understand any other merely by utilizing the prejudices already transmitted to it by that past time. Certainly Gadamer affirms that human being is finite, that consciousness is itself affected by and part of Wirkungsgeschichte, and that understanding is always prejudiced by some history. But that does not imply it is prejudiced by every history or therefore that the coherence of history (its continuity with present understanding) can be assumed as a given, prior to understanding. Quite the contrary, Gadamer

---

41. Ricoeur links this notion, the course of events, to writing, for both show how meaning is not limited to an origin—i.e., the event in its initial context or, for texts, an authorial intention ("The Model of the Text," p. 325).

assumes that historical difference and disintegration are not to be denied. There are many histories, to some of which any particular historian does not belong. These too can be understood, but for their understanding, true prejudices are not given already. They must be made.

Wirkungsgeschichte alone is not enough to explain how it is possible to understand traditions in which the historian does not already participate. There must also be *wirkungsgeschichtliches Bewusstsein*.[42] This phrase refers to the fact that not only is consciousness (*Bewusstsein*) affected by history but that it is also conscious of that fact. It is self-conscious. Yet we need to remember that "being historical means never dissolving into self-knowledge" (285 / 269). There is always a remainder, an excess of what we are beyond what we know of ourselves, that makes self-consciousness incomplete. For just this reason it is always possible to become more aware of our own historical situation, the situation in which understanding takes place. Having such awareness does not mean that once the situation has become more fully conscious, we can step outside it, any more than seeing our shadow means that we can outrun it. Rather our shadow moves along with us. The situation of understanding can also be called our horizon. It marks the limit of everything that can be seen from a particular point of view, but the idea of a horizon also implies that we can see beyond our immediate standpoint. To acquire a horizon means that we acquire a far-sightedness which, though limited, is not merely myopic.

The question arises as to whether acquiring a historical horizon means placing ourselves within the horizon of a past tradition so that we could understand it with its own eyes, from its own perspective. Clearly, acquiring a historical horizon does not mean that at all. We exist nowhere but in our own time, within our own horizon, and there is no magical time machine that can transport us anywhere else. Not only is it impossible, moreover, it is also undesirable that we should place ourselves in another time or assume another's standpoint. We would thereby forfeit the benefits of temporal distance; and by assuming another's standpoint as that of another, we would merely fortify our own, making it safe and untouchable. "In that one views a tradition from a historical standpoint, that is, tries to place oneself in the historical situation and to reconstruct the historical horizon, one thinks he is understanding. In truth one has fundamentally

42. For various translations of Wirkungsgeschichte and wirkungsgeschichtliches Bewusstsein, see Bruns, *Inventions*, p. 181; Hoy, *Critical Circle*, p. 63; Palmer, *Hermeneutics*, p. 191; and Rorty, *Philosophy and the Mirror of Nature*, p. 359.

given up the claim to find in the tradition a truth valid and intelligible for oneself. Such recognition of the otherness of the other, which makes him the object of objective knowledge, is to that extent a fundamental suspension of his claim to truth'' (287 / 270). Objectifying the other's point of view proves that we do not, and insures that we will not, share it; but only what we share can be true. The other per se is not in possession of the truth, for there is no truth such that we would not believe it too—along with him. If objectifying something means that we stand outside it, that we do not share it, or necessarily credit it, there can be no objective knowledge of the truth.

All knowledge of the truth is shared knowledge, and all knowledge of the truth of history is shared truth. This fact implies that all understanding of history posits, as the condition of historical knowledge, a single shared horizon that embraces times.[43] Though there can be and often are two different horizons, one of the historian and the other of the tradition he wants to understand, this does not mean that they are, or should be, alienated from each other. It does not mean that the historian needs to place himself in the other horizon in any other sense than that he needs to place *himself* in it—that is, try to understand what the other is saying as true. And the truth always means what is true from the historian's own viewpoint, within his own horizon, as well as within the other's. "Understanding is always the fusion of these horizons supposedly existing in themselves" (289 / 273). Understanding always projects the unity of a shared truth, even if the single horizon enabling understanding is not given in advance.

But neither is the autonomy and fixity of the two horizons given in advance. Our own horizon is constantly in the process of formation, not least through our encounters with the past. It does not remain static, nor is its limit permanently circumscribed like a circle in which we are forever enclosed.[44] When we understand the past, we do not simply apply our particular criteria unthinkingly as if they were eternal verity; nor do we automatically reject them as obvious falsehood or irrelevancy. Rather, coming to a shared understanding "always means rising to a higher universality that overcomes not only our own particularity

43. Here the influence of Hegelian universal history on Gadamer is most apparent and the critique of Pannenberg (see n. 18 above) perhaps most apropos.

44. "The hermeneutic consciousness," Bleicher writes, "regards the conception of unitary epochs with a closed horizon as an abstraction. . . . Both the interpreter and the part of tradition he is interested in contain their own horizon; the task consists, however, not in placing oneself within the latter, but in widening one's own horizon so that it can integrate the other" (*Contemporary Hermeneutics*, p. 112). For the contrary of this hermeneutic view, see Foucault, *The Archaeology*

but that of the other as well'' (288 / 272).[45] Wirkungsgeschichtliches Bewusst-sein, the awareness that one's own understanding is affected by history, is consciousness that one has a horizon and understands within a particular situa-tion.[46] Being conscious of this fact, the historian does not assume the identity of past and present but rather assumes that there is a tension between the two. ''The hermeneutic task consists not in covering up this tension in a naive assim-ilation but rather in developing it consciously'' (290 / 273).[47] If there is to be assimilation and a shared understanding, the historian must apply his own stand-ards; and yet if he is not naively to conceal the tension and difference of past and present, the standards so applied cannot be simply those given in advance. The historian can presume neither that the criteria already familiar to him are correct and univocally applicable to the past, nor that those of the past are correct and univocally applicable to the present. This, then, is the problem of application endemic to all understanding—to find a common sense between the strange and the familiar.

UNDERSTANDING BY APPLYING

(2.2.2.A) To the traditional division of hermeneutics into understanding and interpretation, the Pietist hermeneutics of J. J. Rambach added a third division, application. Gadamer is not concerned to rigidify this threefold division; quite the contrary.[48] Yet he affirms that there are in fact three elements in hermeneutics. Among the deficiencies of romantic hermeneutics, as Gadamer describes them, is that it overlooked the historicity of the interpreter and the tension between

of Knowledge, pp. 8–9. Note that only when historical difference is absolutized into discontinuity is historical relativism possible.

45. When Gadamer uses this Hegelian language of rising above the particular to the universal, he seems to imply some kind of progress in understanding. Yet, in a letter to Grondin, he writes, ''I would rather not speak of an expansion of horizon achieved in understanding but instead only of a displacement. . . . Gain and loss appear woven into each other, and on just this depends the historicity of effective history'' (Grondin, *Hermeneutische Wahrheit*, p. 160).

46. ''What I mean [by *wirkungsgeschichtliche Bewusstsein*] is first that we do not raise ourselves out of the event and, as it were, approach it in such a way that the past becomes an object to us'' (''Die Kontinuität der Geschichte,'' p. 41).

47. ''The best reading,'' Steiner writes, ''the best criticism will serve the poem or the play by making visible, by making analytically expressive, the distance which separates it from the object of its attention'' (*On Difficulty*, pp. 156–57).

48. Hirsch, by contrast, segregates the ''Three Dimensions of Hermeneutics.'' See his essay of that title in *The Aims of Interpretation*, pp. 74–92.

past and present that this historicity necessitates. Thus it also overlooked the problem of application where this tension is most manifest.

In the pre-romantic hermeneutics of Chladenius, we recall, interpretation is an occasional activity in the sense that it is required only on those occasions when understanding is not immediate and automatic. For this reason, interpretation and understanding are not, for Chladenius, the same thing. In the romantic hermeneutics of Schleiermacher, by contrast, the assumption is that misunderstanding, not understanding, is automatic. Thus whenever there is to be understanding, there must be interpretation. Understanding is never immediate but always mediated by interpretation; and since this is always the case, understanding is indivisible from interpretation. With this conclusion Gadamer concurs, though not for the same reasons: in his view misunderstanding is no less mediated than its contrary. Yet because romantic hermeneutics fused understanding and interpretation into a unity, the third element—application—was segregated and relegated to a position ancillary and subsequent to hermeneutics proper. What Gadamer proposes, then, is not a return to the threefold division of Pietism, nor to the twofold unity of romantic hermeneutics. He suggests rather that hermeneutics is best understood as the triunion of understanding and interpretation with application in one integral unit.

We have seen, too, in Gadamer's exposition that historical hermeneutics from Schleiermacher to Dilthey understood history as an aesthetic text, a literary work; and therefore historiography borrowed its methods primarily from philology. But there is also a legal and theological hermeneutics.[49] The interpretation of law and Scripture, unlike that of literature, cannot be explained merely by reference to the part–whole process, however, because even if this process is fully realized and the whole is understood in itself, nevertheless understanding is not yet complete. The seemingly extrinsic application of law and Scripture to something else is in fact part of what we mean by understanding them in themselves, intrinsically. Understanding the law and Scripture means understanding them in relation to the present, for one has not yet understood them until they can be applied to the situation at hand. In legal and theological hermeneutics, it is clearest that application is integral with, and indivisible from, interpretive understanding.

Law and Scripture cannot be understood merely aesthetically or merely historically because their claim on the present, their claim to be applicable, is

---

49. *Text und Applikation*, ed. Manfred Fuhrmann et al., offers virtually a casebook on the questions surrounding theological and legal as well as literary application.

part of what they are. Any understanding that ignores this claim is bound to be abstract and reductive. But since both historicism and aesthetics were premised on the elimination of the normative claims of tradition, the legal and biblical traditions were moved to the periphery of hermeneutics and displaced by the safer, more controllable, and less imposing model offered by literary tradition. To reunite them, however, implies that we are not safe from literature either. It too exerts a claim and can therefore be interpreted only by being applied. If law and Scripture cannot be interpreted merely aesthetically or historically, that is because we have misunderstood art and history too. For they too exert a claim to truth and a claim on us, a claim which becomes evident when the interpretation of art and history is reunited with that of law and Scripture. But that reunion becomes possible only when we admit the involvement of application in all interpretive understanding.

The claim of law and Scripture is imposing; it is a superior claim. Interpreting what has such a normative claim never involves merely imposing our own standards. The interpreter does not merely allow his prejudices to go untested and unchecked, nor does he merely apply his own pre-given criteria, because law and Scripture are themselves norms and criteria that apply to the interpreter and his situation. Application is reciprocal. The judge applies his understanding to the law—that is, tries to understand the law according to his best lights with reference to the case at hand; but he also applies the law to his understanding, for he wants to understand the case at hand with reference to the law and not to his own understanding alone. The law is properly understood when it is properly applied to the case, and so too Scripture is understood when, in preaching, it is brought home to the particular situation of the congregation. This reference to the case at hand implies that there is always a tension between the sense of the legal or biblical text as it is written and the sense arrived at by its application to the particular situation, the particular case. The situation of application is continually varied and continually new; and if the text to be applied cannot be understood independently of the particular situation to which it is applied, then it must be understood in every situation in a new and different way.

To affirm the contrary, to affirm that the cognitive is divisible from the normative, that understanding precedes application, and that the text is first understood in itself and only subsequently understood in relation, is merely to affirm that at some point law and Scripture do not apply. This point, at which they apply to nothing, occurs precisely in one's own understanding of them. The thesis that application of the law is subsequent to understanding it is a claim that one's own understanding is exempt from the law—that the law does not apply to it. But isn't this purported exemption already a misunderstanding of the law and not at all the condition of its perfect understanding? Understanding is not an exception that breaks the law because it too is subject to the law. So also the understanding of history is not only ideally but also actually subject to history and tradition. It is always the understanding of a finite historical being.

Gadamer's affirmation of human finitude implies that understanding is always tied to a concrete historical situation, a particular case: it is always applied understanding, even when application is not the interpreter's conscious purpose.[50] There is therefore an insuperable tension between the self-sameness of the text to be understood and the multiplicity of different situations to which it applies and in which it is understood. That this tension is insuperable means that it cannot be collapsed into identity (the identity of understandings among themselves or with their object), nor can the tension be magnified into unrelatedness (the independence of understanding in itself from the object in itself). For finite understanding, there is similarity, not identity; difference, not unrelatedness. These two terms of the tension are complementary. When Gadamer writes that the text is understood differently (as applied to different situations) if it is understood at all, he clearly implies also that it is understood similarly, for all difference implies similarity and vice versa.[51] We understand at once similarly and differently. We understand *as*.

(2.2.2.B) *As* marks the tension between past and present, and also between general and particular. In this respect, Gadamer asks whether understanding can adequately be conceived of as consisting in the application of a general text— a tradition, law, or religious principle—to a particular situation. This is a question that Aristotle addresses as well in the *Nichomachean Ethics*. Gadamer explicates hermeneutics through the ethics of Aristotle because ethics, like hermeneutics, involves the problem of applied knowledge. Does this mean that the past is understood when it subsumes the present, as a general ethical law is understood when it subsumes a particular instance? Or is that a misconception of ethical as well as historical application?

---

50. In identifying application in the broad sense with the situatedness of understanding and its practical interests, Gadamer is not unique, Hoy suggests, for "Wittgenstein also emphasizes the way understanding is grounded in and constituted by the meaning contexts provided by forms of life. Nor does he think a sharp wedge can be driven between understanding and application. In the *Philosophical Investigations* he argues that understanding a rule is *at the same time* understanding how to apply it" (*Critical Circle*, p. 56).

51. Compare Heidegger on this topic in *Identity and Difference*.

Plato and Socrates equate *arete* with logos, virtue with knowledge. This equation implies that knowledge of a general ethical principle, an eternal eidos of right action, is in itself knowledge of how to act in the particular ethical situations it governs. There is essentially no variety or difference among such situations rightly understood, for right ethical understanding consists in selecting and applying a permanent ethical idea to the case at hand, subsuming it as an instance of this unalterable universal. Such a conception of ethics denies the reality of history and difference. Aristotle too affirms that ethical action requires and involves knowledge, but Gadamer finds Aristotle's ethics specially apropos to hermeneutics because the moral knowledge that Aristotle describes is not detached from history and becoming but itself involved in it.

The question is what ethical knowledge is knowledge of. It is not knowledge of an object or objective knowledge. One does not merely size up the situation; one does not want merely to know what is the case or to determine what would be the right reaction. The ethical situation is not detached like an object from the person trying to understand it, for it presents a choice that he himself has to make. It requires a decision, not only knowledge but action and involvement. For the same reason, the knowledge implicit in successful ethical decision and action cannot be merely theoretical, a contemplative knowledge of the moral rule per se. Moral knowledge is not epistemic knowledge like that of pure mathematics—that is, pure knowledge essentially divorced from any application. On the contrary, ethical knowledge is acquired precisely in application, and this application is not like applied mathematics either. For mathematics can be applied only to what accords with its own unchanging regularity; but ethical knowledge— the knowledge that governs moral action—must be applied in historical life that is not always the same but also different. If historical difference is real, knowledge of a self-identical ethical universal is never sufficient to determine what is right in any particular instance. If we do nevertheless come to right ethical decisions, that means that the knowledge involved is not self-identical but continually different. This, for Socrates and Plato, is mere contradiction: real knowledge is always permanent knowledge of the permanent. But if so, history is either unreal or unknowable. What Gadamer suggests through Aristotle, by contrast, is that history is productive of real knowledge that is applicable because it differs and that differs because it is applied.

In that ethical knowledge is intrinsically applied, it is closer to *techne* than to *episteme* developed without regard to application.[52] Techne, like ethics, is

52. "The problem of the application of science already presupposes that science as such possesses its self-certain and autonomous existence prior to all application and free from all reference to possible application; but thanks to just this freedom from purpose, its knowledge is available for

applied knowledge: it is the knowledge of a craftsman who makes something. He has a general idea of what this thing is supposed to be and what purposes it is to serve, and he guides his labors accordingly. In addition to this idea of the ends of his work, the craftsman also has the practical knowledge of the means necessary to accomplish them. Such know-how can be acquired through experience (which does not alter the fact that it is still *techne*, still knowledge), or technique can be acquired through a technical education. This education is not theoretical, Gadamer reminds us, though it is called *theoretisch* in German usage. Technical education is intrinsically oriented toward application; the knowledge thereby gained is not pure but already fitted to application and taught by those who are experienced in its use.

Moral knowledge too is something between pure theory and pure experience.[53] Experience alone, being experienced, or having long experience is not itself sufficient for making right ethical decisions; there must also be knowledge of what is right prior to experience to guide those decisions. And yet that prior knowledge cannot be refined into a universal rule independent of experience because ethical knowledge also involves knowledge of the concrete situation. It requires experience. Although techne also requires experience, however, moral knowledge—phronesis—is clearly something different. One does not fashion oneself ethically as a craftsman fashions a thing. What accounts for this difference is first that one fashions, precisely, oneself. Phronesis, the ethical knowledge involved, is neither pure, theoretical, epistemic knowledge that is an end in itself; nor is it technical knowledge in which means are applied to something else as an end. Rather it is knowledge applied to oneself, self-knowledge. Thus means and ends are fused.

Like the craftsman, the person faced with an ethical decision always begins with a general idea. In ethics, however, this idea is not the craftsman's idea of the form of a thing, its purpose, or use, but an idea of what is generally right. The ideals of ethical conduct can be and are taught in homes and schools and in the anonymous instruction of tradition and custom. Since this education occurs long before the age of decision making or the experience thereof, the ethical ideals so inculcated are therefore necessary prejudices. It should be quite clear by this time that recognizing a prejudice as such does not at all mean that it is false. Without moral prejudices, there are no ethical decisions. Such decision is

any application whatsoever, precisely because science has no competence to preside over its application" (Gadamer, "Welt ohne Geschichte," in *Truth and Historicity*, p. 8).

53. "One of the points that Gadamer and Habermas have in common," Howard writes, is that "truth is not contemplative at any level, and an account of knowing must not be such as to leave *theoria* and *praxis* in a state of estrangement" (*Three Faces of Hermeneutics*, p. 130).

application, and we can apply only a knowledge that we already possess, prior to the decision. Yet blind obedience to the dictates of the tribe has already lost its ethical quality, for a moral decision must be one's own.[54] Moreover, if it is not merely impulsive, ethical action must take account of the particular situation which required decision in the first place. Whereas the idea of the thing to be made by the craftsman can be fully determined beforehand (this is what makes mass production possible), the idea of what is morally right "cannot be fully determined independently of the situation that demands what is right from me" (300 / 283). If there is no ethical mass production, this means that even if our ethical principles, our moral prejudices, are right, they cannot be unthinkingly imposed on any and all situations. For there is a courage that avoids the fight as well as one that engages in it, a dignity that abases itself as well as one that refuses to stoop, and there is always a loyal disobedience as well as obedience. The choice that is right cannot be determined in advance or apart from the particular situation, for the situation itself partly determines what is right.

For this reason, what is right cannot be definitively codified. And the same is true of what is just, however clearly the law is written. Certainly if there is to be rule of law and not of men, laws must be enacted beforehand, open to all because they apply to all. Unless laws are given in advance, there can be no legal but only personal judgment—and hence no justice. Yet there is no way so to specify law beforehand as to obviate the need for judgment. Not only must there be a jury to determine questions of fact but also a judge to determine questions of law—and there are always such questions. A judge who exercises no judgment or poor judgment or snap judgment always applies the law too strictly or too leniently. We are always tempted to take judgment out of the hands of the judge and write it into the law when felons are released on technicalities or judges take no cognizance of extenuating circumstances. But though a law can always be made more perfect, it cannot be made so perfect as to render justice automatic or judgment unnecessary. Laws written in advance are necessarily general, and what is general is imperfect in that it requires interpretation and judgment with respect to the particular circumstances. Justice can be perfectly served only when both the general law and the particular case are taken into account.

The idea of perfect justice Aristotle calls equity. This is the most general

---

54. Larmore faults Gadamer's traditionary conception of moral judgment for not allowing for creative insight ("Moral Judgment," p. 293). Yet Gadamer's emphasis on phronesis as knowledge means precisely that one learns something in making moral judgments, whether that can be called creative insight or not.

law, for it governs all special laws about taxes, robbery, property, or whatever. Yet the law of equity has never been enacted; nor is there any reason to do so, because this law, though completely universal, is also completely tautological and empty: equity says only that justice shall be just. Yet we know what this means, and what it says is of the highest importance. It means that justice is not always served in abiding by the letter of the law, that if on a particular occasion a judge does not insist on the full rigor of the law, he may yet be abiding by a higher law, the most general law, that of equity. And if this law is not in fact empty, that is because the universal of equity is fulfilled by the concreteness of the particular occasion. The most general law is also the most concrete.

The craftsman who has to revise his plans and adapt them to particular circumstances does so because he finds obstructions and difficulties, and so he either works around them or settles for an inferior product. In either case, his prior knowledge of what is to be made is not improved in the application of it. By contrast, a judge who adapts the law to particular circumstances cannot "work around" either the law or the circumstances. Nor if justice is to be served can he settle for an "inferior product." Quite the contrary, the circumstances must be understood within the law, and it is precisely within the law that he must find the better law that fits the occasion. The judge determines questions of law. He determines the law itself as it applies to the particular case, and this means that in the very process of application the knowledge of what is lawful and just is continually determined, improved, and completed.

Whenever judgment is necessary, whenever there is no rule for the application of rules, what a rule means (its interpretation) will be indivisible from, and in part determined by, the instances to which it is applied. Moral knowledge, like legal, requires judgment: the skill (for which there is no rule) to apply rules. Judgment is needed because there is always a tension between the general rule and the particular instance; and thus, though it is always necessary, it is never sufficient to know the general rule. For not only is the general applied to the particular in the act of judgment, but also the particular is applied to the general. They supplement and complement each other reciprocally. Such judgment is not impulsive but deliberate. It cannot merely subsume the particular under the general, and thus it requires a weighing of both. It requires reflecting and deliberating with oneself. This is phronesis, the virtue of reflective deliberation that determines right application.

In Aristotle's description of phronesis Gadamer discerns a way of solving the hermeneutic problem of application. Whether one considers the interpreter's prejudices as the generalities to be applied to the particular text, or the text as the generality to be applied to the interpreter's particular situation, in neither case is application merely subsequent to understanding, nor for that reason, is application reductive or distortive. As the analysis of phronesis shows, the general cannot be understood in advance, and application to the particular cannot be subsequent, because not only is the particular subsumed under the general but also the general under the particular. Thus the general is not a pre-given universal that could be pre-known, because it is continually determined by the particular, even as it determines the particular. Application is not reductive but productive—precisely because it is not unilateral. If we want to know whether the interpreter applies himself to the text or applies the text to himself, the answer is always each to the other. "In order to understand, he cannot disregard himself and the concrete hermeneutic situation in which he exists. He must relate the text to this situation if he wants to understand at all" (307 / 289).

(2.2.2.C) The bilateral relation involved in application is what Gadamer understands by the term *dogmatics*. Because the relation is reciprocal, dogmatics is not forced interpretation, sheer imposition of meaning on an empty form waiting to be given content by the meaning-endowing interpreter. Rather the force is bilateral because dogmatics is the interpretation of that which is itself in force, whether law or Scripture. This implies too that, since the force is bilateral, dogmatics cannot be conceived as the construction of pure doctrine per se and apart from its application. For that is merely either to deny the force of applied understanding or to deny that the doctrine is in force in the very understanding of it.

"Legal hermeneutics was divorced from theory of understanding as a whole because it had a dogmatic purpose, just as, conversely, theological hermeneutics was dissolved into philological-historical method when it gave up its ties to dogma" (308 / 290). Thus to the end of reuniting all four—the interpretation of law, Scripture, literature, and history—in one unified hermeneutic, Gadamer asks whether the difference between dogmatic and historical interest can be rigidified into antithesis.

With respect to law, the question is whether the dogmatic, applied understanding of the judge can finally be differentiated from that of the legal historian.[55] If not, the judge is something of a historian as the historian is something of a

---

55. For comments on Gadamer by two theoreticians of legal interpretation, see the works of Esser and Hruschka cited in the bibliography.

judge. Certainly it is necessary for the judge to know what the law means, and that includes its original meaning. If nothing has changed since the law's enactment, then to understand its present meaning is also to understand its historical meaning. But if there is not this direct and unaltered continuity, the judge can neither enact a new law nor dispense with the old one. Nor can he ignore the case at hand, however it differs from that envisioned by the original legislators. On the contrary, in understanding the law that is still in force he must be aware of the tension between past and present. He must be aware of the change in circumstances and, conscious of this change, determine how the law is to be presently understood and applied. The judge cannot afford to be a mere historian because, by reason of his office, he cannot afford the luxury of relegating justice to history.

The legal historian has no such office or duty of application.[56] Does the fact that he has no legal practice make him more of an authority, more objective than the judge? Perhaps not, but it does not make him less objective either, for he too exercises judgment, though not in a courtroom. As a historian, his intent is to establish the original meaning of the law as such. This aim does not imply that he can ignore application, for the original application determines in part the original meaning. But even if he must take into consideration the original applications, yet the original applications, like the original meaning, are to be distinguished from those of the law as it is presently enforced. The historian is the guardian of difference, for his task of understanding the past as such involves exposing the putative identity of past and present. If they were identical, there would be no historical task per se, no historians of law but only judges. Because past and present are not identical, the judge can neither overlook historical change nor content himself with being a mere historian. But neither can the historian. Because the judge is concerned primarily with the present, he must see that present in its tension with the past. Because the historian is concerned primarily with the past, he must see that past in tension with the present. There is absolutely no way to understand the difference beween the past and the present that does not presume an understanding of the present from which the past is to be differentiated. There is no understanding whatsoever of the original meaning of a law in itself. That original meaning per se is no more nor less than not-the-present meaning, but this negation too involves mediation with the present. The

---

56. Betti distinguishes very strictly between the judge, whose task is practical, and the legal historian, whose task is purely contemplative (cf. Bleicher, ed., *Contemporary Hermeneutics*, p. 83).

historian, like the judge, must be concerned with the present in its difference from the past; and insofar as he is intrinsically concerned with the present, he is not solely a historian.

The judgment of the historian is exercised in differentiating the past from the present; but this difference is a relation, and thus the difference cannot be absolutized into unrelatedness. The historian must relate the past to the present in order to determine its difference, and in doing so he is involved in application. Unrelatedness cannot be conceived as even an ideal of history, the ideal differentiation. The legal historian has a broader purview than the judge in that he concerns himself not only with laws still in force but with those that are no longer so. Difference is already given in the lapse of such laws' validity. Yet it is not the triumph of the historian to show that these laws have no relation whatsoever to the present. Quite the contrary, it is especially clear in precisely the cases that seem to be of purely historical interest that the task of the historian is not just to differentiate but to discern relation, to find similarity and establish relevance where there appear to be none. "The real object of historical understanding is not events but their significance" (311 / 293). Significance is applicability; and for the historian, application—relation to the present—is not only the means to the end of differentiation but itself the end. In discerning the force of what is not currently in force, history finds its ideal.

Thus Gadamer takes legal hermeneutics as the model for the unity of dogmatic and historical interest and so also for the unity of hermeneutics as a whole. It is a model also for the way a tradition changes and further determines itself from within—that is, for the way understanding a tradition alters it precisely by belonging to it. Understanding belongs to tradition as application (for example, precedent) belongs to the meaning of the law. A law is not enacted by the legislators once and for all. It is also "enacted" when the judge acts on it, applies it; and thus there is no knowledge of the law that excludes knowledge of precedent, the law's preceding applications. In an application that sets precedent, the judge determines the law, not just what it was but what it is and will be. He revises the law, not by enacting a new law, but precisely in understanding the law already in force. Such revision is clearly not outside the law in question. It is through the understanding of this very law itself that the law is changed. The judge cannot set his understanding outside the law, for he too is subject to it, not only in his private life but also and especially in his public and official judgments. His understanding is itself governed by the law that is superior to him. There can be justice only if he acknowledges this superiority and is so constrained that, even in revising the law, his interpretation belongs to the law and is the law's own interpretation. His understanding is the law precisely because it belongs to the law and not because it is the arbitrary pronouncement of an understanding that is a law unto itself. Indeed we can divorce the law from the understanding of it only in a dictatorship, in which the dictator stands above the law and can understand it in any way he pleases. But this means he is not *understanding* it at all.

Understanding is necessary only where there is the rule of law, and such rule implies that the law is universally binding, not only on the accused but on the judge in his very understanding of it. The law applies to him too, for without this self-application there is no rule of law and, as in the case of the dictator, no understanding of it. This bears repeating: without application there is no understanding. Application varies and so does understanding, but (except in a dictatorship) the law is the understanding of it by those who are themselves under the law. It is precisely because understanding belongs to the law that the law changes. This, Gadamer contends, is true of every tradition. Understanding is not outside tradition but rather, because it involves self-application, understanding belongs to tradition. Thus the understanding of tradition is itself an event in that tradition, the very event by which the tradition is carried on. It is in this way that understanding is itself rightly to be understood. All understanding of tradition is self-application, self-understanding. All self-understanding is the understanding of some tradition, by which understanding the tradition is also furthered. Understanding makes the traditions of which it is made; and since it is productive, understanding—even if it is understanding of the whole—adds itself to the whole that is to be understood. For this reason self-understanding is always to be achieved.

This model of understanding is designed to comprehend not only legal but also theological, philosophical, and historical hermeneutics. Bultmann remarks, "The interpretation of scripture is subject to no other conditions than any other literature" (314 / 295).[57] By this, he (like Schleiermacher) means that there is no specifically biblical hermeneutics. Yet he also suggests that the understanding of Scripture presupposes a relation to what it says. As Gadamer affirms, "It presupposes that the word of scripture addresses us and that only the person who

---

57. That Gadamer's hermeneutics shares much with Bultmann's notion of demythologizing is unmistakable, yet the two cannot be exactly equated. Of demythologizing Gadamer writes, "It is still a matter of practical exegesis and does not directly concern the hermeneutical principle of *all* exegesis. The general hermeneutical implication of this theological concept of myth is that we cannot dogmatically establish a definite concept of myth and then determine once and for all which aspects of Scripture are to be unmasked by scientific explanation as 'mere myth' for modern man" (*PH* 52).

is addressed—whether believing or doubting—understands" (315 / 297).[58] But if there is not specifically biblical hermeneutics, the same must be true of every scripture, every literature, as is true of every law—namely, that understanding universally involves application.[59] A judge applies the law to himself in the very understanding of it because he recognizes its superiority to his own understanding, and this recognition of authority is all the more true of the theologian interpreting the word of God.

But it seems that there is no such acknowledgment of superiority and hence no corollary self-application in the realm of philology and literary criticism. The reason for this apparent absence is that, as historiography appropriated the methods of philology, so also the study of literature came to be equated with literary history and thus became a sub-species of history generally. So conceived, literary criticism is the attempt merely to understand what a literary artist once wrote, and not its truth. To this end it is necessary to eliminate the critic's prejudices, so that his understanding has no effect on the text, and by the same token the text is permitted no effect on his understanding. Bilateral application is thus ideally precluded. Yet there remains a tension between literary criticism and history generally.[60] The historian is always using literary texts as a means, looking through them at something larger, of which they are only a part or an expression. From the viewpoint of the historian, the literary critic lends too much credence and too much autonomy to the individual text. As Dilthey observes, "Philology would like to see rounded off existence everywhere" (318 / 300), and this is indeed the case. There remains among students of belles lettres a resistance to the idea that the great works should be homogenized and leveled off with everything written or, still worse, with the vast plain of history generally. This resistance registers the fact that for the critic literature still possesses an exemplary

58. Macquarrie explains "being addressed" as follows: "No matter how far we may be in time or in language or in outlook from any text, we could never enter into any understanding of it unless there were at least some minimum of common ground between ourselves and the text. If it is to mean anything to us, there must be some continuity between its subject-matter and what we already understand" (*Scope of Demythologizing*, p. 45). See also Palmer, *Hermeneutics*, p. 189.

59. Arthur ("Gadamer and Hirsch") links literary and biblical authority through the notion of canonicity. Hartman does so by appeal to imitation: "It is possible that pleasure may return to the critic if he imitates older, more sacred modes of commentary. Something of this sort is indeed happening; but the pleasure of it will remain highly qualified. For our imitation of sacred exegesis is consciously archaic or a mock-up unless we believe in authority: that of the sacred text and, by extension, of our own, critical text" (*Criticism in the Wilderness*, p. 176).

60. This tension is even more marked between history and theology. As Ebeling writes, "If there were now only historical theology, there would be theology no more" (*Word and Faith*, p. 431).

character, a qualitative independence from, and superiority to, the ordinary and quotidian. Great books even now retain, though faintly, the character of standards to be met—models not only of form and eloquence but also of truth. And the important thing is that the critic even measures himself and his own writing by reference to these standards. He applies them to himself, not automatically, as if they were given and patent standards, but because he remains committed to them and considers himself bound by them. "The philologist weaves further, as it were, the great carpet of tradition that supports us all" (321 / 302). His understanding is itself an event in, and, because it includes self-application, a furtherance of, the tradition to which it belongs.

But even if literary history can be assimilated to legal and theological hermeneutics since it too acknowledges a claim superior to its own and includes an element of application, there remains the problem of history generally. The historian does not affirm that great books have a normative validity for anyone; still less do they exert a claim on him. He does not admit the truth claim of the individual classic, even and especially if it is a classic of history. Certainly he listens to the classics of history as of art, for they, like all relicts, are expressive of history. What the classics express always exceeds what they mean or intend, and it is in this excess that the historian expects to find the truth. The historian listens for what a text betrays above and beyond what the author is himself trying to portray. The historian interrogates the text at a distance and maintains his superiority and suspicion. He cannot trust the historians who were his predecessors or accept the truth of what they said, for if he did, his own labors would be superfluous. Thus historiography traces the pathology of the historical text. The historian is like a physician who is not at all bound by the diagnosis of the patient, or a clinical psychologist who takes the patient's own diagnosis as itself a symptom to be interpreted and understood in a larger context than the patient is aware of.

This larger context is ultimately the totality of all the expressions that history offers. The historian does not trust what any individual text says; in fact, he trusts more to relicts that are not texts and have no intent of their own but which, as symptoms, nevertheless tell him something about the past.[61] Yet precisely insofar as non-texts too can be interpreted and understood as expressions, the historian has no choice but to read everything as if it were something like a text.

---

61. Cf. Betti: "Because of the absence of any conscious intent at representation, [practical activity] provides the most genuine and reliable indication of the attitude of their author by allowing safe inferences as to the underlying mentality" ("Hermeneutics," p. 55).

The historian's text is the totality of all sub-texts, and historical understanding proves to be a philology—not of great books, to be sure, but of the great book of history.

This was Dilthey's conclusion, and Gadamer affirms it. But although Dilthey criticized philology for rounding off literary works into self-contained wholes, yet when he assimilates history to philology, he makes the same mistake. Dilthey sees history as a complete whole that permits complete understanding and allows the historian to stand completely outside it. That distance is his objectivity. He does not touch history and it does not touch him: there is no application. Yet it seems clear that the great book of history does not lie open to the perusal of any historian at all. It is too great, too manifold and various, for anyone to understand it comprehensively, at a single glimpse. Thus it always remains a projected whole, and that projection involves the prejudices of the historian. It involves applying himself to history. But even assuming that he projects a true prejudice and thereby understands the whole as it truly is, nevertheless what is true of the historian's predecessors is also true of him and his own history. It too becomes one more text, one more expression, of which the history is still to be written. It becomes one more event in history itself. Thus not only does the historian apply himself and his prejudices to history; history also applies to him. Every study of history belongs to history not only in that it belongs to the past and the prejudices of the past, but also in that it belongs to the future, for it is always still to be interpreted. The understanding of history is history itself.

This is Hegel's conclusion, and Gadamer affirms it. But although both concur that understanding history is in itself history, Hegel views history as the history of understanding, of reason, and of the growth of self-consciousness perfected in the transparent self-presence of absolute spirit. For Hegel, history belongs to understanding. For Gadamer, understanding belongs to history. The reason for Gadamer's conclusion is this: precisely because understanding is itself an event in history, it extends, furthers, and carries on history. Understanding makes history. Even if it is an understanding of the whole, it adds itself and integrates itself with the whole, which therefore always remains to be understood. History necessarily exceeds the understanding of it, and therefore there is no overcoming or subsuming history in a perfected understanding. Mind is finite, not absolute, precisely because it is always in the process of creating history, creating the conditions of self-consciousness, and therefore deferring the achievement of perfect self-consciousness indefinitely into the future.

Application is the "adding" either of present understanding to the past event to be understood or of present history to present understanding: this is the operation of prejudice and the basis of Wirkungsgeschichte. Application is also the adding of present understanding to future history, always still to be understood. But can we really speak of applying future history to present understanding? Indeed this is what projection is : the anticipation of possibility before its realization, a future that operates on the present. What is projected is prejudice, tradition, the already familiar; but it is projected as a possibility, not a given. Projective understanding jumps the gun, as we have said; it runs ahead of itself and therefore has always to catch up with itself. If this is true of all understanding, it is not just the great book of history that exceeds the understanding of it. "Application happens in all reading so that the person who reads a text is himself within the meaning he apprehends." He adds his own understanding to the text. Therefore, Gadamer continues, "the line of sense that reveals itself to him as he reads will always break off in an open-ended indeterminacy." The circle does not close because the aspect of the text that he does not fully understand is precisely that which he has contributed to it. "He can and indeed must admit that coming generations will understand differently what he has read in the text." But this difference need not be just another way. If his reading of the text sets precedent, then what future generations will need to understand is precisely his understanding of the text: what he has added to the text, the self-application, is the possibility for future interpretations. "What is true of every reader is also true of the historian. Only that for him is at issue the whole of historical tradition which he must mediate with the present of his own life if he wants to understand and which he thereby holds open toward the future" (323 / 304). Understanding is itself an event in historical tradition; and, like every event, it gives occasion for future understanding as it also arises from the past. If understanding is at all a special event in history, that is only because, in projecting a past tradition that it already understands, understanding projects it not as a mere continuance of the familiar but as a possible future that it does not yet understand.

QUESTIONING EXPERIENCE

(2.2.3.A) History always and necessarily exceeds the understanding of it because understanding contributes to and belongs to the ongoing course of history. Clearly it is possible for us to be aware of this fact. This awareness Gadamer calls wirkungsgeschichtliches Bewusstsein: the consciousness that consciousness is affected by history. What the historian studies is Wirkungsgeschichte. He knows that every event is effected by history, that it has a pre-history and does not appear ex nihilo; and he also knows that it effects history, that it has a post-history and does not disappear ad nihilum either. In investigating the pre-history and post-history of an event, it is not something else that he is studying but the history of the event itself. So too if he is studying a work, a conscious event, he knows that that consciousness has not only a focus of attention on what is present to it but also a temporal horizon that shades off into the before and after, past and future. Moreover, if the historian realizes that the same is true of himself and his own work, this awareness is wirkungsgeschichtliches Bewusstsein.

It is not only consciousness of a historical object but self-consciousness and self-understanding that the historian achieves in such a realization. But does not this self-consciousness imply that history no longer can have a direct effect on the historian but that everything is filtered and mediated through consciousness? History then is nothing but the consciousness of it. It would seem that it is precisely wirkungsgeschichtliches Bewusstsein that precludes the historian from being himself an element of Wirkungsgeschichte. Hegel contends for this reason that history is an element of consciousness: history dissolves into the thought of it, and the perfect knowledge of history consists in the fusion in thought of the whole past with the present, the absolute fusion of history with truth. Gadamer, as we have noted before, does not at all overlook the fact that his view has a good deal in common with Hegel's. He too refuses to dissociate history from understanding and truth. But given this similarity it would seem that Gadamer is open to the same critique as that directed at Hegel—of forgetting the actual and material that cannot be subsumed into consciousness. If that is not the case, it is because Gadamer conceives of wirkungsgeschichtliches Bewusstsein in such a way that the consciousness of effecting and being effected does not dissolve into a merely reflective reality, into mere thought. Rather the reality Gadamer is concerned to understand marks the limit of the omnipotence of reflection (325 / 307). History exceeds the reflective understanding of it; and yet, in Gadamer's view, history gives rise to truth. Together these two propositions imply that truth exceeds every understanding of it. This is a very strange position to maintain. Yet the excess of truth over understanding, reflection, and self-consciousness is precisely what precludes the equation of truth with method.

We can make the strangeness of Gadamer's position more pointed: he wants to understand a reality that exceeds understanding. This kind of paradox always arises when one tries to break up Hegel's dialectical identification of real and ideal, reality and understanding. If Gadamer is endeavoring to determine the limit of reflection, he runs afoul of Hegel's demonstration that reflection can have no limits. For in order to determine that something is a limit, we must have already gone beyond it, just as we know that a fence is a limit when we see what lies on the other side. Reflection has already jumped the fence in knowing it as a limit; and if the same is true of all limits, then reflection is itself unlimited—infinite. There can, therefore, be no reality that lies essentially outside reflection and no history that necessarily exceeds the understanding of it. To affirm the contrary, as Gadamer does, is to suggest that understanding is never whole but always partial and relative to that part. Yet insofar as the thesis that understanding is never whole claims to be itself the whole truth, it is self-refuting. The falsehood of the thesis of relativism is demonstrated by reflection, by its being bent back reflexively on itself.

We have considered Gadamer's response to this problem at length in the introduction and need not dwell on it again here. It will suffice to recall that the fact that a proposition is reflexively self-refuting does not necessarily imply that it is false, but only that it cannot be understood reflexively. It is entirely possible that all Cretans are liars, even if a Cretan tells us so. "Contradictions are an excellent criterion of truth but, unfortunately, they are not an unambiguous criterion when we are dealing with hermeneutics" (510 / 488). If the fact that a proposition cannot be bent back on itself without self-contradiction does not prove ipso facto that the proposition is meaningless or false, then the reliability of reflection as a gauge of truth becomes suspect. And if not all truths can be understood by reflection, this means that some truths exceed reflective understanding, and we are back to Gadamer's position. Asserting this position may indeed be self-contradictory, but the contrary position, from the same purely logical and formal point of view, is no better. It is circular in that it assumes precisely the reliability of reflection that is at issue.

What is not sufficiently stressed in the introduction, however, is that Gadamer does not relegate Hegel's philosophy to the emptiness of formal logic. "It is concerned not with a formalism of reflection," Gadamer writes, "but with the same thing that we also must hold onto" (328 / 310). Especially in the *Phenomenology* Hegel's concern is not only to discover what can be learned by constructing a formal, logical argument but also what has been learned from history and from experience. Even if in Hegel's view these two are ultimately the same, prior to that ultimacy they are not; and it is in the meantime, in historical time, that pure self-contemplation does not suffice and experience is therefore indispensable.

(2.2.3.B) Samuel Johnson once remarked of a man's second marriage that it exhibited the triumph of hope over experience. In this observation he implies something crucial to Gadamer as well: experience, including the hermeneutic experience of interpreting, has the character of disappointment. If so, experience consists in the disappointment of some expectation or some hope, and thus hope always precedes experience and is its condition. If hope also triumphs over experience, that means it follows disappointment as well as precedes it. Disappointment itself gives rise to hope, as hope leads to disappointment. In Gadamer's view this continuing cycle constitutes the nature of experience. If wirkungsgeschichtliches Bewusstsein is not pure self-contemplation and formal speculation, it too learns from experience, namely the experience of the past and the interpretation of history. No less than the natural sciences, the human sciences are dependent on experience. Thus they too are involved in the cycle of hope and disappointment that defines the character of experience in general.

If experience consists in such a cycle, this suggests that it must be understood in terms of a process and not in terms of its end. Normally we would say that the end of experience is knowledge, and certainly Gadamer concurs that the experience of history leads to historical knowledge. But in his consideration of hermeneutic experience he is concerned to reverse the normal line of thought— that is, he conceives of knowledge in terms of experience and process rather than conceiving of experience in terms of knowledge and result.

We are most familiar with the latter, experience conceived teleologically, from our acquaintance with the theory of induction. Inductive experience leads toward something. The process of induction begins when we notice that something repeats itself and that we have had the same experience twice. As these particular experiences accumulate, we abstract from them a general concept covering all such experiences. What induction leads to then is a concept; and the advantage of concepts is that, once acquired, no further experience is necessary. One need no longer refer back to previous experiences or to the process by which the concept was generated; moreover all future experiences of the type covered by the concept are obviated as well. Inductive experience is fulfilled in the knowledge of the concept—which, in both senses, is the end of experience. Thus, in the teleological view, experience finds its fulfillment in its extinction. The theory of induction implies that confirmation is the primary and most important aspect of experience. The process of experience is essentially an experience of repetition and the identity of experiences. An experience remains valid as long as it encounters no contrary instances; and when such a negative experience does arise, one simply embarks on a new and (one hopes) longer course of confirmation.

In exposing the idols of the tribe so as to clear the ground for more methodical induction, Bacon mentions that the belief in oracles was based on a remarkable ability to remember the true prophecies and an equally remarkable facility to forget the false ones. In this way the belief in oracles was always confirmed and there could be no valid induction. But Gadamer suggests that the theory of induction, whether of Bacon or Aristotle, in fact suffers from this same defect in that it locates the cognitive import of experience in confirmation and considers negative experiences—those of difference, disappointment, and dis-confirmation—as no more than the occasion for getting back on the normal course of repetition. Induction too wants to remember the positive and forget the negative experiences. Like the belief in oracles, the process of induction is an expression of hope—the hope in this case of confirmation. But if all experience is imbued with hope, the question is whether this expectation and anticipation ends at some point. We say that experience ends in knowledge, but if knowledge is not at all the end of hope, that is because knowledge is not the end of experience either. When we conceive of knowledge in terms of experience, rather than the reverse, we see that knowledge involves the hope not only that it will ever after be confirmed. It does not anticipate mere repetition but also new knowledge on the basis of new experience. Thus experience cannot be understood teleologically in terms of a final state in which experience is perfected in being obviated, but only in terms of process.

The process of experience is necessarily one of disappointment, not only the disappointment of never reaching the final end but also the disappointments along the way. In explaining induction, we say that a subsequent experience confirms a prior experience. But these two experiences are not necessarily of the same kind. The subsequent experience is an experience of some thing, but it is also an experience of confirmation. Confirmation presupposes a prior experience of the same thing, but this prior experience need not itself be an experience of confirmation. Indeed there is a real sense in which we can say that when something is repeated and just happens to us again, it is not an experience at all. When something simply accords with our expectations and provides a pure, unsurprising confirmation, it no longer provides an experience. That is to say, only unexpected confirmations are cognitively significant; and if even significant confirmations have this quality of running counter to our expectations, we can conclude that disconfirmation and disappointment always belong to the nature of experience.

Having an experience means that we change our minds, reorient and reconcile ourselves to a new situation. Hegel does justice to this change, which he calls a reversal of consciousness; and Gadamer draws on Hegel's analysis of the negativity implicit in experience. Inductive confirmation, we have said, presupposes two experiences of the same object. Disconfirmation, it would seem, implies acquiring a new concept. The former concept that governed our old expectation is negated and a new one is formed. However, Hegel asks whether the negation pertains only to concepts, whether only our minds are changed. If Kantian noumenalism, the division between appearance and the thing in itself, is mistaken, as Hegel demonstrates, then in the negativity of experience "both change, our knowledge and its object. . . . The new object contains the truth about the old one'' (337 / 318).

In reconciling ourselves to a new and different situation, we also reconcile ourselves to ourselves, a process which for Hegel leads ultimately to an overcoming of all alienation, both from what we know and from ourselves. The fact that for Hegel experience leads to this comprehensive reconciliation implies that he forsees a final reconciliation, a final dissolution of negativity and difference in self-knowledge, even though he emphasizes the negativity of experience, as does Gadamer. Even Hegel conceives the final overcoming of experience as the aim of experience itself. He too conceives experience teleologically in terms of its resultant knowledge. What Gadamer affirms, by contrast, and what he learns from Hegel himself, is that experience is essentially the experience of negation. It consists in disconfirmation and disappointment. We expect regularity and experience irregularity; we expect predictability and experience unpredictability. We expect what our concepts invite us to expect, and if experience consists in negation, what it negates most clearly are our concepts. In this respect, conceptual knowledge is not the end and goal of experience but its antithesis.

Thus Gadamer suggests that the end of experience consists not in knowledge but in experience itself: in being experienced—that is, being open to new experience. Being experienced does not mean knowing this or that but rather knowing how to deal with the unexpected—indeed expecting it. Being perfectly experienced does not mean knowing everything but, quite the contrary, being radically undogmatic, being prepared to have and learn from new experiences. "The dialectic of experience has its own completion not in conclusive knowledge but instead in that openness to experience which is brought into play by experience itself'' (338 / 319). If experience does not reach closure in knowledge, that is because being experienced consists not only in preserving hope to the end but extending it beyond every end and, in an openness to new experience, to the unexpected, to possibility, and to the future.

It is not knowledge that is infinite but the process of experience. This is what Gadamer calls the bad infinite, for which the end keeps delaying its arrival. If this deferral always gives room for hope, yet being experienced means having experienced disappointment, so that one expects that too. What Gadamer has in mind by openness to experience is not exactly the sanguine aestheticism of the Grand Tourist who sets out into the world to seek new experiences. The experienced man has learned from experiences of a kind that neither he nor anyone else seeks out. He learns, as Aeschylus says, through suffering. What he learns is not any particular thing but rather the uncertainty of all plans and predictions, the frustration of all attempts to control or close off the future, and the disap-

pointment of all aspirations to comprehend in a single concept, however inclusive, the infinite process of experience. "Experience is the experience of human
finitude. . . . Experience teaches us to recognize reality. Knowing what is, is the
genuine result of all experience, as of all wanting to know. But what is, is here
not this or that but 'what is not to be overruled' " (339–40 / 320).

Being experienced is the consciousness of finitude. It is the understanding
that something exceeds understanding, a consciousness of history and one's own
historicality. This conscious openness to experience is what Gadamer means by
hermeneutic consciousness, wirkungsgeschichtliches Bewusstsein. It too is a
form of self-knowledge, but not merely narcissistic knowledge of the self by the
self, for there is always something that eludes pure reflection. Since self-contemplation does not suffice, knowledge always requires experience, and self-
knowledge requires experience of an other. Wirkungsgeschichtliches Bewusstsein requires, in particular, hermeneutical experience—that is, understanding of
historical tradition. Tradition is not simply a series of events that one comes to
know; it is expression that one comes to understand. Historical tradition is
language and expresses itself like a Thou who is the other that self-knowledge
requires for self-understanding. Hermeneutic experience consists in dialogue with
tradition; and as in all dialogue through which an understanding is to be achieved
with the other, we do not take what the other says as an expression merely of
his opinion. Nor do we take what he says as an expression of his character or
his nature so that one could make predictions on that basis. Nor do we engage
in a kind of one-up-manship by trying to explain the other's opinion from behind
or above.

In dialogue we take what the other says not as an expression of himself but
of the topic at hand, and we take this expression as addressed to us. Dialogue
consists in mutual concern with a common topic. "A person who reflects himself
out of the reciprocity of such a relationship alters the relationship and destroys
its moral bond. In the same way the person who reflects himself out of a living
relationship to tradition destroys the true sense of this relation" (343 / 324). If
there is to be dialogue, the relationship must be reciprocal; each must belong to
the other, each prepared to listen to what the other says as something addressed
to him. Each is open to what the other has to say, affirming its rightness, even
though it contradicts himself. "Whoever is in this way open to tradition can see
that historical consciousness [historicism] is not really open at all; rather, when
it reads its texts 'historically,' it has fundamentally flattened out tradition beforehand, so that one's own standards can never be put in question by tradition"
(344 / 325). The openness of hermeneutic consciousness, by contrast, consists,
very simply, in the historian's knowing that he himself has something still to

learn from tradition; and it involves the same openness to experience, in this case hermeneutic experience, that characterizes being experienced in general.

(2.2.3.C) Anyone who is aware that he has something still to learn is aware of his finitude and his limits. But how is it that hermeneutic consciousness eludes Hegel's argument concerning the dialectic of the limit—namely, that consciousness has always exceeded the limit in becoming aware of it as such, so that the very consciousness of limits proves itself to be unlimited and infinite? Gadamer concurs that experience consists in negation and that knowledge consists in determinate negation. But since he does not conceive of knowledge as the end of experience, he considers the perfection of experience not as perfect knowledge but as being perfectly experienced. The openness to experience which this perfection implies consists in indeterminate negation. Being experienced means knowing one's limits, but having this knowledge does not imply that one knows some determinate thing. Quite the contrary, being experienced, being open to experience, being conscious of finitude, means knowing that one does not know.

In Socratic dialogue Gadamer discerns a paradigm of the perfection of experience, for Socrates provides the model of indeterminate negation, the knowledge of not knowing, that eludes Hegel's dialectic of the limit. If we begin with Socratic rather than Hegelian dialectic, we can understand experience temporally, in terms of process rather than result. Knowing that he does not know, Socrates puts questions. Whereas in determinate knowledge experience comes to a stand, assumes a fixed state, and takes the form of statement, the dialogue of Socrates and his interlocutors embodies the process of question and answer. A statement or assertion, no doubt, is an answer; but it is an answer to which the question has been forgotten. A statement disguises the fact that it is a reply to a prior question. It conceals the priority of the question and so also its past, the process of conversation by which it arose. Moreover, if a statement claims to be a definitive answer, it closes off the future, for a definitive answer is one that obviates further questioning. This closure of past and future is precisely the contrary of what Gadamer means by being experienced or being open to experience. Thus to explicate the openness of experience he affirms the primacy of process over state and of question over statement.

That experience is negative means that it consists in the discovery that something is not what we thought, not what we expected. But before coming to this conclusion and making this negative statement, there is a moment of hesitation between the positive and the negative, an intermediate stage between the steady course of old expectations confirmed and the disconfirmation that alters that course. At this stage, simply, we are unsure and ask whether the thing we are examining is this way or that. Here is the point of openness, when we know that we do not know, and this openness takes the form of a question. An open question is one that has not received a definitive answer. It is this kind of question that brings something into the open and reveals it. But we must be careful here, for what we usually mean by revelation is full determination, complete knowledge; and that is just the contrary of what is intended here. When something is brought into the open by an open question, its openness consists in the fact that it might be either this way or that. The openness of the thing consists in its still undetermined possibilities.

Genuine questions are distinguished from pedagogical and rhetorical questions in that they not only apparently but actually reveal that something is questionable and bring it into the stage of possibility and openness. Yet the only questions that do this are not fuzzy or vague, completely indeterminate and open-ended. They are bounded by a horizon. Within this horizon, openness consists in the possibility of the thing's being this way or that; but each of these possibilities must have been determined beforehand, and their determinacy marks the limits of a question's horizon. The openness of a question is not infinite because it involves no more than the indeterminacy or hesitation between alternative determinations. A rhetorical question gives its own answer. A pedagogical question implies the direction of its answer but leaves some distance that the student must cross in order to reach the answer. That an open question is not infinitely open means that it too is a leading question and gives direction, but its openness consists in its leading in several possible directions to several possible answers.

As the Socratic dialogues illustrate, because questions give direction, it is even more difficult to ask than to answer them. And it is still more difficult to discern the questionability of something, rather than make confident assertions about it. This is the difficulty of coming to know that we do not know, and it cannot be facilitated by method. "There is no method of learning to question, of seeing what is questionable" (348 / 329). But isn't this what the Cartesian method is, a method of doubting and questioning raised to the perfection of questioning everything? Gadamer does not address the issue here, but his response is nonetheless clearly implied. A universal question, one without limits and without a horizon, has no possible answer. Nor is there a method of more local questioning, for particular questions and doubts arise of their own accord. A genuine doubt is precisely one that is not manufactured.[62] One does not raise

---

62. Peirce's critique of Descartes' program is very close to Gadamer's: "We cannot begin with complete doubt. We must begin with all the prejudices that we actually have when we enter upon the study of philosophy. These prejudices are not to be dispelled by a maxim, for they are things that it does not occur to us *can* be questioned. Hence this initial scepticism will be a mere

it as a matter of general principle, program, or method; rather it arises outside our control, and sometimes even despite it. Genuine questions, like genuine doubts, occur to us. They happen to us and are not something we do.

Socratic dialectic is an art of questioning. But it consists not in a method of making up questions, a technique of putting them, or even of answering them. Rather it consists in remaining open so that questions can still occur to answerer and questioner alike. Openness to this occurrence, to the event of the question, is hermeneutic consciousness, wirkungsgeschichtliches Bewusstsein. The interpreter does not dispense with his prejudices. He puts them at risk. He does not assert his dogma or that of the text but opens it to being challenged and questioned. Even his answers preserve this interrogative quality. They are answers to a prior question certainly, yet they do not render it a closed question but instead open it up. "The art of questioning is the art of being able to ask further questions, that is, it is also the art of thought. It is called dialectic because it is the art of carrying on a real conversation" (349 / 331).

One who has developed the art of conversation does not continually toss out bon mots, even if he can, for they tend to stop conversation; quite the opposite, the art of conversation consists in being able to carry it on, to further it. For the same reason, conversation does not imply the alternation of assertions which collide at loggerheads until one overcomes the other. As the end of a game is the playing of it, so the end of conversation—over coffee, at a party— is simply to carry on the conversation; and dogmatic statements, those not open to discussion, are always out of place. But if it is a substantive conversation in which both partners are concerned to reach a mutual understanding, they cannot avoid the issue or leave it undecided and up in the air. They do not simply carry on a discussion but conduct it. When a discussion is conducted, it is led in some direction and toward some destination. Yet even when, like Socrates, one person leads the conversation or becomes the discussion leader, if it is to remain a conversation and not become a lecture, the discussion leader must himself be a participant.[63] He must be prepared to weigh the other's opinion, even give it added weight, and allow his own opinions to be challenged. In fact, we speak of "partners" in conversation to suggest that in a genuine conversation neither

---

self-deception, and not real doubt. . . . A person may, it is true, in the course of his studies, find reason to doubt what he began by believing: but in that case he doubts because he has a positive reason for it, and not on account of the Cartesian maxim" (*Essential Writings*, p. 86).

63. Habermas, by contrast, argues that only an outside observer can detect misunderstanding when the language itself in which a conversation is conducted is systematically distorted. See "The Hermeneutic Claim to Universality," in Bleicher, eds. *Contemporary Hermeneutics*, p. 191.

one is the leader, nor do both conduct it alternately. "To lead a conversation means to place oneself under the direction of the object toward which both partners are led" (349 / 330). The object of the conversation is what both want to understand, and it is by reference to this object that they reach a mutual understanding. This joint object, not the partners, conducts the conversation. But how can they be led by a mutual understanding that is yet to be reached or by a common object that does not yet exist? One cannot suppose it to be given, for its absence motivated the conversation in the first place. Yet one must suppose mutual understanding of the common object to be possible, for that possibility motivates the partners to engage in conversation as well. Perhaps this double motivation best characterizes conversation: to be impelled from behind by lack and difference but also to be drawn from before by possibility and community.

Gadamer describes the hermeneutic task as "coming into conversation with the text" (350 / 331). This is a task: it does not happen automatically. Yet opening a conversation cannot be mechanized or methodized either. The interpreter is drawn into conversation with the historical text when it says something interesting, something that concerns him too. The interpreter who is thus drawn in no longer stands at a distance or merely makes assertions about the text, but rather engages in a conversation with it. He asks questions of it and so draws the text into conversation as well, draws it out and interprets it. But to draw the text into conversation means that it too no longer consists of statements but instead of answers and questions. The task of hermeneutics is to transform fixed assertion into conversation and to bring the bygone and static past back into the process of history.

In dialogue, questioning is reciprocal, and the same holds of dialogue with tradition. "That a text handed down from tradition becomes the object of interpretation means already that it puts a question to the interpreter" (351 / 333). Initially, the question is this: to what question is this text an answer? The meaning of every sentence, as R. G. Collingwood[64] showed, is determined by the question

64. For Gadamer, one significance of Collingwood's logic of question and answer consists in the doubts it raises about the 'great problems' approach to the history of philosophy represented by the Marburg and southwest German neo-Kantians. (See Gadamer's introduction to *Denken*, the German translation of Collingwood's autobiography, p. x.) Gadamer writes elsewhere that "every question really asked is motivated. One knows why one asks something, and one must know why one is asked something if one is really to understand the question and in a given case to answer it. . . . That a question is actually answerable only when I know why it is asked means, however, that with respect to the great questions [cf. 'great problems'] with which philosophy is never finished, the sense of the question is determined first through the motivation of the question" (*KS* 3:242). See also *KS* 1:54 and *RAS* 47.

to which it replies, and it cannot be construed without understanding that question. Thus the question to which the interpreter construes the text as an answer is of utmost importance. But every question implies several possible answers; and insofar as the text depends on the question it addresses, it possesses not only a focus of statement or assertion but also a horizon of unasserted possibilities of meaning, which are the possibilities of interpretation that exceed what is stated in the text.

To open a conversation with a text means to understand the question to which the text is an answer as an open question. If it is an open and not a closed question, then the answer the text gives is not definitive. Even its answer raises a question, one that is still open to discussion.[65] To open a text to discussion means to open its topic to the interpreter's contributions. It becomes open to interpretation, by which the conversation is furthered. But this does not at all mean that the interpreter supplies the definitive answers which the text of itself cannot provide. Quite the contrary, for the interpreter to enter the conversation means that he does not have the answers but, like the text, is concerned to find them. He does not make assertions but asks questions. Moreover, insofar as the text raises an open question to which the interpreter does not already have the answer, it asks a question of him. The text asks a real question, and its reality consists in the fact that it concerns the interpreter too. The reciprocity of questioning is realized when the interpreter puts a question to the text by which he in turn is put in question.

Thus the question raised by the text merges with the interpreter's own questioning in the dialectical play which Gadamer calls the fusion of horizons. Interpretive inquiry always exceeds what the author had in mind because, in thinking the latter through, the interpreter cannot help noticing the dubiousness of what the author takes for granted, thus converting into a question what was formerly a given. But just as historical events cannot be reduced to the hopes, desires, and intentions of the participants, so also meaning, if it is a historical event, cannot be reduced to the author's intention. History frustrates our predictions and alters our plans. It is what occurs between cup and lip. History is

---

65. Rorty departs from Gadamer in arguing that "the point of edifying philosophy [i.e., hermeneutics] is to keep the conversation going rather than to find objective truth" (*Philosophy and the Mirror of Nature*, p. 377). Gadamer does not differentiate between the search for truth (though perhaps not objective) and the continuance of conversation. Marquard suggests a more practical motivation for keeping the conversation going: "It blunts— potentially deadly—interpretive controversies in that it transforms the authoritative relation to the text into one that is interpretive: into an understanding of the text that—necessarily ad libitum—can be discussed; and the person who is willing to discuss is less likely to kill" (*Abschied vom Principiellen*, p. 130).

the gap between will and consequence, the non-identity of intention and meaning. The finality of dogmatic assertion, therefore, is always premature, for meaning remains in process, open to interpretation.[66] This virtuality derives not from a defect in the author but from the nature of meaning: it is always to be realized. Thus interpretation finds its goal in being such a realization of meaning, though without becoming dogmatic or claiming that it is the full realization. The hermeneutically conscious interpreter knows, on the one hand, that the text did not have the last word, for he contributes his own word to the conversation in which both participate. Yet, on the other hand, he also knows that he himself will not have the last word about the text, and that is not his aim anyway.[67] Moreover he needs the text in order to place his own prejudices at risk and to point out the dubiousness of what he himself takes for granted, thus disclosing new possibilities for questioning and extending his own horizon by fusing it with that of the text. Knowing that he does not know, being cognizant of his finitude, and realizing that he does not have the first word or the last, the interpreter holds himself open to history—that is, to the continuing event of truth.[68]

The interpreter best understands himself as a participant in a continuing conversation, one that pre-dates his own consciousness and will post-date it. He does not impose his own concepts dogmatically but rather holds them open because he knows that they have had and will have a history. Conversation is the process of concept formation, of coming to mutual understanding and reaching a common meaning. But this continuing process in which shared concepts are formed takes place within the language of dialogue. The presupposition of reaching a mutual understanding of a common object is neither a common nature nor a special faculty of empathy but language.[69] It is not that the common object is first known in itself and that a joint understanding is then reached. Quite the contrary, the common object exists nowhere prior to the partners' common

---

66. Much of Bakhtin's work pertains to the virtual nature of meaning. Here, for example, are a few of his comments on the novel: "No matter how distant this object [the novel] is from us in time, it is connected to our incomplete, present-day, continuing temporal transitions, it develops a relationship with our unpreparedness, with our present. But meanwhile our present has been moving into an inconclusive future. And in this inconclusive context . . . [the novel's] sense and significance are renewed and grow as the context continues to unfold" (*The Dialogic Imagination*, p. 30).

67. Bloom cites Rabbi Tarphon's remark: "You are not required to complete the work, but neither are you free to desist from it" (*Map of Misreading*, p. 46).

68. Grondin makes the point that "openness is primarily openness to the arrival of truth" (*Hermeneutische Wahrheit*, p. 24).

69. In the human sciences, Gadamer affirms, "there is no other means by which to distinguish the true from the false than . . . logos, speech" (*KS* 1:45).

understanding. Nor is their understanding first reached and then put into words. Quite the contrary, mutual understanding is reached in conversation itself. "Every conversation presupposes a common language, or better: it creates a common language" (360 / 341). Reaching a common understanding, a common sense, depends on the achievement of a common language in which the partners can communicate. Thus in the final section of *Truth and Method* Gadamer turns his attention from the role of the question in conversation to language in general as what makes understanding possible.

3

Being at Home in Language

Hegel's idea of knowledge, conceived as absolute self-transparency, has something fantastic about it if it is supposed to restore complete at-homeness in being. But could not a restoration of at-homeness come about in the sense that the process of making oneself at home in the world has never ceased to take place? . . . Is not language always the language of the homeland and the process of becoming at home in the world? [*PH* 238–39]

"Sein, das verstanden werden kann, ist Sprache" (450 / 432). Being that can be understood is language. This sentence formulates one of the fundamental conclusions toward which the final part, and indeed the whole, of *Truth and Method* is directed: namely, that the scope of understanding, and of hermeneutics, is coextensive with the all-encompassing universality of language.[1] We will be able to see more clearly what this sentence implies when we follow the path that leads Gadamer to affirm it. But even before considering the sentence in any detail, we can already hear echoes of numerous passages in the later Heidegger, especially his well-known phrase "Language is the house of being." Gadamer also cites the line of Stefan George that fascinated Heidegger: "Kein Ding sei, wo das Wort gebricht" (464 / 445). Further, when Gadamer mentions "the conversation that we are" (360 / 340), one cannot help recalling Heidegger's discussion of Hölderlin.[2] Gadamer's indebtedness to Heidegger in these and many other respects is apparent, and he is at no pains to conceal it.

Indeed Heidegger's influence on Gadamer's conception of language is so pervasive that it comes as some surprise when Gadamer writes, "We have

---

1. Gadamer explicates the sentence in this way in *PH* 103.
2. Gadamer, of course, has himself written on Hölderlin; see his essays in *KS* 2.

213

German romanticism to thank for the presuppositions concerning the systematic significance of the linguisticality of conversation in all understanding" (366 / 350). Gadamer is careful with his phrasing here: the foundations for the recognition of the primacy of language in understanding were laid by German romanticism, though their development was carried out much later, by Heidegger among many others. We recall that in *Being and Time* Heidegger draws directly on the hermeneutics of Dilthey and Yorck; but Gadamer locates his own sources much earlier—in romanticism, and that means primarily in Schleiermacher. Again this is surprising, because in *Truth and Method* Schleiermacher's hermeneutics has figured largely as the initial wrong turn that diverted the human sciences toward methodologism and away from an appropriate self-conception. Directly against Schleiermacher's theory that understanding consists in reconstructing the genesis of the other's opinion, Gadamer writes, "What a text means is not to be compared with an immovable and obstinately maintained idée fixe that suggests only one question to the interpreter: how the other could have come to such an absurd opinion" (365–66 / 350). But if this were in fact all that Schleiermacher's hermeneutics boils down to, it would present Gadamer himself with only one question, the merely historical question concerning the genesis of that absurd theory itself. Precisely because he does not adopt Schleiermacher's program of reconstruction, then, Gadamer finds that it presents him with a great many questions, none of which are merely historical because they are real questions pertinent to and finally integrated with Gadamer's own inquiry.

We can see how closely they are integrated when we observe that Gadamer's climactic conclusion, "Being that can be understood is language," is very nearly a paraphrase of the epigraph from Schleiermacher that stands at the head of this final section: "Everything presupposed by hermeneutics is only language."[3] Between these two sentences, there occurs a fusion of horizons. There is no need to assert that the two are synonymous. Clearly they are different. "Being" *(Sein)*, for example, is not identical to "everything" *(Alles)*,[4] but they are nonetheless closely related. That the sentences are clearly different does not prevent them from being clearly similar; and even if we insist on the difference,

---

3. For Gadamer's reconsideration of the problem of language in Schleiermacher, see his "Das Problem der Sprache in Schleiermachers Hermeneutik," in *KS* 3:129–40. Heidegger comments on Schleiermacher in *On the Way to Language*, pp. 10–11.

4. Gadamer appears to vacillate on this question. On the one hand, he writes that Zeno "could no longer hold onto the philosophical meaning of the doctrine of being and understood 'being' only as 'everything'" (*KS* 3:247). On the other hand he writes, "The principle of hermeneutics simply means that we should try to understand everything that can be understood. This is what I meant by the sentence: 'Being that can be understood is language'" (*PH* 31).

we recall Gadamer's principle that the interpreter understands differently if he understands at all. There is no doubt that Schleiermacher *intends* to make no ontological proposition, but then Gadamer does not attempt to reconstruct Schleiermacher's intention either.

Gadamer's concern with being obviously derives from Heidegger; and when Gadamer reads Schleiermacher, he "back-reads" him through his own prejudices, and specifically through Heidegger. Yet we should not conclude too hastily that Gadamer is therefore guilty of naively and unhistorically modernizing his romantic predecessor. The distance between Heidegger and Schleiermacher is as great as can well be imagined, but this distance is not simply a vast emptiness. It is filled with the continuity of tradition. As Gadamer belongs to the tradition of Heidegger, so also Heidegger's focus on the interpretation of meaning, specifically the meaning of being, allies him to the hermeneutic tradition of Dilthey, and Dilthey in turn found a mentor in Schleiermacher. As each of them contributed to the history of hermeneutics, each altered that history and thereby altered what hermeneutics is. The principle of Wirkungsgeschichte pertains to the history of hermeneutics as it does to every other history, and what this principle implies is that a historical event means what it comes to mean. No one doubts the advantages of historical hindsight and retrospect, the viewpoint of a subsequent time when the repercussions and consequences of an event have become clear.[5] But these are the advantages that accrue from back-reading— that is, reading the past in terms of its future. And when an event has repercussions that reach the historian's own time, it is precisely through his own time that he must back-read the past.

Consider an elementary instance of historical back-reading: the British Stamp Act prepared the way for the American Revolution. This assertion about the act's Wirkungsgeschichte says nothing about what the members of Parliament intended, but it says a great deal about what the act meant. Likewise, to say that Schleiermacher's hermeneutics laid the foundations for Dilthey, Heidegger, and Gadamer implies nothing about Schleiermacher's intentions but only about what happened to his hermeneutics, what became of it. Texts too are historical events and so must be understood historically, in terms of what becomes of them. What happened to Schleiermacher's proposition "Everything presupposed in hermeneutics is only language" is that it has come to mean, "Being that can

---

5. Danto asserts that "it is only retrospectively that we are entitled to say that an episode has a given specific meaning" (*Analytical Philosophy of History*, p. 8; see also ch. 8, "Narrative Sentences," on back-reading). Habermas discusses the coincidence of Danto's and Gadamer's views in his review of *TM*, pp. 346–47.

be understood is language." Schleiermacher's sentence is open to other interpretations, no doubt, but the fact that Gadamer's interpretation is achieved
by back-reading is not of itself sufficient to convict it of misinterpretation.
Quite the contrary, Gadamer's understanding, like that of every historian, is
based on retrospection and hindsight; and that is the condition of its being
right.

The series of reasonings that brings Schleiermacher to the conclusion
that language is the fundamental presupposition of hermeneutics includes,
first, his contention that misunderstanding is automatic. Times change. It is
nevertheless most natural to disregard this change and to apply the standards
of one's own time to the past. Thus misunderstanding follows naturally unless
it is artificially curbed by method, specifically the method of transposition
and reconstruction. From the brief example of the fusion of horizons above,
we can determine the extent to which Gadamer concurs with this contention.
He concurs that times change and that back-reading is natural. But not only
natural, Gadamer contends, it is inevitable and without methodological remedy. And not only inevitable, back-reading is also proper, for the application
of one's own standards, though it can and does foster misinterpretation, is
also the condition of the fusion of horizons. It is the condition of coming to
understanding and agreement which is the goal of interpretation itself. The
application of one's contemporary standards is the condition of interpretation
itself and does not always lead to misinterpretation. Misunderstanding is no
more automatic than understanding.

This brings us to the second premise that leads Schleiermacher to assert the
primacy of language in hermeneutics: since understanding is not automatic,
whenever it does occur, it involves interpretation. Whereas prior to Schleiermacher it was thought that interpretation is necessary only in those occasional
cases where direct, natural understanding fails, Schleiermacher discerns that
understanding is never immediate but on the contrary always mediated by interpretation. Thus understanding and interpretation are indivisible. With this Gadamer certainly concurs. Their difference consists in the fact that Schleiermacher
conceives interpretation as methodically guided understanding, whereas for Gadamer understanding is guided by wirkungsgeschichtliches Bewusstsein, a consciousness of historical finitude which endeavors to enlarge its horizon while at
the same time acknowledging that this horizon cannot be methodologically dissolved or extended to infinity. But the two thinkers agree on the basic idea:
understanding is interpretation.

This premise is not at all obvious. On the one hand, we might object that
interpretation precedes understanding insofar as it is the means by which the end

of understanding is reached.[6] There are two problems here. Since there are no other means and since the end of understanding is never achieved except by means of interpretation, it is impossible to separate the means from the end. Achieving understanding, moreover, does not mark the point where interpretation ceases, for there is always more to understand. If understanding does not end, that implies that understanding occurs in the midst of an ongoing process of interpretation, not after it. On the other hand, against the equation of interpretation and understanding, we might object that interpretation does not precede but rather follows understanding. Here understanding is conceived as a private mental act which, once completed, is then expressed in a public interpretation— for example, in a performance on stage. Interpretive expression in this view reproduces cognitive understanding and presupposes understanding as its condition. The problem with this position is that if we first understand then interpret, it must be possible to understand without interpreting; but this is merely to say in other words that understanding is direct and automatic, that times do not change, and that there is already available a common language that unites them. If historical change is real, however, there is no understanding the past without interpretation. We do not first understand and then select interpretive language from a pre-given pool to express that understanding. Rather the indivisibility of understanding and interpretation implies that interpreting, finding the words for understanding, is understanding itself. Thus Schleiermacher concludes, "Everything presupposed in hermeneutics is only language."

If so, the fusion of horizons consists most concretely in a fusion of languages; and translation, Gadamer suggests, offers a model of this process (365 / 349). It is appropriate that translators should also be called interpreters even though translation is an extreme form of interpretation—extreme in that two alien languages are to be integrated. Yet hermeneutics is always motivated by some degree of alienation; and since for that reason all understanding requires interpretive mediation, it also involves some form of translation (whether between languages or between idiolects).[7] We should note the radicalism of Gadamer's position in this respect. He implies that where there is no translation in the broad sense, there is no understanding. From this premise it follows that in ordinary conversations (say, about the weather) conducted in the mother tongue and common idiolect of the participants, no understanding takes place. In one sense

6. This is Betti's position: interpretation is "the procedure that aims for, and results in, Understanding" ("Hermeneutics," p. 56).

7. For Steiner's comments on translation as a paradigm of hermeneutics, see *After Babel*, pp. 296–301.

the participants understand each other, but there is no event of understanding because they understand each other already, prior to the conversation. The event of understanding creating a common language has already occurred; and, sharing a language, the partners in a sense no longer need to understand that language. They do not need to translate but only to speak. The perfect understanding of a language is reached when the language is no longer thematized as such but allows something else to be expressed through it. To understand a language means to understand what is said and not to understand the language per se at all. In this way, the perfect transparency of our mother tongue renders it oddly opaque, like a foreign language that we do not understand at all. In the one case no translation is needed, in the other none is possible, and in both the absence of translation implies the absence of understanding.

The two situations are clearly different, however. Even if being able to speak does not necessarily mean being able to understand one's own language, yet it does mean understanding what is said in it. In this situation, it would seem, the absence of translation does not prevent but instead promotes the understanding of what is meant. Yet this direct and immediate understanding of what is said contradicts the indirection implied in Gadamer's equation of understanding and interpretation, and the question is therefore how it is possible to conceive of immediate understanding of the thing meant (like the immediate understanding of language) as a kind of non-understanding. Here again there is a transparency and self-evidence of things that obviate understanding them. The thing that we take for granted does not obtrude itself upon our attention and cannot do so until it loses its obviousness, until it becomes unpredictable and asserts itself by countering our expectations. Then we look at it as if for the first time. It is when things change that it becomes clear in retrospect what they really were and are. This change is what makes it necessary to understand them but it is also what makes understanding possible. The understanding that mediates between states or appearances of the thing, as it was and is, is interpretation; and historical retrospection—the understanding of things after they have changed— is a form of translation broadly conceived.

To understand something means to be able to translate it between languages or, more generally, to be able to reword it between two phrasings in the same language. But what is it that is reworded or translated? In the previous two paragraphs we have considered translation with respect to language and with respect to what is meant in it. But it is curiously difficult to determine whether in a translation it is words or things that are translated. When we say that German "Baum" translates English *tree*, it seems clear enough that a word is being translated. Translation means finding a substitute word. As a definition, this is absurdly simplistic, but it is nonetheless basic; the problem it raises is that finding a substitute word means leaving behind the original words. The original does not get carried across, and in that sense it does not get translated at all, only displaced and replaced. If, with Gadamer, we think of the fusion of horizons as a fusion of languages into a common language, the question arises as to whether translation is a good model for this process—whether there occurs in translation any such fusion of languages or merely a displacement of one by the other. If a translation of Chinese turns out as pidgin English, we can detect the fusion plainly enough, but it is also a bad translation. Yet this consideration does not rule out the possibility of fusion; it implies only that in a good translation the fusion will ideally be invisible. Standard Chinese must be translated into standard English. Nor does this process involve the imposition of one standard on another, for the task of the translator is to discover, precisely within the resources of his own language, expressions commensurate with the original. In doing so he does not merely assert the rights and maintain the standards of his own language; he does not merely employ the resources of his own language but also extends them. Translation enlarges the horizon of what can be said in a given language, and this enlargement is the index and function of the fusion of languages.

Where there is genuine translation, the original word does not simply get left behind but is fused into the language of the translator.[8] It is indeed true, then, that in translation words are translated. Yet the displacement theory of translation also has some truth in it, for it implies that it is not so much language but instead the thing meant which is carried across from one language to another. Gadamer's emphasis on the thing meant is so crucial to this final section of *Truth and Method* that it deserves special attention here as well. We recall Gadamer's insistence on what might be called the intentionality of understanding: it always involves coming to an understanding about some thing. Arriving at a common understanding of a common object is a linguistic process that requires achieving a common language. Thus Gadamer concurs with Schleiermacher that "everything presupposed in hermeneutics is only language." But for Schleiermacher, hermeneutics is the attempt to understand not some thing but rather another person, specifically through his expressions. Everything—the sole condition— presupposed by hermeneutics consists in these expressions. To say that they are language is certainly correct, but to say further that they are only language and

---

8. This is true not only of translation between languages but between times: "Archaism to some degree and a displacement of style toward the past are pervasive in the history and craft of translation" (Steiner, *After Babel*, p. 341).

nothing but language is mistaken. The force of this *only* derives from the fact that Schleiermacher conceives language as aesthetic self-expression which expresses only the subjectivity of the person expressing himself. What is only language does not express any thing; and though "everything" in Schleiermacher's proposition sounds perfectly all-inclusive, it actually excludes from the sphere of hermeneutics every thing. "Being that can be understood is language" takes Schleiermacher's proposition literally, but it means almost the opposite. It means at the very least that things, indeed all things, can be understood when we have words for them. To understand language is to understand the thing meant; and it is this common object, and not only language, which unites those trying to reach understanding.

When Gadamer writes that "the thing can scarcely be separated from language" (364 / 349), we must remember that for just this reason the contrary is true as well: language can scarcely be separated from the thing that is meant. Hermeneutics has traditionally been assigned to the sphere of grammar and rhetoric because it is concerned with understanding language, and Gadamer affirms the traditional categorization. But since he also affirms the unity of hermeneutics and dialectic, Gadamer expands the sphere of understanding to include things as well as language. This fact is easily forgotten because of the emphasis on language in this final section. We have seen that interpretation is neither prior nor posterior to understanding, and thus interpretation is the linguistic expression of understanding. But understanding is the understanding of things, and thus interpretation is best conceived as the process by which mind and world are unified in language. In ontological hermeneutics being makes itself understood *as* language.

THE SPIRIT OF THE LETTER

(3.1.A) In moving from conversation to translation as a model of the hermeneutic process, Gadamer turns from oral to written language as the medium of understanding. Translation remains a form of conversation in that it is a common object, the thing meant by original and translation alike, which unites the partners. Yet in the case of translation, the dialogue occurs between an interpreter and a text rather than between two persons. The text is like a silent partner that speaks only through the interpreter.[9] This situation, of course, can make for a very one-

---

9. "The broadest conception of literature and text," Gadamer writes, "is achieved by defining reading as making fixed writing speak" ("Philosophie und Literatur," p. 27). Horst Turk argues that in *TM* there is an ambiguity and vacillation between a conversation- and a text-oriented hermeneutic, and that the former possesses "only a limited explanatory power" ("Wahrheit oder Methode," p. 128).

sided conversation. Texts are in fact helplessly vulnerable to imposition; and unless the interpreter holds himself open to what the text says, there will be no dialogue, but only monologue. Yet it remains true that, in translation and interpretation generally, the interpreter must speak for the text. Its openness to imposition is a necessary consequence of its need for and openness to interpretation, and the interpreter who would fulfill his task cannot do otherwise than involve himself in the meaning of the text by speaking for it.

The object of interpretation is tradition in the form of language, and specifically silent, written language. Non-linguistic tradition is interpretable insofar as it too can be understood as language. But linguistic tradition is, in a special sense, definitively traditional, for it exists only traditionally. Unlike relics and remnants of the past, linguistic tradition (whether oral or written) disappears the moment it ceases to be handed down. An oral tradition never persists by sheer inertia. It cannot be left to endure on its own but requires that impetus be continually added by repetition. Language that exists only traditionally has less physical immediacy than the relics of the past, but the corollary of this deficiency is the advantage that linguistic tradition does not suffer time and change but thrives on it. However, it is not in oral but rather in written tradition that the non-immediacy of language is most fully realized. A book is a physical object subject to decay and destruction, but what is written in it is an ideal entity entirely abstracted from its physical embodiment. The word, not the palpable book, is the bearer of tradition; and written tradition attains a purely intangible, ideal existence that is not dependent on any particular book or any of the particularities of any reader.

The written word, moreover, is abstracted from the immediacy of sound and voice, on which oral tradition depends. Through texts we have direct access to the past without the multiple intermediaries necessitated in oral transmission. But for this reason it seems that texts persist on their own, that they do not require the mediation, the process of handing down so evident in oral tradition. Yet in fact written tradition, like oral, vanishes utterly when it is not interpreted. The waving branches of a tree indicate the wind, a portrait represents the person portrayed, a track in the snow suggests the passage of an animal, regardless of whether anyone interprets them that way or not. But a written word is absolutely meaningless unless and until it is interpreted to have a certain meaning. The ideality of the written word implies its absolute dependence on interpretation. It is not a word except when it is interpreted as such, and it exists nowhere outside the interpretations of it.

"In writing, language attains its true spirituality" (368 / 352). As an ideal entity detached and abstracted from physical embodiment, the letter is spirit. By reading we have direct access to a moment of the past, and this is not partial access through remnants and fragments but access to a whole. When this whole is conveyed in the medium of writing, the past attains the permanence characteristic of spirit, for it is available to every present and to anyone who can read. But more than merely available to readers, written tradition is dependent on them, for writing is meaningless without being interpreted. A text, of itself silent and dumb, needs the interpreter to speak for it; and he must speak in his language, the language of the present. Like a mirror, a text gives the interpreter the clearest possible image of the past, but it is a virtual image and does not exist unless he looks into the mirror—that is, interprets the text. Without the participation of the present, the written past disappears; and thus the reader of the written word does not and need not return to the past, for in reading he is "simultaneously here and there" (368 / 352). Through writing, the past is disembodied, abstracted, and alienated in a purely spiritual existence that makes it permanent and contemporaneous with every present.[10] But the spirit of the letter is empty meaninglessness until it is given flesh, made concrete and real, in each interpretation of it.

"Writing is no mere accident or supplement that qualitatively alters nothing in the continuance of oral tradition" (369 / 353). The difference writing makes is as great as the difference between play and plays, and of the same kind, for writing marks the same transformation as the metamorphosis into form (*Gebilde*) that distinguishes a drama from a game. As ideal, written tradition consists in language detached from voice and speech so that it lives a life of its own independent of the life of the writer and his original readers. The meaningfulness of writing, unlike that of speech, does not require the presence of the writer, and it survives his death. Even if a text, such as a letter, is addressed to a specific recipient, its meaning cannot be confined to what the addressee understands because, as writing, it is intelligible to everyone in any time, whatever the circumstances when it is read. It becomes, as it were, public property, the property of every time and of everyone who can read. Writing can be copied, reproduced, and repeated ad infinitum because it possesses an autonomy of

---

10. Ricoeur explains, "In living speech, the instance of discourse has the character of a fleeting event. The event appears and disappears. This is why there is a problem of fixation, of inscription. . . . This inscription, in spite of its perils, is discourse's destination. What in effect does writing fix? Not the event of speaking, but the 'said' of speaking" ("Model of the Text," p. 318). Gadamer differs from Ricoeur only in that he conceives writing as an abstraction and alienation from the event; thus writing needs to be "re-eventualized" in a new speech act in order to become fully meaningful. For a fuller comparison, see Kirkland, "Gadamer and Ricoeur: The Paradigm of the Text."

meaning independent of the life of the author and his initial audience.[11] "A text," therefore, "is not to be understood as an expression of life" (370 / 354). The ideality of writing detaches meaning from the psyche of the writer and reader, and thus the meaning of written tradition cannot be interpreted psychologically.

When we do not understand something spoken to us, we can ask the speaker for an explanation. But in interpreting a text no such explanation is forthcoming unless we offer it ourselves. Whereas speech interprets itself by intonation, accent, and reference to the circumstances in which it is spoken, the written word is helpless in the absence of such aids to understanding, as Plato rightly saw. Writing is defenseless against misinterpretation. Yet Plato was himself a writer, and he wrote in such a way that the train of thought in the Socratic dialogues follows the course of dialectic: thought is drawn into the peripatetic course of the thing itself as it unfolds itself. The counterpart of the helplessness of writing is that written language is freed from the the contingencies of its origin to follow the track of the thing itself. The reader of a written text need not be distracted from its subject matter by the special psychological situation of a speaker or the particular historical circumstances of his immediate hearers. The peculiarities of its genesis do not determine once and for all the meaning of a text permanently fixed in writing, for it survives them. It forms new relationships and acquires new addressees. For a reader, what is written always appears addressed directly to him. "What he understands is always already more than an alien opinion—it is always already possible truth. This is what becomes manifest through the dissolution of the spoken from the speaker and the lasting permanence that writing bestows" (372 / 356).

(3.1.B) Not only does what is understood, the interpreted object, consist in language; understanding itself is a linguistic process. It is, of course, true that the critic or historian not only reads books but writes them. He writes an interpretation and his understanding is published as a text. But here Gadamer is concerned with the linguistic nature of understanding, regardless of whether pen is ever put to paper. As interpretation, understanding consists in finding words and concepts to explain the meaning of a text or historical event. Those we find first are the readiest to hand, and these words and concepts currently available in common usage we very often employ without considering where they come from or whether they are in fact apt and appropriate. In one sense they are indeed

---

11. Compare Derrida, "Signature Event Context," pp. 179–80.

always applicable. Nothing in the object will prevent us from applying them if we choose to, and yet the danger is always that the past is unconsciously subsumed under the familiar language of the present. The historical past is subordinated to the dominion of the present when the present frame of reference is itself dominated by invisible prejudices. But once we become conscious of this problem and of the possible unsuitability of our own language, the solution is scarcely to drop our contemporary linguistic and conceptual frame of reference or replace it with that of the past. The ideal interpretation of a poem is not a copy of it; quite the contrary, a copy is no interpretation at all. Assuming the words and concepts of the past and abandoning those of the present is simply the abandonment of the attempt to understand. On the one hand, then, subordinating the past to the present leads to misunderstanding; but on the other, returning to the past leads to no understanding whatever.

The alternative to both that makes right understanding possible consists in the fusion of horizons, which we have seen is a fusion of languages. It is this process alone that enables the text to say something, to address us and tell us something that we do not already know. "Through interpretation a text comes to speak. But no text and no book speaks if it does not speak the language that reaches the other" (375 / 358). That an old text does not still speak an intelligible language marks the need and occasion for interpretive understanding; and since it speaks an unintelligible language, simply reproducing and repeating it does not render it any more intelligible. Yet the fact that it does speak a language means that it can indeed be understood—if it is translated. The fusion of languages—not just in translation proper but in any interpretive understanding— does not abandon the words and concepts of the present, for only this linguistic framework is intelligible. The language of the present is always the sole language of understanding, and yet the fusion of language does not involve the subordination of past concepts to those of the present either, because fusion is bilateral. "To think historically always already contains a mediation between those concepts and one's own thought" (374 / 350). When languages are fused in such a mediation, neither remains what it was. Something happens to both, and that event—itself a historical event—is historical understanding.

If we conceive of mediation only as the establishment of a relation between a past and a present, we can see easily enough how and why understanding changes. An interpretation must make a fixed text speak to the mobile present; as times change and the language of the text again falls mute and unintelligible, interpretation must find words within a new language that will enable it to speak again, to a new time. If interpretation is the establishment of relation and the relation changes as what is related changes, "there can therefore be no interpretation correct 'in itself''' (375 / 358). But this conception of mediation as relation leads straight into relativism—the meaning of the fixed past is relative to a changing present. And while Gadamer certainly denies the possibility of a single correct interpretation, he also denies the determinacy of the historical past, its languages, and its meanings. Thus he conceives the mediation of past and present not as a relation of one to the other but as the fusion of both.

In fusion two things blend, merge, and become indivisible. To conceive historical understanding as fusion implies that the historian's interpretation becomes one with the historical object it interprets, and the very fact that this process of unification is linguistic shows at the same time how fusion is possible and why understanding is not relative. We have seen that in naive interpretation, the historian's words and concepts are employed unselfconsciously, as if they were self-evidently applicable and transparent. In sophisticated interpretation, by contrast, the interpreter's universe of discourse becomes conscious, its limits become apparent, and its once obvious appropriateness becomes dubious. If that does not mean he either can or should abandon it, then he must consciously bend his language, adapt his concepts, and expand his universe of discourse by assimilating and fusing it with that other universe he wants to understand. Insofar as this warping remains a manifest distortion of the interpreter's language (recall the example of pidgin English), fusion has to that degree failed and is incomplete. We can still differentiate the two things, the interpretation and what it interprets. That is, the interpretation still insists on its own separate existence. When genuine understanding occurs, however, the interpreter's language does not call attention to itself but rather directs attention to what is meant. Interpretation does not set up a second sense of its own to which the sense of the text would be relative: such duality signals rather the failure of interpretation. ''The interpretive concepts are not at all thematized as such. It is their function rather to disappear behind what they bring to speak in interpretation. Paradoxically, an interpretation is right when it is able to disappear in this way'' (375–76 / 359).

A perfect mediation is one in which the medium disappears. A correct interpretation is one that is transparent and thus cannot be differentiated from what it interprets. This non-differentiation is fusion, understanding. Paradoxically, the mark of its occurrence is that it goes and should go unremarked, and this unremarkability defines the character of language, including interpretive language, when it is functioning properly.

Naive interpretation lacks the consciousness of language, as of all prejudice. Wirkungsgeschichtliches Bewusstsein, however, is the interpreter's consciousness of language's effects on himself and on what he interprets. Yet all the effort that goes into building the hermeneutic consciousness of language is directed toward making the interpreter's words and concepts just as transparent and invisible as they are in naive interpretation. Understanding reaches its highest sophistication in this second naivete—when it recedes, effaces itself, and simply lets the text speak through it, without interference.

Gadamer's exposition of fusion offers the positive counterpart to his critical argument against the ideal of historical objectivity, the divorce of interpretation from what it interprets, and also against aesthetic differentiation, which involves the same schism. When we watch the performance of a play and the production is good, it is the play itself that we see, not the interpretation of it. It is an interpretation that is presented, of course, but we do not see it as that. We now understand that this same invisibility ideally holds true for academic interpretation of the play in books and articles. "There is then no basic difference between the interpretation which a work experiences in its reproduction and that which the philologist performs" (377 / 361).

The same is the case with respect to music, painting, and the plastic arts. Yet non-verbal art seems most clearly to raise doubts about the equation of interpretation and understanding because it calls into question the adequacy of language to understanding. We are most likely to appeal to the principle of ineffability when confronted with non-literary works of art. 'Words cannot express . . . ' is the phrase that comes to mind—which does not mean that the work is meaningless or unintelligible. On the contrary, by this phrase we want to say that we do understand the work and that our understanding outstrips and exceeds the possibilities of language to express it. The difficulty that non-verbal art poses, the objection it implies to the unification of understanding and interpretive language, marks a critical juncture in Gadamer's argument. It is easy enough to conceive of literary interpretation as rewording or paraphrase. Without much more difficulty we can conceive of it as translation, though the question arises as to whether there are certain words and phrases—or even all poetry—that defy translation or interpretation from one language to another. But with respect to non-literary art this problem is especially acute, for here the question is whether it is possible to "translate" the non-verbal into words.

But isn't this the question of language generally—of how it is possible to word things? Non-verbal art poses no special problem of ineffability that is not already posed by the meanest pebble on the shore. There are indeed many moments, and not just in art interpretation, when we feel constricted by the expressive capacity of common usage. Yet the very critique of these common forms is itself expressed in the form of language, and language contains within it a principle of growth whereby common usage continually expands to meet the needs of thought and understanding.[12] To this enlargement there are no insuperable limits. Though it is sometimes true that 'words cannot express,' yet nothing that can be understood is necessarily and of itself ineffable; and when we do understand something, that is the point when we can *say* what we understand, the unity of thought and word and thing.

Precisely the integrity of this union accounts for the difficulty of translation. The very transparency and perfect suitability of our own language to things has as its counterpart that it seems impossible that any other language could possess the same appropriateness. The tightness of this bond between language and things makes it appear that reason is therefore bound to and bound by one language. The plurality of languages makes it clear, however, that things are dependent on no particular language, and the fact is that reason is not either. "Hermeneutic experience is the corrective through which thinking reason withdraws from the bonds of the linguistic, and is itself linguistically constituted" (380 / 363). Though difficult, translation is always possible; and if it becomes too unwieldy, then it is possible to learn the foreign language so thoroughly that it becomes one's own language and translation is no longer necessary. But even were these two alternatives not available, there is no boundary to a language, no limit that it cannot overstep so that understanding would be inescapably imprisoned in it. "Every language, despite its difference from other languages, can say everything it wants" (380 / 363). Hermeneutics is what enables it to say what other languages want to say as well. Hermeneutics, that is, is the very process by which the expressive capacity of a language is enlarged and its universe of discourse expanded. Through hermeneutics a language becomes able to say something which it could not say before.

The fact that interpretation is an event in the history of a language (because during interpretation something happens to the interpreter's language) can, and even should, go entirely unnoticed. In both the first and second naivete, the interpreter's words and concepts do not become manifest as objects in themselves. In being applied to things, these words and concepts are themselves modified because application, as we have seen above, is not the subsumption of a particular under a universal that leaves the universal unchanged. Rather application involves a continual process of language formation and conceptual development. Without

---

12. The point Gadamer is making here is that no critique of language from outside language is possible, and furthermore none is needed. Note that this argument parallels Gadamer's discussion of history, and for good reason: Language is the concretization of Wirkungsgeschichte.

the consciousness of language, this process goes on behind our back; and the same happens despite the heightening of linguistic consciousness resulting from modern philosophy of language.

In fact, Gadamer suggests, philosophy of language has not gotten beyond the first naivete. "The path from the complete unconsciousness of language in classical Greece leads to the instrumentalist devaluation of language in modernity" (381 / 365). Certainly there has been an increased consciousness and increased sophistication with respect to language, but Gadamer finds this to be a false sophistication precisely insofar as philosophy or linguistics endeavors to become conscious of language as an object in itself. Their very identity as sciences requires them to make language an object of research. Yet this, in Gadamer's view, is impossible. To investigate language as such and in itself means that it must be purified and separated from the things it means. It becomes a form without, and opposed to, a content. Cassirer calls it a symbolic form, and this formalism is brought to perfection when Saussure conceives of language as a set of pure differences—that is, differences without termini that are differentiated.[13] If language as a system of formal differences can be studied without regard to the conversations in which it is employed and the situations to which it is applied, that implies the forms are not affected by the content they express. We pick them up, employ them, and then return them in the same condition until they are needed again. That is to say, the objectification of language as a formal system leads to a naive instrumentalism—naive because it has no choice but to ignore the effect of application, the back-pressure of the content on the form, since the elimination of that content was the condition of objectification.

Language, Gadamer argues, is not an instrument because, unlike a tool, it does not exist as such apart from its use; and there is no more objective science, no higher consciousness of language than that already implicit in speaking it and applying it to things. But being able to speak implies being able to say what we mean and no longer having to think about the words per se. Despite the work of grammarians, linguists, philologists, and philosophers of language, "unconsciousness of language has not ceased to be the genuine mode of being of speaking" (382 / 366). Even when we are talking about language, our own words recede from view and hide themselves precisely in expressing the thing meant. Language is most itself when it is transparent and self-concealing, when it reveals not itself but its object; and if there are fundamentally no bounds to language, then language "is never a mere object but comprehends everything

---

13. See Saussure's *Course in General Linguistics*, pp. 117–18.

that can ever be an object'' (382 / 365). All consciousness, as Husserl showed, is consciousness of something. What Gadamer suggests is that language exceeds consciousness and its control because language is the condition of the consciousness of all objects whatsoever.

THE RISE OF "LANGUAGE"

(3.2.A) We have seen that hermeneutic consciousness, wirkungsgeschichliches Bewusstsein, finds its paradigmatic realization in the interpreter's awareness that the words and concepts he employs are historically conditioned and that they prejudice his interpretation. For this reason, he does not automatically accept their validity or assume their eternal verity; rather he inquires into their origin and history.[14] *Language* is itself a word and concept, and an especially important one for Gadamer and modern interpretation generally. That language too has a history and origin which require our attention becomes obvious when we recall that classical Greek has no word for it. Language existed long before "language," and to the early history of the latter, from classical Greece to the Middle Ages, Gadamer now directs our attention.

Modern instrumentalism has its source, Gadamer contends, in Greek thought, specifically in Plato's *Cratylus*. Here the indivisible unity of word, meaning, and thing is first called into question. In Greek, a word is *onoma*, noun or name. A name belongs to the person who answers to it. It is part of him and in fact says who he is. To consider all words as names in a pre-philosophical way presumes the unity of language and things, the name with what it names. "Greek philosophy, we can almost say, began with the recognition that the word is only a name, that is, it does not substitute for true being" (383 / 366). Thus the unity of word and object became dubious, and the *Cratylus* discusses two theories about their possible relation, neither very satisfactory.

Both theories begin with the object. Once we have the object, we might say on the one hand that the word is given to it or, on the other, that the word is found for it. In the first view, an object is given a name. It is christened, as

---

14. Gadamer considers all words as shifters, as occasional expressions such as "here," whose meaning is completed by their usage in concrete situations and can be understood only when those situations are understood. "Is it not true of every meaning that, as what the word means, it always stands within the horizon of determinate situations? Is it not characteristic of the meaning of every word that its formation has a determinate history? . . . Thus is there not in every meaning a piece of history? . . . And are they not all completed only through the situation, the context, in which they stand?" (*Über die Ursprunglichkeit der Philosophie*, p. 22).

a child that comes into the world without a name later receives one, even a specially made up one; and this name can be subsequently changed virtually at will. Yet it is obvious, if also somewhat curious, that so-called proper names are a great deal easier to alter than common ones, which remain comparatively permanent. But only comparatively. All words change in the course of time; and even if objects are never actually christened with words, yet it is quite plausible that language accrues to things by a societal and impersonal act of institution and convention.

In the second view, however, words are not made up and given to things but rather are found for them. Whereas the conventionalist theory supposes no reason but only the fact of the connection between word and object, the idea of finding words to express something implies the idea of finding the right words. Even if finding means only selecting a word from an available pool, this decision supposes a criterion of selection; and insofar as the selection theory differs from the conventionalist theory, its criterion of appropriateness is not simply conventionality, a criterion that takes its cue from other speakers. Rather the criterion of selection is similarity, naturalness, or agreement with the thing. The problem with this view is that, even if what constitutes the adequacy of word to thing could be clearly defined, it is still difficult to explain the mutability and plurality of words and languages. The conventionalist theory does most justice to our sense of the variability and arbitrariness of words for a given thing, but does least justice to our sense that certain words are right and others not. The advantage and disadvantage of the selection theory are just the reverse.

Plato's *Cratylus* raises doubts about both, and perhaps for the same reason. Both views presume the givenness of the object and inquire only about how words are subsequently joined to something already known, prior to its verbalization. The fact that neither theory of language is accepted in the *Cratylus* directs us away from language and toward the non-linguistic knowledge of the Ideas. In this way Plato hoped to preserve that knowledge from the doubts cast on it by the verbal paradoxes and linguistic aporias typical of the sophists. To obviate these problems it was necessary to obviate words. Thus the consequence of his reaction against the sophists was that "Plato's discovery of the Ideas covered up the real essence of language even more completely than the sophist theoreticians" (385 / 369).

Plato does not affirm either theory of language, but he does not absolutely deny them either because he shares their common premise, and it is this premise— the priority of knowledge to language—which links the *Cratylus* to modern instrumentalism. Nor does Gadamer deny them ultimately, because each, by reason of its inadequacy, summons the aid of the other; and the insufficiency of both suggests the unity of word and thing that is Gadamer's thesis. On the one hand, it is clear that in general Plato retains a preference for the selection or resemblance theory insofar as the model of copy and original is his standard model of knowledge. But it is precisely with respect to ideal, rational entities— for example, numbers—that correctness defined as similarity runs into the most obvious difficulties, for there can be no resemblance between the sound of a word and a number or any idea. The names of numbers must therefore owe their existence to convention alone. Socrates reduces the similarity principle ad absurdum when he insists that, if a word resembles its object, so also must its letters. It is evident that no knowledge about the thing is conveyed in the letters of its name, and there is none conveyed in words either. Socrates implies in this way that the locus of truth is therefore not words but rather the logos.

Gadamer concurs that truth is not to be found in individual words or even in all the words in a language, but for him this admission does not require the abandonment of language as the locus of truth in favor of a wordless logos. As letters first become meaningful when they are linked in words, so words first become capable of being true when they are organized in discourse. There can be no decomposition of veridical units into their elements because truth can occur only when a certain level of organization has been reached. Socrates is right, then, that there is no truth in individual words, but that is not because truth exists somewhere outside language but rather because truth belongs to discourse. That truth is not to be found in a dictionary says nothing against its presence in language, for language is not to be found there either but instead in speaking and writing.

Socrates takes us in the opposite direction. In his emphasis on the logos as the exclusive bearer of knowledge and truth, "we see that the real paradigm of the noetic is not the word but the number whose naming is obviously pure convention and whose 'exactitude' consists in the fact that it is defined by its place in the series, that is, by its being a pure structure of intelligibility, an ens rationis" (390 / 373). "One" can be spoken but "1" cannot. What a number means can only be thought; it is only mute logos not language. If logos is best represented in the rational sequence of numbers, then (Socrates implies) words best serve their purpose when they function like numbers, pure signs. A copy (the basis of the similarity theory) exists in its own right even when the original is absent or no longer exists at all; by means of its own characteristics a copy resembles its original. But by contrast to the copy, the purity of a pure sign consists in the fact that ideally it points or refers without existing. It means without being. Or if it must have some existence in order to signify at all, then a sign's purity means that its specific characteristics do not matter. They can be varied at will, as accords with the conventionalist theory. If it is not convenient to write "eighteen," then we can write "XVIII" or "18" or "*n*." The only question is utility, for if language is a system of pure signs, then it is a mere tool that either serves its purpose or else is replaced with a better tool. The epoch-making decision about language implied in the transition from language as *eikon* to language as *semeion* in the *Cratylus* leads to the universal language schemes of the seventeenth and eighteenth centuries and also to the more ambitious construction of artificial languages in the twentieth. It leads to the notion that language is a means in the service of techne. In Plato's emphasis on the silent logos, in his insistence on the independence of thought and its object from words, there was already implicit the technologization of language.

In Gadamer's view, however, language is not an instrument at the disposal of will, desire, consciousness, or subjectivity generally. Thus he affirms that, as with the mimesis theory of art, there is still something right about the iconic theory of language. This affirmation does not imply that he asserts some visual or aural similarity between discourse and its object, only that they belong together. Gadamer never denies the maxim of Luther that prefaces the second part of his book: "Qui non intelligit res, non potest ex verbis sensum elicere." No one who does not understand the thing is able to elicit meaning from the words. Yet Gadamer suggests that the reverse is also true, that, as George writes, "Kein Ding sei, wo das Wort gebricht" (464 / 445). Where the word breaks off, no thing can be. There is no understanding of things apart from language, and no understanding of language apart from things. They belong together.

The defect of artificial language schemes, such as Leibniz's *characteristica universalis*, is their presumption that knowledge can be constructed in advance of experience.[15] "Yet it is universally the case that human imperfection does not permit adequate knowledge a priori, and experience is indispensable" (393 / 376). One cannot devise a language in advance of experience. But if not prior, language is not posterior to experience either. "Experience is not wordless at first and then made an object of reflection by being named. . . . Rather seeking and finding words to express it belongs to experience itself" (394 / 377). One advantage of the resemblance theory is that it recognizes this indivisible reciprocity between discourse and thing. A second advantage is that a copy does not betray the embarrassment over its own existence that one finds in the sign.

---

15. "After Gödel," writes Apel, "a single world calculus on the basis of a single formalized language of science, the dream of neoleibnizianism, proved utopian" (in Bubner, ed., *Hermeneutik und Dialektik*, p. 106).

A pure sign ideally means without being; and insofar as language is conceived of as semiotic, its own being seems always an obstacle to be gotten around, superseded, or merely concealed. But if semiotics finds its ideal in forgetting the being of language, the iconic theory serves as a corrective and reminder that even the purest sign must exist in order to be a sign. And in that existence the sign is like a copy, which—however it effaces itself in deference to the original—nevertheless conveys meaning through its own characteristics and its own existence. Conceived of as iconic, language is a thing that means, a being that can be understood.

(3.2.B) Though Plato's philosophy of the logos involves the attempt to overcome language and hence to forget its existence, the Christian idea of incarnation reasserts the importance of the word, for Christianity begins with the advent, the Incarnation when the Word was made flesh. The philosophy of the logos corresponds to the Platonic and Pythagorean idea of embodiment—which, Gadamer explains, is quite distinct from incarnation and implies a different theory of language as its analogue. In embodiment, the soul maintains an identity separate from the body. It does not become body but temporarily resides there and retains, during migration, a distinctness from each of its embodiments until it is finally released from them all. The relation of soul and body is something like that between content and form, or the thing in itself and its appearance. The content can take on any number of forms but it is not itself any one of them. Among modern semantic theories, embodiment corresponds most closely to the class theory of meaning, in which the meaning of a sentence (its proposition) consists in what is meant by the class of all sentences synonymous with it.[16] Not the actual sentence but the ideal proposition (like the logos) is the bearer of truth and falsehood, and no sentence in the class is the proposition, it only means it. The proposition itself is ineffable.

In incarnation, by contrast, the Word becomes flesh. When Christ manifested himself to men in human form, this form was not a mere manifestation or appearance, a mere form either concealing or revealing a content different from itself. Whereas the Greek gods appeared in human guise, the doctrine of the church is that Christ became a man, without diminution of his divinity. Whereas the idea of embodiment implies that the soul is not pure until it is released from the flesh, "in the incarnation the reality of spirit first comes into

16. Hirsch draws on this theory of meaning to support the intentionalist criterion of correct interpretation in *The Aims of Interpretation*, pp. 50–73.

its full perfection" (396 / 379). Spirit is not lessened but instead realized by its incarnation. The advent, moreover, is an event which, like all historical events, is unique; and thus in contrast to the ideality of the disembodied logos, the Christian doctrine of the incarnate Verbum insists on the reality of history. In the event of incarnation the word is uttered, spoken, and thereby realized.

It is the act or event of speech that is here drawn to our attention. If the class theory of meaning is analogous to the idea of embodiment, the closest modern correlate of incarnation is speech act theory. The class theory takes as its model the constative sentence, a statement or assertion whose meaning is located in a proposition itself ineffable. J. L. Austin's speech act theory, on the other hand, takes the performative utterance (for example, a command or promise) as its paradigm. This paradigm is actually more inclusive insofar as even statements and assertions need to be stated and asserted, and thus they too are performatives. The contrast between the two theories becomes apparent when we see that there can be no such thing as an ineffable performative. A promise becomes binding—that is, it first becomes a promise—when it is spoken. Its being uttered, performed, and incarnated in a speech act is not something secondary but instead a necessary condition of its meaning. Saying makes the word flesh, makes it concrete, and only then is it real. The act of making a promise is the promise itself. A speech act is an event that both is and means.

It is not to Austin,[17] however, but to Augustine and especially Aquinas that Gadamer turns for an understanding of the relation of thought and word implied in incarnation. The Christian Verbum, we have seen, is distinguished from the Greek logos by the fact of the advent, the unique fact of history that is the Incarnation. The logos does not occur; it is fixed, permanent, and eternal. Yet we read in John's gospel that the Word was with God from the beginning—and in that respect it is, like the Platonic logos, eternal. One problem, then, is how to reconcile the eternality of the Verbum with the historicity of the advent. This apparent contradiction is what draws Gadamer's interest away from the disembodied and non-temporal logos toward the incarnate Verbum, for the Incarnation raises precisely the question about the advent of truth that is Gadamer's own: If truth is one and the same, like God the Father, how can truth occur in time, like God the Son?

When the church fathers affirmed the Trinity and rejected the doctrine that

---

17. Gadamer cites Austin for the first time in the third edition of *WM* (p. 404n). Misgeld differentiates Austin and Gadamer in that "Gadamer does not emphasize the concept of rule in his analysis of dialogically proceeding inquiry" ("Discourse and Conversation," p. 328).

the Son was subordinate to the Father, they denied the subordination of the word to what it reveals, and Gadamer (in contrast to Plato) denies this as well. It is the union of Father and Son that the theologians maintain, just as Gadamer maintains the union of thought and language. But the problem remains that the spoken word is implicated in time, history, variety, and multiplicity. Thus to explain the fact that the Word was with God from all eternity, the church fathers distinguish the inner, mental, or rational word from the external, spoken word; and it is by appeal to the former that they elucidate the mysterious unity of the Trinity. God the Father is related to God the Son as thought is related to the mental word. They are indivisibly one yet not identical. When Augustine elevates the mental word and depreciates the spoken word to a secondary importance, he preserves the superiority of the one Word above the multiplicity of imperfect languages actually spoken by men. In this way, however, he turns the verbum back into the silent, atemporal logos. Gadamer agrees that thought is not bound to any particular language, for it is always possible to expand one's language or learn a new one. Yet thought always takes place in some language, and that language is tied to a particular place and time. Like Plato and influenced by him, Augustine does not do justice to the facticity and temporality of the word that become most apparent when it is spoken.

Aquinas too begins with the inner word and, influenced indirectly by Plato through Aristotle, finds the concept of the logos again appropriate to explicate the Trinity. Yet for Thomas the verbum remains something different from the logos. Even though it is silent and belongs to no particular language, the mental word and thought itself, according to Thomas, have a temporal character that is overlooked by Augustine. As the word is never a single word but a sequence, so thought is not intuitive but discursive. Since finite understanding does not comprehend in a single intuition what it comes to know, it requires a train of thoughts or mental words. We have mentioned above that words become meaningful and veridical only when a certain level of organization has been reached— that is, in discourse. What Thomas shows is that this discursiveness, along with the temporality and plurality it implies, is necessitated by the finitude of the human intellect.[18]

---

18. Cf. Gadamer: "What Heidegger's provocative formulation ["die Sprache spricht"] means is the precedence of language to every individual speaker. Thus one can say in a certain sense . . . that language possesses a certain, though limited, pregivenness with respect to thought. The reasonable meaning of 'language speaks' appears to me to be included in the neoplatonic moment that the one word, which is, however, truly the word of thought, articulates itself in words and discourse" (KS 4:169).

For Thomas, the Son is related to the Father not merely as the mental word is to thought, but as thoughts (or words) are related to other thoughts (or words) in a discursive sequence. Despite the fact that discursiveness is a mark of finitude, Thomas considers it an apt metaphor for the Trinity because it addresses both aspects of the issue: the Son is with the Father from the beginning, yet is born of the Father. Discursiveness is able to display both these aspects because the sequence it involves is not merely a series of one thing after another, an association of unrelated ideas. Rather Thomas's paradigm of discursive thought is the syllogism. This model catches the successive nature of thought, the fact that it is necessary to proceed through a series of premises in order to reach a conclusion; yet the syllogism also suggests that the conclusion was implied in the premises from the beginning. The Son emanates from the Father as a conclusion from the premises.

When Aquinas allies the process of syllogistic reasoning to the neoplatonic concept of emanation, he focuses attention on an aspect of the verbum that distinguishes it from the logos. Emanation is a process of proliferation by which the one becomes many. Whereas in Plato's philosophy (or Hegel's) this plurality is a sign of some degeneration, denaturing, or deficiency in the one, its need for reintegration, no such lack is implied in the emanation of the Son from the Father. They are two but also one. The Son is both the same and different from the Father: the Word (and the word) is both the same and different from what it reveals. As the Word was with the Father from the beginning and yet is independent, so also is the human word neither identical nor unrelated, neither prior nor posterior, to the thing it means. If Gadamer too believes that in the beginning was the word, it is because he conceives of the process of historical emanation whereby one thing emerges from another as the discursive process whereby word emerges from word. In both cases, it is a movement from the actual to the actual. We have seen above that Gadamer reasserts the iconic theory of language, in which an existent means an existent. Now, with the aid of St. Thomas, he can further conceive of meaning, the relation of original to copy, as process. It is still a relation of concrete to concrete, but now that relation is understood to be a historical process. The movement of original to copy is a discursive emanation from the actual to the actual.

From his consideration of Aquinas, Gadamer draws several inferences. The nature of finitude, as disclosed by the discursiveness of human intellect, consists in the fact that finite mind never arrives at complete self-presence. That thought is discursive and not intuitively immediate means that there is always a delay, a path to be traversed, before the conclusion can be reached. Thought is in process essentially, always on the way, and it must always defer its conclusions until the process is unfolded. As a historian must await the outcome, the consequences of an event, before he can understand it, so also there is a deferral, more general but of the same type, endemic to discursive thought itself. Waiting, being inbetween, having set out but not yet having arrived, is the condition of finite mind that is not present to itself or its object but is rather processual and historical—that is, dependent on past and future. But though discursiveness betrays the finitude of thought, it also discloses its infinite freedom. There is always room for further interpretation. The fact that the human word is not one but many, the fact that the object of thought is not wholly realized in any one of its conceptions, impels it constantly forward toward further words and concepts, and gives it an essentially unlimited freedom to produce new ones.

(3.2.C) For Aquinas, we have seen, discursiveness (and rational thought itself) finds its paradigmatic expression in the syllogism, as it did for Aristotle as well. When Gadamer considers the relation of language to the process of concept formation, however, he calls into question the supposition that logic, whether deductive or inductive, plays the primary role in this process. If, with Gadamer, we conceive of thought as language rather than logic, then we can see the inadequacy of both deduction and induction as models of thought in general. It is clear that words have a preestablished meaning, a general sense, that precedes their use in a particular instance. Thus it seems that the application of a word to a particular object consists in subsuming the particular under the general concept, which concept is the meaning of the word. Application conceived of in this way as subsumption accords with the deductive model. But subsumption allows for no change in the concept and produces no new concept beyond those already implicit in the premises. Thus it cannot explain where concepts come from or the continuing process of concept formation that is always taking place as language is used. Since it is focused on the opposite, deduction takes no account of the determination of the universal by the particular, the dependency of meaning on context, or the back-formation of concepts through the application of words to concrete instances by a particular speaker in a specific situation.

But it seems, therefore, that the inadequacy of deductive subsumption simply refers us to the inductive schema, which describes the generation of concepts precisely through the determination of the universal by the particular. The inductive model does not, like the deductive, begin with the concept but rather ends with it, and thus its problem is the reverse. Here the correlate and opposite of subsumption is what induction supposes is an origin in wordless, conceptless experience which then subsequently acquires conceptual language by a process of abstracting the element common to many such experiences. This view, how-ever, places the advent of word and concept too late. We need not and do not wait on the process of abstraction, the discovery of the common de-nominator, to render the similarity of experiences linguistically expressible and concep-tualizable. It is possible to say that man is a wolf without knowing that both are mammals or rapacious. Even before we have a generic term for what is common to two things, we can connect them metaphorically by transferring the name of the one to the other.

If thought is indivisible from language, then thought is more fundamentally metaphorical than logical. Metaphor is a specifically linguistic process of concept formation (*Bildung*), since a concept is altered and expanded when a *word* is transferred from one thing to another so that the new thing becomes intelligible. Yet the process is not merely verbal because it is the new *thing* to which the word is applied that changes and enlarges the concept, the meaning of the word. Metaphor is the linguistic basis of the bilateral and reciprocal nature of application that Gadamer underlines so strongly. Induction and deduction, by contrast, are unilateral, hierarchical, and unidirectional: they proceed either from the particular to the universal or vice versa, but not both. Metaphor, by contrast, consists in a reversible, oscillating, circular movement. If pages are like leaves, then leaves are also like pages. Each sets up a resonance in the other, thereby leveling the hierarchy. Whereas induction and deduction are vertical models of thought, concerned with the "higher" universal and the "lower" particular, metaphorical transference operates horizontally. Like the iconic relation of existent to existent or the emanation of the real from the real, metaphor connects two things on the same plane. To say that a table has legs does not subsume it to the body; to say that the human body has a trunk does not abstract something common to it and a tree. Neither descending nor ascending, neither subsumption nor abstraction, metaphor is a lateral movement. Like deduction, metaphor begins with a concept, but the concept is changed by the transferred application; like induction, it ends with a new concept, but by the metamorphosis of a previous one.[19] Because it is horizontal, metaphor flattens out the difference between particular and general, unfamiliar and familiar. If we have a very particular experience, one that is new and strange, and we want to express it in all its novelty as it was never expressed

---

19. "For the theory of metaphor," Gadamer writes, "Kant's hint in paragraph 59 [of the *Critique of Judgment*] still seems to me the most profound; metaphor basically does not compare two contents but rather 'transfers reflection beyond the object of intuition to a completely different concept, to which perhaps an intuition can never directly correspond'" ("Anschauung und Anschau-lichkeit," p. 13).

before, we reach almost automatically for metaphor. But even in such defamiliarizing transferences as "the pages of the tree," the unique appeals back to the familiar and the singular to the common.

The horizontal character of metaphor is related to the fact that it is an exclusively discursive phenomenon.[20] No word is in itself metaphorical but only in combination with others. Yet this does not mean that language is in itself unmetaphorical, for it too is discursive and does not consist in individual words but rather in their being woven together in texts and contexts, spoken and written. Each word modifies, determines, and is determined by the others in the discursive sequence. If we take the mutually interpretive relation of text and context, neither of which can be understood without the other, as the standard version of the hermeneutic circle, we can see that metaphorical transference is a paradigm of this continuing back-and-forth oscillation. When a word carries over from one sphere of reference to another, when leaves become pages and pages leaves, neither is left unchanged; and because of this reciprocity it becomes difficult and finally impossible to determine which is the tenor and which the vehicle, which text and which context. For the same reason, it is ultimately impossible to separate language into literal and metaphorical, for the literal consists in forgotten metaphor, the forgotten fusion of two spheres of discourse into identity. This phrase already suggests that in metaphor we find a model of the fusion of horizons, which is itself a version of the hermeneutic circle. So too metaphorical transference (*Übertragung*) is the linguistic analogue[21] of tradition (*Überlieferung*): both involve the same process of carrying over in which not only concepts are formed but a common sense. Finally, the centrality of the hermeneutic *as* in *Truth and Method* indicates how fundamental is the importance of metaphor.

Indeed, if we reconsider the book's earlier sections we can see that metaphor is not merely a central concept for Gadamer but also a mode of thought. Art is considered as play, plays, and tragedy. Each is a figure of art and, as becomes clear in retrospect, also of history and truth. Gadamer's figurative, sometimes even allegorical, mode of thought makes *Truth and Method* particularly rich but also particularly difficult to understand. When he writes about playing, for instance, he writes entirely about playing and makes significant contributions to the theory of play itself; and yet at the same time the reader is perfectly aware that playing is not at all his primary concern, even when he is writing about nothing else. We sense the same ambiguity in the previous section on the Trinity.

---

20. Ricoeur makes this point in *The Rule of Metaphor*, pp. 21, 97.
21. Gadamer makes this analogy explicit in *Die Aktualität des Schönen*, p. 64.

Aquinas employs the human word as a figure of the divine Word. Gadamer, it would seem, employs the divine Word as a figure of the human word. That is, he apparently reads—even misreads—Aquinas's metaphor in reverse, as if the vehicle were the tenor. And yet it is not at all clear that Gadamer takes the divine merely as a metaphor of the human. All his emphasis on human finitude, to name only one aspect of his thought, militates against that idea. Gadamer is of direct interest to theologians[22] because in this and other passages, he is writing theology—while at the same time contributing to a specifically human hermeneutics; and might not the same reversibility hold for Aquinas?

Even in the concept of metaphor itself we find this metaphoric ambivalence of focus. I have said above that metaphor offers a paradigm of the hermeneutic circle, a model of the fusion of horizons, the analogue of tradition. Metaphor, in sum, is a metaphor of hermeneutics. Yet here too tenor and vehicle exchange places. Language, Gadamer argues, is fundamentally metaphorical (404 / 389); it is, moreover, the concretion of wirkungsgeschichtliches Bewusstsein (367 / 351). Gadamer's emphasis on the primacy of language and metaphor suggests that they are the reality—of which hermeneutics is the metaphor. But this reading is also too simple, too hierarchical, and too unilateral because it needs to be reversed again, and yet again, as play continues.

We have not yet mentioned the obvious relevance of metaphor to poetry. Gadamer is concerned to show that metaphorical transference is a basic feature of language generally, not one that is specific to poetry. Speech is not especially ordinary language nor poetry specially extraordinary. When Aristotle consigns metaphor to poetics and rhetoric, this delimitation already signals his distrust of the ongoing process of concept formation that occurs in language prior to logical formalization. It is true that Aristotle's metaphysical categories are parts of speech; and to that extent he implies the unity of speech and thought, and the priority of language to logic. Yet his conception of knowledge is dominated by the ideal of proof and logical ordering. The consequence is that for Aristotle the conceptual advance-work performed by language must be tested at the bar of logic before it can be admitted as knowledge, and logic must distinguish between proper and transferred meaning. Aristotle's allotment of metaphor and poetry itself to the special realms of grammar, rhetoric, and poetics indicates that language has been denied cognitive import. Language is judged (and found wanting) by reference to the order of things, and that is a logical order.

---

22. For an extensive bibliography of theological materials relevant to Gadamer's hermeneutics, see Hilberath, *Theologie Zwischen Tradition und Kritik.*

It is clear that language as it is spoken does not model itself on a logical, syllogistic pattern. And it is just as clear that it goes its own way in apparent obliviousness to the order of things as that is scientifically determined; and so long as this order remains the criterion by which spoken language is judged, it will appear faulty. Common usage lags interminably behind scientific discovery, and not simply because time is needed for dissemination of knowledge first available only to specialists. The sun still "rises" and "sets" despite the centuries that have passed since Copernicus. Regardless of biological classification, peanuts are still nuts, koalas and pandas are bears, spiders are insects, and dolphins are still (should one now say, metaphorically?) fish. Yet is it the case that whales are truly, properly, and correctly called mammals—or does that biologically accurate term express merely one way of looking at them, and perhaps not the most important? Is "leviathan" somehow less accurate? The question is whether the discrepancy between language and the scientific order is ascribable merely to ignorance, obtuseness, or the sheer inertia of language.

If it is certainly true that language lags behind science, it is no less certain that it often races far ahead. Although not the smallest fraction of the charted stars have scientific names, there are, for instance, half a dozen common words describing a running horse, though no scientific terms at all. Alongside metaphor as one aspect of the creativity of language, there is also this ability to proliferate locutions and concepts far beyond what scientific classification strictly requires. One need only think of the numerous Eskimo names for snow or the two hundred African words for camel, although there are, if I recall correctly, only two biological species. This generativity of language is the other side of its apparent poverty with respect to the scientific order; its poverty is not mere deficiency but rather registers the fact that language goes its own way because it answers the immediate needs of its speakers and expresses what they find most important, regardless of the scientific order.

By allying the creativity of language to the divine creativity that speaks the world into being, Nicholas of Cusa is able to conceive of the multiplicity of human locutions and languages positively. He understands them not merely as mental words, as Aquinas did, but as actual spoken languages; and even these, he implies, are—however many—still not a mere dispersion and enfeeblement of the one true Word. Whereas the neoplatonic schema of emanation implies degeneration in the process whereby the one proliferates into the many, and whereas the story of Babel explains the division of languages as a punishment, Cusanus suggests that the positive side of human finitude is displayed in the creative fecundity of language, its fundamentally unlimited capacity to generate new expressions and ideas. Historical variation, discursiveness, synonymy, the variety of tongues—all examples of the plurality of language—seem accidental when judged against the one true order of things as it would appear to the atemporal intuition of an infinite mind. Yet Cusanus conceives of linguistic plurality as a gradual unfolding or explication of that unity, as an interpretive process which, precisely because the human mind is not infinite, continues ad infinitum. Thus human language and languages are revelations of that unity, but they also follow the human aspects of it, and these are many. Languages express and address the specific needs, interests, and priorities of human communities in a variety of concrete circumstances and historical situations. In registering what is humanly important, the diversity of words and languages finds its justification. This plurality is contingent or accidental only if human finitude is so. There is a range of necessary and legitimate variation in words within and among languages, yet all articulate the one divine order in the variety of its aspects and appearances to men. Even if the discrepancy among words implies a corresponding discrepancy, variance, or inexactness with respect to the thing—a certain room for play—nevertheless for Nicholas of Cusa thought and language remain intimately related to the one truth. Despite the variety of languages, he does not retreat into relativism.

LANGUAGE AND BEING: DIFFERENCE WITHOUT DISTINCTION

(3.3.A) One reason Cusanus scarcely felt a temptation in the direction of relativism is that for him the peculiarities or differences of the various languages do not possess any interest or significance in themselves but only insofar as they are all consonant with each other and with the one truth. The temptation toward relativism becomes much stronger, however, when in modern comparative linguistics the particular characteristics of national languages become precisely the focus of inquiry. Now specific languages are the object of research, which involves marking off language in general from the object-domains of other sciences, distinguishing language from what is said in it, and discriminating each language from the others. Wilhelm von Humboldt does not entirely segregate a language from the world expressed in it; on the contrary, he taught that every language presents its own world view (416 / 398). The discrimination among languages implies the individuation of world views and national psychologies. If each language community, moreover, inhabits not only a distinct but an unbreachable world of its own, then the way is paved for a kind of monadological idealism implying an irreconcilable plurality of windowless worlds, each determined by and relative to the language in which it is expressed. Linguistic determinism and relativism, however, are not what Gadamer has in mind in celebrating the multiplicity and fecundity within and among languages. His problem, then, is to maintain the non-relativism of Cusanus while fully acknowledging the real differences between language worlds which Humboldt and his successors have made it impossible to overlook.

The power of language, Humboldt states in one of his richest formulations, consists in making "infinite use of finite means" (417 / 399). It is not just that the sounds, letters, words, and syntactic patterns are finite while capable of unlimited variation. What is more important is that the power of language always exceeds whatever is and has been said in it; and since it surpasses the content to which it is at any moment applied, language, Humboldt concludes, must be conceived as a form[23] consisting of infinite permutations and combinations of finite elements detached from any specific content. For Humboldt, each language expresses a world as a form expresses a content; and even if he does not himself follow this path to the end, it is the form–content dichotomy that leads, first, to an instrumentalist notion of language as a formal means; second, to the notion that the world is one thing and language another such that they can be relative to each other; and third, to the notion that, given the infinite power of language, each world is not only relative to its language but determined by it. Each of these consequences, as well as the form–content split itself, is entailed by the initial move that institutes linguistic science: the creation of language as an object in itself and apart from what it means.

Language can be considered as an object, however, only when it is idling and abstracted from its use. In use, when language is performing work, its forms disappear as such because they are working. They are full with what they mean, and there is no form–content split. In use, language is always saying something. Children do not first learn the universal forms of their tongue and then how to apply them to particular cases; rather they learn horizontally, from use to use. From speech they learn to speak, and from application to apply. Language is most itself, Gadamer suggests, when it is least objectified, when form and content, discourse and world are not distinguished.

The lateral nature of native language acquisition also has implications for

---

23. "To take form as the starting point in language," Palmer writes, "is to make essentially the same error as to take form as the starting point in aesthetics. The event character of the phenomenon and its temporality are lost, and, most importantly, one falls into the error of designating the human subject, instead of the nature of the thing coming to expression, as the fixed point of reference" (*Hermeneutics*, p. 204).

learning a foreign language. Humboldt writes, "Only because we always carry over our own worldview, even our linguistic view, more or less into a foreign language, this experience is never purely or completely successful" (418 / 400). Certainly Humboldt is right about the fact of the carry-over. Gadamer calls it the fusion of horizons, the paradigm of hermeneutic experience by which, without leaving the old one, we acquire a new horizon that allows an expansion of what is possible to see, learn, and understand. But the linguist, almost reversing the story of Babel, conceives of the perfection of each language in its separateness and distinction from every other. It is almost to be regretted that, since we cannot do so perfectly, we are at all capable of learning foreign languages, for in that way the purity of both languages is sullied by the intercourse between them.

Regrettable or not, however, the fact remains that such fusion occurs. English, for example, acquired many Latin and French terms during the late Middle Ages and Renaissance; now French is acquiring English terms, and the process goes on. What is an imperfection from the point of view of the linguistic purist, however, becomes from the hermeneutic point of view a distinct advantage: any language can be learned by the speakers of any other. Even if we never just drop one language when we acquire another, no speaker is necessarily trapped within the confines of his mother tongue because that language itself is capable of merging with others. We do not need to liberate ourselves from our native language or break out of it, but rather only to avail ourselves of its openness and intrinsic capacity for development.[24] Because of this capacity, languages possess the possibility of infinite expansion and cannot be conceived of as windowless enclosures. It is certainly true that each presents a world view of its own, but the very fact of this multiplicity means that other languages and other worlds offer multiple concrete possibilities for the expansion of our own insofar as we can learn to live and speak in them. When we do learn them, they are fused with our own; and the fact of fusion suggests that languages cannot be conceived as irremediably incommensurate and essentially segregated, for they are always merging into each other.

If we refuse to accept the form–content split, finally, there follows what is for Gadamer the most important consequence, that the fusion of languages is a fusion of worlds. Humboldt himself denies this split when he considers the origin of language, for he sees it as coinciding with the origin of humanity. The word

---

24. Even if, as Habermas argues, languages as such are systematically distorted and deceptive, there is no need for hermeneutics to change into a critique of ideology (see Habermas' review of *TM*, p. 360). Language has the capacity to correct itself from within.

was with man from the beginning. Neither given to man nor instituted by him, language does not advene to humanity because there is no human world without it. For Gadamer, as for Humboldt, the coincidence of language with the human world is not merely chronological but essential. It implies that language is not one among many human possessions, for it is not a possession at all but rather constitutive of what it means to be human. Language is not one among other things in the world, for the relation of language and world is reciprocal. "The world is world only insofar as it comes to language, but also language has its own real existence in that the world is presented in it" (419 / 401).

This is a specifically human world. An animal is dependent on and a product of its environment; so also human societies are influenced by their language world. The difference between animal environment and human world, however, is that because the human world is linguistically constituted, there is a human freedom vis-à-vis the world that is absent in animals.[25] This freedom is evident in the fact that the relation of language and world is not fixed. Not only is there a variety of languages, but even if a particular language presents a particular world, its speakers are still at liberty to say the same thing in any number of ways. This freedom too belongs to the plurality of language: there is never only one way, or even a single right way, to describe any given set of circumstances. The world does not prescribe the language for it. Since language is our relation to the world, there is room for play that precludes our being determined by the world as an animal by its environment. The same is true of the human world as a world of language. The freedom for a variety of words and locutions precludes any linguistic determinism of thought within a language, just as without it such determinism is obviated by our freedom to learn other languages.

Our freedom from the world implies at the same time that the world is free from us and from the locutions in which it is expressed. Precisely because any given word is not prescribed or motivated by the thing it means, the word means the thing itself, independent of the particular word that means it. Because any particular locution is undetermined with regard to the thing, the locution is not self-reflexive; it does not point to itself, for any given word could have been another. There is always implied something like: "I mean that ———, or whatever you call it." Since there is a difference and distance between language and world that gives language room for play, for calling things by any number of names, language also gives the world its own freedom and presents it as it

---

25. For Ricoeur's corollary distinction between *Welt* (world) and *Umwelt* (environment), see "The Model of the Text," p. 321.

truly is, undetermined by and independent of the peculiarities of the speaker and the particular locutions he employs. Language, in brief, can represent matters of fact (421 / 403). This does not imply a world apart from language. We always need some word: each human world is linguistically constituted, but it is not determined by or relative to the particular language in which it becomes intelligible.

Yet there is another version of relativism which we have not yet considered. Language constitutes a world's horizon of intelligibility, the limit of everything that can be understood in that world, which is to say, the limit of the world itself. This Humboldt already knew, but the problem is that it leaves us with an unsurpassable plurality of worlds, each of which is apparently relative and incomplete with respect to the one world in itself. Certainly, Gadamer agrees, each language community lives in its own world. These language worlds, moreover, alter so radically in the course of history that, for instance, even native English speakers cannot now understand Old English except by learning it as a "foreign" language. Yet every language world, because it is linguistically constituted, can be learned and can learn others. Although a language marks the horizon, the limit of intelligibility, it is, as we have seen, a flexible limit because languages are open to enlargement. For the same reason, language worlds too are open to expansion. "Such worldviews are not relative in the sense that one could set then against them the 'world in itself,' as if the right view from a possible standpoint outside the human language world were able to encounter it in its being in itself" (423 / 405).[26]

There is no such standpoint and none is necessary. Each language presents no more nor less than a view of the world itself, and therefore a partial view. Yet each of the many language worlds implies the one common world, independent of that particular language; each implies the unity of the one world understood from whatever point of view and whatever it is called. Every language world implies this totality not only negatively, because it is partial, but positively as its own possibility. The plurality of language worlds cannot be conceived of as relativities opposed to the one absolute world because they cannot be opposed to each other. Since every such world is constituted linguistically and is therefore open to others, "each of them contains in it potentially all others, that is, each can expand itself into every other. It can understand and comprehend from itself the 'view' of the world as it offers itself in other languages" (424 / 406). Nothing lies essentially beyond the horizon of what can be understood in language.

26. Wolff is seriously mistaken in asserting that Gadamer "fully endorses the Humboldtian theory of linguistic relativity" (*Hermeneutic Philosophy*, p. 114).

Nothing is in itself necessarily unintelligible, for language—not some abstract language in general, the silent logos, or even the divine Word—but each spoken, human language is potentially infinite. At this point we are prepared to understand better what Gadamer means by the fundamental hermeneutic principle "Being that can be understood is language." "The linguistic character of our experience of the world . . . exhibits an experience that is always finite but that nowhere encounters a barrier at which something infinite is intended that can barely be surmised and no longer spoken. Its own operation is never limited, and yet is not a progressive approximation of an intended meaning. There is rather a constant representation of this meaning in every one of its steps" (*PH* 80).

The potential infinity of language does not, however, imply the infinity of consciousness. We need to recall that language is the locus of history, tradition, prejudice, and all the forces that operate on thought prior to conscious reflection.[27] There is no doubt that thought is conditioned by such linguistic forces; and even though we are aware of this fact, "the consciousness of being conditioned in no way removes this conditionedness [*hebt keineswegs auf*]" (424 / 406). While language, as we have seen, is always able to overcome its own inadequacies and deficiencies, our awareness of the potential infinity of language does not remedy the finitude of consciousness. From the fact that language infinitely exceeds every use to which it is put and every content to which it is applied, Humboldt infers that language is a formal power. Gadamer draws a different inference. If every consciousness is a consciousness of an object, then it becomes clear that language is not to be identified with consciousness, for language precedes consciousness essentially, since the horizon of language embraces everything that can be an object. In language "becomes visible what is real beyond every individual consciousness" (425 / 407).

This reality comprehends the entire real world, not just the real facts and objects verifiable by science but also real appearances such as the two hundred kinds of camel and the setting of the sun. Language not only comprehends everything that can be an object but presents also what cannot be objectified. It is not mind that is absolute but language. "In language the world presents itself. The linguistic experience of the world is 'absolute.' It transcends all relativities in the positing of being because it comprehends all being in itself, in whatever relationships (relativities) it shows itself" (426 / 408). Each objective science,

27. "We are always already biased in our thinking and knowing by our linguistic interpretation of the world. To grow into this linguistic interpretation means to grow up in the world. To this extent, language is the real mark of our finitude" (*PH* 64). See also *KS* 3:239 and "Die Stellung der Philosophie," p. 14.

Gadamer suggests, posits such a relativity. Though, like physics, each science attempts to be global and to include in principle all possible objects, yet each posits being in its own way, as the sphere of everything objectifiable by and commensurate with its own methods of research. But even if there were only one scientific method, joining all objective sciences into one omnicomprehensive super-science which, like an ideal metaphysics, would be the science of all beings and of all possible objects of consciousness, nevertheless, its sphere of knowledge would still not be the whole. The sphere of this super-science cannot be complete because, as objective, it must exclude the researcher, his method, and the science itself. This, at its simplest, is what objectivity means: keeping the subject outside and separate from the object—and since every objective science must therefore exclude itself from its sphere of research, no objective science can be a science of the whole. Each must necessarily be relative.

Human science, however, is not objective because it is circular. It is itself what it studies; and for precisely the same reason it is not subjective. Nor is it relative in the same way as natural science. Though finite and perpetually incomplete, human science that includes itself is nonetheless a science of the whole—the whole world, which can never be objectified because we live in it, belong to it, and are part of it. It is language that is capable of revealing this whole because its relation to world is not objective. Our linguistic experience of the world is prior to everything that can be known and addressed as existing. The fundamental relatedness of language and world, therefore, does not mean that the world becomes the object of language. Rather what is the object of knowledge and statement is always already within the world horizon of language. "The linguisticality of our experience of the world does not include the objectification of the world" (426 / 408). Language exceeds consciousness not only because it makes possible the objectification of every being within the world, every possible object of consciousness, but also because it reveals the absolute, irrelative world; and this is not an object of consciousness. The language world can be understood, but only from within, by living in it, and therefore not objectively.

Hermeneutics, human science, is the paradigmatic instance of such understanding. Language makes understanding possible. We have seen above that language is both the medium and the focus of hermeneutics, but in this respect hermeneutic experience exemplifies our life in the language world generally. Language is the concretion of Wirkungsgeschichte; and just as interpretation does not objectivize the history that affects it because interpretation is an event which belongs to that history and furthers it, so also world is not objectivized in language. The process by which a tradition is made to speak once again in interpretive language is the same process by which things in general are worded. Like traditions, things too become speakable and understandable, long before being objectified, when they are part of the language world to which consciousness also belongs.

(3.3.B) *Zugehörigkeit*—the belonging of thought to language and language to world—is Gadamer's word for the prior ground that makes possible adequation and correspondence; that is, belonging is the ground of truth.[28] It is the truth of truth: in Heidegger's terms, the *Lichtung*, the place of disclosure. For Gadamer, language is the locus of belonging in that it is the place where subject and object, thought and world, meet—or, more precisely, where they are at home together prior to being split asunder by conscious reflection.[29] Language presents this primordial whole. Yet the problem remains that in fact language is finite. It does not develop teleologically by gravitating toward a pre-given order of things as it would appear to an infinite mind; rather, as we have seen, it goes its own way. If language is not governed by an eternal order, however, no more is it subject to human will, for language is not a tool of thought that could be constructed or replaced at will. Even if thought is not the tool of language either, yet so intimately are they related that the historical specificity of languages reflects that of the men who speak them. Because they are finite, both language and thought are in a constant process of development and are open to new experience. But if language marks the home where subject and object meet and originally belong together, the question is why the finitude of language does not imply the relativization of truth.

"In metaphysics, belonging refers to the transcendental relation between being and truth; knowledge is considered as a moment of being itself and not primarily as an act of the subject" (434 / 416). Metaphysics does not begin with a worldless subject which stands over against its object, the spiritless world.

---

28. Bleicher rightly aligns Zugehörigkeit with a great many of Gadamer's other terms: "The linguisticality of Being found expression with Gadamer in such concepts as *Wirkungsgeschichte* (effective history), *Zugehörigkeit* (belongingness), *Spiel* (game), and *Gespräch* (dialogue)—which are almost completely interchangeable and point at the possibility of truth as disclosure, or *Horizontverschmelzung* (fusion of horizon) as Gadamer refers to it" (*Contemporary Hermeneutics*, p. 118).

29. Being at home is Gadamer's preferred metaphor for our situation in language: "As [language] is the one word or the unity of discourse, it is that wherein we ourselves are so completely at home that even our dwelling in the word is not at all conscious to us" (*KS* 4:83). "Language is an 'element' within which we live in a very different sense than reflection is. Language completely surrounds us like the voice of home which prior to our every thought of it breathes a familiarity from time out of mind" (*HD* 97). See also *RAS* 51 and *PH* 238–39.

Rather it begins with them already belonging together. At this level of generality, Gadamer is himself in accord with the tradition of metaphysics; but the differences quickly become clear. From Plato to Hegel, truth consists in the complete revelation of the thing, its full presence to an infinite mind; and insofar as the human mind approaches this infinity, it knows the truth. Dialectic, the path of this approach, is not direct but more like the course of a tacking ship which proceeds forward by continually reversing its direction. Since in Greek metaphysics thought belongs to being, the sudden reversals which thought experiences are not a function of the imperfections of subjectivity. Rather than dialectic of the logos follows the dialectical course of the thing itself.

For Gadamer, by contrast, dialectic takes place not in the wordless realm of the logos but instead in spoken language, not in the opposition of statement and counterstatement but in the exchanges of conversation and dialogue, in question and answer rather than assertion. Hermeneutic experience, which is the paradigm of our experience of the world, takes place in language and consists in conversation with a text itself linguistic. The dialectical character of hermeneutic experience is evident not only in the to and fro, the play, between the interpreter and the text onto which interpretations are continually projected, retracted, and emended. No less fundamental is the dialectical process of question and answer. For as the interpreter puts a question to the text from which he expects an answer, so also the text puts a question to the interpreter. It puts his questions in question, and thus the interpreter becomes the interpreted. In these respects hermeneutic experience is dialectical. But the decisive difference between hermeneutics and logos philosophy is that in the hermeneutic conversation something happens. "Etwas geschieht" (437 / 419). An event occurs. Tradition is not only investigated but furthered and produced. Interpretation contributes to and thus belongs to the tradition.

Negatively put, the fact that hermeneutic interpretation is an event in the tradition it interprets means that nothing is revealed. Nothing is discovered, if that implies that a previously existing thing is now uncovered and disclosed as the thing in itself. Prior to the interpretation, the tradition did not exist in the way it is now understood. Hermeneutics, therefore, is not teleological. It leads nowhere but onward and does not progress toward any complete revelation of the thing, its presence to an infinite intellect. The mode of being of linguistic tradition is not presence but history; it is always *to be* made and formed. In positive terms, then, in the event of interpretation tradition itself happens. The dialectical changes that occur in the process of interpretation are not a function of the interpreter's subjectivity but of tradition. The path of interpretation is the dialectical course of the tradition itself as it is understood in new contexts and new circumstances by new interpreters. If interpretation does not discover anything, that is because when, through interpretation, "tradition comes to speak anew, something emerges and exists from then on that did not exist before" (437–138 / 419). History is made in the event of understanding tradition, but this history is not the mere passage of time, for in interpretation tradition comes into being. There is an access of being in the same way as when, in a genuine conversation, something occurs to both partners that had not occurred to either of them before. When they come to an understanding, something new is conceived. Something new happens, and what occurs in hermeneutic conversation is being.

We come to realize that belonging is an ontological way of talking about the condition achieved by the fusion of horizons. When horizons are so fused that the interpretation belongs to what it interprets, the resulting whole is, as it were, greater than the sum of its parts. There is a birth and growth of something reducible to neither the interpreter, nor the text, nor their conjunction. If the continuing advent of tradition does not progress toward any destination, then interpretation cannot be adjudged imperfect or incomplete for failing to reach it. There is no remainder that need necessarily be overlooked. The history of interpretation is neither gradual nor partial but at each moment in principle already whole. There is nothing more to know about a tradition than what emerges in its continuing interpretations, its Wirkungsgeschichte. And though there are always other traditions to understand, or the same traditions to be interpreted again, there is nothing in itself inaccessible to language; there is no object that cannot be worded, spoken, and heard. Hearing is a universal sense because it does not, like sight, distance subject from object. Listening (zuhören) to a tradition when it speaks to us and addresses us in the language of interpretation is already belonging to it (Zugehörigkeit).

But if interpretative understanding is in principle complete, if listening is attentive to the whole of things, does not this infinity belie the finitude of hermeneutic experience? That it does not becomes clear in Gadamer's further discussion of the dialectics of language. As the fundamental hermeneutic experience, listening too has a dialectical element in that it endeavors to be undistracted, even by itself and its own prejudices (441 / 422). For genuine listening is not obstinate insistence on one's own point of view but a willingness to consider it negatively. Reversals of understanding are apparent in the process of conjecture and revision, projection and re-projection, that allows the thing itself to emerge for the interpreter. But this dialectic involves more than allowing one partial interpretive statement to be counterbalanced by another on the opposite side of the question. Interpretation, in Gadamer's view, does not in fact consist in statements, assertions, and propositions; and this, as we will see, explains why "the word that interpretively encounters the sense of the text brings the whole of this sense to speak,"—that is, allows "an infinity of sense to be presented in the finite" (441 / 423).

The relation of finite and infinite mediated by the interpretive word Gadamer calls a speculative relation, a mirror relation. The mirror, of course, has been the dominant metaphor of mimesis since Plato; but Gadamer means by it something more than that language is the mirror, the representation, of things. The virtuality of the mirror image metaphorically expresses the disappearance of interpretive language, its invisibility in itself, and its dissolution into what it interprets. But what the mirror reflects is also an image, an appearance, of the thing. The mirror and what it reflects are each images of the other, as language and world are also reciprocally definitive. The speculative person, unlike the dogmatic, does not limit himself to the obvious, to the answer that is immediately available, or to a dogma already fixed and determined; rather he considers, reflects, listens, and keeps himself open to alternatives and possibilities.

Reflection, moreover, is fundamental to speculative philosophy and, most relevant here, to Hegel's speculative dialectic. Hegel demonstrates how speculative reflection operates in the reversals and oscillations within dialectical propositions that reveal the dialectical structure of the thing itself. For Hegel, the speculative finally dissolves into the dialectical. The distinction between them is not preserved because, as heir of the Greek logos philosophy, Hegel confines his attention to propositions. He therefore subordinates language to statement[30] and thereby subordinates speculative relation (which retains the difference between a reflection and what it reflects) to dialectical identity, unmediated by language.

The language of the hermeneutic conversation, however, does not consist in statements and the counterstatements at odds with them; and it is to nonpropositional language that Gadamer turns in order to consider the speculative aspect of language finally overlooked by Hegel. A poem is speculative, Gadamer suggests, but not because it mirrors some existent thing. The speculative relation does not inhere in the reflection of particular things by particular words. "Every word breaks forth as from a center and is related to the whole through which alone it is a word. Every word resonates with the whole of language to which it belongs and reveals the whole of the worldview that informs it. As the event

---

30. For Heidegger's critique of *apophansis* (statement, assertion), see *Being and Time*, pp. 201ff.

of the moment, every word therefore brings with it the unsaid, which it answers and summons. The occasionality of human speech is not the temporary imperfection of its expressive power; it is in fact the logical expression of the living virtuality of speech, which brings into play a whole of meaning without being able to say it wholly. All human speech is finite in such a way that there is laid up in it an infinity of meaning to be explicated and laid out'' (434 / 415–16).

The speculative nature of speech consists in the fact that, unlike the proposition, it always reflects more than it says. The said reflects the unsaid; the part mirrors the whole—the whole truth that is virtually present in each act of speech.[31] The virtuality of speech, like the virtuality of the mirror image, consists in the fact that its meaning cannot be grasped, determined, and encapsuled in statements. Speech is speculative in that the finite and occasional event of speech reflects virtually the infinity of the unspoken. This virtuality is the expectancy of speech, its appeal to the future. It gives impetus to interpretation, to saying what always still remains to be said.[32] This should not be taken to imply that interpretation succeeds where speech fails, for both belong to the one conversation; and interpretation succeeds or fails in the same way as speech does. Like the poet, the interpreter too says what he means. But ''to say what one means, to make oneself understood, . . . binds the said together with the infinity of the unsaid in the unity of meaning and lets it be so understood. . . . Someone speaks speculatively when his words do not copy beings but express a relationship to the whole of being and let it come to speak'' (444–145 / 426). To speak clearly so that the whole of what one means can be understood is not to make statements about states or affairs or matters of fact, whether in poetry or interpretation; to speak speculatively is not to reflect an existent reality but being.

In that a text has meaning by appealing to the unsaid, it invites interpretation; and if that infinity of the unsaid is the whole of being, as Gadamer suggests,

---

31. Since the whole truth is virtually present in each act of speech, language ''is the omni-comprehensive preinterpretedness of the world. The process of concept formation which arises within this linguistic preinterpretedness is never a first beginning . . . because it is always a thinking further in the language which we speak and a laying out of the world that is laid up within it'' (KS 3:239).

32. Gadamer elaborates: ''Just as the speculative statement demands dialectical 'exposition,' the work of art demands interpretation, even though its content may never be exhausted in any particular interpretation. My point is that the speculative statement is not a judgment restricted in the content of what it asserts any more than a single word without a context or a communicative utterance torn from its context is a self-contained unit of meaning. The words which someone utters are tied to the continuum which determines the word to such an extent that it can even be 'taken back.' Similarly, the speculative statement points to an entirety of truth, without being this entirety or stating it'' (HD 96).

then being is what calls for interpretation. Hermeneutic ontology is the interpretation of being, and the interpretation of tradition symbolizes this process
because it shares in it. Whether with respect to being or texts, it is important to
stress that interpretation is called for. Tradition calls for the discursive, historical
process in which it is unfolded, explicated. It needs interpretation when it becomes different from and alien to the dispositions and suppositions peculiar to
the interpreter's own situation. The finitude of the interpreter, as marked by
these particularities, does not imply that all understanding is misunderstanding.
Difference is the condition of interpretation. We understand differently if we
understand at all, for unless there is some difference to be integrated, some gap
to be bridged, the interpreter will have nothing to say and no interpretation will
be possible. By reason of its indigence, tradition still calls for interpretation,
invites it. Interpretation begins not only in the middle of historically conditioned
prejudices and preconceptions, it begins as a response to the text's invitation.
In both ways, interpretation is situated within an ongoing process which it did
not originate and will not complete. In this respect the finitude of interpretation
consists in its inability to begin at the beginning, to begin with nothing, indeed
to begin at all. Lacking a beginning, interpretation is finite also in that it foresees
no end and no telos. The finitude of interpretation, its lack of beginning or end,
implies at the same time its historical infinitude and open-endedness. This end-
lessness has profound consequences for our conception of truth, for it suggests
that if there is any truth at all, it occurs not at the beginning or the end but in
the process of interpretation.[33] Once we really abandon the notion of archaeology
or teleology as the locus of truth—once we acknowledge that "there is no possible
consciousness, however infinite, for which the tradition would appear in the
light of eternity" (448 / 430)—then we are in a position to see that tradition is
indeed precisely what it appears to be in the light of history. Tradition, and
being itself, exists historically; and the historical interpretation of it offers real
knowledge. It offers truth.

(3.3.C) It is to be emphasized that interpretation, like play, cannot be
understood as an activity of the interpreting subject nor as a method in which
the subject exerts control over himself in order to control an object. In Gadamer's
hermeneutics as in Greek dialectic, the interpretation that yields truth consists

---

33. "In dialectic," Grondin writes, "thought continually takes on new forms without there
being postulated unconditionally a process of successive approximation to the truth. In philosophical
hermeneutics, this infinite process is designated as 'truth'" (*Hermeneutische Wahrheit*, p. 24).

rather in the movement of the thing to be understood. A correct interpretation is an interpretation of the thing itself, its own interpretation, its self-interpretation. Things make themselves understood in their interpretations—that is, in language that speaks to us here and now. If genuine language reflects not some thing but being, then it is being that makes itself understood in language. Being interprets itself in an intelligible language which mirrors not some previously given existent but rather something that exists henceforward as understandable. Intelligible beings are the historical interpretations of being, its appearances and self-presentations. Being makes itself accessible by presenting itself in beings that can be understood, and they are its self-presentations, its language. "Being that can be understood is language" (450 / 432).

If so, being exhibits the speculative structure of language. It multiplies itself in the infinity of its historical reflections and yet is nonetheless one. It retains its unity because what is expressed in language does not acquire a second existence; but rather its expression in language, as in a mirror, is the appearance of the thing itself. "What something presents itself as, belongs indeed to its own being" (450 / 432). That this *as* belongs to its being means that (rather than being self-identical) it differs from itself: it is / not itself, and this is the case of everything that exists historically. It has a mirror relation to itself, a rift in its identity, which means that existing historically, as always something different, is its way of being. Yet, Gadamer writes, precisely because this is a mirror relation, the multiplicity of historical interpretations do not disintegrate into mere plurality, for they all are still reflections of the thing itself. "Everything that is language has a speculative unity, a difference in itself between its being and its self-presentation, a difference however that is in fact no difference" (450 / 432). Any language—anything that can be interpreted and understood—contains a split between what it is and what it means. What a word means is not what it is; and yet if we divorce the meaning from the word in order to determine what the word is in itself, when it no longer means anything, then it is simply no longer a word. Language does not exist in itself but only in relation. A word is most a word when it is understood, when it means something other than itself and when what it is disappears into what it means, its interpretation.

Whatever can be understood does not exist in itself but in the unity of its understandings. This is of fundamental importance to both aesthetic and historical hermeneutics. As Gadamer has shown in previous discussion, if the work of art can be understood, it does not exist in itself. It exists rather as understood; and what the work is, therefore, cannot be divided from the way it presents itself in its reproductions and interpretations. So also if history is understandable, "the significance of an event or the meaning of a text is no fixed object in itself that only has to be determined'' (451 / 432). Like art, the past in general is indivisible from the history of its interpretations, its Wirkungsgeschichte. Now in this final section Gadamer extrapolates the conclusions drawn from aesthetic and historical hermeneutics to the universal realm of ontology. That being can be understood means it exists historically: it presents itself as something continually different from itself, yet this difference allows no distinction between being and its understanding.

Difference without distinction—this unity in multiplicity is what is implied by the hermeneutic *as* which bridges (without closing) the rift in being. If hermeneutic ontology involves a paradox, that is because it reflects the paradox implicit in all interpretation, namely that the tradition it interprets is ''one and the same and yet different'' (448 / 430).[34] The hermeneutic paradox resulting from the historicity of being is no less offensive to logic than the hermeneutic circle with its double bind of part and whole. Yet even though hermeneutics is guided by a language prior to logic, Gadamer does not content himself with mere contradiction or illogicality. Rather he turns once again to tradition for a non-paradoxical way of thinking about the difference-without-distinction implicit in historical being.

Despite the fact that the Platonic dialogues are the embodiment of the substantialist metaphysics (based on a permanent, self-identical, underlying substance) that he resists, Gadamer finds in Plato's thought about the one and the many an analogue of his own thought about the same and the different. The crux in Platonic metaphysics occurs at the point of transition from the realm of the idea to that of its sensible appearances. How can these many appearances be true? That is, how can they all be appearances of the one idea? The beautiful offers an answer to these questions. With reference to the idea of the good, appearances can be illusory and deceptive. That someone seems to be good does not necessarily mean that he is so. Yet this is not the case with the idea of beauty: if something seems beautiful, it is beautiful. There is no distinction between real and apparent beauty. Since it belongs to the nature of beauty to appear, the idea of beauty has the ontological function of mediating between idea and appearance, for in each appearance of the beautiful, the idea of beauty is immediately present. Beauty makes itself apparent. One does not need to search behind beautiful appearances in order to discover real beauty, for beauty

---

34. Compare *HD* 58: ''It is clear then that what appears as this differentiation of the undifferentiated has life's structure of splitting in two and becoming identical with itself. . . . Life is the identity of identity and difference.''

itself is present in each of them. Each is really beautiful. Each appearance is true. The difference between the multiplicity of beautiful appearances and the one idea of beauty is without a distinction, and thus (especially in the *Symposium*) beauty best explains how the sensory realm has access to the ideative or, to be more exact, how the two realms are indivisible.

Like the idea of beauty, being—whether aesthetic, historical, or ontological—is indivisible from its historical manifestations. Like being, beauty has the character of light in that it makes itself apparent in its appearances. It shines on them, lights them up, and makes them beautiful; and by so doing, it makes itself manifest. The speculative structure of being, its mirror relation to its appearances, finds its analogue in the reflective self-revelation of light. As light becomes visible itself only when it makes something else visible, so being manifests itself (and is) only in the historical process of disclosing beings that can be understood—that is, in language. This process is the continuing event of truth, *aletheia*, the self-revelation of being that speaks directly to historical men living in diverse times and places. "The light that lets everything emerge in such a way that it is enlightening and understandable in itself is the light of the word" (458 / 440).[35] Being presents itself in the light of words which reflect it as it truly is, just as beauty is revealed in what it makes beautiful.

Beauty, then, serves as a symbol of truth, the fundamental truth achieved in the interpretive sciences. This is the truth which, like beauty, is characterized by its being immediately apparent—that is, by its self-evidence. It offers itself in evidence and, like beauty, cannot and does not need to be proved because its truth is already clear prior to demonstration. Achieving this clarity requires not proof but insight, the experience of sudden enlightenment when things appear in a new light and the horizon of intelligibility is thereby extended. "Hermeneutic experience belongs in this realm because it too is the event of a genuine experience. Wherever something speaks to us from tradition, in what is said there is something enlightening, without its being in all respects certified, judged, and decided. Tradition asserts its own validity in being understood and displaces the horizon which until then had enclosed us" (460 / 442). From interpretive insight into a tradition is formed a common sense, a shared and evident truth that possesses its own kind of certainty. Such insight is an event, the experience of understanding; and this is the mode of knowledge that belongs exclusively to finite, historical minds that require experience since they neither comprehend all

---

35. For Heidegger's critique of Descartes' conception of beings as what are lit by the subject rather than Being as light itself, see the "Letter on Humanism" in *Basic Writings*, p. 211.

in a single intuition nor develop all knowledge out of themselves by self-contemplation. Insight cannot be controlled or produced at will because it is not something we do, an activity of the knowing subject, but rather an event: in an insight something occurs to us. Something that is prior to knowledge speaks to us. When things suddenly become clear, manifest, and evident—when we see them truly for the first time—then their very visibility discloses the light that makes insight possible. The event of understanding reflects and responds to the continuing self-presentation of being in tradition.

Truth occurs as a response to a tradition that addresses us in a language we can understand. Being presents itself in and as this language, and in order to understand the event of truth that occurs in this self-presentation Gadamer draws on the Platonic tradition which suggests that the event of *aletheia*, disconcealment, is the essence of the beautiful. "The beautiful . . . makes itself apparent in its being; it presents itself. What thus presents itself is not different from itself when it presents itself. It is not something for itself and something else for others . . . . It makes no difference whether it 'itself' or its reflection appears" (462 / 443–44). What we understand in tradition is a view or aspect or appearance of being, but it is nonetheless a true appearance and an appearance of truth because it is in the nature of being (as of beauty) to present itself and appear. Because it interprets itself, its interpretations are not something other than it is. Being presents itself in the very representations by which it is understood. Like the work of art it exists only in the history of its representations. Being speaks in a language accessible to finite mind, and understanding it "is indeed a genuine experience, that is, a confrontation with something that validates itself as truth" (463 / 445).

This truth is something we neither possess nor make, a product of consciousness, but rather something that happens to us and in which we participate, as when we get caught up in a game. Truth happens when we lose ourselves and no longer stand over against it as a subject against an object. When we are caught up in the game that is played with us, it is then, even before we are aware of it, that we have joined in the continuing event of truth. "The one who understands is always already drawn into the event whereby the meaningful validates itself. . . . When we understand, we are drawn into an event of truth and we come, as it were, too late if we want to know what we are supposed to believe" (465 / 446). We *already* know. We are always already prejudiced by tradition, which asserts its validity prior to consciousness. The fact that we never completely rid ourselves of prejudice certainly marks the finitude of historical being—but some prejudices are true. The fact that the knower's own being comes into play in his knowledge certainly betrays the limitation of objectivity and method, but it does not prevent truth. Despite our will to be methodical and objective, despite our desire to remain a bystander detached from the game, despite our attempts to prevent it, the truth of tradition occurs to us.

Selected Bibliography

Altieri, Charles. *Act and Quality: A Theory of Meaning and Humanistic Understanding.* Amherst: University of Massachusetts Press, 1981.

Apel, Karl-Otto. *Analytic Philosophy of Language and the Geisteswissenschaften.* Dordrecht: Reidel, 1967.

————. "The A Priori of Communication and the Foundation of the Humanities." In Dallmayr and McCarthy, ed., *Understanding and Social Inquiry,* pp. 292–315.

————. *Towards a Transformation of Philosophy.* Trans. Glyn Adey and David Frisby. London: Routledge and Kegan Paul. 1980.

Apel, Karl-Otto, et al., ed. *Hermeneutik und Ideologiekritik.* Frankfurt: Suhrkamp, 1973.

Arthur, Christopher E. "Gadamer and Hirsch: The Canonical Work and the Interpreter's Intention." *Cultural Hermeneutics* 4 (1977):183–97.

Bacon, Francis. *Complete Essays.* New York: Washington Square Press, 1963.

Bakhtin, M. M. *The Dialogic Imagination: Four Essays.* Trans. Caryl Emerson and Michael Holquist. Austin: University of Texas Press, 1981.

Bartsch, Hans Werner, ed. *Kerygma and Myth: A Theological Debate.* Trans. Reginald H. Fuller. London: SPCK, 1953.

Baumann, Zygmunt. *Hermeneutics and Social Science: Approaches to Understanding.* London: Hutchinson, 1978.

Bernard, J. H. Introduction to Kant's *Critique of Judgment.* New York: Hafner Press, 1951.

Bernstein, Richard. *Beyond Objectivism and Relativism: Science, Hermeneutics, and Praxis*. Philadelphia: University of Pennsylvania Press, 1983.

Betti, Emilio. "Hermeneutics as the General Science of the *Geisteswissenschaften*." In Bleicher, ed., *Contemporary Hermeneutics*, pp. 51–94.

Bleicher, Josef, ed. *Contemporary Hermeneutics: Hermeneutics as Method, Philosophy, and Critique*. London: Routledge and Kegan Paul, 1980.

Bloom, Harold. *A Map of Misreading*. New York: Oxford University Press, 1975.

Bohler, Dietrich, "Philosophische Hermeneutik und Hermeneutische Methode." In Fuhrmann et al., ed., *Text und Applikation*, pp. 483–512.

Bruns, Gerald L. *Inventions: Writing, Textuality, and Understanding in Literature and History*. New Haven: Yale University Press, 1982.

Bubner, Rüdiger. "Theory and Practice in Light of the Hermeneutic-Criticist Controversy." *Cultural Hermeneutics* 2 (1975):337–52.

Bubner, Rüdiger; Konrad Cramer; and Reiner Wiehl, ed. *Hermeneutik und Dialektik*. 2 vols. Tübingen: J. C. B. Mohr (Paul Siebeck), 1970.

Buck, Günther. "The Structure of Hermeneutic Experience and the Problem of Tradition." Trans. Peter Heath. *New Literary History* 10 (1981):31–47.

Burke, Edmund. *Reflections on the Revolution in France*. Ed. Conor Cruise O'Brien. Baltimore: Penguin, 1968.

Byrum, Charles Stephen. "Philosophy as Play." *Man and World* 8 (1975):315–26.

Carr, David. "Interpretation and Self-Evidence." *Analecta Husserliana* 9 (1979):133–47.

Cavell, Stanley. *Must We Mean What We Say?* New York: Scribners, 1969.

Collingwood, R. G. *An Essay on Metaphysics*. Oxford: Clarendon Press, 1940.

––––––. *The Idea of History*. Oxford: Clarendon Press, 1946.

Dallmayr, Fred R., and Thomas A. McCarthy, ed. *Understanding and Social Inquiry*. Notre Dame: University of Notre Dame Press, 1977.

Danto, Arthur C. *Analytical Philosophy of History*. Cambridge: University Press, 1965.

Deely, John. *Introducing Semiotic: Its History and Doctrine*. Bloomington: Indiana University Press, 1982.

de Man, Paul. *Allegories of Reading: Figural Language in Rousseau, Nietzsche, Rilke, and Proust*. New Haven: Yale University Press, 1979.

––––––. "The Rhetoric of Temporality." In Charles S. Singleton, ed., *Interpretation: Theory and Practice*, pp. 173–209. Baltimore: Johns Hopkins University Press, 1969.

Derrida, Jacques. *Of Grammatology*. Trans. G. C. Spivak. Baltimore: Johns Hopkins University Press, 1974.

––––––. "Signature Event Context." *Glyph 1* (1977):172–97.

––––––. *Writing and Difference*. Trans. Alan Bass. Chicago: University of Chicago Press, 1978.

de Saussure, Ferdinand. *Course in General Linguistics*. Trans. Wade Baskin. New York: McGraw-Hill, 1959.

Descartes, René. *Philosophical Writings*. Ed. Elizabeth Anscombe and Peter T. Geach. Indianapolis: Bobbs-Merrill, 1971.

Dockhorn, Klaus. "Hans-Georg Gadamer's *Truth and Method*." *Philosophy and Rhetoric* 13 (1980):160–80.

Dreyfus, Hubert L. "Holism and Hermeneutics." *Review of Metaphysics* 34 (1980):3–23.

Ebeling, Gerhard. *Word and Faith*. Philadelphia: Fortress Press, 1963.

Erickson, Stephen A. *Language and Being: An Analytic Phenomenology*. New Haven: Yale University Press, 1970.

Ermarth, Michael. "The Transformation of Hermeneutics: 19th-Century Ancients and 20th-Century Moderns." *Monist* 64 (1981):175–94.

———. *Wilhelm Dilthey: The Critique of Historical Reason*. Chicago: University of Chicago Press, 1978.

Esser, Josef. *Vorverständnis und Methode in der Rechtsfindung: Rationalitätsgarantien der Richterlichen Entscheidungspraxis*. Frankfurt: Athenäum, 1970.

Feigl, Herbert, and Wilfrid Sellars, ed. *Readings in Philosophical Analysis*. New York: Appleton-Century-Crofts, 1949.

Feyerabend, Paul. *Against Method: Outline of an Anarchistic Theory of Knowledge*. London: NLB, 1975.

Foucault, Michel. *The Archaeology of Knowledge*. Trans. A. M. Sheridan Smith. New York: Harper and Row, 1976.

Frank, Manfred. *Das Individuelle Allgemeine: Textstructurisierung und -interpretation nach Schleiermacher*. Frankfurt: Suhrkamp, 1977.

Fuhrmann, Manfred, et al., ed. *Text und Applikation: Theologie, Jurisprudenz und Literaturwissenschaft im Hermeneutischen Gespräch*. Poetik und Hermeneutik 9. Munich: Fink, 1981.

Gadamer, Hans-Georg. *Die Aktualität des Schönen: Kunst als Spiel, Symbol, und Fest*. Stuttgart: Reclam, 1977.

———. "Anschauung und Anschaulichkeit." *Neue Heft für Philosophie* 18 / 19 (1980):1–13.

———. "Being, Spirit, God." In *Heidegger Memorial Lectures*, ed. Werner Marx, trans. Steven W. Davis. Pittsburgh: Duquesne University Press, 1982, pp. 55–74.

———. *Dialogue and Dialectic: Eight Hermeneutical Studies on Plato*. Trans. P. Christopher Smith. New Haven: Yale University Press, 1980.

———. *Hegel's Dialectic: Five Hermeneutical Studies*. Trans. P. Christopher Smith. New Haven: Yale University Press, 1976.

———. "Hermeneutics and Social Science." *Cultural Hermeneutics* 2 (1975):307–16, followed by a discussion, pp. 317–36.

———. "The Hermeneutics of Suspicion." In Shapiro and Sica, ed., *Hermeneutics: Questions and Prospects*, pp. 54–65.

————. "Historical Transformations of Reason." In Theodore F. Geraets, ed.,
Rationality To-day. Ottawa: University of Ottawa Press, 1979.

————. Introduction to Collingwood's *Denken* [autobiography]. Trans. Hans-
Joachim Finkeldei. Stuttgart: Koehler, 1955.

————. Introduction to *Der Ursprung des Kunstwerks* by Martin Heidegger.
Stuttgart: Reclam, 1967.

————. *Kleine Schriften 1: Philosophie—Hermeneutik*. 2nd ed. Tübingen: J.
C. B. Mohr (Paul Siebeck), 1976.

————. *Kleine Schriften 2: Interpretationen*. 2nd ed. Tübingen: J. C. B. Mohr
(Paul Siebeck), 1979.

————. *Kleine Schriften 3: Idee und Sprache: Plato, Husserl, Heidegger*. Tübingen: J. C. B. Mohr (Paul Siebeck), 1972.

————. *Kleine Schriften 4: Variationen*. Tübingen: J. C. B. Mohr (Paul Siebeck), 1977.

————. "Die Kontinuität der Geschichte und der Augenblick der Existenz."
In *Geschichte: Element der Zukunft*. Tübingen: J. C. B. Mohr (Paul Siebeck),
1956, pp. 33–49.

————. *Philosophical Hermeneutics*. Trans. David E. Linge. Berkeley: University of California Press, 1976.

————. "Philosophie und Literatur." In E. W. Orth, ed., *Was ist Literatur?*
Phenomenologische Forschungen 11, pp. 18–45. Freiburg: Abber, 1981.

————. *Philosophische Lehrjahre: Eine Rückschau*. Frankfurt am Main: Klos-
termann, 1977.

————. "The Problem of Historical Consciousness," *Graduate Faculty Philosophy Journal* 5 (1975):8–52.

————. *Reason in the Age of Science*. Trans. Frederick G. Lawrence. Cambridge: MIT Press, 1981.

————. *Rhetorik und Hermeneutik*. Göttingen: Vandenhoeck and Ruprecht,
1976.

————. "Die Stellung der Philosophie in der Heutigen Gesellschaft." In *Das
Problem der Sprache*. Deutscher Kongress für Philosophie. Munich: Fink,
1967.

————. *Truth and Method*. Ed. Garrett Barden and John Cumming. New York:
Seabury Press, 1975.

————. *Über die Ursprunglichkeit der Philosophie*. Berlin: Chronos, 1948.

————. *Wahrheit und Methode: Grundzüge einer Philosophischen Hermeneutik*.
4th ed. Tübingen: J. C. B. Mohr (Paul Siebeck), 1975.

Gadamer, Hans-Georg, ed. *Truth and Historicity*. The Hague: Nijhoff, 1972.

Garrett, Jan Edward. "Hans-Georg Gadamer on 'Fusion of Horizons'." *Man
and World* 11 (1978):392–400.

Gerber, Uwe, ed. *Hermeneutik als Kriterium für Wissenschaftlichkeit?* Loccumer
Kolloquien 2. Loccum: n.p., 1972.

Gödel, Kurt. "Some Metamathematical Results on Completeness and Consistency of Formally Undecidable Propositions of *Principia Mathematica* and Related Systems," In van Heijenoort, ed., *From Frege to Gödel*, pp. 592–617.

Grimm, Gunter. *Rezeptionsgeschichte: Grundlegung einer Theorie*. Munich: Fink, 1977.

Grondin, Jean. *Hermeneutische Wahrheit? Zum Wahrheitsbegriff Hans-Georg Gadamers*. Königstein/Ts.: Forum Academicum, 1982.

Habermas, Jürgen. *Communication and the Evolution of Society*. Trans. Thomas McCarthy. Boston: Beacon Press, 1976.

———. "The Hermeneutic Claim to Universality." In Bleicher, ed., *Contemporary Hermeneutics*, pp. 181–212.

———. *Knowledge and Human Interests*. Trans. Jeremy Shapiro. Boston: Beacon Press, 1971.

———. "A Postscript to *Knowledge and Human Interests*." *Philosophy of the Social Sciences* 3 (1973):157–89.

———. "A Review of Gadamer's *Truth and Method*." In Dallmayr and McCarthy, ed., *Understanding and Social Inquiry*, pp. 335–63.

Hamburger, Käte. *Wahrheit und Aesthetische Wahrheit*. Stuttgart: Klett-Cotta, 1979.

Hans, James S. "Hans-Georg Gadamer and Hermeneutic Phenomenology." *Philosophy Today* 22 (1978):3–19.

———. "Hermeneutics, Play, Deconstruction." *Philosophy Today* 24 (1980):299–317.

Hartman, Geoffrey H. *Criticism in the Wilderness: The Study of Literature Today*. New Haven: Yale University Press, 1980.

Heidegger, Martin. "The Age of the World View." *Measure* 2 (1951):269–84.

———. *Basic Writings*. Ed. David Farrell Krell. New York: Harper and Row, 1977.

———. *Being and Time*. Trans. John Macquarrie and Edward Robinson. New York: Harper and Row, 1962.

———. *Identity and Difference*. Trans. Joan Stambaugh. New York: Harper and Row, 1969.

———. *Poetry, Language, Thought*. Trans. Albert Hofstadter. New York: Harper and Row, 1971.

———. *On the Way to Language*. Trans. Peter D. Hertz. New York: Harper and Row, 1971.

Hempel, Carl G. "The Function of General Laws in History." In Feigl and Sellars, ed., *Readings*, pp. 459–71.

Hesse, Mary. "In Defense of Objectivity." In *Revolutions and Reconstructions in the Philosophy of Science*, pp. 167–86. Bloomington: Indiana University Press, 1980.

Hilberath, Bernd Jochen. *Theologie zwischen Tradition und Kritik: Die Philosophische Hermeneutik Hans-Georg Gadamers als Herausforderung des Theologischen Selbstverständnisses.* Düsseldorf: Patmos, 1978.

Hinman, Lawrence M. "Quid Facti or Quid Juris: The Fundamental Ambiguity of Gadamer's Understanding of Hermeneutics." *Philosophy and Phenomenological Research* 40 (1980):512–35.

Hirsch, E. D., Jr. *The Aims of Interpretation.* Chicago: University of Chicago Press, 1976.

————. *Validity in Interpretation.* New Haven: Yale University Press, 1967.

Hofstadter, Douglas R. *Gödel, Escher, Bach: An Eternal Golden Braid.* New York: Vintage Books, 1979.

Hogan, John. "Gadamer and the Hermeneutical Experience." *Philosophy Today* 20 (1976):3–12.

How, Alan R. "Dialogue as Productive Limitation in Social Theory: The Habermas-Gadamer Debate." *Journal of the British Society for Phenomenology* 11 (1980):131–43.

Howard, Roy J. *Three Faces of Hermeneutics: An Introduction to Current Theories of Understanding.* Berkeley: University of California Press, 1982.

Hoy, David Couzens. *The Critical Circle: Literature, History, and Philosophical Hermeneutics.* Berkeley: University of California Press, 1978.

Hruschka, Joachim. *Das Verstehen von Rechtstexten: Zur Hermeneutischen Transpositivität des Positiven Rechts.* Munich: Beck, 1972.

Hufnagel, Erwin. *Einführung in die Hermeneutik.* Stuttgart: Kohlhammer, 1976.

Hyde, Michael J. "Philosophical Hermeneutics and the Communicative Experience." *Man and World* 13 (1980):81–98.

Jansen, Paul. "Die hermeneutische Bestimmung des Verhaltnisses von Natur- und Geisteswissenschaft und ihre Problematik." In Kurt Hübner und Albert Menne, ed., *Natur und Geschichte.* Deutscher Kongress für Philosophie, pp. 363–70. Hamburg: Meiner, 1973.

Japp, Uwe. *Hermeneutik.* Theorie und Geschichte der Literatur und der Schönen Künste 47. Munich: Fink, 1977.

Jauss, Hans Robert. *Toward an Aesthetic of Reception.* Trans. Timothy Bahti. Minneapolis: University of Minnesota Press, 1982.

Juhl, P. D. *Interpretation: An Essay in the Philosophy of Literary Criticism.* Princeton: Princeton University Press, 1980.

Kant, Immanuel. *Critique of Pure Reason.* Trans. Norman Kemp Smith. London: Macmillan, 1961.

Kermode, Frank. *The Classic.* London: Faber and Faber, 1975.

————. *The Genesis of Secrecy: On the Interpretation of Narrative.* Cambridge: Harvard University Press, 1979.

Kirkland, Frank M. "Gadamer and Ricoeur: The Paradigm of the Text." *Graduate Faculty Philosophy Journal* 6 (1977):131–44.

Kisiel, Theodore. "The Happening of Tradition: The Hermeneutics of Gadamer and Heidegger." *Man and World* 2 (1969):358–85.

———. "Ideology Critique and Phenomenology." *Philosophy Today* 14 (1970):151–60.

———. "Repetition in Gadamer's Hermeneutics." *Analecta Husserliana* 2 (1972):196–203.

Kleene, Stephen Cole. *Mathematical Logic*. New York: Wiley, 1967.

Kresic, Stephen, ed. *Contemporary Literary Hermeneutics and Interpretation of Classical Texts*. Ottawa: Ottawa University Press, 1981.

Kuhn, Thomas S. *The Essential Tension: Selected Studies in Scientific Tradition and Change*. Chicago: University of Chicago Press, 1977.

———. *The Structure of Scientific Revolutions*. 2nd ed. Chicago: University of Chicago Press, 1970.

Laing, R. D. *The Divided Self: An Existential Study in Sanity and Madness*. London: Tavistock, 1960.

Lakatos, Imre. "Falsification and the Methodology of Research Programmes." In Sandra G. Harding, ed. *Can Theories Be Refuted?* Dordrecht: Reidel, 1976.

Larmore, Charles. "Moral Judgment." *Review of Metaphysics* 35 (1981):275–96.

Laudan, Larry. *Progress and Its Problems: Toward a Theory of Scientific Growth*. Berkeley: University of California Press, 1977.

Lawrence, Frederick. "Gadamer and Lonergan: A Dialectical Comparison." *International Philosophical Quarterly* 20 (1980): 25–47.

Linge, David E. "Dilthey and Gadamer: Two Theories of Historical Understanding." *Journal of the American Academy of Religion* 41 (1973): 536–53.

McCarthy, Thomas. "On Misunderstanding 'Understanding'." *Theory and Decision* 3 (1973):351–69.

MacIntyre, Alasdair. "Contexts of Interpretation: Reflections on Hans-Georg Gadamer's *Truth and Method*." *Boston University Journal* 24 (1976):41–46.

Macquarrie, John. *The Scope of Demythologizing: Bultmann and His Critics*. New York: Harper and Row, 1966.

Magliola, Robert. *Phenomenology and Literature: An Introduction*. West Lafayette: Purdue University Press, 1973.

Marquard, Odo. *Abschied vom Principiellen: Philosophische Studien*. Stuttgart: Reclam, 1981.

Misgeld, Dieter. "Discourse and Conversation: The Theory of Communicative Competence and Hermeneutics in the Light of the Debate Between Habermas and Gadamer." *Cultural Hermeneutics* 4 (1977):321–44.

———. "On Gadamer's Hermeneutics." *Philosophy of the Social Sciences* 9 (1979):221–39.

Murray, Michael. *Modern Critical Theory: An Introduction*. The Hague: Nijhoff, 1975.

————. *Modern Philosophy of History: Its Origin and Destination*. The Hague: Nijhoff, 1970.

Murray, Michael, ed. *Heidegger and Modern Philosophy: Critical Essays*. New Haven: Yale University Press, 1978.

Nagel, Ernst, and James R. Newman. *Gödel's Proof*. New York: New York University Press, 1958.

Nassen, Ulrich. "Hans-Georg Gadamer und Jürgen Habermas: Hermeneutik, Ideologiekritik, und Diskurs." In Ulrich Nassen, ed., *Klassiker der Hermeneutik*. Paderborn: Schoningh, 1982.

Naumann, Manfred, et al. *Gesellschaft, Literatur, Lesen: Literaturrezeption*. Berlin: Aufbau, 1975.

Ong, Walter J. *Ramus, Method, and the Decay of Dialogue*. Cambridge: Harvard University Press, 1958.

Palmer, Richard E. *Hermeneutics: Interpretation Theory in Schleiermacher, Dilthey, Heidegger, and Gadamer*. Evanston: Northwestern University Press, 1969.

————. "Phenomenology as Foundation for a Post-Modern Philosophy of Literary Interpretation." *Cultural Hermeneutics* 1 (1973):207–23.

————. "Toward a Postmodern Hermeneutics of Performance." In Michel Bernamon and Charles Cramello, ed., *Performance in Postmodern Culture*. Madison: Coda Press, 1977.

Pannenberg, Wolfhart. "Hermeneutik und Universal Geschichte." In *Grundfragen Systematischer Theologie: Gesammelte Aufsätze*, 2nd ed., pp. 91–122. Göttingen: Vandenhoech and Ruprecht, 1971.

Peirce, Charles S. *The Essential Writings*. Ed. Edward C. Moore. New York: Harper and Row, 1972.

Peters, Ted. "The Nature and Role of Presupposition: An Inquiry Into Contemporary Hermeneutics." *International Philosophical Quarterly* 14 (1974):209–22.

————. "Truth in History: Gadamer's Hermeneutics and Pannenberg's Apologetical Method." *Journal of Religion* 55 (1975):36–56.

Polanyi, Michael. *Personal Knowledge: Towards a Post-Critical Philosophy*. Chicago: University of Chicago Press, 1958.

Popper, Karl R. *The Logic of Scientific Discovery*. New York: Harper and Row, 1968.

————. *Objective Knowledge: An Evolutionary Approach*. Oxford: Clarendon Press, 1972.

————. *The Poverty of Historicism*. Boston: Beacon Press, 1957.

Richardson, William J. *Heidegger: Through Phenomenology to Thought*. 3rd ed. The Hague: Nijhoff, 1974.

Ricoeur, Paul. *The Conflict of Interpretations: Essays in Hermeneutics*. Trans. Don Ihde. Evanston: Northwestern University Press, 1974.

————. "Ethics and Culture: Habermas and Gadamer in Dialogue." *Philosophy Today* 17 (1973):153–65.

————. "The Hermeneutical Function of Distanciation." *Philosophy Today* 17 (1973):129–41.

————. "The Model of the Text: Meaningful Action Considered as a Text." *Social Research* 38 (1971):529–62. All but the final pages are reprinted in Dallmayr and McCarthy, ed., *Understanding and Social Inquiry*, pp. 316–33.

————. "Phenomenology and Hermeneutics." *Nous* 9 (1975):85–102.

————. *The Rule of Metaphor*. Trans. Robert Czerny et al. Toronto: University of Toronto Press, 1977.

————. "The Task of Hermeneutics." In Murray, ed., *Heidegger and Modern Philosophy*, pp. 141–60.

Rorty, Richard. *Philosophy and the Mirror of Nature*. Princeton: Princeton University Press, 1979.

————. "A Reply to Dreyfus and Taylor." *Review of Metaphysics* 34 (1980):39–46.

Russell, Bertrand. "Mathematical Logic as Based on the Theory of Types." In van Heijenoort, ed., *From Frege to Gödel*, pp. 150–82.

Ryle, Gilbert. *The Concept of Mind*. New York: Barnes and Noble, 1949.

Schuchman, Paul. "Aristotle's Phronesis and Gadamer's Hermeneutics." *Philosophy Today* 23 (1979):41–50.

Seung, T. K. *Semiotics and Thematics in Hermeneutics*. New York: Columbia University Press, 1982.

————. *Structuralism and Hermeneutics*. New York: Columbia University Press, 1982.

Shapiro, Gary, and Alan Sica, ed. *Hermeneutics: Questions and Prospects*. Amherst: University of Massachusetts Press, 1984.

Skinner, Quentin. "Hermeneutics and the Role of History." *New Literary History* 7 (1975):209–32.

————. "Motives, Intentions, and the Interpretation of Texts." *New Literary History* 3 (1971–72):321–42.

Smith, P. Christopher. "Gadamer's Hermeneutics and Ordinary Language Philosophy." *The Thomist* 43 (1979):296–321.

Sontag, Susan. *Against Interpretation and Other Essays*. New York: Farrar, Strauss and Giroux, 1961.

Steiner, George. *After Babel: Aspects of Language and Translation*. London: Oxford University Press, 1975.

————. *On Difficulty and Other Essays*. Oxford: Oxford University Press, 1972.

Strawson, P. F. "Truth." *Analysis* 9 (1949):83–97.

Swearingen, James. "Philosophical Hermeneutics and the Renewal of Tradition." *The Eighteenth Century: Theory and Interpretation* 22 (1981):195–221.

Tarski, Alfred, "The Semantic Conception of Truth." In Feigl and Sellars, ed., *Readings* pp. 52–84.

Taylor, Charles. "Interpretation and the Sciences of Man." *Review of Metaphysics* 25 (1971):3–51.

———. "Understanding in Human Science." *Review of Metaphysics* 34 (1980):25–38.

Toulmin, Stephen. "The Construal of Reality: Criticism in Modern and Postmodern Science." In W. J. T. Mitchell, *The Politics of Interpretation*, pp. 99–117. Chicago: University of Chicago Press, 1983.

———. *Foresight and Understanding: An Inquiry into the Aims of Science.* Bloomington: Indiana University Press, 1961.

———. *The Philosophy of Science.* London: Hutchinson, 1953.

Tugendhat, Ernst. *Der Wahrheitsbegriff bei Husserl und Heidegger.* Berlin: de Gruyter, 1970.

Turk, Horst. "Wahrheit oder Methode? H. G. Gadamers 'Grundzüge einer Philosophischen Hermeneutik'." In Hendrik Birus, ed. *Hermeneutische Positionen.* Göttingen: Vandenhoeck and Ruprecht, 1982.

van Heijenoort, Jean, ed. *From Frege to Gödel: A Source Book in Mathematical Logic, 1879–1931.* Cambridge: Harvard University Press, 1967.

von Wright, Georg Henrik. *Explanation and Understanding.* Ithaca: Cornell University Press, 1971.

Walker, Marshall. *The Nature of Scientific Thought.* Englewood Cliffs, N.J.: Prentice-Hall, 1963.

Warning, Rainer, ed. *Rezeptionsästhetik: Theorie und Praxis.* Munich: Fink, 1975.

Weinsheimer, Joel. "Burke's *Reflections*: On Imitation as Prejudice." *Southern Humanities Review* 16 (1982):223–32.

———. "The Heresy of Metaphrase." *Criticism* 24 (1982):309–26.

———. *Imitation.* London: Routledge and Kegan Paul, 1984.

———. " 'London' and the Fundamental Problem of Hermeneutics." *Critical Inquiry* 9 (1982):303–22.

White, Hayden. *Metahistory: The Historical Imagination in Nineteenth-Century Europe.* Baltimore: Johns Hopkins University Press, 1973.

———. *Tropics of Discourse: Essays in Cultural Criticism.* Baltimore: Johns Hopkins University Press, 1978.

Whitehead, Alfred North. *The Function of Reason.* Boston: Beacon Press, 1958.

Wisdom, John O. *Philosophy and Its Place in Our Culture.* New York: Gordon and Breach, 1975.

Wittgenstein, Ludwig. *Philosophical Investigations.* Trans. G. E. M. Anscombe. New York: Macmillan, 1953.

————. *Tractatus Logico-Philosophicus* Trans. C. K. Ogden. Introduction by Bertrand Russell. London: Kegan Paul, Trench, Trubner, 1922.

Wolff, Janet. *Hermeneutic Philosophy and the Sociology of Art*. London: Routledge and Kegan Paul, 1975.

Index

Abbild. See copy
absolute knowledge, 37, 39, 40, 53
absolute spirit, 37, 38, 39, 151, 152, 198
abstraction, 92, 95, 238
Aeschylus, 204
aesthetics, 2, 92, 255–56; aesthetic rationalism, 6–7; aesthetic consciousness, 65, 93,
   112, 131, 146–47; subjectivization of, 81,
   89; aesthetic differentiation, 93, 100, 118,
   120, 121–22, 127, 130; aesthetic distance,
   116; in art history, 122–23. *See also* art; autonomy; judgment
aletheia, 39, 257, 258
alienation (*Fremdheit*), 5, 15, 92, 125, 126,
   159, 204; from historical world, 87–88; of
   historical distance, 137, 139
allegory, 89–90, 91, 97
anamnesis, 68
Anspruch, 85, 86
application, 33, 74; in historicism, 185–86,
   187; of knowledge, 188–92; in legal hermeneutics, 192–96; in past/present mediation,
   198–99; in language, 227–28, 238. *See also*
   dogma
appropriation, 131, 159
Aquinas, St. T., 234, 235, 236–37

architecture, 119, 126–27
arete, 188
Aristotle, 42, 94, 116, 187, 191, 237, 240
art, 2, 4, 17, 26; nature of, 84, 89, 90, 130;
   non-art, 92, 100, 120, 130; as historical
   interpretation, 97–98; as play, 102, 103. *See
   also* being; experience; history; interpretation; truth; truth claim
artificial language, 16, 41, 42, 43, 53, 232;
   object-language, 55, 58, 59; metalanguage,
   55–56, 58, 59
as-structure, 94, 95, 105, 122, 187, 255,
   256
assimilation, 130, 131, 132, 159, 178, 184
Aufhebung. See sublation
Augustine, St., 234, 235
Ausbildung, 72, 74
Auslegung. See interpretation
Austin, J. L., 234
authority, 74, 170–71
autobiography, 150
autonomy, 14, 45, 92, 121; of aesthetics, 66,
   78–79, 85, 116
awareness, 38
axiomatization, 43, 44, 45, 49, 50, 52; of language, 55, 58

"back-reading," 215–16
Bacon, F., 2, 8, 9, 20, 21–22, 202
bad infinite, 37, 38, 39, 204
Baumgarten, A. G., 76
beauty, 81, 82, 256–58; in nature and art, 83, 84–85
being, 9, 10; being at home, 4, 5, 70; historical, 11, 15, 158, 162; of art, 66, 101, 110; of spirit, 70–71; reflected by language, 214, 215, 255, 256, 258
being-there. See Dasein
belonging, 28; to language, 249–50, 251
Bewusstein. See consciousness
Bild. See picture
Bildung (education), 68–70, 71–72, 79, 80, 107; aesthetic, 92–93, 94. See also human sciences; prodigal son
biography, 150
Bultmann, R., 195
Burke, E., 73, 74

Carnap, R., 3, 29
Cassirer, E., 228
catharsis, 116
certainty, 12, 13; of historian, 153, 154, 156
Chladenius, 139, 140, 185
classics, 133, 136, 174, 175
Collingwood, R. G., 209–10
commitment, 28–29
common sense, 72–73, 74, 75, 79, 80, 92, 111, 139
community (common ground), 75, 80, 82, 93, 117; in language, 242–43. See also common sense
confirmation, 23, 26, 27, 29, 203
consciousness, 10, 11, 13, 15, 38, 39, 156. See also objectivity; understanding
contemporaneity, 114–15
context. See horizon
continuity, 149, 150
contradiction, 48, 49, 201. See also self-contradiction
convention, 90
conversation. See dialogue
copy, 119, 120, 121–22
Cusanus, N., 241–42, 243

Dasein, 71, 161–64. See also understanding
decoration, 126–27
Derrida, J., 101
Descartes, R., 2, 7, 9–10, 11, 42, 75; on authority and reason, 170–71
determinism. See linguistics
dialectic, 37, 39–40, 42, 140, 206; in hermeneutic experience, 250–52, 253

dialogue, 1, 37, 40, 42, 90, 208, 210, 223; with tradition, 205–06; understanding through, 209–10, 212; access of being in, 250, 251, 252–53
Dilthey, W., 6, 17, 20, 67–68, 185; on Erlebnis, 87, 89; on tradition and dogma, 134, 136; on history as science, 148–52; on finitude, 152–53; on philology, 196–97, 198
discontinuity, 97
discourse, 74
discursiveness, 236, 237, 239, 241–42
disintegration, 97
divination, 141
dogma: in interpretation, 134, 135–36, 141, 142, 168
doubt, 10, 13
drama, 106, 109–10, 222
Droysen, J., 144, 147, 148

ecstasis, 115, 116
effect in history. See Wirkungsgeschichte; wirkungsgeschichtliches Bewusstsein
eidos, 119, 188
eikon, 232–33
Einbildungskraft (imagination), 68, 81, 83
Einstein, A., 19
eleos, 116
emanation, 236, 238, 241
embodiment, 233, 234
Enlightenment, the, 90, 167, 168, 169, 173
Epimenides, 45, 48
episteme, 41, 188–89
epistemology, 4, 5, 15, 156, 162
equity (perfect justice), 190–91
Erlebnis, 86–87, 88. See also experience
error, 7, 8, 26, 170
escape, 92
ethics, 78, 188, 189–90
Euclid, 42, 43
event, 237; historical, 34, 200, 210, 211, 227; of truth, 100, 113, 211
excursion, 92, 94, 125, 159
existentialism, 28
experience, 17, 20, 23, 33, 44; historical, 148–50, 152, 154, 155; aesthetic, 91, 103, 104; disappointment in, 201–02, 203, 205. See also openness
experiment, 22, 24. See also Popper, K., expression, 41, 147–48, 155

facticity, 35, 235; hermeneutics of, 161, 162, 163
falsificationism, 18, 19, 24, 25, 27, 28–29, 43, 134

festival (*Fest*): permanence in change, 113–14, 115

Feyerabend, P., 36

Fichte, J., 86

finitude, 45, 132; human, 37, 53, 187, 235–36; of reason, 74, 171; of consciousness, 117, 127; consciousness of in historicism, 152, 155, 205, 206, 211, 216; of interpretation, 253–54

Fremdheit. See alienation

Freud, S., 38

fusion, 175, 244, 226; of language, 219, 224, 225

fusion of horizon, 183–84, 210, 211, 251; in language, 214, 216, 217

Galileo, 42

game. *See* play, concept of

Gebilde (structure), 68, 107, 109, 112, 113, 222

Geisteswissenschaften. See human sciences

genius, 7, 67; in art, 85, 86, 91, 95; of interpreter, 141, 157

George, S., 232

Gestalt psychology, 94

Gibbon, E., 172, 173, 174

Gödel, K., 3, 49–50, 51–52, 57, 58, 111; Gödel's number, 50, 51; Gödel's proofs, 50, 53

Goethe, J., 68, 87, 88

Hamann, J. G., 94

hap, 8, 11, 15, 116

Hegel, G., 11, 37–38, 45, 91; on *Bildung*, 69–70; hermeneutics of, 131–32; views of history of, 143, 145–46, 198; on truth, 160–61; on reflection, 200–01; on experience, 203–04; on dialectic, 206, 252

Heidegger, M., 6, 20, 28, 37, 38, 161; ready-to-hand, 30–31; on interpretation, 71–72; on hermeneutic of facticity, 161–63; on language, 213, 214, 215

Helmholtz, H., 66–67, 72, 74, 75

Hempel, C., 16

Heraclitus, 70

hermeneutic circle, 23, 49, 98. *See also* question and answer

hermeneutic consciousness, 205, 206, 208; of language, 225–26, 227. *See also* wirkungs-geschichtliches Bewusstsein

hermeneutic conversation, 252–53

hermeneutic nihilism, 96–97

hermeneutic reflection, 32

hermeneutics: philosophical, 7–8, 28; history of, 15, 160, 161; universality of, 17, 36, 140, 143; aesthetics in, 130–32; Reformation, 134, 135, 136; romantic, 143, 154, 178, 184; historical, 150, 185; as method, 177–78; biblical, 195–96. *See also* application; interpretation; understanding

hierarchy of levels, 58

Hilbert, D., 44–45, 50, 53

historian, 150, 159; of law, 7, 192, 193–95; of art, 123, 124; as interpreter of texts, 197–98

historical being, 149, 150

historicism, 27, 59, 132, 143, 151–52, 154, 160; and relation of past to present, 173–74

historicity, 37; of understanding, 164–65; of interpreter, 184–85; of being, 255–56

historiography, 2, 27, 160, 172, 173, 196, 197

history, 2, 26, 36, 40; objectification of, 13–14, 15; truth in, 59, 139, 143, 144, 154, 155; as art, 117, 146, 148, 151–52; teleological view of, 143, 144, 145, 202, 203, 204; historic deeds, 145, 146; as universal, 145, 152; as expression, 147–48; as science, 149, 150; coherence of, 149, 181–82

Hofstadter, D., 52

Hölderlin, F., 213

horizon: concept of, 157–58, 182, 207. *See also* fusion of horizon

human sciences, 4, 20, 28, 64; nature of, 26, 33, 35, 36; objectivity of, 58, 248; method in, 66–67; *Bildung* in, 70, 71

humanistic tradition, 2, 66; concepts of, 72–75, 76–77, 79–80. *See also* common sense; judgment; tact; taste

Humboldt, W. von, 242, 243, 244, 246, 247

Husserl, E., 20, 87, 150, 156, 157–58, 160

iconic theory of language, 233, 236

idealism, 144–45, 154, 158, 160–61

illusion, 92

image, 120. *See also* mirror; picture

imagination. *See Einbildungskraft*

imitation. *See* mimesis

incarnation, 233–34

incompleteness theorem, 3

individuality, 137, 139, 147

induction, 20–21, 28, 67; as method in natural sciences, 21, 202–03

insight, 257–58

integration, 159, 160

intentionality of understanding, 156, 219–20

interpretation, 95–96, 125, 129–30, 140, 211; process of, 71–72; variety and freedom in, 104–07, 111, 112, 124; of drama, 110–11; true, 111, 112, 113; of history, 139–40; objectivity of, 166, 175, 176; in dialogue, 210–12; misinterpretation, 216, 223; nature

of, 225, 227; as access to truth, 254–55.
  See also law; tradition; translation

judgment, 75, 78, 92, 93, 111, 129, 159, 201;
  aesthetic, 76, 81, 82, 83, 91; legal, 190,
  192–95
justice. *See* equity

Kant, I., 6, 20, 80–81, 99, 148; epistemology
  of, 65–66; on judgment, 75–76; on aesthetics, 77, 78–79, 82–84, 85, 86, 87; on genius, 95–96
Kierkegaard, S., 97
knowledge. *See* absolute knowledge; application; ethics; moral knowledge
Kuhn, T., 18, 25–26, 27, 28, 33, 35

Lakatos, I., 18–19, 28
language, 39, 40, 68, 213; history of, 1, 229–
  33; instrumentalist theory of, 30n24, 57,
  228–29, 232, 243; as transparent, 31, 218,
  227, 228; natural, 43, 57n48, 58; "closed,"
  54–55, 58; hierarchy of, 56, 58; as opaque,
  218; and non-verbal art, 226–27; resemblance theory of, 232–33; plurality of, 235,
  236, 242, 245, 246; nature of, 237–38;
  creativity of, 241–42; infinitude of, 243,
  244, 246–47; teleological view of, 249,
  250. *See also* artificial language;
  axiomatization
language world, 242, 246
Laudan, L., 18
law, 185–87, 190; legal interpretation, 191–
  92, 193–95
Leibniz, G. W., 3, 232
life, 157, 158–59, 160
life-world, 36, 157, 158
light, 257–58
linguistics, 214, 220, 227, 242–43, 247, 248;
  linguistic process, 219, 223; linguistic tradition, 221, 222, 223; linguistic determinism,
  242–43, 245
listening, 251, 257
literary criticism, 196
literature, 127–30. *See also* texts; tragedy;
  world literature; written word
Locke, J., 75
logic, 3, 20, 29, 36, 42, 50, 55; mathematical,
  41, 43, 44, 45
logos, 39, 231–32, 233, 234, 235
Lukács, G., 96, 97
Luther, M., 113, 135, 136, 232

mapping, 44–45, 50, 55
Marx, K., 38

mathematics, 26, 41–42, 49, 50. *See also*
  logic
meaning, 46, 49, 162–63
mediation, 34–35, 68, 148, 224–25; of past
  and present, 132, 133–34, 193, 194, 206.
  See also application; performance
memory, 74
metamathematics, 45, 50, 51, 53
metaphor, 238, 239, 240
metaphysics, 37, 148, 248, 249–50, 256
method, 4–7, 41; as access to truth, 2, 15, 43;
  as control of self, 7, 9, 12; as control of
  world, 7, 12; universality of, 8, 15, 17, 20,
  37; in natural sciences, 16, 17, 20, 22, 32;
  methodization, 29, 38; in understanding,
  139–40; in human sciences, 156–57, 163,
  164; and prejudices, 175–76. *See also* experiment; induction; truth
methodologism, 41, 66, 74–75, 214
Mill, J. S., 20–21, 67
mimesis, 109, 117, 118, 121, 232, 253; double mimesis, 112–13, 118, 126, 128
mirror, 222, 252, 253
misunderstanding, 137, 166; as automatic,
  175, 216
monologue, 37, 221
moral knowledge, 171, 188, 189, 190, 191
"moral sciences," 20. *See also* human
  sciences
Morris, C., 3, 53
myth, 168

Nachbild. See reproduction
Nagel, E., 44, 50, 51, 52
natural sciences, 2–3, 26, 27, 33–34; hermeneutics in, 32, 35–36, 41; objectivity of,
  57–58; universality of, 64, 65. *See also*
  method; truth
Newman, J., 44, 50, 51, 52
Newton, I., 19, 42
Nietzsche, F., 38, 101
nominalism, 47
noumenalism, 119, 203
numbers, 231–32

objective spirit, 38, 40
objectivity, 5, 14, 28, 29, 31–32, 153, 259;
  objectivism, 5, 6, 29–30; objectification, 14,
  27–28, 30, 38, 39, 48, 49, 183. *See also*
  history; human sciences; interpretation; natural sciences; self-consciousness
ontology: in hermeneutics, 220, 254. *See also*
  being
openness, 107, 208, 244; to truth of art, 65,
  124; in interpretation, 106–07, 167; to experience, 204, 205, 206–07

oral tradition, 127, 221
original (*Urbild*), 68, 119; of a picture, 120, 121–22

painting. *See* picture
paradox, 41, 44, 52; liar paradox, 45, 46, 51; semantic paradox, 50, 54–55
part-whole process, 141, 152, 154–55, 185, 175–76, 177, 253. *See also* wholeness
Peirce, C., 10, 75
perception, 94, 95
performance, 107, 109–10; as mediation, 115, 123, 125–26
performing arts, 109–10, 119, 123, 125
permanency, 153, 156
personification, 84
phenomenology, 87, 94, 160, 162
philology, 136–37, 196
philosophy, 2, 18, 151; of science, 19, 20. *See also* hermeneutics
phobos, 116
phronesis, 73, 189, 191–92
picture, 68, 119, 120–22, 124
Pietism, 184, 185
Plato, 42, 118, 188, 223, 233, 256; *Cratylus*, 229, 230, 232
play, concept of, 81, 101, 102, 118, 122; in games, 102, 104, 107–08; as representation-of, 105–06; becomes a play, 106, 107
play. *See* drama
plurality of language. *See* language
poetry, 119, 224, 240
Polanyi, M., 18, 28; on truth in science, 29, 30–32, 33
Pope, A., 86, 108
Popper, K., 18, 19, 21, 28, 29, 33, 35, 44, 52; on experiment, 22–23, 24, 25
positivism, 3, 16, 17, 19–20, 25, 35
pragmatics, 53
prejudice, 10, 11, 12–13, 139, 158, 198; in science, 21–22; in understanding history, 167, 168, 170, 180–81; moral, 189–90; of interpreter, 191–92; in tradition, 258–59
presence-at-hand, 5, 95
preservation: as *Bewährung*, 174
prodigal son: as paradigm of *Bildung*, 70
progress, 24–25, 27, 28
projection, 163, 165–66, 176–77
proposition, 48, 49
Pythagoras, 233

question and answer, 22–23, 207, 208, 209–10, 211

Rambach, J. J., 184

Ranke, L. von, 144, 145, 146, 167
rationalism, 83, 169, 170
ready-to-hand, 30–31
reality, 150–51
reason, 148, 169, 170, 174. *See also* finitude
recognition, 108–09, 115–16
reconstruction, 5, 134, 138, 141, 160, 214
reduction, 158, 162
reflection, 30, 32, 38, 41, 43, 47, 153; limits of, 200–01
reflexivity, 48, 49, 54, 58n49, 201
relativism, 40–41, 47, 57–58, 110, 201, 225; in art history, 124–25
repeatability, 23, 114; of artwork, 108, 109, 112, 113, 114
repetition, 108, 109, 114, 115
representation, 105–06, 107, 118, 123, 128, 223. *See also* drama
reproduction, 68, 118, 130
research, 28, 33, 34, 172, 173, 174
return, 70–71, 92, 94, 125, 126
revelation, 39
rhetoric, 74, 75, 90, 97, 240
romanticism, 168, 169, 185
rules for interpretation, 140
Russell, B., 3, 44, 50, 53, 57, 58; liar paradox, 45–46; theory of types, 46–47, 48, 49
Ryle, G., 39

Sartre, J. P., 28
Saussure, F. de, 228
Schelling, F. von, 86
Scherer, W., 87
Schiller, F. von, 86, 92, 97
Schleiermacher, F.: on tradition, 131, 132, 185; on basis of understanding, 136–39; on language, 214, 215, 216, 220
Scripture, 90, 142, 143; interpreting, 136, 139, 185–87
self-consciousness, 5, 11, 15, 37, 53, 160; objectivity in, 38, 48, 49; incompleteness of, 39, 40; historical, 153, 162–63, 198, 200
self-contradiction, 48, 53, 54, 57, 58, 59, 98
self-knowledge, 11, 53, 54
semantics, 53, 54
semiotics, 130
sensus communis, 76, 81, 82. *See also* common sense; community
Shaftesbury, Earl of, 76
Sichverhalten, 9
sign, 233
significance, 5, 84, 87, 150
simultaneity, 93, 114n35, 131
situatedness, 161–62
Socrates, 42, 188, 206, 207, 208, 231–32

speech, 40, 241, 243, 253
speech act theory, 234
Spinoza, B., 139, 140
spirit, 144, 151, 152. *See also* absolute spirit;
    objective spirit
Sterne, L., 1
structure. *See Gebilde*
subjectivity, 40, 57, 116, 146, 158, 250; sub-
    jectivism, 5, 6, 112; of art, 101–03
sublation (*Aufhebung*), 98
subsumption, 34, 72, 187, 198, 200, 237–38;
    in judgment, 76, 77–78
superstition, 168
syllogism, 42, 236, 237, 241
symbol, 42, 50, 88–89, 97
syntactics, 53

tact, 72–73
Tarski, A., 3, 53–55, 56, 57, 58
taste, 76, 77–78, 81, 85, 92, 111, 112
Taylor, C., 16–17
techne, 188–89, 232
technologism, 35
technology, 33, 34
teleology, 25, 26, 37, 56, 250, 254. *See also*
    history; language
telos, 24, 145
temporal distance, 179–80, 182
temporality, 13, 35, 113, 114, 150, 235
texts, 14, 135, 136, 143, 167
theology, 136
thought: as tool of language, 249
thrownness, 10, 11, 163
time, 163, 182
time-consciousness, 157
totalization, 3, 43, 56–57
Toulmin, S., 18, 21
tradition, 2, 12, 131, 132, 186; truth in, 30,
    40, 65, 258–59; role of allegory in, 90–91;
    in interpretation, 135, 142, 250–51, 254;
    prejudice in, 167–68, 169, 171; in historical
    research, 171–72, 173; as source of under-
    standing, 205–06. *See also* humanistic tradi-
    tion; linguistics
tragedy, 116, 117, 118
translation, 217, 218, 219, 227; as form of
    conversation, 220–21
Trinity, the, 234–35, 236
truth, 1, 2, 37, 139; in natural sciences, 9–10,
    17, 28, 29, 63–64; *v* method, 19–20, 41,
    49, 52; redundancy theory of, 31, 54–55;
    affirmation theory of, 31–32, 54; Tarski's
    theory of, 52–53; in art, 257–58. *See also*
    event; history; language; method; Polanyi,
    M.; tradition

truth claim: of history, 64, 66, 133–34, 135,
    151–52, 180–81, 211; of art, 64–65, 66, 79,
    81, 98, 99, 100
types, theory of, 3, 45, 46–47, 48, 49, 53, 56.
    See also Russell, B.

Übertragung (metaphor), 239
uncertainty, 5
understanding, 24, 49, 81, 165, 178–79; as
    joining in tradition, 30, 135–36, 163–64; of
    history, 35–36, 198–99; universal theory of,
    137–39; as self-understanding, 165–66;
    shared understanding of truth, 183–84;
    through dialogue, 217–18; intentionality of,
    219–20; as linguistic process, 223–25
Unified Science movement, 3
universal history. *See* history
Urbild. See original
Urteil, 86
Urteilung, 159
utilitarianism, 83

Valéry, P., 96, 97
verbum, 234, 235
verification. *See* confirmation
Vico, G., 74, 149, 152
Vienna Circle, 16
Vorbild (examplar), 68

Walker, M., 17–18, 34
Weltverhalten, 9
Whitehead, A. N., 45, 50
wholeness, 177–78
Willenbestimmung, 9
Winckelmann, J., 144, 145
Wirkung, 116, 181
Wirkungsgeschichte, 181, 182, 198, 200, 215,
    248, 251, 256
wirkungsgeschichtliches Bewusstsein: in histo-
    ricism, 182, 184, 199, 200, 202, 205, 208;
    in language, 216, 229, 240
Wisdom, J., 16
Wittgenstein, L., 16, 41, 101
word: understood, 255
Wordsworth, W., 5
world: being-in-the-world, 161–62; language
    world, 245–46, 247. *See also* life-world
world literature, 128, 129
written word, 221, 222, 223

Yorck, Count P., 158, 159, 214

Zeno, 45
Zugehörigkeit. See belonging